Rick Steves

BEST OF

IRELAND

Rick Steves & Pat O'Connor

Contents

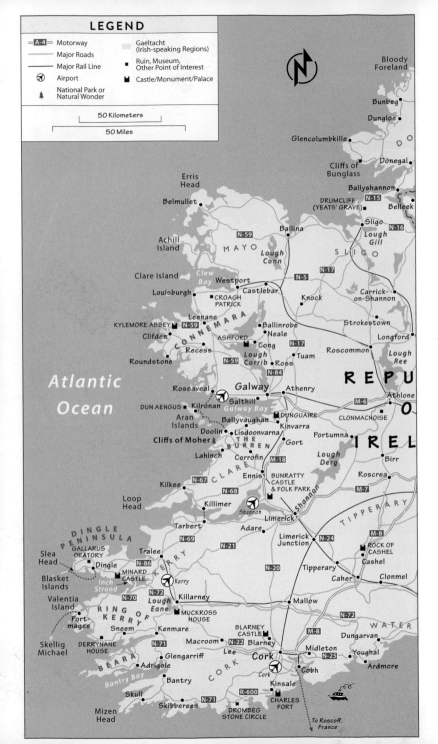

LEGEND

🚐 A-4 Motorway

Major Roads

Major Rail Line

✈ Airport

🌲 National Park or
Natural Wonder

Gaeltacht
(Irish-speaking Regions)

■ Ruin, Museum,
Other Point of Interest

▉ Castle/Monument/Palace

50 Kilometers

50 Miles

N

Atlantic Ocean

Bloody
Foreland

Bunbeg

Dungloe

Glencolumbkille

DO

Cliffs of
Bunglass

Donegal

Ballyshannon

DRUMCLIFF
(YEATS' GRAVE)

N-15

Belleek

Sligo

N-16

*Lough
Gill*

SLIGO

Erris
Head

Belmullet

Ballina

N-59

MAYO

*Lough
Conn*

Carrick-
on-Shannon

Knock

Strokestown

Longford

*Lough
Ree*

Achill
Island

Clare Island

*Clew
Bay*

Westport

Castlebar

N-5

N-17

Louisburgh

CROAGH
PATRICK

Leanane

Roscommon

KYLEMORE ABBEY

N-59

CONNEMARA

Ballinrobe

Neale

ASHFORD

Cong

N-17

Clifden

Recess

Ross

N-84

Tuam

Roundstone

*Lough
Corrib*

N-59

Rossaveal

Galway

Athenry

Athlone

M-6

REPU

Kilrónan

Salthill

Galway Bay

CLONMACNOISE

O

DUN AENGUS

Aran
Islands

Ballyvaughan

DUNGUAIRE

Kinvarra

IREL

Doolin

Lisdoonvarna

Gort

Portumna

Birr

Cliffs of Moher

THE
BURREN

*Lough
Derg*

Lahinch

Corrofin

CLARE

M-18

Roscrea

Kilkee

N-67

Ennis

BUNRATTY
CASTLE
& FOLK PARK

M-7

N-68

Shannon

TIPPERARY

M-8

Loop
Head

Killimer

Shannon

Limerick

ROCK OF
CASHEL

Tarbert

Limerick
Junction

N-24

Cashel

DINGLE
PENINSULA

N-69

Adare

N-21

N-20

Tipperary

Caher

Clonmel

GALLARUS
ORATORY

Tralee

N-86

Caher

Slea
Head

Dingle

MINARD
CASTLE

KERRY

Kerry

Limerick

Mallow

N-72

Blasket
Islands

*Inch
Strand*

N-70

*Lough
Eane*

Killarney

WATER

Valentia
Island

RING
OF
KERRY

MUCKROSS
HOUSE

BLARNEY
CASTLE

M-8

Dungarvan

N-72

Port-
magee

Sneem

Kenmare

Macroom

N-22

Blarney

Midleton

N-25

Youghal

Skellig
Michael

DERRYNANE
HOUSE

Lee

Cork

Cobh

Ardmore

BEARA

Glengarriff

CORK

N-71

Adrigole

Cork

Kinsale

Bantry Bay

Bantry

CHARLES
FORT

Skull

N-71

R-600

Mizen
Head

Skibbereen

DROMBEG
STONE CIRCLE

To Roscoff,
France

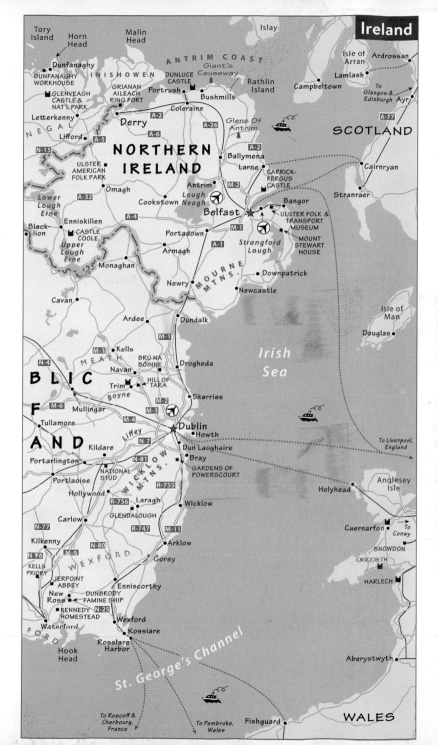

Introduction

Flung onto the foggy fringe of the Atlantic pond like a mossy millstone, Ireland drips with mystery, drawing you in for a closer look. You won't find the proverbial pot of gold, but you will treasure the engaging and feisty Irish people. Irish culture—with its unique language, intricate art, and mesmerizing music—is as intoxicating as the famous Irish brew, Guinness.

The Irish revere their past and love their proverbs (such as "When God made time, he made a lot of it"). Ireland is dusted with prehistoric stone circles, beehive huts, and standing stones—some older than the pyramids. While much of Europe has buried older cultures under new, Ireland still reveals its cultural bedrock.

Today's Ireland is vibrant, cosmopolitan, and complex. The small island (about the size of Maine) holds two distinctly different Irelands: the Republic of Ireland (an independent nation that's mainly Catholic) and Northern Ireland (part of the United Kingdom, roughly half Protestant and half Catholic). No visit is complete without a look at both.

Want to really get to know Ireland? Belly up to the bar in a neighborhood pub and engage a local in conversation. The Irish have a worldwide reputation as talkative, musical, moody romantics with a quick laugh and a ready smile. Come join them.

THE BEST OF IRELAND

In this selective book, I recommend Ireland's top destinations—a mix of lively cities, cozy towns, and natural wonders—along with the best sights and experiences they have to offer.

The biggie on everyone's list is Dublin, the energetic, friendly capital of the Republic of Ireland. But there's so much more to see. The island is dotted with Celtic and Christian ruins, cliffside fortresses, and prehistoric sites. Brú na Bóinne's burial mounds are older than Stonehenge. There's the proud town of Kilkenny, the historic Rock of Cashel, colorful Kinsale, and two peninsula loops:

the famous Ring of Kerry and the more intimate Dingle Peninsula. Youthful Galway is a good launch pad for dramatic scenery: the sheer Cliffs of Moher (in County Clare) and craggy Aran Islands.

In Northern Island, historic Belfast sheds light on the political Troubles that once bitterly divided this country. The lush Antrim Coast delights visitors, with fun-loving Portrush serving as a handy home base.

In some cases, when there are interesting sights or towns near my top destinations, I cover these briefly (as "Near" sights), to help you enjoyably fill out a free day or a longer stay.

Beyond the major destinations, I'll briefly cover the Best of the Rest: the

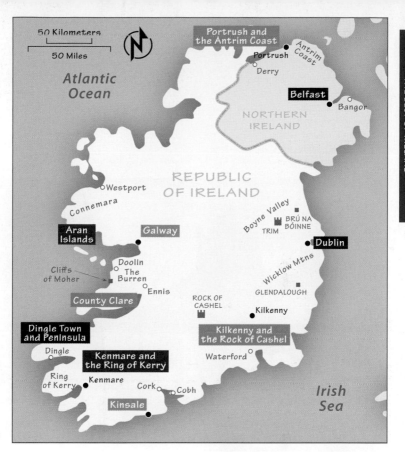

50 Kilometers
50 Miles

Atlantic
Ocean

**Portrush and
the Antrim Coast**

Portrush

Antrim
Coast

Derry

NORTHERN
IRELAND

Belfast

Bangor

REPUBLIC
OF IRELAND

Westport

Connemara

Boyne Valley

BRÚ NA
BÓINNE

TRIM

**Aran
Islands**

Galway

Dublin

Doolin
The
Burren

Cliffs
of Moher

Wicklow Mtns

GLENDALOUGH

Ennis

ROCK OF
CASHEL

County Clare

Kilkenny

**Dingle Town
and Peninsula**

**Kilkenny and
the Rock of Cashel**

Dingle

**Kenmare and
the Ring of Kerry**

Waterford

Ring
of Kerry

Kenmare

Cork

Cobh

Kinsale

Irish
Sea

region of Connemara and the town of
Derry. These great destinations don't quite
make my top cut, but are worth seeing if
you have more time or specific interests.

To help you link the top sights, I've
designed a two-week itinerary (on page
24), with tips to help you tailor it to your
interests and time.

THE BEST OF DUBLIN

The bustling capital of the Republic of Ireland is a fascinating concoction of treasured Dark Age gospels, Celtic artifacts, and rambunctious pubs. It shows its heart in its sights—from the Kilmainham Gaol (where the English imprisoned Irish rebels and paupers) to the Guinness Storehouse, which deifies the national beer. Its musical tradition and writers' heritage fuel "trad" and literary pub crawls. While its greatest sight is the medieval Book of Kells, the best thing about Dublin is its people.

❶ *Christ Church Cathedral sits atop Norman crypts and anchors the historic heart of Dublin.*

❷ *The friendly pulse of this vibrant city is best felt in its many traditional pubs.*

❸ *The Ha' Penny Bridge, just beyond the inn, replaced ferries and charged locals a half-penny toll.*

❹ *Turreted Dublin Castle was the center of dominant English control in Ireland for almost eight centuries.*

❺ *The popular Musical Pub Crawl introduces Irish traditional sessions to tune-loving travelers.*

❻ *Monastic scribes copying scriptures painstakingly created the Book of Kells during the Dark Ages.*

❼ *Grafton Street is a pedestrian shopping mecca, inviting for a stroll on a sunny day.*

THE BEST OF KILKENNY AND THE ROCK OF CASHEL

Two fine stops between Dublin and Dingle are medieval Kilkenny and the massive Rock of Cashel. Kilkenny is a sturdy, hardworking town, with a castle, cathedral, and atmospheric pubs featuring live traditional folk music. The evocative Rock of Cashel has majestic hill-topping ruins worth exploring and pondering. South of Kilkenny, you can make excursions to an old abbey, a replica of a famine ship, and the birthplace of Waterford crystal.

❶ *The ruins of the **Rock of Cashel** are the most evocative sight in Ireland's interior.*

❷ ***Waterford's crystal craftsmanship** draws enthusiastic visitors from around the world.*

❸ *Colorful shop fronts and unpretentious pubs line the medieval streets of **Kilkenny.***

THE BEST OF KINSALE

Quaint Kinsale has served as a port since prehistoric times. Stroll the pedestrian-friendly medieval quarter and take the excellent walking tour that makes the town's history come alive. The squat Charles Fort on the harbor offers great bay views and an engrossing museum that covers rugged British military life. Kinsale is also Ireland's gourmet capital; try to fit in three meals. Nearby, the historic town of Cobh has a special appeal for visitors with Irish roots.

❶ **Kinsale,** long a historic port, has a fun, fresh look.

❷ **Cobh**'s docks once creaked with Titanic passengers and US-bound emigrants.

❸ **Walking tours** transform Kinsale's back lanes with tales of former maritime glory.

THE BEST OF KENMARE AND THE RING OF KERRY

The colorful town of Kenmare, known for tidiness and lacework, is a good base for side-stepping the throngs flocking to Ireland's famous scenic loop. Allow a full day to tour the 120-mile Ring of Kerry, exploring ancient ring forts, peaceful towns with names like Sneem and Portmagee, and dramatic islands. Time it right and drive clockwise around the peninsula to avoid the parade of tour buses going in the opposite direction.

❶ Serene **Staigue Fort,** *dating from the Iron Age, lies 10 minutes' drive off the Ring of Kerry.*

❷ *Visitors to* **sheep ranches** *can observe shearing and shepherd-dog training.*

❸ **Muckross House** *hosted Queen Elizabeth I and attracts garden lovers today.*

❹ **Kenmare** *offers a respite from crowds and a base for exploring the Ring of Kerry.*

THE BEST OF DINGLE TOWN AND PENINSULA

My favorite Gaelic village—Dingle—welcomes you to my favorite Irish peninsula. Wander the town's charming lanes, check out the stained-glass windows in the chapel, look for the resident dolphin in the harbor, and sound out the Gaelic signs. You're in a Gaeltacht, a region where the traditional Irish language and ways are prized. The 30-mile loop around the peninsula is awash with beehive huts, prehistoric stone pillars, and ancient ring forts. Look up to see the rugged hills; look down to see the surging waves. And slow down… to take it all in.

❶ A bodhrán *drum, sold at Dingle's music shops, helps keep the beat in* **traditional Irish music.**

❷ *The cute* **town of Dingle** *delights travelers.*

❸ **Fungie the dolphin** *is a playful ambassador for boat tours around Dingle harbor.*

❹ *Early Christians gathered on the peninsula at holy places like the* **Gallarus Oratory.**

❺ *Art Nouveau stained-glass artistry adorns Dingle's convent* **chapel of Díseart.**

THE BEST OF COUNTY CLARE

This county on the rugged western coast offers the thrilling Cliffs of Moher, prehistoric structures in the wildflower wonderland of the Burren, and several musical towns. Little Doolin attracts music lovers with a trio of trad pubs, while Kinvarra hosts a medieval banquet for the lord or lady in you.

❶ *The 650-foot-high* **Cliffs of Moher** *drop dramatically into the Atlantic.*

❷ **Dunguaire Castle,** *standing sentry beside Galway Bay, offers memorable castle banquets.*

❸ *The little crossroads of* **Doolin** *sports lively* **trad music sessions** *in three steamy pubs.*

❹ *In* **the Burren,** *the* **Poulnabrone Dolmen** *was a tomb built 5,000 years ago.*

THE BEST OF GALWAY

Galway is a youthful university town with a great street scene and lively nightlife, punctuated by pubs and street musicians. It's also a springboard to the Cliffs of Moher and the Burren to the south, the Aran Islands offshore, and the region of Connemara to the north.

❶ Banners for the original 14 Norman founding "tribes" of Galway grace **Eyre Square.**

❷ The **Spanish Arch** slices through the town's medieval wall.

❸ A youthful international college population energizes Galway's **pedestrian corridor.**

❹ Proud Irish step dancing is fun to watch in Galway's **music pubs.**

THE BEST OF THE ARAN ISLANDS

The windswept Aran Islands have a stark and rugged beauty. From Galway, make a memorable crossing to Inishmore by ferry or flight. The island has simple towns, hiking trails, and a slew of early churches, but all roads lead to Dun Aengus, an Iron Age fort at the edge of a high cliff. The smaller island of Inisheer, with a hilltop castle, church ruins, and an evocative shipwreck, makes a fine excursion from Doolin.

❶ Walls of jagged limestone define winding lanes across **Inishmore**'s windswept interior.

❷ Islander-owned minivans greet travelers at the dock and scoot them efficiently around Inishmore.

❸ About 1,200 years ago, devoted pilgrims flocked to Inishmore and rest now near the **Seven Churches.**

❹ The small isle of **Inisheer** sees fewer visitors and offers peaceful solitude to modern hermits.

THE BEST OF BELFAST

Once the center of the Troubles, the no-nonsense capital of Northern Ireland has come a long way. Political murals depict its fractured past, but today's Belfast has a hopeful future, with bustling pedestrian zones, a cosmopolitan restaurant scene, and a bold, shiny *Titanic* museum that draws crowds.

❶ *The high-tech* **Titanic exhibition** *tells one of history's most famous stories.*

❷ *The stately* **Victorian grandeur** *of City Hall hints at former Industrial Revolution wealth.*

❸ *Rural craftsmanship is kept alive in simple village dwellings at* **Cultra Folk Park.**

❹ *The historic* **Crown Liquor Saloon** *offers private snugs in which to enjoy your mellow pint.*

THE BEST OF PORTRUSH AND THE ANTRIM COAST

With old-time amusement arcades and waterfront dining, the small-town beach resort of Portrush is the gateway to the wonders of the lovely Antrim Coast. Explore the stunning basalt Giant's Causeway, stroll the ruins of Dunluce Castle, and test your nerve crossing the Carrick-a-Rede Rope Bridge, suspended high over a watery channel below.

❶ *Pleasant* **Portrush** *thrives on summer crowds exploring the scenic Antrim Coast.*

❷ *Hikers and birdwatchers thrill to the lofty* **Carrick-a-Rede Rope Bridge.**

❸ **Dunluce Castle** *perches on a sea stack accessed by a strategic bridge.*

THE BEST OF THE REST

With extra time or interest, splice the following destinations into your trip. The region of Connemara has abbey ruins, a lakeside mansion, a pilgrimage mountain, and the genteel town of Westport. Derry is a revitalized Northern Ireland town that's come to terms with the Troubles.

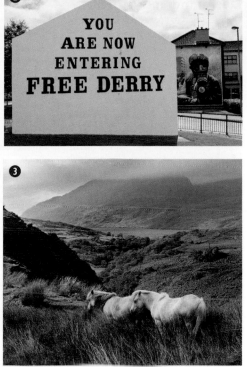

❶ *Colorful and passionate (often political) murals decorate* **Derry**'s *buildings.*

❷ *During the Troubles, this* **sign** *marked a popular gathering point for speakers to address crowds.*

❸ **Connemara**'s *rugged vistas attract painters, naturalists, hikers, and photographers.*

❹ *Prim* **Westport** *makes a good stop or a home base when exploring Connemara.*

TRAVEL SMART

Approach Ireland like a veteran traveler, even if it's your first trip. Design your itinerary, get a handle on your budget, make advance arrangements, and follow my travel strategies on the road. For my best advice on sightseeing, accommodations, restaurants, and transportation, see the Practicalities chapter.

Designing Your Itinerary

Decide when to go. Peak season, June through August, offers long days and a busy schedule of tourist fun. Cruise-ship crowds affect Dublin, the Cobh region, and Belfast.

Travelers in "shoulder season" (mid-April through May, plus Sept through early Oct) experience smaller crowds, decent weather, and all the sights and fun. Prices, crowds, and temperatures drop off-season (early Oct through mid-April); city sightseeing is generally fine, though in towns, some sights have shorter hours or shut down.

No matter when you go, expect rain. Just keep on traveling and take full advantage of "bright spells."

Choose your top destinations. My itinerary (on page 24) gives you an idea of how much you can reasonably see in 14 days, but you can adapt it to fit your own interests and time frame.

Bustling, rollicking Dublin is a must for its museums, street scene, and nightlife.

Music lovers follow their ear to pubs playing live traditional music. The top musical towns are—in this order—Dingle, Doolin, Galway, Westport, and Dublin. Foodies favor Kinsale, but won't go hungry elsewhere.

Historians choose among sights prehistoric (such as the Boyne Valley, the Burren, and the Dun Aengus cliff-edge fortress), medieval (Rock of Cashel and Glendalough), and modern (from the independence movement in Dublin to the Troubles in Belfast).

Seekers of nonstop beauty visit the Republic's rugged west coast—the Dingle Peninsula, Ring of Kerry, Cliffs of Moher, and Aran Islands—and Northern Ireland's scenic Antrim Coast. Photographers want to go everywhere.

If you have time to explore only one idyllic peninsula, choose the Dingle

Peninsula over the more famous Ring of Kerry. If you want to include both, this book will help you do it efficiently and enjoyably.

Draft a rough itinerary. Figure out how many destinations you can comfortably fit in the time you have. Don't overdo it—few travelers wish they'd hurried more. Allow enough days per stop: Figure on at least one to two days for major destinations.

Staying in a home base—like Galway or Dublin—and making day trips can be more time-efficient than changing locations and hotels. Minimize one-night stands, especially consecutive ones; it can be worth taking a late-afternoon train ride or drive to get settled into a town for two nights.

Connect the dots. Link your destinations into a logical route. Determine which cities you'll fly into and out of; begin your search for transatlantic flights at Kayak.com. All direct flights from the US to Ireland land in Dublin, low-key Shannon (good for cautious drivers), or Belfast.

Decide if you'll travel by car or public transportation. For the efficiency and freedom, I recommend driving. You won't need a car in big cities (park it), but it's ideal for exploring regions, stopping wherever you like.

If relying on public transportation, these destinations are easiest—Dublin, Dingle, Galway, Aran Islands, and Belfast—using a combination of trains, buses, taxis, and minibus tours, plus a flight or boat to the islands. Trains don't cover the entire island, and bus travel is slow due to multiple connections and/or frequent stops.

Allot sufficient time for transportation in your itinerary. Whether you travel by train, bus, or car, it'll take a half-day to get between most destinations.

To determine approximate transportation times between your destinations, study the driving chart (on page 352) or Google.com/maps. To look at train and bus schedules in advance, go online (www.discoverireland.ie, select "Getting Around"). If your trip extends beyond

Ireland, check Skyscanner.com for cheap flights within Europe.

Plan your days. Finetune your trip; write out a day-by-day plan of where you'll be and what you want to be sure to see. To help you make the most of your time, I've suggested day plans for destinations. But check the opening hours of sights; avoid visiting a town on the one day a week that your must-see sight is closed. Research whether any holidays or festivals will fall during your trip—these attract crowds and can close sights (for the latest, visit Ireland's tourist website, www.discoverireland.ie).

Give yourself some slack. Nonstop sightseeing can turn a vacation into a blur. Every trip, and every traveler, needs downtime for doing laundry, picnic shopping, relaxing, people-watching, and so on. Pace yourself. Assume you will return.

Ready, set... You've designed the perfect itinerary for the trip of a lifetime.

Trip Costs

Run a reality check on your dream trip. You'll have major transportation costs in addition to daily expenses.

Flight: A round-trip flight from the US to Dublin costs about $1,000-2,000.

Car Rental: Figure on at least $300 per week, not including tolls, gas, parking, and insurance. Rentals are cheapest if arranged from the US.

Public Transportation: For a two-week trip, allow $200 per person for buses and trains. Because Ireland's train system has gaps, a rail pass probably won't save you money, but buying train tickets online in advance can save as much as 50 percent.

Budget Tips: You can cut your daily expenses by taking advantage of the deals you'll find throughout Ireland and mentioned in this book.

Transit passes (for all-day or multiple-day usage) in bigger cities decrease your cost per ride. In Dublin and Belfast, using a hop-on, hop-off bus to get around isn't

THE BEST OF IRELAND IN 2 WEEKS

This unforgettable trip will show you the very best Ireland has to offer.

DAY	PLAN	SLEEP IN
	Arrive in Dublin	Dublin
1	Sightsee Dublin	Dublin
2	Dublin	Dublin
3	Rent a car at Dublin Airport, drive to Kilkenny for lunch, visit the Rock of Cashel, and end in Kinsale	Kinsale
4	Kinsale	Kinsale
5	Drive to Kenmare for lunch, then visit sheep farm and Muckross House, and end in Dingle town	Dingle
6	Dingle town	Dingle
7	Drive the Dingle Peninsula loop	Dingle
8	Drive to the Cliffs of Moher, then through the Burren, ending in Galway	Galway
9	Day-trip by plane or boat to Inishmore (Aran Islands)	Galway
10	Drive to Portrush. (Or add another day to explore— and overnight in—Connemara or Derry en route to Portrush.)	Portrush
11	Antrim Coast	Portrush
12	More Antrim Coast, then drive to Belfast	Belfast
13	Belfast	Belfast
14	Drive to Boyne Valley to visit Brú na Bóinne	Trim
	Return car at Dublin Airport and fly home	

Notes: Even if you're flying into Dublin, you don't need to start there; you can rent a car at the airport and drive to small-town Trim for an overnight, then tour Ireland, drop the car at the airport, and enjoy Dublin as your trip finale.

If you want to add the Ring of Kerry to this itinerary, spend the night in Kenmare on Day 5 and do the Ring on Day 6, ending in Dingle town that night.

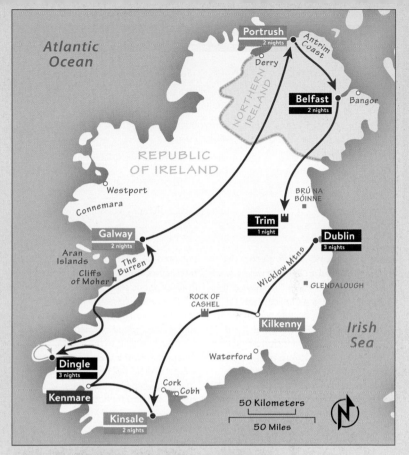

Atlantic Ocean

Portrush
2 nights

Antrim Coast

Derry

NORTHERN IRELAND

Belfast
2 nights

Bangor

REPUBLIC OF IRELAND

Westport

Connemara

BRÚ NA BÓINNE

Trim
1 night

Dublin
3 nights

Galway
2 nights

Aran Islands

The Burren

Cliffs of Moher

Wicklow Mtns

GLENDALOUGH

ROCK OF CASHEL

Kilkenny

Irish Sea

Waterford

Dingle
3 nights

Kenmare

Cork

Cobh

Kinsale
2 nights

50 Kilometers

50 Miles

Average Daily Expenses per Person: $200

Cost	Category	Notes
$85	Lodging	Based on two people splitting the cost of a $170 double room (including breakfast)
$60	Meals	$20 for lunch, $30 for dinner, $10 for snacks or Guinness
$40	Sights and Entertainment	An average of $40 a day works for most people
$15	City Transit	Buses or taxi
$200	**Total**	(applies to cities, figure on less for towns)

cheap, but it provides a live guide, a city introduction, and an efficient way to reach far-flung sights (cheaper than taxis and less time-consuming than city buses).

Avid sightseers consider two different sightseeing passes—the Heritage Card and the Heritage Island Visitor Attractions Guide—that cover dozens of sights across Ireland (see "Sightseeing Passes" in the Practicalities chapter). On a smaller scale, some cities offer combo-tickets or passes that cover multiple museums, though you'll need to sightsee briskly to make them pay off. If a town doesn't offer deals, visit only the sights you most want to see, and seek out free sights and experiences (people-watching counts).

Some businesses—especially hotels and walking-tour companies—offer discounts to my readers (look for the RS% symbol in the listings in this book).

Book your rooms directly with the hotel via email or phone for the best rates. Some hotels give you a discount if you pay in cash and/or stay three or more nights (check online or ask). Rooms cost less outside of peak season (mid-June-Aug). And even seniors can sleep cheap in hostels (some have double rooms) for about $30 per person. Or check Airbnb-type sites for deals.

It's no hardship to eat cheap in Ireland. You can get hearty, affordable meals at pubs and early-bird dinner deals at nicer restaurants. Cultivate the art of picnicking in atmospheric settings.

When you splurge, choose an experience you'll always remember, such as the Dunguaire Castle medieval banquet or a flight to the Aran Islands. Minimize souvenir shopping—how will you get it all home? Focus instead on collecting vivid memories, wonderful stories, and new friends.

Before You Go

You'll have a smoother trip if you tackle a few things ahead of time. For more info on these topics, see the Practicalities chapter and check www.ricksteves.com for book updates, more travel tips, and helpful talks.

Make sure your passport is valid. If it's due to expire within six months of your ticketed date of return, you need to renew it. Allow up to six weeks to renew or get a passport (www.travel.state.gov).

Arrange your transportation. Book your international flights. Figure out your main form of transportation within Ireland: You can rent a car, or buy train and bus tickets (either as you go, or you can book train tickets in advance online at a discount). Younger and older drivers may face age restrictions; see page 350.

Book rooms well in advance, especially if your trip falls during peak season

Book rooms well in advance.

Travel light and happy.

or any major holidays or festivals.

Reserve or buy tickets ahead for major sights, saving you from long ticket-buying lines, particularly for Dublin's Book of Kells and Kilmainham Gaol, Newgrange (the best Boyne Valley burial mound), and Belfast's Titanic museum.

Consider travel insurance. Compare the cost of the insurance to the cost of your potential loss. Check whether your existing insurance (health, homeowners, or renters) covers you and your possessions overseas.

Call your bank. Tell them you'll be using your debit and credit cards in Europe. Ask about transaction fees, and get the PIN number for your credit card. You won't need to bring along euros (for the Republic of Ireland) or pounds (for Northern Ireland)—instead, withdraw currency from cash machines while traveling.

Use your smartphone smartly. Sign up for an international service plan to reduce your costs, or rely on Wi-Fi in Europe instead. Download any apps you'll want on the road, such as maps, transit schedules, and the free Rick Steves Audio Europe app (see page 356).

Pack light. You'll walk with your luggage more than you think. Bring a single carry-on bag and a daypack. Use the packing checklist in Practicalities as a guide.

Travel Strategies on the Road

If you have a positive attitude, equip yourself with good information, and expect to travel smart, you will.

Read—and reread—this book. To have an "A" trip, be an "A" student. Study up on sights, and note opening hours, closed days, crowd-beating tips, and whether reservations are required or advisable. Check the latest at www.rick steves.com/update.

Be your own tour guide. As you travel, get up-to-date info on sights, reserve tickets and tours, reconfirm hotels and travel arrangements, and check transit connections. Find out the latest from tourist-information offices (TIs), your hoteliers, checking online, or phoning ahead. Upon arrival in a new town, lay the groundwork for a smooth departure; confirm the train, bus, or road you'll take when you leave.

Give local tours a spin. Your appreciation of a city or region and its history can increase dramatically if you take a walking tour in any big city or even hire a private guide. If you want to learn more about any aspect of Ireland, you're in the right place with experts happy to teach you in a language you understand.

Plan for rain. No matter when you go, the weather can change several times in a day. Bring a jacket and dress in layers. A spell of rain is the perfect excuse to go into a pub and meet a new friend.

Outsmart thieves. Although theft isn't a major problem outside of Dublin, it's still smart to wear a money belt. Tuck it under your clothes, and keep your cash, credit cards, and passport secure inside it. Carry only a day's spending money in your front pocket. In case of loss or theft, see page 332.

To minimize potential loss, keep your expensive gear to a minimum. Bring photocopies or screen shots of important documents (passport and cards) to aid in replacement if they're lost or stolen. While traveling, back up your digital photos and files frequently.

Guard your time and energy. Taking a taxi can be a good value if it saves you a long wait for a cheap bus or an exhausting walk across town. To avoid long lines,

take advantage of the crowd-beating tips in this book (such as visiting sights early or late).

Be flexible. Even if you have a well-planned itinerary, expect changes, sight closures, sore feet, and so on. Your Plan B could turn out to be even better. And when problems arise (bad food, a late bus, or rainy days), keep things in perspective. You're on vacation in a beautiful country.

Connect with the culture. Interacting with locals carbonates your experience. Enjoy the friendliness of the Irish people; most interactions Most interactions are accompanied by fun banter, especially at pubs, where lively conversations fueled by beer are called *craic* (crack). Ask questions—many locals are as interested in you as you are in them. Slow down, step out of your comfort zone, and be open to unexpected experiences. When an interesting opportunity pops up, say "yes."

Hear the fiddler playing? Taste the Guinness? Your next stop...Ireland!

Welcome to Rick Steves' Europe

Travel is intensified living—maximum thrills per minute and one of the last great sources of legal adventure. Travel is freedom. It's recess, and we need it.

I discovered a passion for European travel as a teen and have been sharing it ever since—through tours, my public television and radio shows, and travel guidebooks. Over the years, I've taught thousands of travelers how to best enjoy Europe's blockbuster sights—and experience "Back Door" discoveries that most tourists miss.

Written with my talented co-author, Pat O'Connor, this book covers the highlights of the entire island, offering a balanced mix of exciting cities and great-to-be-alive-in small towns. And it's selective—there are plenty of music-loving villages, but we recommend only the best ones. Our self-guided museum tours and city walks give insight into the country's vibrant history and today's living, breathing culture.

We advocate traveling simply and smartly. Take advantage of our money- and time-saving tips on sightseeing, transportation, and more. Try local, characteristic alternatives to expensive hotels and restaurants. In many ways, spending more money only builds a thicker wall between you and what you traveled so far to see.

We visit Ireland to experience it—to become temporary locals. Thoughtful travel engages us with the world, as we learn to appreciate other cultures and new ways to measure quality of life.

Judging from positive feedback from readers, this book will help you enjoy a fun, affordable, and rewarding vacation—whether it's your first trip or your tenth.

Happy travels! *Taisteal sásta!*

Rick Steves

Republic

The modern Irish state has existed since 1922, but its inhabitants proudly claim their nation to be the only contemporary independent state to sprout from purely Celtic roots (sprinkled with a few Vikings and shipwrecked Spanish Armada sailors to spice up the gene pool). The Romans never bothered to come over and organize the wild Irish. Through the persuasive and culturally enlightened approach of early missionaries such as St. Patrick, Ireland is one of the very few countries to have initially converted to Christianity without much bloodshed. The religious carnage came a thousand years later, with the Reformation. Irish culture absorbed the influences of Viking raiders and Norman soldiers of fortune, eventually enduring the 750-year shadow of English domination (1169-1922).

For most of the 20th century, Ireland was an isolated, agricultural economic backwater that had largely missed out on the Industrial Revolution. Things began to turn around when Ireland joined the European Community (precursor to the EU) in 1973, and really took off during the "Celtic Tiger" boom years (1995-2007), when American corporations saw big tax and labor advantages in locating here. Ireland's "Silicon Bog" became the European home to such big names as IBM, Intel, Microsoft, Apple, Facebook, and Google.

Today, the Republic of Ireland attracts both expatriates return-

# of Ireland

ing to their homeland and new foreign investment. As the only officially English-speaking country to have adopted the euro currency, Ireland makes an efficient base from which to access the European marketplace. About 35 percent of the Irish population is under 25 years old, leading many high-tech and pharmaceutical firms to locate here, taking advantage of this young, well-educated labor force.

Until recently, Ireland was one of the most ethnically homogenous nations on earth, but the Celtic Tiger economy changed all that. A recent census found that over 15 percent of Ireland's population had been born elsewhere.

Everyone here speaks English, though you'll encounter Irish Gaelic (commonly referred to as "Irish") if you venture to the western fringe of the country. The Irish love of conversation shines through wherever you go. All that conversation is helped along by the nebulous concept of Irish time, which never seems to be in short supply. Small shops post their hours as "9:00ish 'til 5:00ish." The local bus usually makes a stop at "10:30ish." A healthy disdain for being a slave to the clock seems to be part of being Irish. And the warm welcome you'll receive has its roots in ancient Celtic laws of hospitality toward stranded strangers. You'll see the phrase "Céad míle fáilte" in tourism brochures and postcards throughout Ireland—it translates as "a hundred thousand welcomes."

Republic of Ireland Almanac

Official Name: The Republic of Ireland (a.k.a. "Ireland" or, in Irish, Éire).

Area: With 27,000 square miles—half the size of New York State—it occupies the southern 80 percent of the island of Ireland. The country is small enough that radio broadcasts cover traffic snarls nationwide.

Population: Ireland's 4.8 million people are of Celtic stock. They speak English, though Irish Gaelic is spoken in pockets along the country's west coast. Nearly eight in ten are nominally Catholic, though only one in three attends church.

Geography: The isle is mostly flat, ringed by a hilly coastline. The climate is moderate, with cloudy skies about every other day.

Latitude and Longitude: 53°N and 8°W. The latitude is equivalent to Alberta, Canada.

Biggest Cities: The capital of Dublin (550,000 people) is the only big city; more than one in four Irish live in the greater Dublin area (1.9 million). Cork has about 125,000 people, Limerick 94,000, Galway 79,000, and Waterford 53,000.

Economy: The Gross Domestic Product is $294 billion, and the GDP per capita is $62,562—one of Europe's highest and 30 percent more than Britain's. Major moneymakers include tourism and exports (especially to the US and UK) of machines, medicine, Guinness, glassware, crystal ware, and software. Traditional agriculture (potatoes and other root vegetables) is fading fast, but dairy still does well.

Government: The elected president appoints the Taoiseach (TEE-shock), or prime minister, who is nominated by Parliament. The Parliament consists of the 60-seat Senate, chosen by an electoral college, and the House of Representatives, with 166 seats apportioned after the people vote for a party. Major parties include Fianna Fáil, Fine Gael, and Sinn Fein—the political arm of the (fading) Irish Republican Army. Ireland is divided into 28 administrative counties (including Kerry, Clare, Cork, Limerick, and so on).

The Average Irish: A typical Irish person is 5'7" and 37 years old, has 1 or 2 kids, and will live to be 80. An Irish citizen consumes nearly five pounds of tea per year and spends $5 on alcohol each day.

The flag of the Republic of Ireland

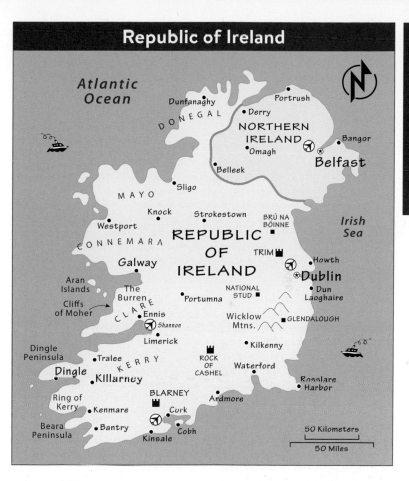

Republic of Ireland

Atlantic Ocean

Dunfanaghy
Portrush
DONEGAL
Derry
NORTHERN IRELAND
Omagh
Bangor
Belfast
Belleek

Sligo
MAYO
Knock
Strokestown
BRÚ NA BÓINNE
Irish Sea

Westport
CONNEMARA
REPUBLIC OF IRELAND
TRIM
Howth
Galway
Dublin

Aran Islands
The Burren
Portumna
NATIONAL STUD
Dun Laoghaire
Cliffs of Moher
CLARE
Ennis
Shannon
Wicklow Mtns.
GLENDALOUGH
Limerick
Kilkenny

Dingle Peninsula
Tralee
KERRY
ROCK OF CASHEL
Waterford
Dingle
Killarney
Rosslare Harbor
Ring of Kerry
Kenmare
BLARNEY
Ardmore
Beara Peninsula
Bantry
Cork
Cobh
Kinsale

50 Kilometers
50 Miles

As time has passed, relations between Ireland and her former colonial master Britain have improved. In May 2011, Queen Elizabeth II became the first British monarch to visit the Republic of Ireland since Ireland's 1921 split from the United Kingdom, which occurred during her grandfather's reign. Her four-night visit (to Dublin, Cashel, and Cork) unexpectedly charmed the Irish people and did much to repair old wounds between the two countries, establishing them, in the words of the Queen, as "firm friends and equal partners."

The big question now is how "Brexit" (Britain's impending exit from the EU) might complicate Ireland's easy trading relationship with their UK neighbors. Although the UK as a whole voted to leave the EU, the citizens of Northern Ireland voted to remain (recognizing the advantage of their soft border with the Republic). A possible "hardening" of this border is generally seen as a step backwards that both countries want to avoid.

At first glance, Ireland's landscape seems unspectacular, with few mountains higher than 3,000 feet and an interior consisting of grazing pastures and peat bogs. But its seductive beauty slowly grows on you. The gentle rainfall, called "soft weather" by the locals, really

RTE: The Voice of Ireland

Many a long drive or rainy evening has been saved by the engaging programs I've happened upon on RTE: Raidió Teilifís Éireann. What the BBC is to Britain, RTE is to Ireland: This government-owned company and national public broadcaster produces a wide range of programs on television, radio, and online. Look for it as you travel (via RTE's smartphone apps, on the radio in your car, or on TV at your B&B).

First hitting the airwaves on New Year's Eve 1961, today's RTE TV broadcasts are all digital and in the English language on RTE channels 1 and 2. But don't shy away from channel 4 (TG4), with Irish language TV shows subtitled in English—it's a great way to get a feel for the sound of the language. You couldn't find a richer or more accessible introduction to Irish culture.

Got a serious appetite for all things Irish? Online at www.rte.ie/archives, you'll find a treasure trove of fascinating archived RTE programs—everything from coverage of JFK's 1963 visit, to recollections of the 1916 Rising, to the poetry of Seamus Heaney, to Gaelic sports.

does create 40 shades of green—and quite a few rainbows as well. Ancient, moss-covered ring forts crouch in lush valleys, while stone-strewn monastic ruins and lone castle turrets brave the wind on nearby hilltops. Charming fishing villages dot the coast near rugged, wave-battered cliffs.

The resilient Irish character was born of dark humor, historical reverence, and a scrappy, "we'll get 'em next time" rebel spirit. The influence of the Catholic Church is less apparent these days, as 30 percent of Irish weddings are now civil ceremonies. But the Church still plays a part in Irish life. The average Irish family spends almost €500 on celebrations for each of their children's first communions. And the national radio and TV station, RTE, pauses for 30 seconds at noon and at 18:00 to broadcast the chimes of the Angelus bells—signaling the start of Catholic devotional prayers. The Irish say that if you're phoning heaven, it's a long-distance call from the rest of the world, but a local call from Ireland.

Dublin's Leinster House is the seat of Irish government.

Channel TG4 broadcasts Irish language TV shows subtitled in English.

Dingle Peninsula

Dublin

With reminders of its stirring history and rich culture on every corner, Ireland's capital and largest city is a sightseer's delight. This fair city will have you humming, "Cockles and mussels, alive, alive-O."

As the seat of English rule in Ireland for 750 years, Dublin was the heart of a "civilized" Anglo-Irish area known as "the Pale." Anything "beyond the Pale" was considered uncultured and almost barbaric...purely Irish.

The Golden Age of English Dublin was the 18th century. The British Empire was on a roll, and the city was right there with it. Those glory days left a lasting imprint on the city. Squares and boulevards built in the Georgian style, such as Merrion Square, give the city an air of grandeur. The National Museum, the National Gallery, and many government buildings are in the Georgian section of town.

Throughout the 19th century, as Ireland endured the Great Potato Famine and saw the beginnings of the modern struggle for independence, Dublin was treated—and felt—more like a British colony than a partner. The tension culminated in the Easter Rising of 1916, followed by a successful guerilla war of independence against Britain and Ireland's tragic civil war. With many of its grand streets in ruins, war-torn Dublin emerged as the capital of the British Empire's only former colony in Europe.

While bullet-pocked buildings and dramatic statues keep memories of Ireland's struggle for independence alive, the city is looking ahead to a brighter future. In the last decade, the tentative "green shoots" of a hoped-for financial recovery from the devastating 2008 crash have sprouted into a forest of cranes sweeping over booming construction blocks and expanding light-rail infrastructure. Dubliners are energetic and helpful, and visitors enjoy a big-town cultural scene wrapped in a small-town smile.

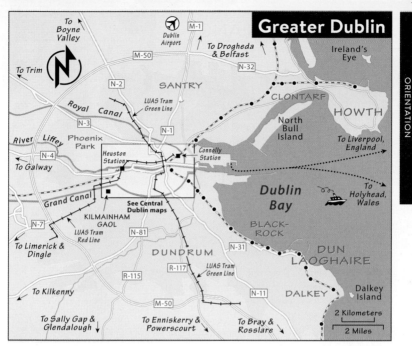

DUBLIN IN 2 DAYS

Sprawling, bustling Dublin has a compact core containing most of the sights, making it easy to enjoy. This city is a must for travelers interested in Celtic or Viking artifacts, Irish literature, or rebel history. If that's not you, head for the charm of smaller towns.

For most people, Dublin deserves three nights and two days. You can connect many of the sights with a hop-on, hop-off sightseeing bus tour.

Day 1: Visit the Book of Kells and Trinity Old Library when it opens at 9:00, hopefully ahead of midmorning crowds. Then take the guided Historical Walking Tour. Browse Grafton Street and have lunch. Head to the National Museum's Archaeology branch (closed Mon). Nearby parks for exploring or relaxing are Merrion Square and St. Stephen's Green.

On any evening: Have an early-bird special at a nice restaurant. Go for an evening guided pub tour (musical or literary). Drop in on Irish music in the rowdy Temple Bar area. Catch a concert or play, or try the storytelling dinner at The Brazen Head.

Day 2: Tour Kilmainham Goal (reserve ahead), then take the Dublin Castle tour. Grab a pub lunch, then follow the self-guided O'Connell Street Stroll, taking in the GPO Witness History exhibit en route (in the General Post Office).

With extra time: Choose among the National Gallery of Ireland, writers' sights (Chester Beatty Library, Dublin Writers Museum), the *Jeanie Johnston* Tall Ship and Famine Museum, and more.

ORIENTATION

Greater Dublin sprawls with well over a million people—more than a quarter of the country's population. But the center of tourist interest is a tight triangle between O'Connell Bridge, St. Stephen's Green, and Christ Church Cathedral. Within or near this triangle, you'll find

DUBLIN AT A GLANCE

▲▲▲**National Museum: Archaeology** Interesting collection of Irish treasures from the Stone Age to today. **Hours:** Tue-Sat 10:00-17:00, Sun from 14:00, closed Mon. See page 54.

▲▲▲**Kilmainham Gaol** Historic jail used by the British as a political prison—today a museum that tells a moving story of the suffering of the Irish people. **Hours:** Guided tours daily June-Aug 9:00-18:45, Sept-May 9:30-17:30. See page 71.

▲▲▲**Book of Kells in the Trinity Old Library** An exquisite illuminated manuscript, Ireland's most important piece of art from the Dark Ages. **Hours:** May-Sept Mon-Sat 8:30-17:00, Sun from 9:30; Oct-April Mon-Sat 9:30-17:00, Sun 12:00-16:30. See page 50.

▲▲**Historical Walking Tour** Your best introduction to Dublin. **Hours:** April-Oct daily at 11:00, May-Sept also at 15:00; Nov-March Fri-Sun at 11:00. See page 44.

▲▲**Traditional Irish Musical Pub Crawl** A fascinating, practical, and enjoyable primer on traditional Irish music. **Hours:** April-Oct 19:30 daily, Nov and Jan-March Thu-Sat only. See page 44.

▲▲**Chester Beatty Library** American expatriate's sumptuous collection of literary and religious treasures from Islam, Asia, and medieval Europe. **Hours:** Mon-Fri 10:00-17:00, Sat from 11:00, Sun from 13:00; closed Mon Nov-Feb. See page 62.

▲▲**GPO Witness History Exhibit** Immersive presentation on the 1916 Easter Rising and its impact on Irish history, situated in the building that served as the rebel headquarters. **Hours:** Mon-Fri 9:00-17:30, Thu until 19:00 in July-Aug, Sat-Sun 10:00-17:30. See page 71.

▲▲**Temple Bar** Dublin's rowdiest neighborhood, with shops, cafés, theaters, galleries, pubs, and restaurants—a great spot for live (though touristy) traditional music. See page 66.

▲▲**Trinity College Tour** Ireland's most famous school, best visited with a 30-minute tour led by one of its students. **Hours:** Departs every 30 minutes daily 9:15-16:00, Feb-April and Oct-Nov Sat-Sun only. See page 50.

▲▲**O'Connell Street** Dublin's grandest promenade and main drag, packed with history and ideal for a stroll. See page 45.

▲▲**Epic: The Irish Emigration Museum** Creative displays about the Irish diaspora that highlight the emigrants' influences on their new homelands. **Hours:** Daily 10:00-18:45. See page 67.

▲**Dublin Castle** The city's historic 700-year-old castle, featuring ornate English state apartments (interior tourable only with a guide). **Hours:** Mon-Sat 10:00-16:45, Sun from 12:00. See page 60.

▲**Guinness Storehouse** The home of Ireland's national beer, with a museum of beer-making, a gallery of clever ads, and Gravity Bar with panoramic city views. **Hours:** Daily 9:30-19:00, July-Aug until 20:00. See page 73.

▲**National Gallery of Ireland** Fine collection of top Irish painters and European masters. **Hours:** Mon-Sat 9:30-17:30, Thu until 20:30, Sun 11:00-17:30. See page 58.

▲*Jeanie Johnston* **Tall Ship and Famine Museum** Floating exhibit on the River Liffey explaining the famine period that prompted desperate transatlantic crossings (by tour only). **Hours:** Daily April-Sept 10:00-16:00, Oct-March 11:00-15:00. See page 67.

▲**Grafton Street** The city's liveliest pedestrian shopping street. See page 59.

▲**St. Stephen's Green** Relaxing park surrounded by fine Georgian buildings. See page 59.

▲**Dublinia** A fun, kid-friendly look at Dublin's Viking and medieval past with a side order of archaeology and a cool town model. **Hours:** Daily 10:00-18:30, Oct-Feb until 17:30. See page 64.

▲**Merrion Square** Enjoyable and inviting park with a fun statue of Oscar Wilde. See page 59.

▲**Hugh Lane Gallery** Modern and contemporary art, starring Monet, Bacon, and Irish artists. **Hours:** Tue-Thu 10:00-18:00, Fri-Sat until 17:00, Sun 11:00-17:00, closed Mon. See page 70.

▲**Dublin Writers Museum** Connoisseurs' collection of authorial bric-a-brac. **Hours:** Mon-Sat 9:45-17:00, Sun from 11:00. See page 68.

▲**National Museum: Decorative Arts and History** Shows off Irish dress, furniture, silver, and weaponry with a special focus on the 1916 rebellion, fight for independence, and civil war. **Hours:** Tue-Sat 10:00-17:00, Sun from 14:00, closed Mon. See page 75.

▲**Gaelic Athletic Association Museum** High-tech museum of traditional Gaelic sports such as hurling and Irish football. **Hours:** Mon-Sat 9:30-17:00, June-Aug until 18:00, Sun 10:30-17:00 year-round. On game Sundays, it's open to ticket holders only. See page 75.

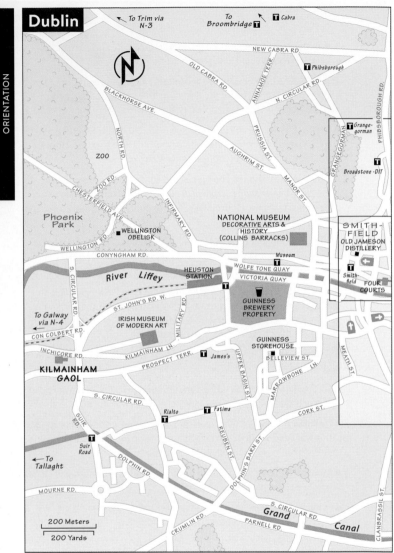

Dublin

To Trim via N-3

To Broombridge

Cabra

NEW CABRA RD.

Phibsborough

OLD CABRA RD.

ANNAMOE TERR.

N. CIRCULAR RD.

PHIBSBOROUGH RD.

BLACKHORSE AVE.

PRUSSIA ST.

AUGHRIM ST.

MANOR ST.

Grangegorman

Broadstone -DIT

NORTH RD.

ZOO

ZOO RD.

CHESTERFIELD AVE.

INFIRMARY RD.

SMITH-FIELD
OLD JAMESON DISTILLERY

Phoenix Park

WELLINGTON OBELISK

NATIONAL MUSEUM
DECORATIVE ARTS & HISTORY
(COLLINS BARRACKS)

WELLINGTON RD.

CONYNGHAM RD.

Museum

River Liffey

HEUSTON STATION

WOLFE TONE QUAY

VICTORIA QUAY

Smithfield

FOUR COURTS

S. CIRCULAR RD.

ST. JOHN'S RD. W.

GUINNESS BREWERY PROPERTY

To Galway via N-4

IRISH MUSEUM OF MODERN ART

MILITARY RD.

CON COLBERT RD.

INCHICORE RD.

KILMAINHAM LN.

PROSPECT TERR.

James's

GUINNESS STOREHOUSE

BELLEVIEW ST.

MEATH ST.

KILMAINHAM GAOL

S. CIRCULAR RD.

UPPER BASIN ST.

MARROWBONE LN.

SUIR RD.

Rialto

Fatima

CORK ST.

REUBEN ST.

Suir Road

To Tallaght

DOLPHIN RD.

DOLPHIN'S BARN ST.

CLANBRASSIL ST.

MOURNE RD.

S. CIRCULAR RD.

Grand Canal

CRUMLIN RD.

PARNELL RD.

200 Meters

200 Yards

Trinity College (Book of Kells), a cluster of major museums (including the National Museum: Archaeology), touristy and pedestrianized Grafton Street, Temple Bar (touristy nightlife center), Dublin Castle, and the hub of most city tours and buses. The major sights outside this easy-to-walk triangle are the General Post Office ("GPO" to locals; north of the center),

and Kilmainham Gaol and the Guinness Storehouse (both west of the center).

The River Liffey cuts the town in two, and most of your sightseeing will take place on its south bank. Many long Dublin streets change names every few blocks, including the wide main axis that cuts north/south through the tourist center. North from the O'Connell Bridge, it's called O'Connell

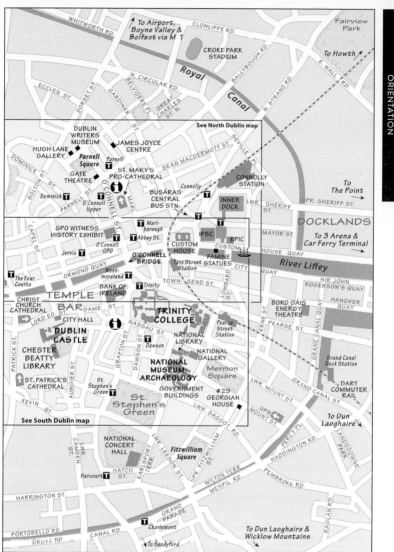

Street; south of the bridge, it becomes Westmoreland, passes Trinity College, and becomes the pedestrian-only Grafton Street to St. Stephen's Green.

Tourist Information

Dublin's busy main TI has lots of info and brochures on Dublin and all of Ireland (Mon-Sat 9:00-17:30, Sun 10:30-15:00,

a block off Grafton Street at 25 Suffolk Street, tel. 01/884-7700, www.visitdublin. com). A smaller but equally helpful TI is just past the Spire, on the east side of O'Connell Street (Mon-Sat 9:00-17:00, closed Sun). Watch out for other shops that claim to be TIs, especially on O'Connell Street. They're aiming to sell you tours and collect commissions.

Maps: At any TI, you can pick up the free Dublin Pocket Guide, but the best free city map is the one created by the Kilkenny Shop (6 Nassau Street, bordering the south side of the Trinity College campus)—available at tourist outlets throughout the city.

Sightseeing Pass

The **Dublin Pass** covers 25 sights and landmarks (but not the Book of Kells); hop-on, hop-off buses; and the Aircoach airport bus—one-way from the airport to the city only (€52/1 day, multiday options available, purchase online and collect at TIs, or buy at TIs, www.dublin-pass.ie). If you want to use the pass on the Aircoach bus into Dublin, buy it in advance online.

Tours

The **Historical Walking Tour,** rated ▲▲, is your best introductory walk to Dublin. A group of hardworking history graduates enliven Dublin's basic historic strip—Trinity College, Old Parliament House, Dublin Castle, and Christ Church Cathedral. All walks last 90 minutes and cost €12 (April-Oct daily at 11:00, May-Sept also at 15:00; Nov-March Fri-Sun at 11:00, ask for discount with this book, free for kids under 14, departs from front gate of Trinity College, private tours available, www.historicalinsights.ie).

The **Traditional Irish Musical Pub Crawl,** rated ▲▲, visits the upstairs rooms of three pubs; there, you'll listen to two entertaining musicians talk about, play, and sing traditional Irish music. In the summer, this popular 2.5-hour tour frequently sells out, but it's easy to reserve ahead online (€14, ask for discount with this book—use code RSIRISH online, beer extra, at 19:30 April-Oct daily, Jan-March Thu-Sat only, no shows in Dec, meet upstairs at Gogarty's Pub at the corner of Fleet and Anglesea in the Temple Bar area, tel. 01/475-3313, www.musicalpubcrawl.com). They also offer

a dinner-show version; for details and location, see page 82.

Dublin City Bike Tours cover five miles of this flat city and visit 20 points of interest north and south of the River Liffey. Designed for riders of average fitness, they set a casual pace, and rarely let a little rain stop them (€27 includes bike, helmet, snack, and water; ask for discount with this book; cash only, reserve in advance, 2.5 hours; March-Nov daily at 10:00, additional tours Fri and Sat at 14:00; departs Isaac's Hostel a half-block west of Busáras bus station at 2 Frenchman's Lane—see map on page 69, mobile 087-134-1866, www.dublincitybiketours.com).

Taking a ▲ **hop-on, hop-off bus tour** is an excellent way to orient yourself on arrival in Dublin. Several companies running roofless double-deckers do similar 1.5-hour circuits of the city (up to 30 stops, buses circle every 10-15 minutes daily 9:00-17:00, usually until 19:00 in summer). This type of tour, with running commentaries (either live or recorded), is made-to-order for Dublin, and buses run so frequently that they make your sightseeing super-efficient. Stops include the far-flung Guinness Storehouse and Kilmainham Gaol. Each company offers various discounts to museums and sights in town, and two kids ride free with each adult. Choose from **Do Dublin** (green buses, €19/24 hours, €23/48 hours, tel. 01/703-3028, www.dublinsightseeing.ie), **Dublin CityScape** (yellow buses, €15/24 hours, €18/72 hours, tel. 01/465-9972, http://cityscapetours.ie), or **City Sightseeing Dublin** (red buses, €19/24 hours, €25/48 hours, also a €10 nonstop evening tour with narration and music, tel. 01/898-0700, https://citysightseeingdublin.ie).

Helpful Hints

Pickpockets: Irish destinations, especially Dublin, are not immune to this scourge. Be on guard—use a money belt or carefully zip things up.

Festivals: Book ahead during festivals and for any weekend. **St. Patrick's Day** is a four-day March extravaganza in Dublin (www.stpatricksday.ie). June 16 is **Bloomsday,** dedicated to the Irish author James Joyce and featuring the Messenger Bike Rally (www.jamesjoyce.ie). Hotels raise their prices and are packed on rugby weekends (about four per year), during the all-Ireland Gaelic football and hurling finals (Sundays in Sept), and during summer rock concerts.

Meet a Dubliner: The **City of a Thousand Welcomes** offers a free service that brings together volunteers and first-time visitors. Sign up online in advance and pick an available time slot. In Dublin you'll meet your "ambassador," head for a nearby tearoom or pub, and enjoy a drink (paid for by the city) and a friendly, informal conversation (of up to an hour). It's a great way to get oriented to the city (meet at Little Museum of Dublin, 15 St. Stephens Green—see map on page 83, tel. 01/661-1000, www. cityofathousandwelcomes.com).

Laundry: **Krystal Launderette,** a block southwest of Jurys Inn Christ Church on Patrick Street, offers same-day full service (daily, tel. 01/454-6864). The **All-American Launderette** offers self- and full-service options (daily, 40 South Great George's Street, tel. 01/677-2779).

O'CONNELL STREET STROLL

This self-guided walk, worth ▲▲, follows Dublin's grandest street from the O'Connell Bridge through the heart of north Dublin. Since 1794, it's been Dublin's main drag.

❷ Self-Guided Walk

• *Start your walk on the...*

❶ **O'Connell Bridge:** This bridge—actually wider than it is long—spans the River Liffey, which historically has divided the wealthy, cultivated south side of town from the working-class north side. While there's plenty of culture on the north

bank, even today the suburbs (a couple of miles north of the Liffey) are considered rougher and less safe. Dubliners joke that "north-siders" are known as "the accused," while "south siders" are addressed as "your honor."

From the bridge, look as far upstream (west) as you can. On the left in the distance, the **concrete building** before the green dome marks the birthplace of the city. It squats on the still-buried site of the first Viking settlement, established in Dublin in the ninth century. On the right side of the river, a pleasant boardwalk leads upriver to the elegant iron **Ha' Penny Bridge.** That bridge leads into the Temple Bar nightlife district (on the left).

Turn 180 degrees and look downstream (east) to see the tall **Liberty Hall** union headquarters (16 stories tall, some say in honor of the 1916 Easter Rising). Modern Dublin is developing downstream. During the Celtic Tiger boom that started in the mid-1990s, the Irish subsidized and revitalized this formerly dreary quarter. While "the Tiger" died with the great recession of 2008-2009, Dublin's economy is booming again—as illustrated by the forest of cranes marking building sites in the east end of town.

A short walk downstream along the north bank leads to a powerful series of gaunt statues memorializing the Great Potato Famine of 1845-1849. Beyond, you'll see the masts of the *Jeanie Johnston,* a replica transport ship (see page 67).

O'Connell Bridge

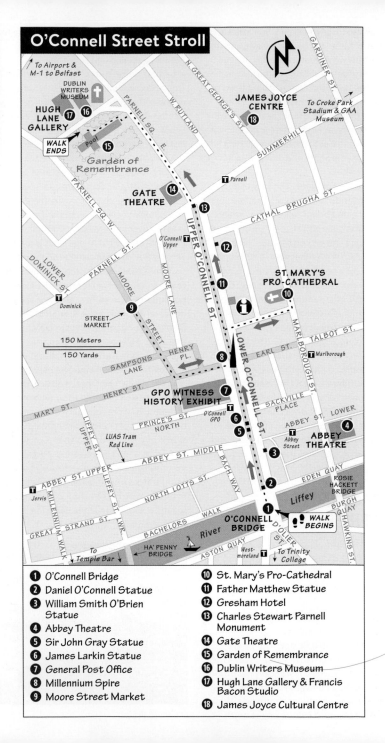

O'Connell Street Stroll

1. O'Connell Bridge
2. Daniel O'Connell Statue
3. William Smith O'Brien Statue
4. Abbey Theatre
5. Sir John Gray Statue
6. James Larkin Statue
7. General Post Office
8. Millennium Spire
9. Moore Street Market
10. St. Mary's Pro-Cathedral
11. Father Matthew Statue
12. Gresham Hotel
13. Charles Stewart Parnell Monument
14. Gate Theatre
15. Garden of Remembrance
16. Dublin Writers Museum
17. Hugh Lane Gallery & Francis Bacon Studio
18. James Joyce Cultural Centre

• *Now start north up O'Connell Street, walking on the wide, tree-lined median strip toward the spike in the sky.*

Statues and Monuments: Ireland's history is celebrated all along O'Connell Street. The median is dotted with statues remembering great figures from Ireland's past—particularly the century (c. 1830-1930) when Ireland rediscovered its roots and won its independence. At the base of the street stands the man for whom Dublin's main street is named—**❷ Daniel O'Connell** (1775-1847). He was known as the "Liberator" for founding the Catholic Association and demanding Irish Catholic rights in the British Parliament. He organized thousands of nonviolent protestors into "monster meetings," whose sheer size intimidated the British authorities.

Farther along is **❸ William Smith O'Brien,** O'Connell's contemporary and leader of the Young Ireland Movement, who was more willing to use force to reach his goals.

At Abbey Street, a one-block detour to the east (right) leads to the famous **❹ Abbey Theatre,** where turn-of-the-century nationalists (including the poet-playwright W. B. Yeats) staged Irish-themed plays.

• *Continue up O'Connell Street.*

Look for the statue of **❺ Sir John Gray,** who, as a newspaperman and politician, was able to help O'Connell's cause. The statue of **❻ James Larkin,** arms outstretched, honors the founder of the Irish Transport Workers Union.

• *On your left is the...*

❼ General Post Office (GPO): This is not just any P.O. It was from here that Patrick Pearse read the Proclamation of Irish Independence in 1916, kicking off the Easter Rising. The building itself—a kind of Irish Alamo—was the rebel headquarters and scene of a bloody five-day siege that followed the proclamation. The post office was particularly strategic because it housed the telegraph nerve center for the entire country. Its pillars are still pockmarked with bullet holes. The engaging GPO Witness History exhibit, on your right as you go inside, brings the dramatic history of this important building to life (see page 71).

• *Arch way back (at the intersection of O'Connell and Henry streets) and marvel up at...*

Busy O'Connell Street

❽ The Spire: There used to be a monument here to the British hero of Trafalgar, Admiral Horatio Nelson. It was blown up in 1966—the IRA's contribution to the local celebration of the Easter Rising's 50th anniversary. The spot is now occupied by the Spire: 398 feet of stainless steel. While it trumpets rejuvenation on its side of the river, it's a memorial to nothing and has no real meaning. Dubliners call it the tallest waste of €5 million in all of Europe. Its nickname? Take your pick: the Stiletto in the Ghetto, the Stiffy on the Liffey, the Pole in the Hole, or the Poker near the Croker (after nearby Croke Park).

• Detour a block west (left) down people-filled Henry Street (Dubliners' favorite shopping lane), then wander to the right into the nearby...

❾ Moore Street Market: Many merchants here have staffed the same stalls for decades (Mon-Sat 8:00-18:00, closed Sun). Start a conversation. It's a great workaday scene. You'll see lots of mums with strollers—a reminder that Ireland is one of Europe's youngest countries, with about 35 percent of the population under the age of 25. At the end of the 1916 Easter Rising, the rebel leaders retreated from the burning post office to 14-17 Moore Street, where they finally surrendered to British troops (see plaque high up).

• Return to O'Connell Street. A block east (right) of O'Connell, down Cathedral Street, detour to...

❿ St. Mary's Pro-Cathedral: Although this is Dublin's leading Catholic church, it isn't a cathedral but a "pro-cathedral" (as in "provisional")—essentially a parish church serving temporarily as a cathedral. The pope declared Christ Church to be a cathedral in the 12th century—and later, gave St. Patrick's the same designation (and they remain "cathedrals" even though they haven't been Catholic for centuries). For two centuries, St. Mary's has been part of the stage upon which Irish history has played out: Daniel

O'Connell gave a rousing speech here in 1825 at its dedication, and he lay in state here in 1847. It hosted the funeral Mass of Michael Collins in 1922, and Éamon de Valera (a leader of the Easter Rising) lay in state here in 1975.

• Back on O'Connell Street, head up the street (north) until you find the statue of...

⓫ Father Matthew: A leader of the temperance movement of the 1830s, Father Matthew was responsible, some historians claim, for enough Irish peasants staying sober to enable Daniel O'Connell to organize them into a political force.

Nearby, the fancy **⓬ Gresham Hotel** is a good place for an elegant tea or beer. In an earlier era, the beautiful people alighted here during visits to Dublin.

• Standing boldly at the top of O'Connell Street is a monument to...

⓭ Charles Stewart Parnell: Ringing the monument are the names of the four ancient provinces of Ireland and all 32 Irish counties (north and south, since this was erected before Irish partition). It's meant to honor Charles Stewart Parnell (1846-1891), the member of Parliament who nearly won Home Rule for Ireland in the late 1800s (and who served time at Kilmainham Gaol). A Cambridge-educated Protestant of landed-gentry stock, Parnell envisioned a modern, free Irish nation of Catholics—but not as a religious state. The Irish people, who remembered their grandparents' harsh evictions during the famine, came to love Parnell (despite his privileged birth) for his tireless work to secure fair rents and land tenure. Momentum seemed to be on his side. With the British prime minister of the time, William Gladstone, favoring a similar form of Home Rule, it looked as if Ireland was on its way toward independence as a Commonwealth nation, similar to Canada or Australia.

Then a sex scandal broke around Parnell and his mistress, the wife of another Parliament member. The press, egged on by the powerful Catholic bishops (who didn't want a secular, free Irish state), battered away at the scandal until finally Parnell was driven from office. Wracked with exhaustion and only in his mid-40s, Parnell died broken-hearted

After that, Ireland became mired in the conflicts of the 20th century: an awkward independence (1921) featuring a divided island, a bloody civil war, and sectarian violence for decades afterward.

• *Continue uphill, straight up Parnell Square East. At the* ⓴ *Gate Theatre (on the left), actors Orson Welles, Geraldine Fitzgerald, and James Mason had their professional stage debuts. One block up, on the left, is the...*

⓯ Garden of Remembrance: Honoring the victims of the 1916 Rising, this spot was where the rebel leaders were held before being transferred to Kilmainham Gaol. The park was dedicated in 1966 on the 50th anniversary of the revolt that ultimately led to Irish independence. The bottom of the cross-shaped pool is a mosaic of Celtic weapons, symbolic of how the early Irish proclaimed peace by breaking their weapons and throwing them into a lake or river. The Irish flag flies above the park: green for Catholics, orange for Protestants, and white for the hope that they can live together in peace (park open daily 8:30-18:00).

One of modern Ireland's most stirring moments occurred here in May 2011, when Queen Elizabeth II made this the first stop on her historic visit to Ireland. She laid a wreath at the **Children of Lir** sculpture under this flag and bowed her head in silence out of respect for the Irish rebels who had fought and died trying to gain freedom from her United Kingdom. This was a hugely cathartic moment for both nations. Until this visit, no British monarch had set foot in the Irish state since its founding 90 years earlier.

• *Your walk is over. Two excellent museums are nearby, standing side-by-side: the* ⓰ *Dublin Writers Museum (in a splendidly restored Georgian mansion, see page 68)*

Ⓐ *General Post Office*

Ⓑ *The Spire*

Ⓒ *Moore Street Market*

Ⓓ *Statue of Charles Stewart Parnell*

Garden of Remembrance

and the art-filled ⑰ *Hugh Lane Gallery (page 70). Here at the north end of town, it's also convenient to visit the* ⑱ *James Joyce Centre (a short walk away, see page 70), or the Gaelic Athletic Association Museum at Croke Park Stadium (described on page 75, a 20-minute walk or short taxi ride away). Otherwise, hop on your skateboard and zip back to the river.*

SIGHTS

South of the River Liffey
▲▲TRINITY COLLEGE TOUR

Founded in 1592 by Queen Elizabeth I to establish a Protestant way of thinking about God, Trinity has long been Ireland's most prestigious college. Originally, the student body was limited to rich Protestant men. Women were admitted in 1903, and Catholics—although allowed entrance by the school much earlier—were only given formal permission by the Catholic Church to study at Trinity in the 1970s.

Trinity students lead 30-minute tours of their campus (look just inside the gate for posted departure times and a ticket seller on a stool). You'll get a rundown of the mostly Georgian architecture; a peek at student life past and present; and the enjoyable company of your guide, a witty Irish college kid.

Cost and Hours: €6, €14 combo-ticket also covers Book of Kells (where the tour leaves you), cash preferred; tours run daily 9:15-16:00, Sat-Sun only in Feb-April and Oct-Nov, no tours Dec-Jan; tours depart roughly every 30 minutes, weather permitting, https://www.tcd.ie/visitors/tours/.

▲▲▲BOOK OF KELLS IN THE TRINITY OLD LIBRARY

The Book of Kells—a 1,200-year-old version of the four gospels—was elaborately inked and meticulously illustrated by faithful monks. Combining Christian symbols and pagan styles, it's a snapshot of medieval Ireland in transition. Arguably the finest piece of art from what is generally called the Dark Ages, the Book of Kells shows that monastic life in this far fringe of Europe was far from dark.

Rick's Tip: *Lines at the* **Book of Kells** *are longest at midday (roughly 11:00-14:30). Those with online tickets skip the queue. To have it all to yourself, be there at opening.*

Cost and Hours: €13, €10 off-peak ticket is good before 10:00 and after 15:00, €14 combo-ticket also covers tour—see details above; May-Sept Mon-Sat 8:30-17:00, Sun from 9:30; Oct-April Mon-Sat 9:30-17:00, Sun 12:00-16:30; audioguide-€5, tel. 01/896-2320, www.tcd.ie/visitors/book-of-kells.

❷ SELF-GUIDED TOUR

Your visit has three stages: 1) an exhibit on the making of the Book of Kells, including poster-sized reproductions of its pages (your best look at the book's detail); 2) the Treasury, the darkened room containing the Book of Kells itself and other, less ornate contemporaneous volumes; and, upstairs, 3) the Old Library (called the Long Room), containing historical objects.

Background: The Book of Kells was a labor of love created by dedicated Irish monks cloistered on the remote Scottish island of Iona. They slaughtered 185 calves, soaked the skins in lime, scraped off the hair, and dried the skins into a cream-colored writing surface called vellum. Only then could the tonsured monks pick up their swan-quill pens and get to work.

The project may have been underway in 806 when Vikings savagely pillaged and burned Iona, killing 68 monks. The survivors fled to the Abbey of Kells (near Dublin). Scholars debate exactly where the book was produced: It could have been made entirely at Iona or at Kells, or started in Iona and finished at Kells.

For eight centuries, the glorious gospel sat regally atop the high altar of the monastery church at Kells, where the priest would read from it during special Masses. In 1654, as Cromwell's puritanical rule settled in, the book was smuggled to Dublin for safety. Here at Trinity College, it was first displayed to the public in the mid-1800s. In 1953, the book got its current covers and was bound into four separate volumes.

The Exhibit: The first-class "Turning Darkness into Light" exhibit, with a one-way route, puts the illuminated manuscript in its historical and cultural context, preparing you to see the original book and other precious manuscripts in the treasury. Make a point to spend time in the exhibit (before reaching the actual Book of Kells). Especially interesting are the short, continuously running video clips that show the ancient art of bookbinding and the exacting care that went into transcribing the monk-uscripts. Don't miss these as they vividly show the skill and patience needed for the monks' work.

The Book: The Book of Kells contains the four gospels of the Bible (typically only two of the gospels are on display at any given time). Altogether, it's 680 pages long (or 340 "folios," the equivalent of one sheet, front and back). The Latin calligraphy—all in capital letters—follows ruled lines, forming

Tour at Trinity College

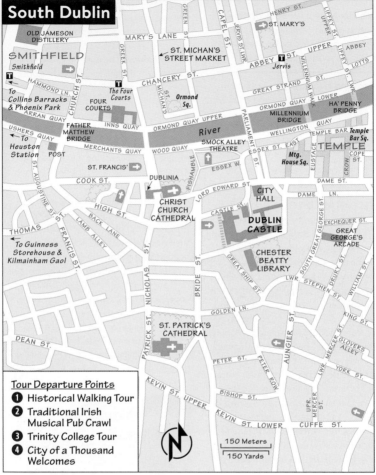

South Dublin

OLD JAMESON DISTILLERY

SMITHFIELD

Smithfield

To Collins Barracks & Phoenix Park

HAMMOND LN.

ARRAN QUAY

FATHER MATTHEW BRIDGE

USHERS QUAY

To Heuston Station

GREEK ST.

MARY'S LANE

ST. MICHAN'S STREET MARKET

CHANCERY ST.

The Four Courts

FOUR COURTS

INNS QUAY

MERCHANTS QUAY

GREEN ST.

CAPEL ST.

JERVIS ST.

HENRY ST.

ST. MARY'S

ABBEY ST. UPPER

Jervis

ABBEY

LIFFEY ST. LWR.

LOTTS

GREAT STRAND ST.

ORMOND QUAY LOWER

MILLENNIUM BRIDGE

HA' PENNY BRIDGE

QUAY

River

Ormond Sq.

ORMOND QUAY UPPER

WELLINGTON

TEMPLE BAR

Temple Bar Sq.

WOOD QUAY

SMOCK ALLEY THEATRE

ESSEX ST. EAST

TEMPLE

POST

ST. FRANCIS'

COOK ST.

ESSEX W.

Mtg. House Sq.

COPE ST.

CROW ST.

DUBLINIA

CHRIST CHURCH CATHEDRAL

LORD EDWARD ST.

DAME ST.

CITY HALL

DAME

LN.

HIGH ST.

BACK LANE

LAMB ALLEY

THOMAS

To Guinness Storehouse & Kilmainham Gaol

CASTLE ST.

DUBLIN CASTLE

EXCHEQUER ST.

GREAT GEORGE'S ARCADE

CHESTER BEATTY LIBRARY

GREAT SHIP ST.

LWR. STEPHEN ST.

STEPHEN

WILLIAM ST.

DRURY ST.

NICHOLAS ST.

BRIDE ST.

GOLDEN LN.

KING ST.

ST. PATRICK'S CATHEDRAL

PATRICK ST.

DEAN ST.

PETER ST.

PETER ROW

AUNGIER ST.

MERCER ST.

GLOVERS ALLEY

YORK ST.

KEVIN ST. UPPER

BISHOP ST.

KEVIN ST. LOWER

CUFFE ST.

UPR. MERCER ST.

Tour Departure Points
1 Historical Walking Tour
2 Traditional Irish Musical Pub Crawl
3 Trinity College Tour
4 City of a Thousand Welcomes

150 Meters

150 Yards

N

---

neat horizontal bars across the page. Sentences end with a "period" of three dots. The black-brown ink was made from the galls of oak trees.

The text is elaborately decorated— of the hundreds of pages, only two are without illustration. Each gospel begins with a full-page depiction of the Evangelists and their symbols: Matthew (angel), Mark (lion), Luke (ox), and John (eagle). The apostles pose stiffly, like Byzantine-style icons, with almond-shaped eyes and symmetrically creased robes. The true beauty lies in the intricate designs that surround the figures.

The colorful book employs blue, purple, red, pink, green, and yellow pigments (all imported)—but no gold leaf. Letters and borders are braided together. On most pages, the initial letters are big and flowery, like in a children's fairytale book.

Notice how the playful monks might cross a "t" with a fish, form an "h" from a spindly-legged man, or make an "e" out of a coiled snake. Animals crouch between sentences. It's a jungle of intricate designs, inhabited by tiny creatures both real and fanciful.

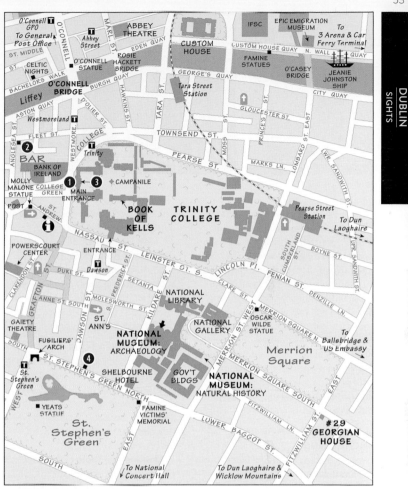

Scholars think three main artists created the book: the "goldsmith" (who did the filigree-style designs), the "illustrator" (who specialized in animals and grotesques), and the "portrait painter" (who did the Evangelists and Mary). Some of the detail work is unbelievably minute.

The Old Library: The Long Room, the 200-foot-long main chamber of the Old Library (from 1732), is stacked to its towering ceiling with 200,000 books. Among the displays here, you'll find one of a dozen surviving original copies of

the **Proclamation of the Irish Republic.** Patrick Pearse read out its words at Dublin's General Post Office on April 24, 1916, starting the Easter Rising that led to Irish independence. Notice the inclusive opening phrase ("Irishmen and Irishwomen") and the seven signatories (each of whom was executed).

Another national icon is nearby: the oldest surviving Irish **harp,** from the 15th century (sometimes called the Brian Boru harp, although it was crafted 400 years after the death of this Irish king). The brass pins on its oak and willow frame once

Book of Kells

Old Library, Trinity College

held 29 strings. In Celtic days, poets—highly influential with kings and druid priests—wandered the land, uniting the people with songs and stories. The harp's inspirational effect on Gaelic culture was so strong that Queen Elizabeth I (1558-1603) ordered Irish harpists to be hung and their instruments smashed. Even today, the love of music is so intense that Ireland is the only country with a musical instrument as its national symbol. You'll see this harp's likeness on the back of Irish euro coins, on government documents, and (respectfully reversed) on every pint of Guinness.

▲▲▲NATIONAL MUSEUM: ARCHAEOLOGY

Showing off the treasures of Ireland from the Stone Age to modern times, this branch of the National Museum is itself a national treasure. The soggy marshes and peat bogs of Ireland have proven perfect for preserving old objects. You'll see 4,000-year-old gold jewelry, 2,000-year-old bog mummies, 1,000-year-old Viking swords, and the collection's superstar—the exquisitely wrought Tara Brooch. Visit here to get an introduction to the rest of Ireland's historic attractions: You'll find a reconstructed passage tomb like Newgrange, Celtic art like the Book of Kells, Viking objects from Dublin, a model of the Hill of Tara, and a sacred cross from the Cong Abbey. Hit the highlights of the following self-guided tour, then browse the

exhibits at will, all well-described throughout. For background information on Irish art, see page 326.

Cost and Hours: Free, Tue-Sat 10:00-17:00, Sun from 14:00, closed Mon, €3 audioguide covers only Treasury room, good café, between Trinity College and St. Stephen's Green on Kildare Street, tel. 01/677-7444, www.museum.ie.

❂ SELF-GUIDED TOUR

• *On the ground floor, enter the main hall and get oriented (with the help of this book's map): In the center (down four steps) are displays of prehistoric gold jewelry. To the left are the bog bodies, to the right is the Treasury, and upstairs is the Viking world. We'll start at Ireland's beginning.*

❶ **Stone Age Tools:** Glass cases hold flint and stone axeheads and arrowheads (7,000 B.C.). Ireland's first inhabitants—hunters and fishers who came from Scotland—used these tools. These early people also left behind standing stones (dolmens) and passage tombs.

❷ **Reconstructed Passage Tomb:** At the corner of the room, you'll see a typical tomb circa 3,000 B.C.—a mound-shaped, heavy stone structure, covered with smaller rocks, with a passage leading into a central burial chamber where the deceased's ashes were interred. This is a modest tomb; the vast passage tombs at Newgrange and Knowth (see pages 93 and 94) are similar but many times bigger.

❸ **The Hill of Tara:** The famous

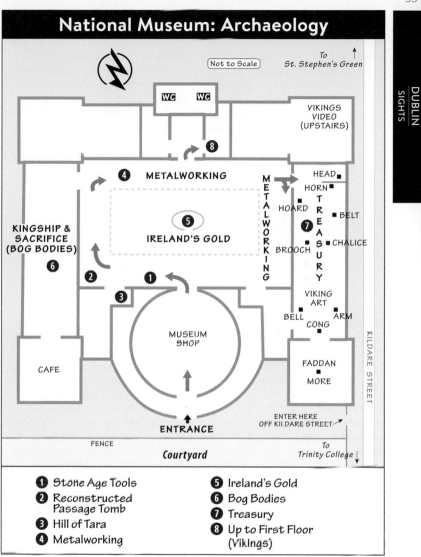

National Museum: Archaeology

Not to Scale

To
St. Stephen's Green

WC   WC

VIKINGS
VIDEO
(UPSTAIRS)

8

4 METALWORKING

HEAD

HORN

M
E
T
A
L
W
O
R
K
I
N
G

HOARD

T
R
E
A
S
U
R
Y

BELT

5
IRELAND'S GOLD

7

BROOCH

CHALICE

KINGSHIP &
SACRIFICE
(BOG BODIES)

6

2

3

1

VIKING
ART

BELL   ARM
CONG

MUSEUM
SHOP

FADDAN
MORE

CAFE

KILDARE STREET

ENTER HERE
OFF KILDARE STREET

ENTRANCE

FENCE

Courtyard

To
Trinity College

- **1** Stone Age Tools
- **2** Reconstructed Passage Tomb
- **3** Hill of Tara
- **4** Metalworking
- **5** Ireland's Gold
- **6** Bog Bodies
- **7** Treasury
- **8** Up to First Floor (Vikings)

passage-tomb burial site at Tara, known as the Mound of the Hostages, was used for more than 1,500 years as a place to inter human remains. The cases in this side gallery display some of the many exceptional Neolithic and Bronze Age finds uncovered at the site.

Over the millennia, the Mound became the very symbol of Irish heritage. This is where Ireland's kings claimed their power, where St. Patrick preached his deal-clinching sermon, and where, in 1843, Daniel O'Connell rallied Irish patriots to demand their independence from Britain (see illustration in poster on the left wall).

4 The Evolution of Metalworking:
Around 2500 B.C., Ireland discovered how to make metal—mining ore, smelting it

in furnaces, and casting or hammering it into shapes. The rest is prehistory. You'll travel through the Bronze Age (axeheads from 2000 B.C.) and Iron Age (500 B.C.) as you examine assorted spears, shields, swords, and war horns. The cauldrons made for everyday cooking were also used ceremonially to prepare elaborate ritual feasts for friends and symbolic offerings for the gods.

❺ Ireland's Gold: Ireland had only modest gold deposits, mainly gathered by prehistoric people panning for small nuggets and dust in the rivers. But the jewelry they left, some of it more than 4,000 years old, is exquisite. The earliest fashion choice was a broad necklace hammered flat (a *lunula,* so called for its crescent-moon shape). This might be worn with accompanying earrings and sun-disc brooches. The Gleninsheen Collar (c. 700 B.C.) was found by a farmer in a crevice of the exposed bedrock of the Burren. It's thought that this valuable status symbol was hidden there during a time of conflict, then forgotten (or its owner killed)—if it had been meant as an offering to a pagan god it more likely would have been left in a body of water (the portal to the underworld). Later Bronze Age jewelry was cast from clay molds into bracelets and unique "dress fasteners" that wearers would slip into buttonholes to secure a cloak. Some of these gold objects may have been gifts to fertility gods.

❻ Bog Bodies: When the Celts arrived in Ireland (c. 500 B.C.-A.D. 500), they brought with them a mysterious

practice: They brutally murdered sacrificial slaves or prisoners and buried them in bogs. Four bodies (each in its own tiny theater with a description outside)—shriveled and leathery, but remarkably preserved—have been dug up from around the Celtic world.

Clonycavan Man is from Ireland. One summer day around 200 B.C., this twentysomething man was hacked to death with an axe and disemboweled. In his time, he stood 5'9" tall and had a Mohawk-style haircut, poofed up with pine-resin hair product imported from France. Today you can still see traces of his hair. Only his upper body survived; the lower part may have been lost in the threshing machine that unearthed him in 2003.

Why were these people killed? It appears to have been a form of ritual human sacrifice of high-status people. Some may have been enemy chiefs or political rivals. The sacrifices could have been offerings to the gods to ensure rich harvests and good luck. Other items (now on display) were buried along with them—gold bracelets, royal cloaks, and finely wrought cauldrons.

❼ Treasury: Irish metalworking is legendary, and this room holds 1,500 years of exquisite objects. Working from one end of the long room to the other, you'll journey from the world of the pagan Celts to the coming of Christianity, explore the stylistic impact of the Viking invasions (9th-12th century), and consider the resurgence of ecclesiastical metalworking (11th-12th century).

Pagan Era Art: The **carved stone head** of a mysterious pagan god greets you (#19, circa A.D. 100). The god's three faces express the different aspects of his stony personality. This abstract style—typical of Celtic art—would be at home in a modern art museum. A **bronze horn** (#17, first century B.C.) is the kind of curved war trumpet that Celts blasted to freak out the Roman legions on the Continent (the Romans never invaded Ireland). The fine objects

Bog mummy

of the **Broighter Hoard** (#15, first century B.C.) include a king's golden collar decorated in textbook Celtic style, with interlaced vines inhabited by stylized faces. The tiny boat was an offering to the sea god. The coconut-shell-shaped bowl symbolized a cauldron. By custom, the cauldron held food as a constant offering to Danu, the Celtic mother goddess, whose mythical palace was at Brú na Bóinne.

Early Christian Objects: Christianity officially entered Ireland in the fifth century (when St. Patrick converted the pagan king), but Celtic legends and art continued well into the Christian era. You'll see various crosses, shrines (portable reliquaries containing holy relics), and chalices decorated with Celtic motifs. The **Belt Shrine** (#32)—a circular metal casing that held a saint's leather belt—was thought to have magical properties. When placed around someone's waist, it could heal the wearer or force him or her to tell the truth.

The **Ardagh Chalice** (#30) and the nearby **Silver Paten** (#31) were used during Communion to hold blessed wine and bread. Get close to admire the elaborate workmanship. The main bowl of the chalice is gilded bronze, with a contrasting band of intricately patterned gold filigree. It's studded with colorful glass, amber, and enamels. Mirrors below the display case show that even the underside of the chalice was decorated. When the priest grabbed the chalice by its two handles and tipped it to his lips, the base could be admired by God.

Tara Brooch: A rich eighth-century Celtic man fastened his cloak at the shoulder with this elaborate ring-shaped brooch (#29), its seven-inch stick-pin tilted rakishly upward. Made of cast and gilded silver, it's ornamented with fine, exquisitely filigreed gold panels and studded with amber, enamel, and colored glass. The motifs include Celtic spirals, snakes, and stylized faces, but the symbolism is neither overtly pagan nor Christian—it's art for art's sake. Despite its name, the brooch probably has no connection to the Hill of Tara. In display cases nearby, you'll see other similar (but less impressive) brooches from the same period—some iron, some bronze, and one in pure gold.

Viking Art Styles: When Vikings invaded Dublin around A.D. 800, they raped and pillaged. But they also opened Ireland to a vast and cosmopolitan trading empire, from which they imported hoards of silver (see the display case of ingots). Viking influence shows up in the decorative style of reliquaries like the **Lismore Crozier** (#43, in the shape of a bishop's ceremonial shepherd's crook) and the **Shrine of St. Lochter's Arm** (raised in an Irish-power salute). The impressive **Bell of St. Patrick** (#24) was supposedly owned by Ireland's patron saint. After his death, it was encased within a beautifully worked shrine (displayed above) and kept safe by a single family, who passed it down from generation to generation for 800 years.

Cross of Cong: "By this cross is covered the cross on which the Creator

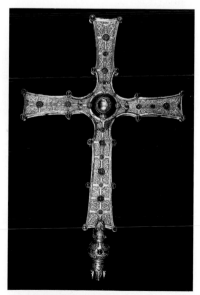

Cross of Cong

of the world suffered." Running along the sides of the cross (#44), this Latin inscription tells us that it once held a sacred relic, a tiny splinter of the True Cross on which Jesus was crucified. That piece of wood (now lost) had been given in 1123 to the Irish high king, who commissioned this reliquary to preserve the splinter (it would have been placed right in the center, visible through the large piece of rock crystal). Every Christmas and Easter, the cross was fitted onto a staff and paraded through the abbey at Cong, then placed on the altar for High Mass. The extraordinarily detailed decoration features gold filigree interspersed with colored glass, enamel, and (now missing) precious stones. Though fully Christian, the cross has Celtic-style filigree patterning and Viking-style animal heads (notice how they grip the cross in their jaws).

Before leaving the Treasury, enter the room behind the Cross of Cong and check out the **Faddan More Psalter**—a (pretty beat-up) manuscript of the Book of Psalms from the same era as the Book of Kells.

• *Now head up to the first floor to the Viking world. Start in the long hall directly above the Treasury, with the informative 25-minute video on the Viking influence on Irish culture.*

❽ **Viking Ireland** (c. 800-1150): Dublin was born as a Viking town. Sometime after 795, Scandinavian warriors rowed their long ships up the River Liffey and made camp on the south bank, around the location of today's Dublin Castle and Christ Church. Over the next two centuries, they built "Dubh linn" ("black pool" in Irish) into an important trading post, slave market, metalworking center, and the first true city in Ireland. (See a model of Dublin showing a recently excavated area near Kilmainham Gaol.)

The state-of-the-art Viking boats worked equally well in the open ocean and shallow rivers, and were perfect for stealth invasions and far-ranging trading. Soon, provincial Dublin was connected with the wider world—Scotland, England, northern Europe, even Asia. The museum's displays of swords and spears make it clear that, yes, the Vikings were fierce warriors. But you'll also see that they were respected merchants (standardized weights and coins), herders and craftsmen (leather shoes and bags), fashion-conscious (bone combs and jewelry), fun-loving (board games), and literate (runic alphabet). What you won't see are horned helmets, which, despite the stereotype, were not Viking. By 1050, the pagan Vikings had intermarried with the locals, become Christian, and were melting into Irish society.

▲**NATIONAL GALLERY OF IRELAND**
This gallery, adjacent to the archaeology branch, is not as extensive as national galleries in London or Paris, but its collections are well worth your time. The beautifully renovated museum boasts an impressive range of works by European masters and displays the works of top Irish painters, including Jack B. Yeats (brother of the famous poet).

Cost and Hours: Free, Mon-Sat 9:30-17:30, Thu until 20:30, Sun 11:00-17:30, Merrion Square West, tel. 01/661-5133, www.nationalgallery.ie.

Tours: Take advantage of the free audioguide (donations accepted) as well

Caravaggio, The Taking of Christ

as free 45-minute guided tours (Sat at 12:30; Sun at 12:30 and 13:30).

Visiting the Museum: Be sure to walk through the series of rooms on the ground floor devoted to Irish painting and get to know artists you may not have heard of before. Visit the National Portrait Gallery on the mezzanine level for an insight into the great personalities of Ireland. You'll find European masterworks on the top floor, including a rare Vermeer (one of only 30-some known works by the Dutch artist), a classic Caravaggio (master of chiaroscuro and dramatic lighting), a Monet riverscape, and an early Cubist Picasso still life.

Perhaps the most iconic of all the Irish art in this museum is the melodramatic (and huge) c. 1854 depiction of the *Marriage of Strongbow and Aiofe* by Daniel Maclise. It captures the chaotic union of Norman and Irish interests that signaled the start of English domination of Ireland 850 years ago. Notice how the defeated Irish writhe and lament in the bright light of the foreground, while the scheming Norman warlords skulk in the dimly lit middle ground. The ruins of conquered Waterford smolder at the back.

St. Stephen's Green and Nearby
▲MERRION SQUARE

Laid out in 1762, this square is ringed by elegant Georgian houses decorated with fine doors—a Dublin trademark. (If you're inspired by the ornate knobs and knockers, there's a shop by that name on nearby Nassau Street.) The park, once the exclusive domain of the residents (among them, Daniel O'Connell at #58 and W. B. Yeats at #82), is now a delightful public escape and ideal for a picnic. To learn what "snogging" is, walk through the park on a sunny day, when it's full of smooching lovers. Oscar Wilde, lounging wittily on a boulder on the corner nearest the town center and surrounded by his clever quotes, provides a fun photo op.

▲GRAFTON STREET

Once filled with noisy traffic, today's Grafton Street is Dublin's liveliest pedestrian shopping drag and people-watching paradise. A 10-minute stroll past street musicians takes you from Trinity College to St. Stephen's Green.

You'll pass two venerable department stores: the Irish Brown Thomas and the English Marks & Spencer. Johnson's Court alley leads to the Powerscourt Townhouse Shopping Centre, which tastefully fills a converted Georgian mansion. The huge, glass-covered St. Stephen's Green Shopping Centre and the peaceful green itself mark the top of Grafton Street.

▲ST. STEPHEN'S GREEN

This city park was originally a medieval commons, complete with gory public executions. The park got its start in 1664, when the city leased some of the land as building lots—and each tenant was obligated to plant six trees. Gradually the green was surrounded with fine Georgian buildings. Today (like New York's Central Park) it provides a grassy refuge for

St. Stephen's Green

Modern Ireland's Turbulent Birth

Imagine if our American patriot ancestors had fought both our Revolutionary War and our Civil War over a span of seven chaotic years...and then appreciate the remarkable resilience of the Irish people. Here's a summary of what happened when.

Easter Rising, 1916: A nationalist militia called the Volunteers (led by **Patrick Pearse**) and the socialist Irish Citizen Army (led by **James Connolly**) join forces in the Easter Rising, but they fail to end 750 years of British rule. The uprising is unpopular with most Irish, who are unhappy with the destruction in Dublin and preoccupied with the "Great War" on the Continent. But when 16 rebel leaders (including Pearse and Connolly) are executed, Irish public opinion reverses as sympathy grows for the martyrs and the cause of Irish Independence.

Two important rebel leaders escape execution. Brooklyn-born **Éamon de Valera** is spared because of his American passport (the British don't want to anger their potential ally in World War I). **Michael Collins,** a low-ranking rebel officer who fought in the Rising at the General Post Office, refines urban guerrilla-warfare strategies in prison, and then blossoms after his release as the rebels' military and intelligence leader in the power vacuum that followed the executions.

General Election, 1918: World War I ends and a general election is held in Ireland (the first in which women can vote). Outside of Ulster, the nationalist **Sinn Fein** party wins 73 out of 79 seats in Parliament. Only four out of 32 counties vote to maintain the Union with Britain (all four lie in today's Northern Ireland). Rather than take their seats in London, Sinn Fein representatives abstain from participating in a government they see as foreign occupiers.

War of Independence, 1919: On January 19, the abstaining Sinn Fein members set up a rebel government in Dublin called Dáil Éireann. On the same day, the first shots of the Irish War of Independence are fired as rebels begin ambushing police barracks, which are seen as an extension of British rule. De Valera is

Dubliners. At the northwest corner (near the end of Grafton Street) you'll be confronted by a looming marble arch erected to honor British officers killed during the Boer War. Locals nicknamed it "Traitor's Arch," as most Irish sympathized with the underdog Boers.

During the 1916 Easter Rising, a group of passionate rebels—a mishmash of romantic poets, teachers, aristocratic ladies, and slum dwellers—dug trenches in the park to hunker down, believing they were creating fortified positions. They hadn't figured on veteran British troops easily trumping their move by placing snipers atop the Shelbourne Hotel (with a bird's-eye view into the trenches).

On a sunny afternoon, this open space is a wonderful world apart from the big city. When marveling at the elegance of Georgian Dublin, remember that it was the second-most important city in the British Empire in that era.

Dublin Castle and Nearby
▲DUBLIN CASTLE

Built on the spot of the first Viking fortress, this castle was the seat of English

elected by the Dáil to lead the rebels, with Collins as his deputy. Collins' web of spies infiltrates British intelligence at Dublin Castle. The Volunteers rename themselves the **Irish Republican Army;** meanwhile the British beef up their military presence in Ireland by sending in tough WWI vets, the Black and Tans. A bloody and very personal war ensues.

Anglo-Irish Treaty, 1921: Having lived through the slaughter of World War I, the British tire of the extended bloodshed in Ireland and begin negotiations with the rebels. De Valera leads rebel negotiations, but then entrusts them to Collins (a clever politician, De Valera sees that whoever signs a treaty will be blamed for its compromises). Understanding the tricky position he's been placed in, Collins signs the Anglo-Irish Treaty in December, lamenting that in doing so he has signed his "own death warrant."

The Dáil narrowly ratifies the treaty (64 to 57), but Collins' followers are unable to convince De Valera's supporters that the compromises are a stepping stone to later full independence. De Valera and his antitreaty disciples resign in protest. **Arthur Griffith,** founder of Sinn Fein, assumes the presidential post.

Irish Civil War, 1921: In June, the antitreaty forces, holed up in the Four Courts building in Dublin, are fired upon by Collins and his pro-treaty forces—thus igniting the Irish Civil War. The British want the treaty to stand and even supply Collins with cannons, meanwhile threatening to reenter Ireland if the antitreaty forces aren't put down.

Aftermath, 1922/23: In August 1922, Griffith dies of stress-induced illness, and Collins is assassinated 10 days later. Nevertheless, the protreaty forces prevail, as they are backed by popular opinion and better (British-supplied) military equipment. By April 1923, the remaining IRA forces dump (or stash) their arms, ending the civil war...but many bitter IRA vets vow to carry on the fight. De Valera distances himself from the IRA and becomes the dominant Irish political leader for the next 40 years.

rule in Ireland for 700 years. Located where the Poddle and Liffey rivers came together, making a black pool (*dubh linn* in Irish), Dublin Castle was the official residence of the viceroy who implemented the will of the British royalty. In this stirring setting, the Brits handed power over to Michael Collins and the Irish in 1922. Today, it's used for fancy state and charity functions (which may sporadically close it to the public).

Cost and Hours: Visiting the courtyard is free, €10 for one-hour guided tour, €7 to visit on your own (state apartments

Dublin Castle

only); Mon-Sat 10:00-16:45, Sun from 12:00, tours depart every 30 minutes; tickets sold in courtyard under portico opposite clock tower, tel. 01/645-8813, www.dublincastle.ie.

Visiting the Castle: Standing in the courtyard, you can imagine the ugliness of the British-Irish situation. Notice the statue of justice above the gate—pointedly without her blindfold and admiring her sword. As Dubliners say, "There she stands, above her station, with her face to the palace and her arse to the nation."

The fancy interior is viewable on a guided tour, which offers a fairly boring room-by-room walk through the lavish state apartments of this most English of Irish palaces. The tour also includes a look at the foundations of the Norman tower as well as original Viking defenses, and the best remaining chunk of the 13th-century town wall.

▲▲CHESTER BEATTY LIBRARY

This library—located in the gardens of Dublin Castle (follow the signs)—is an exquisite, delightfully displayed collection of rare ancient manuscripts and beautifully illustrated books from around the world, plus a few odd curios. These treasures were bequeathed by Alfred Chester Beatty (1875-1968), a rich American mining magnate who traveled widely, collected 66,000 objects assiduously, and retired to Ireland.

Cost and Hours: Free; Mon-Fri 10:00-17:00, Sat from 11:00, Sun from 13:00, closed Mon Nov-Feb; library's Silk Road Café is fine for a light lunch—see listing under "Eating in Dublin"; tel. 01/407-0750, www.cbl.ie.

◉ SELF-GUIDED TOUR

Start on the ground floor, with a 10-minute film about Beatty. Then head upstairs to the second floor to see the treasures he left to his adopted country. Note that exhibits often rotate, so they may not be on display in the order outlined here.

Sacred Traditions Gallery: This space is dedicated to sacred texts, illuminated

manuscripts, and miniature paintings from around the world. The doors swing open, and you're greeted by a video highlighting a diverse array of religious rites—a Christian wedding, Muslims kneeling for prayer, whirling dervishes, and so on.

• *Tour the floor clockwise, starting with Christian texts on the left side of the room. There you'll find several glass cases containing...*

Ancient Bible Fragments: In the 1930s, Beatty acquired these 1,800-year-old manuscripts, which had recently been unearthed in Egypt. The Indiana Jones-like discovery instantly bumped scholars' knowledge of the early Bible up a notch. There were Old Testament books, New Testament books, and—rarest of all—the Letters of Paul. Written in Greek on papyrus more than a century before previously known documents, these are some of the oldest versions of these texts in existence. Unlike most early Christian texts, the manuscripts were not rolled up in a scroll but bound in a book form called a "codex." On display you may see pages from a third-century Gospel of Luke or the Gospel of John (c. A.D. 150-200). Jesus died around A.D. 33, and his words weren't recorded until decades later. Most early manuscripts date from the fourth century, so these pages are about as close to the source as you can get.

Letters (Epistles) of Paul: The Beatty has 112 pages of Saint Paul's collected letters (A.D. 180-200). Paul, a Roman citizen (c. A.D. 5-67; see Albrecht Dürer's engraving of the saint), was the apostle most responsible for spreading Christianity beyond Palestine. Originally, Paul reviled Christians. But after a mystical experience, he went on to travel the known world, preaching the Good News in sophisticated Athens and the greatest city in the world, Rome, where he died a martyr to the cause. Along the way, he kept in touch with Christian congregations in cities like Corinth, Ephesus, and Rome with these letters.

Continuing up the left side of the room, you'll find gloriously illustrated **medieval Bibles** and **prayer books,** including an intricate, colorful, gold-speckled Book of Hours (1408).

• *Turn the corner into the center of the room, to find the sacred texts of...*

Islam: Muslims believe that the angel Gabriel visited Muhammad (c. 570-632), instructing him to write down his heavenly visions in a book—the Quran. You'll see Qurans with elaborate calligraphy, such as one made in Baghdad in 1001. Nearby are other sacred Islamic texts, some beautifully illustrated, where you may find the rare illuminated manuscript of the "Life of the Prophet" (c. 1595), produced in Istanbul for an Ottoman sultan.

• *On the right side of the room, you enter the world of...*

East Asian Religions: Statues of Gautama Buddha (c. 563-483 B.C.) and Chinese Buddhist scrolls attest to the pervasive influence of this wise man. Buddha was born in India, but his philosophy spread to China, Japan, and Tibet (see the mandalas). Continuing clockwise, you'll reach the writings from India, the land of a million gods—and the cradle of Buddhism, Hinduism, Sikhism, and Jainism.

• *Your visit continues downstairs on the first floor, in the gallery devoted to the...*

Arts of the Book: The focus here is on the many forms a "book" can take—from the earliest clay tablets and papyrus scrolls, to parchment scrolls and bound codexes, to medieval monks' wondrous illustrations, to the advent of printing and bookbinding, to the dawn of the 21st century and the digital age.

• *Tour the floor clockwise. Immediately to the left, find a glass case containing...*

Egyptian and Other Ancient Writings: A hieroglyph-covered papyrus scroll from the Book of the Dead (c. 300 B.C.) depicts a pharaoh on his throne (left) presiding over a soul's judgment in the afterlife. The jackal-headed god Anubis (center-right) holds a scale, weighing the heart of a dead woman to see if it's light enough for her to level up to the next phase of eternity. Nearby (in a freestanding glass case, near the bottom) are a few small cuneiform tablets and cylinder seals from as far back as 2,700 B.C. These objects from ancient Sumeria (modern-day Iraq) are older than the pyramids and represent the very birth of writing.

• *Continue up the left side of the room, perusing displays on...*

Printing, Illustrating, and Bookbinding: The printing press with movable type was perfected by Johannes Gutenberg in Germany around 1450. The printed sheets were folded, sewn together, and wrapped in a cover. With the engraving process, beautiful illustrations could also be reproduced on a mass scale. Until the 20th century, it was common for a book buyer to acquire the printed sheets and then select a lavish custom-made cover.

• *Turn the corner to the center of the room.*

Islamic World: These are secular books—science textbooks and poetry—many from the rich Persian culture (mod-

Islamic manuscript painting,
Chester Beatty Library

ern-day Iran). Some are richly illustrated with elaborate calligraphy. While Islam avoids representations of living things, as you can see, that restriction doesn't apply to nonreligious texts.

• *Continue to the right side of the room.*

Far East: Besides albums and scrolls, you might see eye-catching Japanese woodblock prints, ornate Chinese snuff bottles, rhino-horn cups, and the silk dragon robes of Chinese emperors of the Qing dynasty (1644-1911). The Qianlong Emperor (r. 1736-1795)—a poet and arts patron—welcomed European Jesuits to his court and commissioned a huge collection of books, including some carved from jade.

DUBLIN CITY HALL

The first Georgian building in this very Georgian city stands proudly overlooking Dame Street, in front of the gate to Dublin Castle. Built in 1779 as the Royal Exchange (where one changed money), it introduced Ireland to the Georgian style then very popular in Britain. In 1852, the building became the City Hall.

Downstairs, don't miss the free **"Story of the Capital" exhibit.** It's excellent, tracing the history of Dublin through artifacts and models as well as video clips, including *The City in Turmoil.*

Cost and Hours: Free, Mon-Sat

Dublin City Hall

10:00-17:15, closed Sun, coffee shop, tel. 01/222-2204.

Dublin's Cathedral Area

Because of Dublin's English past (particularly Henry VIII's Reformation, and the dissolution of the Catholic monasteries in both Ireland and England in 1539), the city's top two churches are no longer Catholic. Christ Church Cathedral and nearby St. Patrick's Cathedral are both Church of Ireland (Anglican). In the late 19th century, the cathedrals underwent extensive restoration. The rich Guinness brewery family forked out the dough to try to make St. Patrick's Cathedral outshine Christ Church—whose patrons were the equally rich, rival Jameson family of distillery fame.

CHRIST CHURCH CATHEDRAL

Occupying the same site as the first wooden church built on this spot by King Sitric in late Viking times (c. 1030), the present structure is a mix of periods: Norman and Gothic, but mostly Victorian Neo-Gothic from the late 19th century.

Cost and Hours: €6.50 includes downstairs crypt exhibition, €14.50 combo-ticket includes Dublinia (described next); Mon-Sat 9:30-17:00, Sun 12:00-14:30; €4 guided tours Mon-Fri at 11:00, 12:00, 14:00, and 15:00; tel. 01/677-8099, www.christchurchdublin.ie.

Church Services and Evensong: There's a full Anglican service Sun at 11:00, and the public is welcome to a 45-minute evensong service, sung by the esteemed Christ Church choir (Wed-Thu at 18:00, Sun at 15:30).

▲DUBLINIA

This exhibit, which highlights Dublin's Viking and medieval past, is a hit with youngsters (but meaty enough for adults as well).

Cost and Hours: €9.50, €14.50 combo-ticket includes Christ Church Cathedral; daily 10:00-18:30, Oct-Feb until 17:30, last entry one hour before closing; top-floor coffee shop, across from Christ Church Cathedral, tel. 01/679-4611, www.dublinia.ie.

Visiting the Exhibits: The displays are laid out on three floors. The ground floor focuses on Viking Dublin, explaining life aboard a Viking ship and inside a Viking house. Viking traders introduced urban life and commerce to Ireland—but kids will be most interested in gawking at their gory weaponry.

The next floor up reveals Dublin's day-to-day life in medieval times, from chivalrous knights and damsels in town fairs to the brutal ravages of the plague. Like so much of Europe at that time (1347-1349), Ireland lost one-third of its population to the Black Death. The huge scale model of medieval Dublin is especially well done. The top floor's "History Hunters" section is devoted to how the puzzles of modern archaeology and science shed light on Dublin's history. From this floor, you can climb a couple of flights of stairs into the tower for so-so views of Dublin, or exit across an enclosed stone bridge to adjacent Christ Church Cathedral.

ST. PATRICK'S CATHEDRAL

This Anglican cathedral is a thoughtful learning experience as well as a living church. The first church here was Catholic, supposedly built on the site where St. Patrick baptized local pagan converts. While the core of the Gothic structure you see today was built in the 13th century, most of today's stonework is 19th century. After the Reformation, it passed into the hands of the Anglican Church. A century later, Oliver Cromwell's puritanical Calvinist troops—who considered the Anglicans to be little more than Catholics without a pope—stabled their horses here as a sign of disrespect.

Cost and Hours: €6.50 donation to church; Mon-Fri 9:30-17:00, Sat-Sun 9:00-18:00—but on Sun it's closed 10:30-12:30 and 14:30-16:30, last entry one hour before closing; at the intersection of Patrick Street and Upper Kevin Street, www.stpatrickscathedral.ie.

Tours: Free guided tours are given several times a day in summer; check website

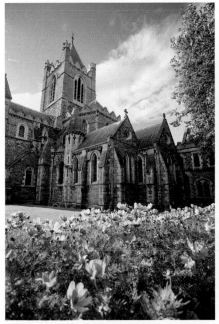

Christ Church Cathedral

St. Patrick's Cathedral interior

for schedule but typically at 10:30, 11:30, 14:30, 15:00, and 15:30.

Evensong: You'll get chills listening to the local "choir of angels" Mon-Fri at 17:30 and Sun at 15:15.

▲▲TEMPLE BAR

This much-promoted area—with shops, cafés, theaters, galleries, pubs with live music, and restaurants—feels like the heart of the old city. It's Dublin's touristy "Left Bank," on the south shore of the river, filling the cobbled streets between Dame Street and the River Liffey.

Three hundred years ago, this was the city waterfront, where tall sailing ships offloaded their goods (a "bar" was a loading dock along the river, and the Temples were a dominant merchant family). Eventually, the city grew eastward, filling in tidal mudflats, to create the docklands of modern Dublin. Once a thriving Georgian center of craftsmen and merchants, this neighborhood fell on hard times in the 20th century. Ensuing low rents attracted students and artists, giving the area a bohemian flair. With government tax incentives and lots of development money, the Temple Bar district has now

become a thriving entertainment (and beer-drinking) hot spot.

Sights and Activities in Temple Bar: Temple Bar Square, just off Temple Bar Street (near Ha' Penny Bridge), is the epicenter of activity. It hosts free street theater and a **Saturday book market.** On busy weekends, people-watching here is a contact sport (and pickpocketing is not).

Irish music fans find great CDs at humble **Claddagh Records** (Cecilia Street, just around the corner from Luigi Malone's, Mon-Sat 11:00-17:30, closed Sun, tel. 01/677-0262). Unlike big, glitzy chain stores, this is a little hole-in-the-wall shop staffed by informed folks who love turning visitors on to Irish tunes. Grab a couple of CDs for your drive through the Irish countryside.

Farther west and somewhat hidden is Meeting House Square, with a lively **organic-produce market** (Sat 10:00-18:00). Bordering the square is the **Irish Film Institute** (main entry on Eustace Street), which shows a variety of art-house flicks. A bohemian crowd relaxes in its bar/café, awaiting the next film (6 Eustace Street, box office daily 13:30-21:00, tel. 01/679-5744, www.irishfilm.ie).

Temple Bar

Less commercial plays can be seen nearby at **Smock Alley Theatre,** with seating surrounding a tiny stage, in a space on the site of the city's first custom-built theater from 1662 (for details, see page 77).

Nighttime Rowdiness: Temple Bar can be an absolute spectacle in the evening, when it bursts with revelers. The noise, pushy crowds and inflated prices have driven most Dubliners away. But even if you're just gawking, don't miss the opportunity to wander through this human circus. For recommendations, see the Temple Bar listings on page 77.

North of the River Liffey

O'Connell Street and the historic core north of the river is covered by the self-guided walk on page 45. After you get oriented with the walk, consider the following sights.

▲▲EPIC: THE IRISH EMIGRATION MUSEUM

Telling the story of the Irish diaspora, this museum celebrates how this little island has had an oversized impact on the world. While the museum has no actual artifacts, this is an entertaining and educational experience.

Cost and Hours: €14, daily 10:00-18:45, last entry at 17:00, one-hour tours at 11:00 and 14:00; in the CHQ building on Custom House Quay (at the modern pedestrian bridge a few steps from the famine statues along the riverfront); tel. 01/906-0861, www.epicchq.com.

Visiting the Museum: The museum fills the wine vaults in the basement of an iron-framed warehouse from the 1820s (where the customs house stood on the River Liffey). Its 20 themed galleries take an interactive, high-tech approach to explain the forces that propelled so many Irish around the globe. Featured illustrious emigrants include labor agitator Mother Jones, Caribbean pirate Anne Bonny, Australian bush bandit Ned Kelly, and musical Chicago police chief Francis

O'Neill. Historic photos of filthy tenements and early films of bustling urban scenes document the plight of the common Irish emigrant. And all along you celebrate Irish heritage in music, literature, sports, and more.

Genealogy Help: Upstairs from the museum, the **Irish Family History Centre** can help you research your Celtic roots (€10 to access research stations, €40 for 30-minute consultation, daily 10:00-17:00, tel. 01/905-9216, www.irishfamilyhistory-centre.com).

Nearby: Today a modern **food court** in the CHQ building serves the glassy office towers. A modern **pedestrian bridge**—shaped like an old Irish harp and designed by Santiago Calatrava—leads to Dublin's strikingly contemporary convention center. Before leaving the riverside area, cross Customs House Quay (the main road) and wander 50 yards up the River Liffey toward the city to contemplate the skeletal sculptures of the city's evocative **Famine Memorial.** A few steps in the opposite direction, downriver, you'll spot the masts of the *Jeanie Johnston* Tall Ship and Famine Museum (see next). A visit here ties in well with the area's emigration theme.

▲*JEANIE JOHNSTON* TALL SHIP AND FAMINE MUSEUM

Docked on the River Liffey, this seagoing sailing ship is a replica of a legendary Irish "famine ship." The original *Jeanie Johnston* embarked on 16 eight-week

Jeanie Johnston *tall ship*

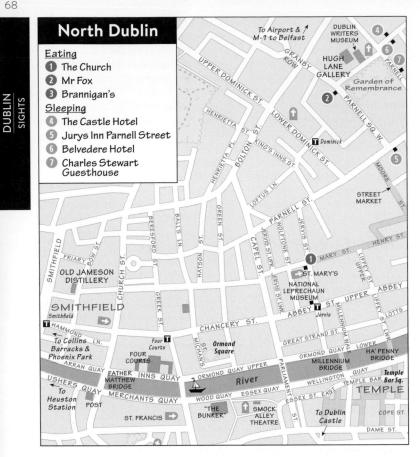

North Dublin

Eating
1. The Church
2. Mr Fox
3. Brannigan's

Sleeping
4. The Castle Hotel
5. Jurys Inn Parnell Street
6. Belvedere Hotel
7. Charles Stewart Guesthouse

transatlantic crossings, carrying more than 2,500 Irish emigrants (about 200 per voyage) to their new lives in America and Canada in the decade after the Great Potato Famine of the 1840s. While many barely seaworthy hulks were known as "coffin ships," the people who boarded the *Jeanie Johnston* were lucky: The ship was Irish owned and crewed, with a humanitarian captain and even a doctor on board, and not one life was lost. Your tour guide will introduce you to the ship's main characters and help illuminate day-to-day life aboard a cramped tall ship 160 years ago.

Note that, because this ship makes goodwill voyages to Atlantic ports, it may be away during your visit—check ahead.

Cost and Hours: €10, visits by 50-minute tour only, easy to book slot in advance online; daily April-Sept 10:00-16:00, Oct-March 11:00-15:00, tours depart on the hour (but no tours at 13:00); on the north bank of the Liffey just east of Sean O'Casey Bridge, tel. 01/473-0111, www.jeaniejohnston.ie.

▲DUBLIN WRITERS MUSEUM

No other country so small has produced such a wealth of literature. As interesting to those who are fans of Irish literature as it is boring to those who aren't, this three-room museum features the lives and works of Dublin's great writers. It's a low-tech museum, where you read informative

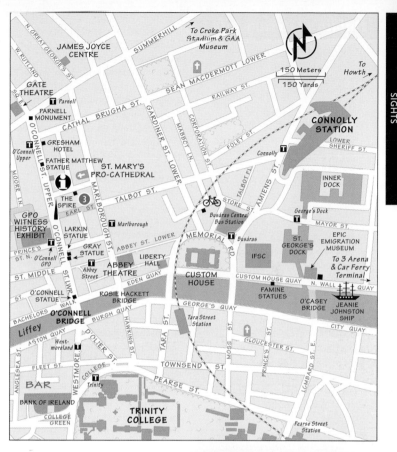

plaques while perusing display cases with minor memorabilia—a document signed by Jonathan Swift, a photo of Oscar Wilde reclining thoughtfully, an early edition of Bram Stoker's *Dracula,* a George Bernard Shaw playbill, a not-so-famous author's tuxedo, or a newspaper from Easter 1916 announcing "Two More Executions Today." If unassuming attractions like that stir your blood—or if you simply want a manageable introduction to Irish lit—it's worth a visit.

Cost and Hours: €7.50, includes helpful 45-minute audioguide; Mon-Sat 9:45-17:00, Sun from 11:00; 18 Parnell Square North, tel. 01/872-2077, www. writersmuseum.com.

Oscar Wilde

Dublin's Literary Life

Dublin in the 1700s, grown rich from a lucrative cloth trade, was one of Europe's most cultured and sophisticated cities. The buildings were decorated in the Georgian style still visible today, and the city's Protestant elite shuttled between here and London, bridging the Anglo-Irish cultural gap. Jonathan Swift (1667-1745) was the era's greatest Anglo-Irish writer—a brilliant satirist and author of *Gulliver's Travels*. He was also dean of St. Patrick's Cathedral (1713-1745) and one of the city's eminent citizens.

Around the turn of the 20th century, Dublin produced some of the world's great modern writers. Bram Stoker (1847-1912) was creator of *Dracula*. Oscar Wilde (1854-1900) penned *The Picture of Dorian Gray* and a clutch of fine plays. George Bernard Shaw (1856-1950) wrote *Pygmalion*, *Major Barbara*, *Man and Superman*, and a host of other dramas. William Butler Yeats (1865-1939) was a prolific poet and playwright on Irish themes. And James Joyce (1882-1941) whipped up a masterpiece called *Ulysses*.

JAMES JOYCE CENTRE

Only aficionados of James Joyce's work will want to visit this micromuseum. Born and raised in Dublin, James Joyce (1882-1941) wrote in great detail about his hometown, and mined the local dialect for his pitch-perfect dialogue. His best-known work, *Ulysses*, chronicles one day (June 16, 1904) in the life of the fictional Leopold Bloom as he wanders through the underside of Dublin. Joyce himself left Dublin (on June 17, 1904) for Paris and lived away from the city for most of his life. He never took up the cause of Irish nationalism and rarely delved into Irish mythology. He instead wrote with a new Modernist focus on linguistic invention and social frankness.

Cost and Hours: €5, Mon-Sat 10:00-17:00, Sun from 12:00, closed Mon Oct-March, two blocks east of the Dublin Writers Museum at 35 North Great George's Street, tel. 01/878-8547, www.jamesjoyce.ie. The center offers walking tours of Joyce sights several times a week.

▲HUGH LANE GALLERY

This stimulating and well-described exhibit of art from the 1870s onward includes a sampling of Impressionist masterpieces from the gallery's founding collection, once owned by Sir Hugh Lane, an Irish art dealer. Genteel and bite-sized, the museum is particularly worth a visit for a well-known Monet painting, an exhibit on modern artist Francis Bacon, and a few select paintings by Irish artists.

Cost and Hours: Free, Tue-Thu 10:00-18:00, Fri-Sat until 17:00, Sun 11:00-17:00, closed Mon, in the Dublin City Gallery on Parnell Square North, tel. 01/222-5550, www.hughlane.ie.

Visiting the Gallery: Head to Room 1, where you'll find **Monet's *Waterloo Bridge*** (1900). On a visit to London, the once-bohemian, now-famous Impressionist Claude Monet checked into Room 618 of the Savoy Hotel and set to work painting Waterloo Bridge at different times of day and in various weather conditions. This painting is just one of 41 versions of the scene. In 1905, Sir Hugh

Monet, Waterloo Bridge

bought Monet's *Waterloo Bridge* as part of his mission to bring modern art to the British Isles and provincial Dublin. Unfortunately, Sir Hugh went down on the *Lusitania* in 1915 and didn't see this gallery open. To see a depiction of dapper Sir Hugh—by the American society portraitist John Singer Sargent—find the room to the right of Room 3.

Francis Bacon Studio: Although he spent most of his life in London, Francis Bacon (1909-1992) was born in Dublin and raised nearby. After his death, his entire London studio was reconstructed here, just as the artist had left it.

After a wandering youth of odd jobs and petty crime, Bacon took up painting in his late thirties. He jumped onto the art stage in 1945 with his bleak canvases of twisted, deformed, screaming-mouthed men caged in barren landscapes—which hauntingly captured the mood of post-WWII Europe. He would become Britain's premier painter, but he continued to live simply. He stayed in his small, cramped flat with an even smaller studio (this one) for his entire life.

▲▲GPO WITNESS HISTORY EXHIBIT

During the Easter Rising in 1916, Irish nationalists took over various buildings in Dublin, including the General Post Office (GPO), which became the rebel headquarters. Initial euphoria led to chaotic street battles and ended with the grim realization among the insurgents that surrender was the best option—trusting that their martyrdom would inspire the country to rise more effectively. This engaging permanent exhibit—in the working GPO—explores that pivotal Easter Week.

Cost and Hours: €12, Mon-Fri 9:00-17:30, Thu until 19:00 in July-Aug, Sat-Sun 10:00-17:30 year-round, last entry one hour before closing, audioguide-€1, tel. 01/872-1916, www.gpowitnesshistory.ie.

Background: A sideshow for European nations preoccupied with World War I, the Easter Rising was critical to Irish nationalists. Almost every Irish generation for the preceding 125 years had launched doomed insurrections. But this one had a lasting effect, although it may not have seemed so in its immediate wake—a couple of weeks later, the patriot leaders who held their ground at the GPO were executed in Kilmainham Gaol (see page 60). Public sympathies shifted seismically. From this point on, after seven centuries of dominance, the British were on a slippery slope leading to the eventual granting of independence to its nearest and oldest colony.

Visiting the Exhibit: You'll find the exhibit, with many interesting artifacts, on the right as you enter the building. It features a fairly balanced view of the rebellion, including the less popular realities (like the lack of widespread support at the beginning of the movement and the civilians who died in the crossfire). Don't miss the excellent 15-minute widescreen depiction of events (called "The Rising") in the tiny theater. An interactive map of Dublin zooms in and out of various neighborhoods, tracking the week's confrontations, with actors dramatizing the events and conversations that shaped the conflict. In video presentations, historians give their take on how the rebellion affected Irish history.

Outer Dublin

The Kilmainham Gaol and the Guinness Storehouse are located west of the old center and can be linked by a 20-minute walk, a five-minute taxi ride, or public bus #40 or #13. (To ride the bus from the jail to the Guinness Storehouse, leave the prison and take three rights—crossing no streets—to reach the bus stop.) Another option is to take a hop-on, hop-off bus, which stops at both sights.

▲▲▲KILMAINHAM GAOL

Opened in 1796 as Dublin's county jail and a debtors' prison, Kilmainham Gaol (pronounced GAY-ol) was considered a model in its day. In reality, this jail was frequently used by the British as a political

From Famine to Revolution

After the Great Potato Famine (1845-1849), destitute rural Irish moved to the city in droves, seeking work and causing a housing shortage. Unscrupulous landlords came up with a solution: Subdivide the city's once-grand mansions, vacated when gentry moved to London after the 1801 Act of Union. The mansions' tiny rooms could then be crammed with poor renters. Dublin became one of the most densely populated cities in Europe—one of every three Dubliners lived in a slum. On Henrietta Street, once a wealthy Dublin address, these new tenements bulged with humanity. According to the 1911 census, one district counted 835 people living in 15 houses (many with a single outhouse in back or a communal chamber pot in the room). In cramped, putrid quarters like this, tuberculosis was rampant, and infant mortality skyrocketed.

Those who could get work tenaciously clung to their precious jobs. The terrible working conditions prompted many to join trade unions. A 1913 strike and employer lockout, known as the "Dublin Lockout," lasted for seven months. The picket lines were brutally put down by police in the pocket of rich businessmen, led by newspaper owner and hotel magnate William Murphy. In response, James Larkin and James Connolly formed the Irish Citizen Army, a socialist militia to protect the poor trade unionists.

Murphy eventually broke the unions. Larkin headed for the US to organize workers there. During World War I, he praised the rise of the Soviet Union and later was persecuted during the postwar "Red Scare" (even doing time in Sing Sing prison for advocating "unlawful means" to overthrow the US government). Meanwhile, Connolly stayed in Ireland and brought the Irish Citizen Army into the 1916 Easter Rising as an integral part of the rebel forces. During the uprising, he slyly had a rebel flag flown over Murphy's prized hotel on O'Connell Street. The uninformed British artillery battalions took the bait and pulverized it.

Connolly was the last of the rebel leaders executed in Dublin in 1916. Unable to stand in front of the firing squad in Kilmainham Gaol (his ankle was shattered by a bullet while he was defending the General Post Office), Connolly was tied to a chair and shot sitting down. Of the 16 rebel executions, his was most often credited with turning Irish public opinion in favor of the rebel martyrs.

Today you'll find heroic Dublin statues to honor both men. James Larkin, arms outstretched, is in front of the post office on O'Connell Street. James Connolly is on Beresford Place, behind the Customs House.

prison. Many of those who fought for Irish independence were held or executed here, including leaders of the rebellions of 1798, 1803, 1848, 1867, and 1916. National heroes Robert Emmett and Charles Stewart Parnell each did time here. The last prisoner to be held in the jail was Éamon de Valera, who later became president of Ireland.

He was released on July 16, 1924, the day Kilmainham was finally shut down. The buildings, virtually in ruins, were restored in the 1960s. Today, it's a shrine to the Nathan Hales of Ireland.

Cost and Hours: €8 includes guided one-hour jail tour and unguided museum visit; daily June-Aug 9:00-18:45, last tour

Kilmainham Gaol

at 17:30; Sept-May 9:30-17:30, last tour at 16:15; tours run 2/hour, tel. 01/453-5984, www.kilmainhamgaolmuseum.ie.

Advance Tickets: In the busy season, be sure to book online a few days before your visit to guarantee a spot on a tour, as walk-up spots go quickly. (You can't book by phone, but you can call to see if tours have seats open.) If you need to wait for your tour departure, visit the museum first (or head across the street and through the park to visit the free Irish Museum of Modern Art—15 minutes on foot).

Getting There: Hop-on, hop-off buses stop here, or take bus #69 or #70 from Aston Quay or #13 or #40 from O'Connell Street or College Green—confirm with driver.

Visiting the Jail: Start your visit with a one-hour guided tour (includes 15-minute prison-history slide show in the prison chapel). It's touching to tour the cells and places of execution—hearing tales of oppressive colonialism and heroic patriotism—alongside Irish schoolkids who know these names well. The museum has

an excellent exhibit on Victorian prison life and Ireland's fight for independence.

Don't miss the dimly lit "Last Words 1916" hall upstairs, which displays the stirring final letters that patriots sent to loved ones hours before facing the firing squad.

▲GUINNESS STOREHOUSE

A visit to the Guinness Storehouse is, for many, a pilgrimage. Arthur Guinness began brewing the renowned stout here in 1759, and by 1868 it was the biggest brewery in the world. Today, the sprawling complex fills several city blocks (64 acres busy brewing 1.5 million pints a day).

Visitors (1.5 million annually) are welcomed to the towering storehouse, where the vibe is glitzy entertainment. Don't look for conveyor belts of beer bottles being stamped with bottle caps, or displays of historic artifacts. Rather than a brewery tour, this is a Disneyland for beer lovers—huge crowds, high decibel music, and dreamy TV beer ads on big screens.

Cost and Hours: €20, includes a €5 pint; daily 9:30-19:00, July-Aug until 20:00, last entry two hours before closing,

The Record-Breaking Records Book

Look up "beer" in the *Guinness World Records*, and you'll discover that the record for removing beer bottle caps with one's teeth is 68 in one minute. But aside from listing records for amazing—or amazingly stupid—feats, this famous record book has a more subtle connection with beer.

In 1951, while hunting in Ireland's County Wexford, Sir Hugh Beaver, then the managing director at Guinness Breweries, got into a debate with his companions over which was the fastest game bird in Europe: the golden plover or the red grouse. That night at his estate, after scouring countless reference books, they were disappointed not to find a definitive answer.

Beaver realized that similar questions were likely being debated nightly across pubs in Ireland and Britain. So he hired a fact-finding team in London to compile a book of answers to various questions. In 1955, the *Guinness Book of Records* (later renamed *Guinness World Records*) was published. By Christmas, it topped the British bestseller list.

In the beginning, entries mostly focused on natural phenomena and animal oddities, but grew to include a wide variety of extreme human achievements.

The iconic books are now available in more than 100 countries and 26 languages, with more than 3.5 million copies sold annually. As the best-selling copyrighted book of all time, it even earns a record-breaking entry within its own pages.

last beer served 45 minutes before closing; tel. 01/408-4800, www.guinness-storehouse.com.

Getting There: Ride the hop-on, hop-off bus (your bus ticket gives you a €1 discount here), or take bus #13, #40, or #123 from Dame Street and O'Connell Street. Enter the brewery on Bellevue Street.

Rick's Tip: *At peak times,* **lines at the Guinness Storehouse** *can be overwhelming, both outside and at various stops within the brewery. To avoid the worst of it, start early and consider* **booking online** *(tickets discounted 20 percent between 9:30 and 10:45).*

Visiting the Brewery: The exhibit fills the old fermentation plant, used from 1902 through 1988, which reopened in 2000 as a huge shrine to the Guinness tradition. Step into the middle of the ground floor and look up. A tall, beer-glass-shaped glass atrium—14 million pints big

(that's about 10 days' production)—soars upward past four floors of exhibitions and cafés to the skylight. Then look down at Arthur's original 9,000-year lease, enshrined under Plexiglas in the floor. At £45 per year, it was quite a bargain.

As you escalate ever higher, you'll notice that each floor has a theme. The first floor is dedicated to cooperage—the making of wooden barrels (with 1954 film clips showing master kegmakers working at their now virtually extinct trade); the second floor has the tasting rooms (described below); the third floor features advertising and a theater with classic TV ads; the fourth floor is where you can pull your own beer (at the Academy); and the fifth floor has Arthur's Bar. The top floor is the Gravity Bar, providing visitors with a commanding 360-degree view of Dublin—with vistas all the way to the sea—and an included pint of the beloved stout.

Claiming Your Beer: Your admission includes a ticket for a beer, which you can

Britain, and Ireland's civil war. Croppies Acre, the large park between the museum and the river, was the site of Dublin's largest soup kitchen during the Great Potato Famine in 1845-1849.

Cost and Hours: Free, Tue-Sat 10:00-17:00, Sun from 14:00, closed Mon, good café; on north side of the River Liffey in Collins Barracks on Benburb Street, roughly across the river from Guinness Storehouse, LUAS red line: Museum stop; tel. 01/677-7444, www.museum.ie.

▲GAELIC ATHLETIC ASSOCIATION MUSEUM

The GAA was founded in 1884 as an expression of an Irish cultural awakening. It was created to foster the development of Gaelic sports, specifically Gaelic football and hurling, and to exclude English sports such as cricket and rugby. The GAA played an important part in the fight for independence. This museum, at 82,000-seat Croke Park Stadium in northeast Dublin, offers a high-tech, interactive introduction to Ireland's favorite games. Relive the greatest moments in hurling and Irish-football history. Then get involved: Pick up a stick and try hurling, kick a football, and test your speed and balance. A 15-minute film (played on request) gives you a "Sunday at the stadium" experience.

Cost and Hours: €7, Mon-Sat 9:30-17:00, June-Aug until 18:00, Sun 10:30-17:00 year-round—except on game Sundays, when the museum is open to ticket holders only; café, located under the stands at Croke Park Stadium, enter from St. Joseph's Avenue off Clonliffe Road, tel. 01/819-2323, www.crokepark.ie/gaa-museum.

Tours: The €14, one-hour museum-plus-stadium-tour option (daily at 11:00, 13:00, and 15:00) is worth it only for rabid fans who want a glimpse of the huge stadium and locker rooms. The €20 rooftop tour offers views 17 stories above the field from lofty catwalks (Mon-Fri at 11:30 and 14:30, Sat-Sun hourly from 10:30 to 14:30; fewer tours Oct-April).

claim on one of three levels. On level 4, you can pull your own pint (and then drink it). On level 5, at Arthur's Bar, you can choose among extra stout (4.2%, carbonated), Dublin Porter (3.8%, 1796 recipe), West Indies Porter (6%, toffee flavor, 1801 recipe), Hop House 13 (4.1%, a hoppy lager), and Black Velvet (half and half sparkling wine and Guinness). On the top floor (where there's the most energy and fun), drinks are limited to the basic stout or soft drinks.

▲NATIONAL MUSEUM: DECORATIVE ARTS AND HISTORY

This branch of the National Museum, which occupies the huge, 18th-century stone Collins Barracks in west Dublin, displays Irish dress, furniture, weapons, silver, and other domestic baubles from the past 700 years. History buffs will linger longest in the "Soldiers & Chiefs" exhibit, which covers the Irish at war both at home and abroad since 1500 (including the American Civil War). The sober finale is the "Proclaiming the Republic" room, offering Ireland's best coverage of the painful birth of this nation. Guns, flags, and personal letters help illustrate the 1916 Easter Rising, the War of Independence against

Ireland's Gaelic Athletic Association

The GAA has long been a powerhouse in Ireland. Ireland's national pastimes of Gaelic football and hurling pack stadiums all over the country. When you consider that 82,000 people—paying about €25 each—stuff Dublin's Croke Park Stadium and that all the athletes are strictly amateur, you might wonder, "Where does all the money go?"

Ireland has a long tradition of using the revenue generated by these huge events to promote Gaelic athletics and Gaelic cultural events throughout the country in a grassroots and neighborhood way. So, while the players (many of whom are schoolteachers whose jobs allow for evenings and summers free) participate only for the glory of their various counties, the money generated is funding children's leagues, school coaches, small-town athletic facilities, and traditional arts, music, and dance—as well as the building and maintenance of giant stadiums such as Croke Park.

In Ireland, sports have a deep emotional connection as a heartfelt expression of Irish identity. There was a time when membership in the GAA was denied to anyone who also belonged to a cricket club (a British game). So intractable was this rule that in 1938, Douglas Hyde (president of Ireland at the time) was kicked out of the GAA for attending an international soccer match.

In 1921, during the War of Independence, IRA leader Michael Collins orchestrated the simultaneous assassination of a dozen British intelligence agents around Dublin in a single morning. The same day, the Black and Tans retaliated. These grizzled British WWI veterans, clad in black police coats and tan surplus army pants, had been sent to Ireland to stamp out the rebels. Knowing Croke Park would be full of Irish Nationalists, they entered the packed stadium during a Gaelic football match and fired into the stands, killing 13 spectators as well as a Tipperary player.

Today Croke Park's "Hill 16" grandstands are built on rubble dumped here after the 1916 Rising; it's literally sacred ground. And the Hogan stands are named after the murdered player from Tipperary. Queen Elizabeth II visited the stadium during her historic visit in 2011. Her warm interest in the stadium and in the institution of the GAA did much to heal old wounds.

EXPERIENCES

Shopping

Shops are open roughly Monday-Saturday 9:00-18:00 and until 20:00 on Thursday. Hours are shorter on Sunday (if shops are open at all). Good shopping areas include:

• **Grafton Street,** with its neighboring streets and arcades (such as the fun Great George's Arcade between Great George's and Drury Streets), and nearby shopping centers (Powerscourt Townhouse and St.

Stephen's Green). Francis Street creaks with antiques.

• **Henry Street,** home to Dublin's top department stores (pedestrian-only, off O'Connell Street).

• **Nassau Street,** lining Trinity College, with the popular Kilkenny Shop (Irish design) and lots of touristy stores.

• **Temple Bar,** worth a browse for art, jewelry, New Age paraphernalia, books, music (try Claddagh Records), and gift shops. On Saturdays, a couple of

Enjoying Dublin's shopping streets

Dublin lights up at night.

markets—one for food and another for books—set up shop. For details on this area, see page 66.

• **Millennium Walk,** a trendy lane stretching two blocks north from the River Liffey to Abbey Street. It's filled with hip restaurants, shops, and coffee bars. It's easy to miss—look for the south entry at the pedestrian Millennium Bridge, or the north entry at Jervis Street LUAS stop.

• **Street markets,** such as Moore Street (produce, noise, and lots of local color, Mon-Sat 8:00-18:00, closed Sun, near General Post Office), and St. Michan Street (food, Tue-Sat 7:00-15:00, closed Sun-Mon, behind Four Courts building).

Theater

Abbey Theatre is Ireland's national theater, founded by W. B. Yeats in 1904 to preserve Irish culture during British rule (performances generally nightly at 20:00, Sat matinees at 14:30, 26 Lower Abbey Street, tel. 01/878-7222, www.abbeytheatre. ie). **Gate Theatre** does foreign plays as well as Irish classics (Cavendish Row, tel. 01/874-4045, www.gatetheatre.ie). The **Gaiety Theatre** offers a wide range of quality productions (King Street South, toll tel. 0818-719-388, www.gaietytheatre. ie). The **Bord Gáis Energy Theatre** is the newest and spiffiest venue (Grand Canal Square, tel. 01/677-7999, www. bordgaisenergytheatre.ie). Intimate little **Smock Alley Theatre** hides at the western fringe of Temple Bar, offering less mainstream performances on the site of

Dublin's first theater (6 Lower Exchange Street, tel. 01/677-0014, www.smockalley. com). Street theater takes the stage in Temple Bar on summer evenings. Browse the listings and fliers at the TI.

Concerts

The **3 Arena,** sited on what was once a dock railway terminus (easy LUAS access), is now sponsored by a hip phone company. Residents call it by its geographic nickname: The Point. It's considered one of the country's top live-music venues (East Link Bridge, toll tel. 01/819-8888, http://3arena.ie).

At the **National Concert Hall,** the National Symphony Orchestra performs most Friday evenings (off St. Stephen's Green at Earlsfort Terrace, tel. 01/417-0077, www.nch.ie).

Pubs and Live Traditional Music

TEMPLE BAR AND NEARBY

The **Temple Bar area** in particular thrives with music—traditional, jazz, and pop. Although it's pricier than the rest of Dublin and extremely touristy, it really is the best place in town to mix beer and music. For locations, see the map on page 82.

Gogarty's Pub has foot-tapping sessions downstairs daily at 13:00 and upstairs nightly from 21:00 (at corner of Fleet and Anglesea, tel. 01/671-1822). Use this pub as a kickoff for your Temple Bar evening.

Most trad sessions include a fiddle.

Dublin nightlife

The **Palace Bar** is a well-preserved gin joint, with almost 135 years of history. It attracted Dublin's literary greats from the start, and contrasts sharply (and refreshingly) with the prefab offerings down the street in the Temple Bar mayhem (east end of Temple Bar, where Fleet Street hits Westmoreland Street at 21 Fleet Street, tel. 01/671-7388, www.thepalacebardublin.com).

Porterhouse has an inviting and varied menu, Dublin's best selection of microbrews, and live music. You won't find Guinness here, just tasty homebrews. Try one of their sampler trays (corner of Essex Street East and Parliament Street, tel. 01/671-5715, check music schedule at www.theporterhouse.ie).

Near Temple Bar: A 10-minute hike up the river west of Temple Bar takes you to two pubs with a local and less touristy ambience. **The Brazen Head,** which claims to be the oldest pub in Dublin, is a hit for an early dinner and late live music (nightly from 21:30), with atmospheric rooms and a courtyard perfect for balmy evenings. They also host great "Food, Folk, and Fairies" storytelling dinner evenings. **O'Shea's Merchant Pub,** just across the street, is encrusted in memories of County Kerry football heroes. It's filled with locals taking a break from the grind. There's live traditional music nightly at 21:30 (the front half is a restaurant, the magic is in the back—enter on Bridge Street, tel. 01/679-3797, www.themerchanttemplebar.com).

EATING

It's easy to find fine, creative eateries all over town. While you can get decent pub grub for under €20 on just about any corner, consider saving that for the countryside. There's just no pressing reason to eat Irish in cosmopolitan Dublin. In fact, going local these days is the same as going ethnic. The city's good restaurants are packed from 19:00 on, especially on weekends.

Rick's Tip: *Eating early (17:30-19:00) saves time and money, as many of Dublin's better places offer an* **early-bird special.**

Fast, Easy, and Cheap in the Center
Near Grafton Street

$$ Cornucopia is a small, earth-mama-with-class, proudly vegetarian, self-serve place two blocks off Grafton. It's friendly and youthful, with hearty lunches and dinner specials (daily generally until 21:00, 19 Wicklow Street, tel. 01/677-7583).

$$$ The Farm is a hardworking and practical place with a passion for fresh, organic, and free-range fare that's affordable and tasty. Lunch and early-bird specials are a smart value (good vegetarian options, Wed-Sat 12:00-23:00, Sun-Tue until 22:00, a half-block south of Trinity College at 3 Dawson Street, tel. 01/671-8654).

$$ **The Hairy Lemon** has a weird name, but its friendly staff, central location, and fun and creative menu keep customers coming back. Hearty eaters will love their famous stew-like Dublin Coddle. Dine in the pub zone or in the brighter annex. Part of the movie *The Commitments* (1991) was filmed here (daily 11:30-22:00, 41 Lower Stephen Street, tel. 01/671-8949).

$$ **O'Neill's Pub** is a venerable, multilevel, dark, and tangled retreat offering good grub, including inexpensive breakfasts and dependable carvery lunches (daily 12:00-22:30, Suffolk Street, tel. 01/679-3656).

$$ **Avoca Café,** on the second floor above the Avoca department store, is a cheap and cheery eatery with healthy foodie plates, great salads, and an enthusiastic local following (Mon-Sat 9:30-17:30, Sun from 11:00, 11 Suffolk Street, tel. 01/672-6019). In the store basement, the $ **Avoca Sandwich Counter** has simple seating and a cheap buffet counter that sells food priced by weight. They also offer deli sandwiches and enticing baked goodies (great for takeaway, daily generally 10:00-18:00).

$$ **The Duke** and **Davy Byrnes,** neighbors on Duke Street, serve reliable pub lunches. Davy Byrnes (at #21, tel. 01/677-5217) feels like pub-meets-diner, and The Duke (at #9, tel. 01/679-9553) has a buffet counter in the back from 12:00 to 16:00. Both are favorites for Irish lit fans whose heroes frequented them (James Joyce, Brendan Behan, and Patrick Kavanagh). Davy Byrnes is where Leopold Bloom ate his gorgonzola cheese sandwich in *Ulysses.*

$$ **Wagamama** is a pan-Asian slurp-a-thon with great and healthy noodle and rice dishes served at long communal tables by energetic waiters (daily 12:00-22:00, South King Street underneath St. Stephen's Green Shopping Centre, tel. 01/417-1878).

$$ **Yamamori** is a plain, mellow, and modern Japanese place serving seas of sushi and noodles (daily 12:00-22:30, 71 South Great George's Street, tel. 01/475-5001).

Near Christ Church Cathedral

$ The **Silk Road Café** at the Chester Beatty Library serves a delightful selection of Middle Eastern and Mediterranean cuisine (in keeping with the theme of the library's collections). The dishes are always fresh, with a good variety of soups, *panini,* falafel, and vegetarian options (Mon-Fri 10:00-16:45, Sat from 11:00, Sun from 12:00, on the grounds of Dublin Castle, tel. 01/407-0770). While you're there, be sure to pop into the amazing (free) library (see listing in "Sights in Dublin").

$ **Queen of Tarts,** with nice outdoor seating, does yummy breakfasts, light lunches, sandwiches, and wonderful pastries (Mon-Fri 8:00-19:00, Sat-Sun from 9:00, just off Dame Street, go 100 yards up from City Hall and left on Cow's Lane, tel. 01/670-7499).

$ **Chorus Café** is a friendly and plain little hole-in-the-wall diner serving salads, *panini,* and pastas (daily 8:30-17:00, 7 Fishamble Street, next door to the site of the first performance of Handel's *Messiah,* tel. 01/616-7088, Cyrus).

$ **Leo Burdock** has been serving authentic fish and chips, in large splittable portions, for more than a hundred years. You'll find it around the corner from Jurys Inn—just follow the line of Dubliners waiting for their haddock (daily 12:00-23:30, no seating—takeaway only, 2 Werburgh Street, tel. 01/454-0306).

Delis and Groceries

Grocery Delis with Seating: If you want to eat fast, cheap, and healthy in the tourist center, two high-end groceries offer fresh sandwiches and a salad bar, and a place to sit while you eat. The **Spar** market (corner of Dame Street and South Great George's Street; more branches throughout the city) is open 24/7 and has huge windows overlooking the Dame Street action. The very proper **Fallon & Byrne Food Hall** is like eating at an upscale Trader Joe's (Mon-Sat 8:00-21:00, Sun until 19:00, 11 Exchequer Street).

Supermarkets: Many of Dublin's grocery stores sell cheap salads, microwaved meat pies, and made-to-order sandwiches. **Dunnes,** at 11 South Great George's Street, is your one-stop shop for assembling a picnic meal (Mon-Sat 8:30-19:00, Sun from 11:00). They have another outlet in the basement of St. Stephen's Green Shopping Centre. **Marks & Spencer** department store has a fancy grocery store in the basement, with fine takeaway sandwiches and salads (daily 8:00-20:00, 20 Grafton Street). **Centra** markets, some open 24 hours, are spread all over Dublin.

Hip and Fun in North Dublin

For locations, see map on page 68.

The Church is a trendy café/bar/restaurant/nightclub/beer garden housed in the former St. Mary's Church. In its former life as a church, it hosted the baptism of Irish rebel Wolfe Tone and the marriage of brewing legend Arthur Guinness. The **$$$ choir balcony** has a huge pipe organ and a refined menu (daily 17:00-22:30). The ground floor **$$ nave** is dominated by a long bar and pub grub (daily 12:00-21:00). A disco thumps away in the bunker-like basement. On warm summer nights, the outdoor terrace is packed. Eating here is as much about the scene as the cuisine (reservations smart Fri and Sat nights, corner of St. Mary's and Jervis Streets, tel. 01/828-0102, www.thechurch.ie).

$$ Brannigan's is an inviting and family-run traditional pub—it's been a "beer emporium since 1909." They offer a nontouristy lunch buffet (Mon-Fri 12:00-15:00), and it's convenient for theatergoers—located roughly halfway between the Gate and Abbey theaters (daily 10:30-23:30, 9 Cathedral Street, just off O'Connell Street 50 yards from the

Spire—tel. 01/874-0137).

$$$ Mr Fox is an elegant and serene little basement operation serving locally sourced dishes created by chef Anthony Smith (Tue-Fri 12:00-14:00 & 17:00-21:30, Sat 17:30-22:00, closed Sun-Mon; behind the Garden of Remembrance at 38 Parnell Square West, tel. 01/874-7778, www.mrfox.ie).

Classy Dining South of Temple Bar

These stylish restaurants serve well-presented food at fair prices. They're located within a block of each other, just south of Temple Bar and Dame Street, near the main TI.

$$$$ Trocadero serves beefy European cuisine to Dubliners interested in a slow, romantic meal. The dressy, red-velvet interior is draped with photos of local actors. Come early or make a reservation—it's a favorite with theatergoers (Mon-Sat 17:00-23:30, closed Sun, 4 St. Andrew Street, tel. 01/677-5545, www.trocadero.ie). The three-course pretheater special is a fine value at €27 (17:00-19:00, leave by 19:45, Robert).

$$$ Eden Bar & Grill lurks on funky William Street with a varied menu from monkfish to pizza, highlighted by especially creative lamb dishes (daily 12:00-16:00 & 17:30-22:00, 7 South William Street, tel. 01/670-6887).

$$$ Boulevard Café is mod, trendy, and likeable, dishing up Mediterranean cuisine that's heavy on the Italian. It's smart to reserve for dinner (Mon-Sat 12:00-22:00, Sun 12:30-20:00, 27 Exchequer Street, tel. 01/679-2131, www.boulevardcafe.ie).

$$$ The Bank wows visitors with its grand Victorian bank-lobby ambience, lit by an arched Tiffany skylight. You'll find great food—the mussel and oyster starters are a hit—in a central location (daily 11:00-23:30, 20 College Green, tel. 01/677-0677).

In Temple Bar

$$ Gallagher's Boxty House is touristy and traditional—a good, basic value with creaky floorboards and old Dublin ambience. They serve stews and corned beef, but the specialty is boxty, the generally bland-tasting Irish potato pancake filled and rolled with various meats, veggies, and sauces (Mon-Fri 12:00-22:00, Sat-Sun from 11:00, reservations wise, 20 Temple Bar, tel. 01/677-2762, www.boxtyhouse.ie).

Rick's Tip: *Restaurants and lodging are* **more expensive** *the closer you get to the* **touristy Temple Bar district.** *In a Temple Bar pub, a pint of beer costs €5—a sobering thought.*

$$ Luigi Malone's, with its fun atmosphere and varied menu of pizza, ribs, pasta, sandwiches, and fajitas, is just the place to take your high-school date (Mon-Sat 12:00-22:00, Sun 13:00-21:30, corner of Cecilia and Fownes streets, tel. 01/679-2723).

$$$ The Shack, while touristy, has a reputation for good quality. It serves traditional Irish, chicken, seafood, and steak dishes (daily 12:00-22:00, in the center of Temple Bar, 24 East Essex Street, tel. 01/679-0043).

$$ The Bad Ass Café serves pizza, pasta, burgers, and salads that are cheap by Temple Bar standards. There's even a fun kids' menu. Their big patio fronts the Temple Bar action, and there's live music nightly in the dark, sprawling, pubby interior (daily 12:00-22:00, 9 Crown Alley, tel. 01/675-3005).

Near the Grand Canal

These places are within a long block of one another in the emerging Grand Canal neighborhood—an area southeast of St. Stephen's Green that's (as yet) undiscovered by the tourist crowds. You'll find them just over the Grand Canal about a 20-minute walk from the center (near the intersection of Baggot Street and Mespil Road).

$$$ Bloom Brasserie & Wine Bar has a woody, candlelit ambience with beautifully presented dishes based on locally sourced meats (beef, lamb, duck)

and seafood (Irish salmon). The modern menu changes with the seasons (Mon-Sat 12:00-14:30 & 17:00-22:30, closed Sun, 11 Upper Baggot Street, tel. 01/668-7170).

$$ Searsons Pub, a sprawling neighborhood favorite, is a gastropub with an open kitchen, a classy-for-a-sports-bar energy, and friendly service. If there's a horse race or rugby match on, it'll be on the screens here (it's located near the rugby stadium and a betting office). You can escape the clamor out back on the patio (daily 12:00-23:30, 42 Upper Baggot Street, tel. 01/660-0330).

$$ Zakura Izakaya is a classy-if-noisy Japanese place—small and tight, like a sushi wine-bar (daily 12:00-22:00, 7 Upper Baggot Street, tel. 01/563-8000).

$$ Langkawi is a cozy, traditional family operation serving Malaysian fusion food, with spicy Indian influences and rice-based Chinese favorites (daily 12:30-14:00 & 18:00-23:30, 46 Upper Baggot Street, tel. 01/668-2760).

Dinner with Entertainment

$$$$ The Brazen Head hosts "Food, Folk and Fairies" evenings, which are more culturally highbrow than the title might suggest, while still remaining fun. Even at €48, the evening is a great value. You get a hearty, four-course meal that's punctuated by soulful Irish history and fascinating Irish mythology, delivered by an engaging local folklorist, with occasional live trad tunes in-between courses (daily 19:00-22:00, Jan-Feb Thu and Sat only, reservations smart; by south end of Father Matthew Bridge, 2 blocks west of Christ Church Cathedral at 20 Bridge Street; pub tel. 01/677-9549, show tel. 01/218-8555, www.irishfolktours.com).

$$$$ The Musical Pub Crawl Dinner Show is a handy intro to Irish traditional music and dancing. Two accomplished musicians take time between tunes to humorously point out what makes this music uniquely Irish—it's a great primer.

Dublin Restaurants

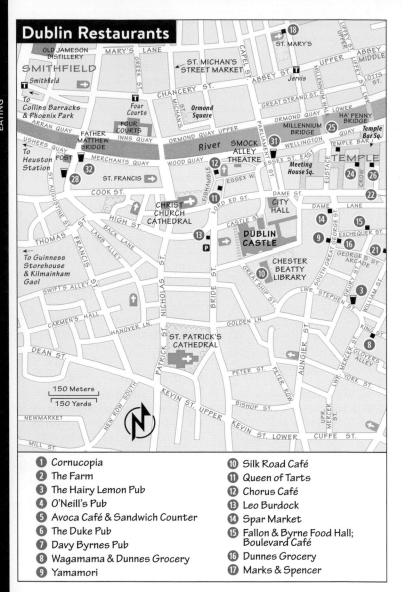

1. Cornucopia
2. The Farm
3. The Hairy Lemon Pub
4. O'Neill's Pub
5. Avoca Café & Sandwich Counter
6. The Duke Pub
7. Davy Byrnes Pub
8. Wagamama & Dunnes Grocery
9. Yamamori
10. Silk Road Café
11. Queen of Tarts
12. Chorus Café
13. Leo Burdock
14. Spar Market
15. Fallon & Byrne Food Hall; Boulevard Café
16. Dunnes Grocery
17. Marks & Spencer

Then you'll move on to dinner with Irish dancing as part of the entertainment (€43, May-Sept Tue-Sat at 18:00, meet at Oliver St. John's Gogarty's on Fleet Street in Temple Bar, tel. 01/475-8345, www. musicalpubcrawl.com).

$$$ Celtic Nights combines traditional music and dancing into a big-stage, high-energy, family-friendly, Irish variety show. This touristy dinner act hits all the clichés, from **Riverdance**-style choreography to fun fiddling and comedic *craic*. It comes with a traditional three-course dinner and lots of audience participation (€35, €15 for children under 12, nightly show at 20:30, downtown by the O'Con-

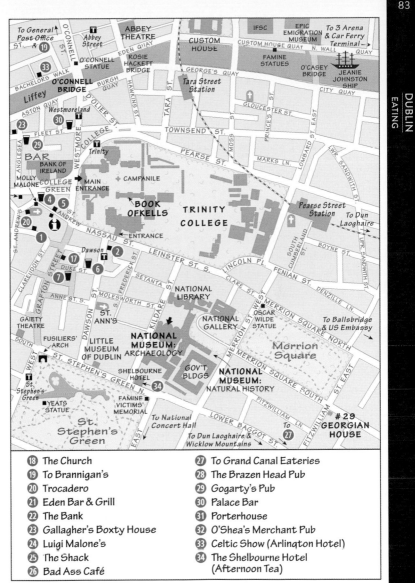

⑱ The Church	㉗ To Grand Canal Eateries
⑲ To Brannigan's	㉘ The Brazen Head Pub
⑳ Trocadero	㉙ Gogarty's Pub
㉑ Eden Bar & Grill	㉚ Palace Bar
㉒ The Bank	㉛ Porterhouse
㉓ Gallagher's Boxty House	㉜ O'Shea's Merchant Pub
㉔ Luigi Malone's	㉝ Celtic Show (Arlington Hotel)
㉕ The Shack	㉞ The Shelbourne Hotel
㉖ Bad Ass Café	(Afternoon Tea)

nell Bridge at the Arlington Hotel, 23 Bachelors Walk, tel. 01/687-5200, www. celticnights.com).

Afternoon Tea

$$$$ The Shelbourne Hotel has been a Dublin landmark since 1824, built to attract genteel patrons and Dublin's

upper-crust socialites. But schlubs like us can dip our toes in the aristocratic fantasy by enjoying the tradition of afternoon tea (no shorts, tank tops, or T-shirts). The menu is a swirl of finger sandwiches, buttermilk scones, clotted cream, strawberry jam, ginger loaf, and fine coffee...as well as 22 varieties of tea. You'll find it in the

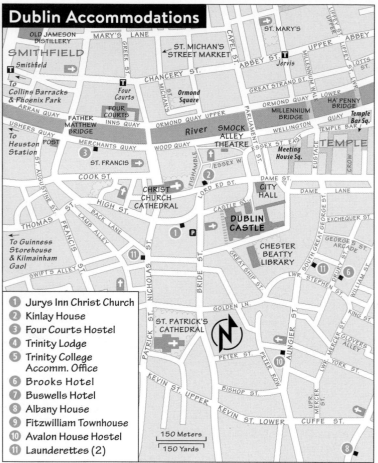

Dublin Accommodations

1. Jurys Inn Christ Church
2. Kinlay House
3. Four Courts Hostel
4. Trinity Lodge
5. Trinity College Accomm. Office
6. Brooks Hotel
7. Buswells Hotel
8. Albany House
9. Fitzwilliam Townhouse
10. Avalon House Hostel
11. Launderettes (2)

ground floor Lord Mayor's Lounge (seatings Mon-Thu at 13:00, 15:15, and 17:30; Fri-Sun at 11:45, 14:00, 16:15, and 18:30; reservations smart, especially on weekends; 27 St. Stephen's Green, tel. 01/663-4500).

SLEEPING

Choosing the right neighborhood in Dublin is as important as choosing the right hotel. All of my recommended accommodations are in safe areas convenient to sightseeing.

Central Dublin is popular, loud, and expensive. You'll find big, practical,

central places south of the river, near Christ Church Cathedral (on the edge of Temple Bar), Trinity College, and St. Stephen's Green. For classy, older Dublin accommodations in a quieter neighborhood, stay a bit farther out, southeast of St. Stephen's Green. North of the river are a few reliable options in an urban area well-served by LUAS streetcars.

South of the River Liffey
Near Christ Church Cathedral
These lodging options cluster near Christ Church Cathedral, a 5-minute

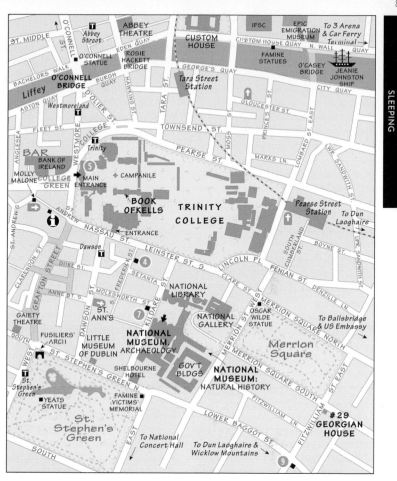

walk from the rowdy and noisy evening scene (at Temple Bar), and 10 minutes from the sightseeing center (Trinity College and Grafton Street). The cheap hostels in this neighborhood have some double rooms.

$$$$ Jurys Inn Christ Church is central and offers business-class comfort in 182 identical rooms. This no-nonsense, American-style hotel chain has a winning keep-it-simple-and-affordable formula. If "ye olde" is getting old—and you don't mind big tour groups—this is a good option. Request a room far from the noisy elevator (breakfast extra, book long in advance for weekends, pay parking, Christ Church Place, tel. 01/454-0000, US tel. 800-423-6953, www.jurysinns.com, jurysinnchristchurch@jurysinns.com).

¢ Kinlay House is the backpackers' choice—definitely the place to go for cheap beds, a central location, and an all-ages-welcome atmosphere. This huge, red-brick, 19th-century Victorian building has 200 metal, prison-style beds in spartan rooms. It fills up most days—reserve well in advance, especially for summer weekends (private and family rooms available, includes continental breakfast, travel desk, kitchen, lots of stairs, Christ Church, 2 Lord

Edward Street, tel. 01/679-6644, www.kin-laydublin.ie, info@kinlaydublin.ie).

¢ **Four Courts Hostel** is a 234-bed hostel well-located immediately across the river from the Four Courts. It's within a five-minute walk of Christ Church Cathedral and Temple Bar. Bare and institutional, it's also spacious and well-run, with a focus on security and efficiency (private rooms available, elevator, game room, some pay parking, 15 Merchant's Quay, from Connolly Station or Busáras Bus Station take LUAS to Four Courts stop and cross river via Father Matthew Bridge, tel. 01/672-5839, www.fourcourtshostel.com, info@fourcourtshostel.com).

Trinity College Area

You can't get more central than Trinity College; these listings offer a good value for the money.

$$$$ Trinity Lodge offers fine, quiet lodging in 26 rooms split between two Georgian townhouses on either side of South Frederick Street, just south of Trinity College (12 South Frederick Street, tel. 01/617-0900, www.trinitylodge.com, trinitylodge@eircom.net).

$$ Trinity College turns its 800 student-housing dorm rooms on campus into no-frills, affordable accommodations in the city center each summer. Look for the Accommodations Office (open Mon-Fri 8:00-18:00) through the door on the right before you come into the courtyard (rooms available late-May-mid-Sept, some en suite rooms but most with shared bath, breakfast extra, tel. 01/896-1177, www.tcd.ie/accommodation/visitors, reservations@tcd.ie).

Near St. Stephen's Green

$$$$ Brooks Hotel is a fine choice for great service, tending 98 plush rooms in an ideal central location. This splurge rarely disappoints (Drury Street, tel. 01/670-4000, www.brookshotel.ie, reservations@brookshotel.ie).

$$$$ Buswells Hotel, one of the city's oldest, is a pleasant Georgian-style haven with 67 rooms in the heart of the city (breakfast extra, between Trinity College and St. Stephen's Green at 23 Molesworth Street, tel. 01/614-6500, www.buswells.ie, info@buswells.ie).

$$$ Albany House's 50 good-value rooms come with high ceilings, Georgian ambience, and some stairs. Ask for a quieter room in back, away from streetcar noise (just one block south of St. Stephen's Green at 84 Harcourt Street, tel. 01/475-1092, www.albanyhousedublin.com, info@albanyhousedublin.com).

$$$ Fitzwilliam Townhouse rents 14 basic rooms in a Georgian townhouse near St. Stephen's Green (family rooms, breakfast extra, 41 Upper Fitzwilliam Street, tel. 01/662-5155, www.fitzwilliamtownhouse.com, info@fitzwilliamtownhouse.com).

¢ **Avalon House Hostel,** near Grafton Street, rents simple, clean backpacker beds (private rooms available, includes continental breakfast, elevator, a few minutes off Grafton Street at 55 Aungier Street, tel. 01/475-0001, www.avalon-house.ie, info@avalon-house.ie).

Away from the Center, Southeast of St. Stephen's Green

This neighborhood—stretching roughly east-west from Leeson Street to Grand Canal Street—is a perfect compromise between busy central lodging options and more sedate choices that are farther out.

$$$$ Number 31 is a hidden gem reached via gritty little Leeson Close (a lane off Lower Leeson Street). Ask Noel about the VIPs who attended dinner parties here 50 years ago. Its understated elegance is top-notch, with 6 rooms in a former coach house and 15 rooms in an adjacent Georgian house; the two buildings are connected by a quiet little garden. Guests appreciate the special touches (such as a sunken living room with occasional peat fires) and tasty breakfasts served in a classy glass atrium (family rooms, free parking, 31 Leeson Close,

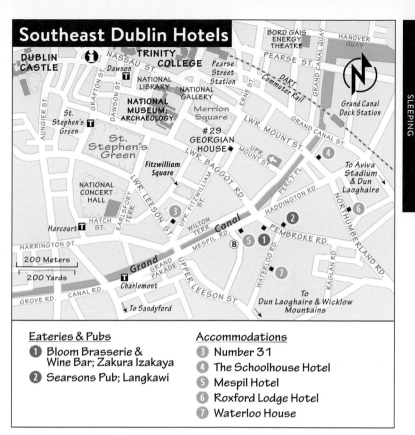

Southeast Dublin Hotels

Eateries & Pubs
1. Bloom Brasserie & Wine Bar; Zakura Izakaya
2. Searsons Pub; Langkawi

Accommodations
3. Number 31
4. The Schoolhouse Hotel
5. Mespil Hotel
6. Roxford Lodge Hotel
7. Waterloo House

tel. 01/676-5011, www.number31.ie, info@number31.ie).

$$$$ The **Schoolhouse Hotel** taught as many as 300 students in its heyday (1861–1969) and was in the middle of the street fight that was the 1916 Easter Rising. Now it's a serene hideout with 31 pristine rooms and a fine restaurant (breakfast extra, book early, 2 Northumberland Road, tel. 01/667-5014, www.schoolhousehotel.com, reservations@schoolhousehotel.com).

$$$ **Mespil Hotel** is a huge, modern, business-class hotel renting 254 identical three-star rooms at a good price with all the comforts. This place is a cut above Jurys Inn (breakfast extra, elevator; small first-come, first-served free parking; 10-minute walk southeast of St. Stephen's Green or take bus #37, #38, #39, or #46A;

50 Mespil Road, tel. 01/488-4600, www.mespilhotel.com, mespil@leehotels.com).

$$$ **Roxford Lodge Hotel** is well managed and a great value. In a quiet residential neighborhood a 20-minute walk from Trinity College, it has 24 tastefully decorated rooms awash with Jacuzzis and saunas. The executive suite is honeymoon worthy (family rooms, breakfast extra, elevator, parking, 46 Northumberland Road, tel. 01/668-8572, www.roxfordlodge.ie, reservations@roxfordlodge.ie).

$$$ **Waterloo House** sits proudly Georgian on a quiet residential street with 19 comfortable and relaxing rooms and a pleasant back garden (family rooms, parking, 8 Waterloo Road, tel. 01/660-1888, www.waterloohouse.ie, info@waterloohouse.ie).

North of the River Liffey
Near Parnell Square

A swanky neighborhood 250 years ago, this is now workaday Dublin with a steady urban hum, made accessible by LUAS streetcars. To locate these hotels, see the map on page 68.

$$$$ The Castle Hotel is a formerly grand but still comfortable Georgian establishment embedded in the urban canyons of North Dublin. A half-block east of the Garden of Remembrance, it's a good value with pleasant rooms and the friendly Castle Vaults pub with live music in its basement (Great Denmark Street, tel. 01/874-6949, www.castle-hotel.ie, info@castle-hotel.ie).

$$$$ Jurys Inn Parnell Street has 253 predictably soulless but modern rooms. It's a block from the north end of O'Connell Street and the cluster of museums on Parnell Square (breakfast extra, tel. 01/878-4900, www.jurysinns.com, jurysinnparnellst@jurysinns.com).

$$$$ Belvedere Hotel has 92 plain-vanilla rooms that are short on character but long on dependable, modern comforts (Great Denmark Street, tel. 01/873-7700, www.belvederehotel.ie, reservations@belvederehotel.ie).

$$$ Charles Stewart Guesthouse, big and basic, offers 60 acceptable rooms in a good location for a fair price (family rooms, breakfast extra, ask for a quieter room in the back, just beyond top end of O'Connell Street at 5 Parnell Square East, tel. 01/878-0350, www.charlesstewart.ie, info@charlesstewart.ie).

TRANSPORTATION

Getting Around Dublin

You'll do most of Dublin on foot, though when you need public transportation, you'll find it readily available and easy to use. With a little planning, sightseers can make excellent use of a hop-on, hop-off bus ticket to link the best sights (see page 44).

You can buy individual tickets for the bus and LUAS light rail, or get a **Leap transit card** that can be used on both (sold at TIs, newsstands, and markets citywide, www.leapcard.ie).

The **Do Dublin** transit and discount card covers the Airlink Express, public buses in Dublin, and the Do Dublin hop-on, hop-off bus (can buy online, at Dublin Airport's Terminal 1, or at Dublin Bus office—see next, www.dodublin.ie).

By Bus

Public buses are cheap and cover the city thoroughly. Most lines start at the four quays (riverfront streets) that are nearest O'Connell Bridge. If you're away from the center, nearly any bus takes you back downtown. Some bus stops are "request only" stops: Be alert to the bus numbers (above the windshield) of approaching buses, and when you see your bus coming, flag it down. Tell the driver where you're going, and he'll ask for €2-3.30 depending on the number of stops. Bring coins, as drivers don't make change.

The **Dublin Bus office** has free route maps and sells transit cards (Mon-Fri 9:00-17:30, Sat-Sun 9:30-14:00, 59 Upper O'Connell Street, tel. 01/873-4222, www.dublinbus.ie).

By Light Rail (LUAS)

The city's light-rail system has two main lines, red and green. The most useful for tourists is the red line, with an east-west section connecting the Heuston and Connolly train stations (15-minute ride apart) at opposite edges of the Central 1 Zone; the Busáras, Smithfield, and Museum stops can be handy. Useful north-south green line stops are at St. Stephen's Green, Trinity College, and both ends of O'Connell Street (€2, buy at machine, 6/hour, runs until 24:45, tel. 1-800-300-604, www.luas.ie).

By Taxi or Uber

Taxis are everywhere and easy to hail. Cabbies are generally honest, friendly, and good sources of information (drop charge—€3.60 daytime, €4 nighttime, €1/ each additional adult, figure about €12-15 for most crosstown rides, €40/hour for guided joyride).

Your Uber app will get you two choices in Dublin: "Uber" is actually a taxi (with the standard metered rate, but no tipping and billed to your account); "Uber Black" is an expensive chauffeur-driven car.

Arriving and Departing
By Train
Dublin has two train stations. **Heuston Station,** on the west end of town, serves west and southwest Ireland (45-minute walk from O'Connell Bridge; take the LUAS light rail or bus #90). **Connolly Station,** which serves the north, northwest, and Rosslare, is closer to the center (15-minute walk from O'Connell Bridge). Each station has ATMs but no lockers.

The train stations are connected by the red line of the LUAS light-rail system and by **bus #90,** which runs along the river (€2, 4/hour). To get from the city center to Heuston Station, catch bus #90 on the south side of the river; to get to Connolly Station and Busáras Central Bus Station, catch #90 on the north side of the river.

TRAIN CONNECTIONS
Note that trains (and buses) generally run less frequently on Sundays. Irish Rail train info: Toll tel. 1850-366-222, www. irishrail.ie.

From Dublin's Heuston Station to: Tralee (every two hours, most change in Mallow but one direct evening train, 4 hours), **Ennis** (11/day, 3-4 hours, change in Limerick, Limerick Junction, or Athenry), **Galway** (8/day, 3 hours).

From Dublin's Connolly Station to: **Waterford** (8/day, 2.5-3 hours), **Portrush** (7/day, 2/day Sun, 5 hours, transfer in Belfast or Coleraine). The **Dublin-Belfast train** connects the capitals in two hours at 90 mph (8/day Mon-Sat, 5/day Sun). Northern Ireland train info: Tel. 048/9089-9400, www.translink.co.uk.

DUBLIN
TRANSPORTATION

By Bus
Bus Éireann, Ireland's national bus company, uses the Busáras Central Bus Station (pronounced bu-SAUR-us). Located next to Connolly Station, it's a 10-minute walk or a short ride on bus #90 to the city center. Bus info: Toll tel. 1850-836-611, www. buseireann.ie.

From Dublin by Bus to: Belfast (hourly, most via Dublin Airport, 3 hours), **Trim** (almost hourly, 1 hour), **Ennis** (almost hourly, 5 hours), **Galway** (hourly, 3.5 hours; faster on CityLink—hourly, 2.5 hours, tel. 091/564-164, www.citylink.ie), **Limerick** (7/day, 3.5 hours), **Tralee** (7/day, 6 hours), **Dingle** (4/day, 8.5 hours, transfer at Limerick and Tralee).

By Plane
Dublin Airport has two terminals located an easily walkable 150 yards apart (airport code: DUB, tel. 01/814-1111, www.dublinairport.ie). Both have ATMs, cafés, Wi-Fi, and luggage storage (www.leftluggage.ie). There is no TI at the airport.

Getting Downtown by Bus: You have two main choices—Airlink (double-decker turquoise bus) or Aircoach (single-deck blue bus). Both pick up on the street directly in front of arrivals, at ground level at both terminals.

Airlink Express: Airlink bus #747 generally runs an east-west route that parallels the River Liffey, and includes stops at the Busáras Central Bus Station, Connolly Station, O'Connell Street, Temple Bar, Christ Church, and Heuston Station. Airlink bus #757 links the airport to the center along a generally north-south axis, including Trinity College, St. Stephen's Green (eastern end), and the National Concert Hall. Ask the driver which stop is closest to your hotel (€7, pay driver, 3-5/hour, about 40 minutes; runs Mon-Sat 5:45-late, Sun from 7:00; tel. 01/873-4222, www.dublinbus.ie). This bus is covered by the Do Dublin transit card, which can be purchased at the airport (see page 88).

Aircoach: This bus generally runs a north-south route that follows the O'Connell and Grafton streets axis. To reach recommended hotels south of the city center, the Aircoach bus #700 or #703 work well (€7 if paying driver, €6 if booked online, covered by Dublin Pass—one-way from the airport to the city only, 3/hour, fewer late-night, runs 24 hours, tel. 01/844-7118, www.aircoach.ie).

By Taxi: Taxis from the airport into Dublin cost about €30.

By Car

It's best to avoid driving in hectic Dublin. If you plan to drive in Ireland, save your car rental for the countryside. Consider renting a car at the airport, where you'll find all the standard car-rental agencies.

M-50 Toll Road: Drivers renting a car at Dublin Airport and heading for the countryside can bypass the worst of the big-city traffic by taking the M-50 ring road south or west. The M-50 uses an automatic tolling system called eFlow. Your rental should come with an eFlow tag installed; confirm this when you pick up your car. The €3.10 toll per trip is automatically debited from the credit card with which you rented the car (for pass details, see www.eflow.ie).

Other Toll Roads: Your rental car's eFlow tag will work only for the M-50 ring road around Dublin. On any other Irish toll roads, you'll have to pay with cash (about €2/toll). These roads mostly run outward from Dublin toward Waterford, Cork, Limerick, and Galway (roads farther west are free).

By Ferry

Irish Ferries and Stena Line combine to make eight daily crossings between Dublin Port (two miles east of O'Connell Bridge) and Holyhead, Wales. Most trips take 3.5 hours (€39), but Irish Ferries offers a twice-daily fast boat that makes the trip in 2 hours (€44). You must board at least 30 minutes before the scheduled sailing time. Since these boats can fill up on summer weekends, book at least a week ahead during the peak period.

Irish Ferries depart at 2:40, 11:50, 14:10, and 17:15 (Dublin tel. 0818-300-400, UK tel. 08717-300-400, www.irishferries.com); **Stena Line** sails at 2:15, 8:20, 15:10, and 20:40 (Dublin tel. 01/907-5555, UK tel. 08447-707-070, www.stenaline.ie).

NEAR DUBLIN

Not far from urban Dublin, the stony skeletons of evocative ruins sprout from the lush Irish countryside. The story of Irish history is told by ancient burial mounds, early Christian monastic settlements, huge Norman castles, and pampered estate gardens.

These sights are separated into two regions:

North of Dublin, the interesting Boyne Valley features the ancient Brú na Bóinne burial site and the medieval town of Trim. It's on my two-week itinerary.

South of Dublin, the Wicklow

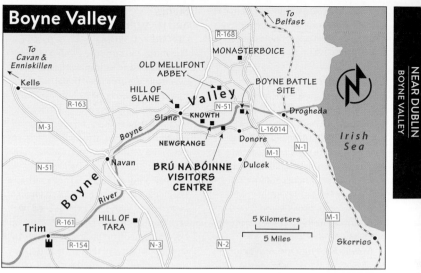

Mountains have the Glendalough monastic settlement, set amid woods and lakes, and the manicured Powerscourt Estate Gardens. The area is enjoyable if you have extra time or interest.

BOYNE VALLEY

The peaceful, green Boyne Valley, 30 miles north of Dublin, is worth a visit for the prehistoric and spiritual sights at Brú na Bóinne. The town of Trim makes an easy overnight stop for drivers (on the first or last night of your trip), and boasts a 13th-century castle—Ireland's biggest.

Brú na Bóinne

The famous archaeological site of Brú na Bóinne—"dwelling place of the Boyne"—is also commonly called "Newgrange," after its star attraction. Here you can visit two ▲▲▲ 5,000-year-old passage tombs— **Newgrange** and **Knowth** (rhymes with "south"). These are massive grass-covered burial mounds built atop separate hills, with a chamber inside reached by a narrow stone passage. Mysterious, thought-provoking, and mind-bogglingly old, these tombs can give you chills.

Planning Your Visit

Access to Newgrange and Knowth is by guided tour only. You'll start your visit at the state-of-the-art visitors center with its excellent museum, then catch a shuttle bus to the tomb sites, where a guide gives a 30-minute tour.

Each tomb site takes about 1.5 hours to visit (30-minute round-trip bus ride plus 30-minute guided tour plus 30 minutes of free time). The museum at the visitors center is well worth an additional 30-60 minutes. If you add in waiting time for the next available shuttle bus, you're looking at a minimum of 2.5 hours to visit one of the tombs (along with the museum), or 4 hours to see both tombs (and museum).

Rick's Tip: *You might* **pick your tomb** *according to whichever shuttle bus is leaving next.*

Which tomb is best? If you can't see both, I'd pick Newgrange because it's more famous and allows you inside. (On the other hand, wait times for the Newgrange shuttle bus can be longer.) Knowth is bigger and flanked by small mounds, but you can't access its narrow passages. Each site is different enough and worthwhile, but for many, seeing just one is adequate.

Orientation

Cost: Newgrange–€7, Knowth–€6, both–€13; museum is included in tomb prices.

Hours: June–mid-Sept daily 9:00-19:00, slightly shorter hours off-season. The last entry to the visitors center is 45 minutes before closing; the last bus to the tombs leaves 1.75 hours before closing. Newgrange is open year-round, while Knowth is open May-Oct only.

Information: Tel. 041/988-0300, www.heritageireland.ie.

Crowd-Beating Tips: Arrive early—ideally before 9:30 in peak season—to avoid the big midday bus-tour crowds from Dublin. Visits are limited, and on busy summer days those arriving in the afternoon may not get a spot on a shuttle bus. An advance reservation system might be in place by the time you visit (check the website). The last bus to the tombs leaves 1.75 hours before closing.

Getting There: By car, drive 45 minutes north from Dublin on N-1 to Drogheda, where signs direct you to the visitors center. If you're using a GPS, input "Brú na Bóinne" rather than "Newgrange" to get to the visitors center, where you must check in.

Getting In: At the visitors center, buy your ticket (to one or both tombs), find out when the next shuttle bus leaves, then spend your waiting time in the excellent museum, grabbing lunch in the cheery downstairs cafeteria, and using the WCs (there are none at the tomb sites).

Tours from Dublin: Newgrange Tours visits Brú na Bóinne (including inside the Newgrange tomb), the Hill of Tara, and the Hill of Slane in a seven-hour trip (€40, daily pickup from several Dublin hotels, book direct via website, mobile 086-355-1355, www.newgrangetours.com, new-grangetours@gmail.com).

Sights

BRÚ NA BÓINNE VISITORS CENTER MUSEUM

The museum introduces you to the Boyne River Valley and its tombs. No one knows exactly who built the 40 burial mounds found in the surrounding hills. Exhibits re-create what these pre-Celtic people might have been like—simple farmers and hunters living in huts, fishing in the Boyne, equipped with crude tools of stone, bone, or wood.

Then around 3200 B.C., someone had a bold idea. They constructed a chamber of large stones, with a long stone-lined passage leading up to it. They covered it with a huge mound of dirt and rocks in successive layers. Sailing down the Boyne to the sea, they beached at Clogherhead (12.5 miles from here), where they found hundreds of five-ton stones, weathered smooth by the tides. Somehow they transported them back up the Boyne, possibly by tying a raft to the top of the stone so it was lifted free by a high tide. They then hauled these stones up the hill by rolling them atop logs and up dirt ramps, and laid them around the perimeter of the burial mound to hold everything in place. It would have taken anywhere from five years to a generation to construct a single large tomb.

Why build these vast structures? Partially, it was to bury VIPs. A dead king might be carried up the hill to be cremated on a pyre. Then they'd bring his ashes into the tomb, parading by torchlight down the passage to the central chamber. The remains were placed in a ceremonial basin, mingled with those of illustrious ancestors.

The museum displays replicas of tools and objects found at the sites, including the ceremonial basin stone and a head made out of flint, which may have been carried atop a pole during the funeral procession. Marvel at the craftsmanship of the perfectly spherical stones (and the phallic one), and wonder at their purpose.

The tombs also served an astronomical

The Newgrange burial tomb predates the Egyptian pyramids.

function; they're precisely aligned to the movements of the sun, as displays and a video illustrate. You can request a short tour and winter solstice light-show demo at a full-size replica of the Newgrange passage and interior chamber.

Since the tombs are aligned with the heavens, it begs the question: Were these structures sacred places where primal Homo sapiens gathered to ponder the deepest mysteries of existence?

▲▲▲NEWGRANGE

This grassy mound atop a hill is 250 feet across and 40 feet high. Dating from 3200 B.C., it's 500 years older than the pyramids at Giza. The base of the mound is ringed by dozens of curbstones, each about nine feet long and weighing five tons.

The entrance facade is a mosaic of white quartz and dark granite. This reconstruction dates to the 1970s; not every archaeologist agrees it originally looked like this. Above the doorway is a square window called the roofbox, which played a key role (as we'll see). In front of the doorway lies the most famous of the curbstones, the 10- by 4-foot entrance stone. Its left half is carved with three mysterious spirals, which have become a

kind of poster child for prehistoric art.

Most of Newgrange's curbstones have designs carved into them. This was done with super-hard flint tools; the Neolithic ("New Stone Age") people had not mastered metal. The stones feature common Neolithic motifs: not people or animals, but geometric shapes—spirals, crosshatches, bull's-eyes, and chevrons.

Entering the tomb, you walk down a narrow 60-foot passage lined with big boulders. Occasionally you have to duck or turn sideways to squeeze through. The passage opens up into a central room—a cross-shaped central chamber with three alcoves, topped by a 20-foot-high igloo-type stone dome. Bones and ashes were placed here in a ceremonial stone basin, under 200,000 tons of stone and dirt.

While we know nothing of Newgrange's builders, it most certainly was a sacred spot—for a cult of the dead, a cult of the sun, or both. The tomb is aligned precisely east-west. As the sun rises around the shortest day of the year (winter solstice, Dec 21), a ray of light enters through the roofbox and creeps slowly down the passageway. For 17 minutes, it lights the center of the sacred chamber (your guide will demonstrate this). Perhaps this was the moment when the souls of the dead were transported to the afterlife, via that ray of life-giving and life-taking light. Then the light passes on, and, for the next 364 days, the tomb sits again in total darkness.

▲▲▲KNOWTH

This site is an impressive necropolis, with one grand hill-topping mound surrounded by several smaller satellite tombs. The central mound is 220 feet wide, 40 feet high, and covers 1.5 acres.

You'll see plenty of mysteriously carved curbstones and new-feeling grassy mounds that you can look down on from atop the grand tomb.

Knowth's big tomb has two passages: one entering from the east, and one from the west. Like Newgrange, it's likely aligned so the rising and setting sun shone down the passageways to light the two interior chambers. Neither passage is open to the public, but you can visit a room carved into the mound by archaeologists, where a cutaway lets you see the layers of dirt and rock used to build the mound. You also get a glimpse down one of the passages.

The Knowth site thrived from 3000 to 2000 B.C. The central tomb dates from about 2000 B.C. It was likely used for burial rituals and sun-tracking ceremonies to please the gods and ensure the regular progression of seasons for crops. The site then evolved into the domain of fairies and myths for the next 2,000 years, and became an Iron Age fortress in the early centuries after Christ. Around A.D. 1000, it was an all-Ireland political center, and later, a Norman fortress was built atop the mound. Now, 4,000 years after prehistoric people built these strange tombs, you can stand atop the hill at Knowth, look out over the surrounding countryside, and contemplate.

Trim

The sleepy, workaday town of Trim, straddling the River Boyne, is marked by the towering ruins of Trim Castle, which seem to say, "This little town was big-time...800 years ago." Trim makes a great landing pad into—or launching pad out of—Ireland. If you're flying into or out of Dublin Airport and don't want to deal with big-city Dublin, this is a perfect alternative—an easy 45-minute, 30-mile drive away. You can rent a car at the airport and make Trim your first overnight base, or spend your last night here before returning your car at the airport.

Orientation

Trim's main square is a traffic roundabout, and everything's within a block or two. Most of the shops and eateries are on or near Market Street, along with banks and a supermarket.

Getting There: Buses run from Dublin's Busáras bus station to Trim nearly hourly, dropping off at the bus shelter next to Trim's TI and the castle entrance on Castle Street (1-hour trip, bus info: tel. 01/836-6111, www.buseireann.ie). Trim has no train station.

Day-tripping drivers can park on the street or in a public lot (pay-and-display system, €1/hour, 2-hour maximum, Mon-Sat 9:00-18:00, free Sun).

Tourist Information: The TI is right next to the castle and has a handy coffee shop (June-Aug Mon-Fri 9:30-17:30, Sat-Sun 12:00-17:00, shorter hours Sept-May, Castle Street, tel. 046/943-7227).

Laundry: The launderette is located close to Market Street (Mon-Sat 9:00-13:00 & 13:30-17:30, closed Sun, Watergate Street, tel. 046/943-7176).

Taxi: Donie Quinn can give you a lift to nearby Boyne sites (tel. 046/943-6009).

Sights
▲▲TRIM CASTLE

This is the biggest Norman castle in Ireland. Set in a grassy riverside park at the edge of this sleepy town, its mighty keep towers above a very ruined outer wall. It replaced a wooden fortification that

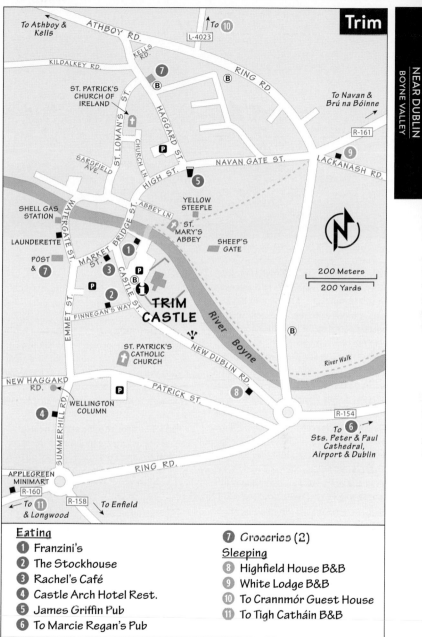

Trim

Eating
1. Franzini's
2. The Stockhouse
3. Rachel's Café
4. Castle Arch Hotel Rest.
5. James Griffin Pub
6. To Marcie Regan's Pub
7. Groceries (2)

Sleeping
8. Highfield House B&B
9. White Lodge B&B
10. To Crannmór Guest House
11. To Tigh Catháin B&B

Trim's huge Norman castle overlooks the Boyne River.

was destroyed in 1173 by Irish High King Rory O'Connor, who led a raid against the invading Normans. The current castle was completed in the 1220s and served as a powerful Norman statement to the restless Irish natives.

Today the castle remains a remarkable sight—so remarkable that it was used in the 1994 filming of *Braveheart* (which was actually about Scotland's—not Ireland's—fight for freedom). The best-preserved walls ring the castle's southern perimeter and sport a barbican gate that contained two drawbridges. The massive 70-foot-high central keep, which is mostly a hollow shell, has 20 sides. This experimental design was not implemented elsewhere because it increased the number of defenders needed to cover all the angles. Make time to take a 15-minute walk outside, circling the castle walls.

Cost and Hours: €5 for entrance to keep and required tour, €2 for gardens only; mid-March-Oct daily 10:00-18:00, Nov-mid-March open Sat-Sun only 10:00-17:00; last entry one hour before closing, 45-minute tours run 2/hour but spots are limited and can fill up—so arrive early in peak season, tel. 046/943-8619, www.heritageireland.ie.

Eating

The restaurants and cafés along Market Street are friendly, wholesome, and unassuming.

$$$ Franzini's has a fun dinner menu and an excellent location next to the castle. They serve pasta, steak, fish, and great salads in a modern, plush space (Mon-Sat 17:00-21:00, Sun 14:00-20:00, on French's Lane across from the castle parking lot, tel. 046/943-1002).

$$$ The Stockhouse serves hearty steaks and poultry, plus creative desserts. Sit upstairs and take in the history of Trim from the walls while you wait (Mon-Thu 17:00-21:00, Fri-Sat until 22:00, Sun 13:00-20:30, Finnegan's Way, tel. 046/943-7388).

$$ Rachel's Café is a good bet along Market Street for salads, sandwiches, and meat pies (Mon-Sat 8:30-17:30, Sun until 17:00, tel. 046/943-1636).

$$ The **Castle Arch Hotel,** popular with locals, serves hearty pub grub at reasonable prices in its bistro on Summerhill Road (daily 12:30-21:00, tel. 046/943-1516).

Pubs: For a fun pub experience, check out Trim's two best watering holes. The **James Griffin** (on High Street) is full of local characters with traditional Irish music sessions on Monday, Wednesday, and Thursday nights. Locals fill the tiny, low-ceilinged **Marcie Regan's,** a creaky, unpretentious pub at the north end of the old Norman bridge over the River Boyne—it's a half-mile stroll outside town, next to the ruins of Newtown.

Supermarkets: Several stores offer picnic supplies. These include **Spar Market** (Mon-Sat 7:30-20:00, Sun 8:30-19:00, Emmett Street) and the larger **Super Valu** (daily 8:00-22:00, on Haggard Street, a bit farther from the town center).

Sleeping

$$ Highfield House B&B, across the street from the castle and a five-minute walk from town, is a stately 210-year-old former maternity hospital, with hardwood floors and 10 spacious, high-ceilinged rooms (family rooms; above the roundabout where Dublin Road hits Trim, just before castle at Castle Street; tel. 046/943-6386, mobile 086 857-7115, www.highfieldguesthouse.com, info@highfieldguesthouse.com, Geraldine and Edward Duignan).

$ White Lodge B&B, a 10-minute walk northeast of the castle, has six comfortably unpretentious rooms with an oak-and-granite lounge (open May-Oct, family room, parking, New Road, tel. 046/943-6549, www.whitelodge.ie, info@whitelodge.ie, Todd O'Loughlin). They also offer a family-friendly self-catering house next door. A handy 300-yard trail leads from across the street to the castle.

These two B&Bs are in the quiet countryside about a mile outside Trim (phone ahead for driving directions). At ivy-draped **$ Crannmór Guest House,** Anne O'Regan decorates five rooms with cheery color schemes (family room; north of the Ring Road on Dunderry Road L-4023, then veer right at the first fork; tel. 046/943-1635, mobile 087-288-7390, www.crannmor.com, cranmor@eircom. net). Anne's professional-guide husband Marc knows all the best fishing holes.

Marie Keane's **$ Tigh Catháin B&B,** southwest of town, has four large, bright, lacy rooms with a comfy, rural feel and organically grown produce at breakfast (cash only, on R-160/Longwood Road, 200 yards past the Applegreen minimart, tel. 046/943-1996, mobile 086-257-7313, www.tighcathain-bnb.com, tighcathain.bnb@gmail.com).

WICKLOW MOUNTAINS

The Wicklow Mountains, while only 15 miles south of Dublin, feel remote—enough so to have provided a handy refuge for opponents to English rule. Rebels who took part in the 1798 Irish uprising hid out here for years. The area only became more accessible in 1800, when the frustrated British built a military road. Today, this same road—now R-115—takes you through the Wicklow area, with the Powerscourt Estate Gardens on the north end and the monastic settlement of Glendalough at the south end.

Getting There

By car or tour, it's easy. It's not worth the trouble on public transport.

By Car: Take N-11 south from Dublin toward Bray, then R-117 to Enniskerry, the gateway to the Wicklow Mountains. Signs direct you to the Powerscourt Estate Gardens and on to Glendalough. From Glendalough, if you're heading west, you can leave the valley (and pick up the highway to the west) over the famous but dull mountain pass called the Wicklow Gap.

By Tour from Dublin: Wild Wicklow Tours packs every minute of an all-day excursion covering the windy military road over scenic Sally Gap and the Glendalough monasteries (€28, ask for discount with this book, runs daily year-round, stop for lunch at a pub—cost not included, several Dublin hotel pickup points, advance booking required, tel. 01/280-1899, www.wildwicklow.ie)

Powerscourt House is surrounded by Italian Renaissance–style gardens.

Do Dublin Tours offers a shorter trip focusing on Glendalough and the Powerscourt Estate Gardens (€22, daily departures from Dublin Bus office, 59 Upper O'Connell Street, tel. 01/844-4265, www.dodublin.ie).

Sights

▲▲ POWERSCOURT ESTATE GARDENS

A mile above the village of Enniskerry, the Powerscourt Estate Gardens (1858-1875) cover 47 acres within a 700-acre estate. While the mansion isn't much (nor open to the public), its aristocratic gardens are Ireland's best.

Upon entry, you'll get a flier laying out 40-minute and one-hour walks. The "one-hour" walk takes 30 minutes at a relaxed amble, with the Great Sugar Loaf Mountain as a backdrop, and a fine Japanese garden, Italian garden, and goofy pet cemetery along the way.

Cost and Hours: €10, daily March-Oct 9:30-17:30, Nov-Feb until dusk, great cafeteria, tel. 01/204-6000, www.powerscourt.ie, info@powerscourt.net.

▲▲ GLENDALOUGH

The steep wooded slopes of Glendalough (GLEN-da-lock, "Valley of the Two Lakes"), at the south end of Wicklow's old military road, hide Ireland's most impressive monastic settlement. Founded by St. Kevin in the sixth century, the monastery flourished (despite repeated Viking raids) throughout the Age of Saints and Scholars until the English destroyed it in 1398. A few hardy holy men continued to live here until it was finally abandoned during the Dissolution of the Monasteries in 1539. But pilgrims kept coming, especially on St. Kevin's Day, June 3. While much restoration was done in the 1870s, most of the buildings date from the 10th to 12th century.

In an Ireland without cities, these monastic communities were mainstays of civilization. At such remote outposts, ascetics gathered to commune with God. Today, Ireland is dotted with the reminders of this age: illuminated manuscripts, simple churches, carved crosses, and about 100 round towers.

The valley sights are split between the

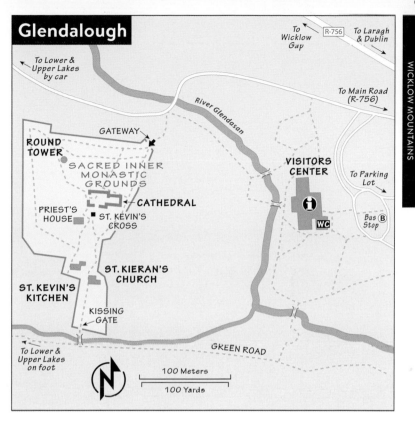

Glendalough

To Wicklow Gap · R-756 · To Laragh & Dublin

To Lower & Upper Lakes by car

To Main Road (R-756)

River Glendasan

GATEWAY

ROUND TOWER

SACRED INNER MONASTIC GROUNDS

PRIEST'S HOUSE

ST. KEVIN'S CROSS

CATHEDRAL

VISITORS CENTER

To Parking Lot

Bus Stop

WC

ST. KIERAN'S CHURCH

ST. KEVIN'S KITCHEN

KISSING GATE

To Lower & Upper Lakes on foot

GREEN ROAD

N

100 Meters
100 Yards

two lakes. The smaller, lower lake is just beyond the visitors center and nearer the best remaining ruins. The upper lake has scant ruins and feels like a state park. Walkers and hikers will enjoy a choice of nine different trails of varying lengths through the lush Wicklow countryside (longest loop takes four hours, hiking-trail maps available at visitors center).

Cost and Hours: Free to enter site, €5 for visitors center, €4 to park at upper lake; open daily 9.30-18:00, mid Oct mid March until 17:00; last entry 45 minutes before closing, tel. 0404/45352.

Visiting Glendalough: Park for free at the visitors center. Visit the center; take the guided tour if possible; wander the ruins surrounding the round tower on your own (free); or walk the traffic-free Green Road a half-mile to the upper lake, and then walk back to the visitors center and your car along the trail that parallels the public road (an easy, roughly one-mile loop). Or you can drive to the upper lake. If you're rushed, skip the upper lake.

The monastic ruins of Glendalough in the lush Wicklow Mountains

Kilkenny
& the
Rock of Cashel

Driving from Dublin (on Ireland's east coast) to Dingle (on Ireland's west coast), the best two stops to break the long journey across the Irish interior are Kilkenny, Ireland's finest medieval town; and the Rock of Cashel, a thought-provoking early Christian site crowning the Plain of Tipperary.

Counties Kilkenny and Tipperary ("Tipp" to locals) are friendly neighbors geographically, yet blood rivals on the hurling field, with the lion's share of the GAA national championships split between them. Watch for kids heading home from school, carrying hurlies (ash-wood sticks with broad, flat ends) and dressed in their local colors (black and yellow, like bumblebees, for Kilkenny; blue and gold for Tipperary).

These two counties also boast some of the finest agricultural land on this rocky and boggy island. These days, farm tractors rumble on the back roads where it's not a long way to Tipperary.

KILKENNY & THE ROCK OF CASHEL IN 1 DAY

With one day, drivers connecting Dublin with Kinsale can get an early start, stop in Kilkenny for lunch, and then tour the Rock of Cashel before ending up in Kinsale to spend the night.

For a longer visit, Kilkenny makes a good overnight for drivers from Dublin who want to visit the Powerscourt Estate Gardens and Glendalough (see previous chapter).

I've listed accommodations for both Kilkenny and at the Rock of Cashel: A night in Kilkenny comes with plenty of traditional folk music in its pubs and lots to do. With extra time, you could visit sights stretching south to Waterford (monastic ruins, a famine ship replica, and crystal factory). But if you're driving between

Kilkenny

KILKENNY & THE ROCK OF CASHEL AT A GLANCE

In Kilkenny

▲▲ **Kilkenny Castle** Historic castle and gardens, later converted into an opulent château. **Hours:** Daily June-Aug 9:00-17:30, shorter hours off-season. See page 104.

▲ **Rothe House and Garden** Sprawling 17th-century merchant's townhouse complex displaying upper-crust Elizabethan life. **Hours:** Mon-Sat 10:30-17:00, Sun 12:00-17:00; Nov-March closes at 16:30 and all day Sun. See page 105.

Between Kilkenny and Waterford

▲▲ **Jerpoint Abbey** Informatively presented abbey ruins with carvings, bringing to life a monastic culture from 850 years ago. **Hours:** Daily 9:00-17:30; Nov-Feb Mon-Fri 9.30-16.00, closed Sat-Sun except in Nov. See page 110.

▲▲ **Kells Priory** Deserted, monastic ruins of a vast complex, with tower houses bordering a huge courtyard, and rock walls that once supported a church, a cloister, and more. See page 110.

▲▲ *Dunbrody* **Famine Ship** Replica of a typical famine ship that brought emigrants to America. **Hours:** Daily 9:00-18:00, Oct-March 10:00-17:00. See page 111.

▲▲▲ **Waterford Crystal Visitor Centre** Popular tour of glass factory with live demos and glittering sales shop. **Hours:** Mon-Sat 9:00-17:00, Sun from 9:30, shorter hours Nov-March. See page 112.

At Cashel

▲▲▲ **Rock of Cashel** Ireland's best tangle of ecclesiastical ruins atop a rocky perch surveying the plains of Tipperary. **Hours:** Daily 9:00-19:00 in summer, closes earlier rest of year. See page 112.

Dublin and Dingle (or Kenmare), the Rock of Cashel is a more direct overnight.

KILKENNY

Lovely Kilkenny gives you a feel for salt-of-the-earth Ireland. Its castle and cathedral stand like historic bookends on a higgledy-piggledy High Street of colorful shops and medieval facades. A night in Kilkenny comes with plenty of traditional folk music in its pubs. It's nicknamed the "Marble City" for its nearby quarry (actually black limestone, not marble), and you can see white seashells fossilized within the black stone steps around town. While a small town today (around 25,000 residents), Kilkenny has a big history: It was the capital of Ireland for a short spell in the turbulent 1640s. And actor George Clooney traces his roots to Kilkenny.

Orientation

Tourist Information: The TI is a block off the bridge in the 16th-century Shee (a wealthy medieval donor family) Alms poorhouse (Mon-Sat 9:00-17:30, Sun 11:00-17:00, shorter hours and closed Sun off-season; Rose Inn Street, tel. 056/775-1500).

Walking Tour: Local guide **Pat Tynan and his staff** offer hour-long town walks that depart from the TI (€10, daily at 11:00 and 14:00, Nov-mid-March by prior arrangement only, mobile 087-265-1745, www.kilkennywalkingtours.ie).

Laundry: The **Laundry Basket** trumpets its existence in vivid red at 21 Patrick Street at the south end of town (Mon-Fri 9:00-18:00, Sat 10:00-15:00, closed Sun, tel. 056/777-0355).

Bike Rentals and Tours: Kilkenny Cycling rents bikes for €20 a day. They provide safety gear, and have route maps for exploring the pastoral charms of County Kilkenny (office behind The Wine Center shop at 15 John Street, mobile 086-895-4961, www.kilkennycyclingtours.com). They also offer **biking and hiking tours**.

Market: The square in front of Kilkenny Castle hosts a friendly produce, cheese, and crafts market on Thursdays (8:00-14:30).

Sights

▲▲KILKENNY CASTLE

Dominating the town, this castle is a stony reminder that the Anglo-Norman Butler

Kilkenny Castle

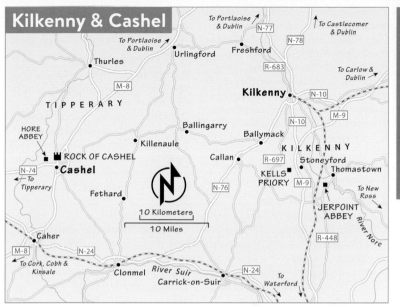

Kilkenny & Cashel

family controlled Kilkenny for 500 years. The castle once had four sides, but Oliver Cromwell's army knocked down one wall when it took the castle, leaving it as the roughly "U" shape we see today.

Cost and Hours: €7, daily June-Aug 9:00-17:30, shorter hours off-season, tel. 056/770-4100.

Visiting the Castle: Enter the castle gate, turn right in the courtyard, and head into the base of the turret. Here you'll find the continuously running 12-minute video explaining how the wooden fort built here by Strongbow in 1172 evolved into a 17th-century château. Then go into the main castle entrance (diagonally across the courtyard from the turret) to buy your entry ticket. You'll be free to walk through the castle. A pamphlet explains the exhibits, and you can also talk to stewards in the important rooms.

Now restored to its Victorian splendor, the castle's highlight is the beautiful family-portrait gallery, which puts you face-to-face with the wealthy Butler family ghosts.

Nearby: The **Kilkenny Design Centre,** across the street from the castle in some grand old stables, is full of local crafts and offers handy cafeteria-style lunches upstairs in the food hall (shops open Mon-Sat 10:00-19:00, Sun until 18:00; food hall open daily 8:30-18:30 tel. 056/772-2118, www.kilkennydesign.com).

▲ROTHE HOUSE AND GARDEN

This is the crown jewel of Kilkenny's medieval architecture: a well-preserved merchant's house that expanded around interior courtyards as the prosperous Rothe family grew in the early 1600s.

Cost and Hours: €5.50; Mon-Sat 10:30-17:00, Sun 12:00-17:00; Nov-March closes at 16:30 and all day Sun; Parliament Street, tel. 056/772-2893, http://rothehouse.com.

Visiting the House and Garden: Check out the graceful top-floor timberwork supporting the roof, which uses wooden dowels (pegs) instead of nails. The museum, which also serves as the County Kilkenny genealogy center, gives a glimpse of life here in late Elizabethan and early Stuart times. The walled gardens at the far back were a real luxury in their time.

The Rothe family eventually lost the house when Oliver Cromwell banished all Catholic landowners, sending them to live on less desirable land west of the Shannon River. In the late 1800s, the building housed the Gaelic League, devoted to the rejuvenation of Irish culture through preservation of the Irish language and promotion of native Irish sports (such as hurling). One of the future leaders of the 1916 rebellion—Thomas McDonagh, who was executed at Dublin's Kilmainham Gaol—taught here.

▲MEDIEVAL MILE MUSEUM

This fine museum covers Kilkenny's brutal yet pious Dark Age past and rounds out the story that the Rothe House (listed above) starts. Housed in the 13th-century St. Mary's Church (much of which was rebuilt in the 1700s), the museum displays medieval artifacts, including ornately carved tomb lids, ceremonial swords and scepters, and neatly penned 800-year-old civic records.

Cost and Hours: €7, €12 with 45-minute tour; open daily 10:00-18:00, Nov-March 11:00-16:30; tours leave daily at 10:30, 12:30, 14:30, and 16:30; 2 Mary's Lane, tel. 056/781-7022, www.medievalmilemuseum.ie.

ST. CANICE'S CATHEDRAL

This 13th-century cathedral is early-English Gothic, rich with stained glass, medieval carvings, and floors paved in history. Check out the model of the old walled town in its 1641 heyday, as well as a couple of modest audiovisuals. The 100-foot-tall **round tower,** built as part of a long-gone pre-Norman church, recalls the need for a watchtower and refuge. The fun ladder-climb to the top affords a grand view of the countryside.

Cost and Hours: Cathedral-€4, tower-€3, combo-ticket-€6; Mon-Sat 9:00-18:00, Sun 13:00-18:00; Sept-May slightly shorter hours and closed for lunch; tel. 056/776-4971, www.stcanicescathedral.com.

SMITHWICK'S EXPERIENCE KILKENNY

Smithwick's (pronounced SMITH-icks) reddish ale was born in Kilkenny...and has been my favorite Irish beer since my first visit to Ireland. Older than Guinness (but now owned by the same parent com-

St. Canice's Cathedral

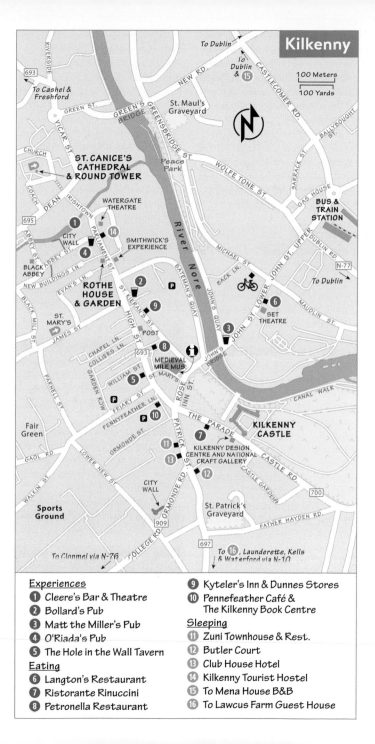

Kilkenny

Experiences
1. Cleere's Bar & Theatre
2. Bollard's Pub
3. Matt the Miller's Pub
4. O'Riada's Pub
5. The Hole in the Wall Tavern

Eating
6. Langton's Restaurant
7. Ristorante Rinuccini
8. Petronella Restaurant
9. Kyteler's Inn & Dunnes Stores
10. Pennefeather Café & The Kilkenny Book Centre

Sleeping
11. Zuni Townhouse & Rest.
12. Butler Court
13. Club House Hotel
14. Kilkenny Tourist Hostel
15. To Mena House B&B
16. To Lawcus Farm Guest House

pany), Smithwick's marked its tercentennial (300th anniversary) in 2010. After a corporate shake-up in 2013, the brewery consolidated its operations in Dublin and opened an "Experience" visitors center here on the former brewery grounds.

Cost and Hours: €13, discount if booked online, entry includes a pint at the tour's end; daily 10:00-18:00, Nov-Feb 11:00-16:00, one-hour tours run hourly, last tour departs one hour before closing; 44 Parliament Street, tel. 056/778-6377, www.smithwicksexperience.com.

Experiences
Pubs and Traditional Music Sessions

Kilkenny has its fair share of atmospheric pubs. Visitors seeking fun trad music sessions can try the first four places listed here. Those seeking friendly conversation in utterly unvarnished Irish surroundings should seek out the memorable duo at the end of these listings. A fun pub crawl could link all of these places with 20 minutes of walking. Check on nightly pub trad session schedules as you explore town during the day (they may change unpredictably).

Starting at the north end of town and working south, **Cleere's Bar & Theatre** is a friendly throwback with surprisingly good pub grub served until 20:00 (music Mon and Wed at 21:30, 28 Parliament Street). **Bollard's Pub,** an unpretentious landmark at the north end of St. Kieran's Street, is a good bet for lively traditional music sessions (Tue and Thu-Fri at 21:00), or sit out front under the awning and enjoy a pint as Kilkenny's humanity flows past you. Just down the same street is **Kyteler's Inn,** with a stony facade and medieval witch-haunted cellar (music nightly in summer at 18:00, 27 St. Kieran's Street). You can saunter over John's Bridge to check out the tunes at **Matt the Miller's Pub,** with its multilevel, dark-wood interior (around 21:00 most nights, next to bridge on John Street across the river from the castle).

Lacking music but high on character, **O'Riada's** is an endangered species—a wonderful, old-fashioned place that your Irish grandfather would recognize and linger in. This is an ideal place to chat with engaging locals (across from the Watergate Theatre at 25 Parliament Street).

At the other end of the conversational spectrum, **The Hole in the Wall** is a tiny, restored Elizabethan tavern (c. 1582) hidden down an alley (capacity 15-20, mostly standing). Charmingly eccentric owner Michael Conway presides over singalongs of Irish classics that include helpful lyrics and explanations of Irish idioms (unpredictable hours but typically Fri-Sat from 20:00 and sometimes weeknights, confirm ahead, look for the alley beside Bourkes shop at 17 High Street, tel. 087/807-5650, www.holeinthewall.ie).

Eating

$$$ Langton's is every local's first choice, serving high-quality Irish dishes under a labyrinthine, multichambered, Tiffany-skylight expanse (daily 12:00-22:00, 69 John Street, tel. 056/776-5133, www.langtons.ie).

$$$$ Ristorante Rinuccini serves classy, romantic, candlelit Italian meals (daily 12:00-14:30 & 17:00-22:00, reservations smart, 1 The Parade, tel. 056/776-1575, www.rinuccini.com).

$$ Petronella Restaurant warms its medieval surroundings with dependable traditional dishes and a welcoming

Kyteler's Inn

vibe (Mon-Sat 12:00-15:00 & 17:00-21:00, closed Sun, Butterslip Lane off High Street, tel. 056/776-1899, www.petronella.ie).

$$$$ Zuni, in one of my recommended accommodations, is a stylish splurge, offering international cuisine (daily 12:30-17:00 & 18:00-20:45, weekend reservations a good idea, 26 Patrick Street, tel. 056/772-3999, www.zuni.ie).

$$$ Kyteler's Inn serves decent pub grub in a timber-and-stone atmosphere with a heated and covered beer garden out back. Visit their fun 14th-century cellar and ask about their witch. Watch your head or risk leaving some of your DNA embedded in the low stone arches (Mon-Sat 12:00-21:00, Sun until 20:00, 27 St. Kieran's Street, tel. 056/772-1064).

$ Pennefeather Café, above the Kilkenny Book Centre, is good for a quick, cheap, light lunch (Mon-Sat 9:00-17:30, closed Sun, 10 High Street, tel. 056/776-4063).

Grocery Store: You'll find an ample selection of supplies for a grassy picnic at Dunnes Stores (a few doors down from Kyteler's Inn on St. Kieran's Street, Mon-Sat 8:00-22:00, Sun 10:00-20:00).

Sleeping

Kilkenny is a popular weekend destination for loud and rowdy "stag" and "hen" (bachelor and bachelorette) parties. For quiet at night, avoid hotels with bars downstairs or nearby, and stick with smaller B&Bs, guesthouses, or rural lodging (especially Fri-Sat nights). Except for the Zuni and Club House, my recommendations should be free of these disturbances.

$$$ Zuni Townhouse, above a fashionable restaurant, has 13 boutique-chic rooms sporting colorfully angular furnishings. Ask about two-night weekend breaks and midweek specials that include a four-course dinner (parking in back, 26 Patrick Street, tel. 056/772-3999, www.zuni.ie, info@zuni.ie).

$$ Butler Court is Kilkenny's best lodging value. Ever-helpful Yvonne and John offer 10 modern, spacious rooms behind the beige, flag-draped archway. Bo the dog quietly patrols the courtyard (wheelchair-accessible, continental breakfast in room, will validate parking in nearby multistory garage on Ormonde Street for length of your stay, 14 Patrick Street, tel. 056/776-1178, www.butlercourt.com, info@butlercourt.com).

$$ Club House Hotel, originally a gentlemen's sporting club, comes with fading Georgian elegance; a musty, creaking ambience; a palatial, well-antlered breakfast room; and 35 comfy bedrooms (secure parking, 19 Patrick Street, tel. 056/772-1994, www.clubhousehotel.com, info@clubhousehotel.com).

¢ Kilkenny Tourist Hostel fills a fine Georgian townhouse with ramshackle fellowship at the north end of the town center, right in the action. It offers 70 cheap beds, a friendly family room, a well-equipped members' kitchen, and a wealth of local information (private rooms available, cash only, pay self-serve laundry, 2 blocks from cathedral at 35 Parliament Street, tel. 056/776-3541, www.kilkennyhostel.ie, info@kilkennyhostel.ie).

Near Kilkenny

$ Mena House B&B is a traditional, good-value option quietly nestled a mile north of town, about a 15-minute walk from the center and easy for drivers (parking, just south of the Kilkenny Golf Club on Castlecomer Road, tel. 056/776-5362, www.menahousebandb.com, menahouse@eircom.net).

$$ Lawcus Farm Guest House is a quirky, seductive confection of rural comfort 10 miles south of Kilkenny between Kells Priory and the village of Stoneyford. A menagerie of friendly pets and farm animals shares the 20-acre property straddling the Kings River. Ask about the tiny secluded tree house (family rooms, cash only, parking, mobile 086-603-1667 or 087-291-1056, www.lawcusfarmguesthouse.com, lawcusfarm@hotmail.com).

Transportation
Arriving and Departing

BY TRAIN OR BUS

Kilkenny's train/bus station is four blocks from John's Bridge, which marks the center of town.

From Kilkenny by Train to: Dublin (6/day, 1.5 hours), **Waterford** (6/day, 45 minutes). For details, see www.irishrail.ie.

From Kilkenny by Bus to: Dublin (8/day, 2.5 hours), **Waterford** (2/day, 1 hour), **Cork** (4-5/day, 2 direct, 3.5 hours), **Tralee** (3/day, 5.5 hours, change in Cork), **Galway** (3/day, 5 hours). For specifics, see www.buseireann.ie.

BY CAR

If you're arriving by car, the Market Yard Car Park behind Kyteler's Inn is handy for a few hours (€1.30/hour, daily 8:00-18:00, entry off Bateman's Quay). The multi-story parking garage on Ormonde Street is the best long-term bet (€1.50/hour, or get the 3-day pass for €10 if staying overnight—it allows you to come and go; open 7:00-23:00, Fri-Sat until 24:00). If parking overnight, wait until you depart to pay since some hotels will validate parking. Otherwise, you can use the pay-and-display meters on the street (€1.50/hour, enforced Mon-Sat 8:00-19:00).

BETWEEN KILKENNY AND WATERFORD

The fast M-9 motorway links Kilkenny and Waterford on a 45-minute drive. But drivers in no rush can savor the journey by spending a couple of enjoyable back-road hours taking in two pastoral sights: Jerpoint Abbey and Kells Priory. Farther along, in the tiny port of New Ross is the *Dunbrody* Famine Ship. And in Waterford itself, you can see one of the most famous glassworks in the world. The rural roads come with old stone bridges spanning placid rivers that weave among tiny villages and abandoned mills. To navigate, bring an Ordnance Survey atlas (available at most bookstores).

▲▲JERPOINT ABBEY

Evocative abbey ruins dot the Irish landscape, but few are as well-presented as Jerpoint (founded in 1180). Its claim to fame is fine stone carvings on the sides of tombs and on the columns of the cloister arcade. If you visit only one abbey in Ireland, make sure it's this one. The well-versed guides bring the place alive again through their insight into the monastic culture that imprinted Ireland 850 years ago. Before leaving, ask for a map to navigate to the more secluded, nearby Kells Priory.

Cost and Hours: €5; daily 9:00-17:30; Nov-Feb Mon-Fri 9:30-16:00, closed Sat-Sun except in Nov; tel. 056/772-4623.

Getting There: It's located about 11 miles (17 km) south of Kilkenny or 2 miles (3 km) south of Thomastown, beside R-700.

Visiting the Abbey: The Cistercian monks, who came to Ireland from France in the 12th century, were devoted reformers bent on following the strict rules of St. Benedict. Their mission was to bring the wild Irish Christian church back in line with Rome. They steamrolled their belief system across the island and stamped the landscape with a network of identical monasteries. The Celtic Christianity that thrived in the Dark Ages was no match for the organization and determination of the Cistercians. For the next 350 years, these monasteries were the local religious authority.

What eventually did them in? King Henry VIII's marriage problems, his subsequent creation of the (Protestant) Church of England, and his eventual dissolution of the (Catholic) monasteries.

▲▲KELLS PRIORY

This place is a wonderful lonely gem. Locals claim that the massive religious complex of Kells Priory (more than 3 acres) is the largest monastic site in

The cloister at Jerpoint Abbey

Europe. It's an isolated, deserted ruin that begs a curious wander, a nimble shutter finger on your camera, and alert side-stepping of sheep droppings.

Cost and Hours: Free, no set hours.

Getting There: You'll find Kells Priory about 9 miles (15 km) south of Kilkenny or 6 miles (10 km) west of Jerpoint Abbey, just off the R-697 road. From Jerpoint Abbey, turn left, then take your first right through the village of Stoneyford. At the end of the village, turn left (at the sign for Kells Priory), then continue straight.

The main parking lot lies on a slope above the south side of the ruins. But I prefer to park beside the Kings River on the north side of the ruins. To get there, cross the pretty stone bridge over the river, and turn right onto the L-5067 road. Drive about 100 yards past the first mill (with a craft shop in an adjacent building); when you come to the second mill (completely shuttered and abandoned), park in the gravel lot in front.

Visiting the Priory: From the parking lot by the abandoned mill (described above),

stroll past the mill's rusty waterwheel and enjoy the wander downstream for the remaining 100 yards along the riverside path. It's a photogenic approach to the priory ruins. Once inside the complex, watch where you walk and explore at your leisure. Consider bringing a picnic to enjoy. But please respect the site and leave no trash.

Founded in 1193 by Norman soldiers of fortune with Augustinian monks in tow, this priory grew into the intimidating structure that locals call "the seven castles" today. These "castles," however, were actually Norman tower houses connected by a wall that enclosed the religious functions within. Inside the walls, the site is divided into two main areas: One is a huge interior courtyard (larger than a football field) dominated by the encircling tower houses; the other is a tangled medieval maze of rock walls (remnants of a cloister, a church, cellars, a medieval dormitory, and a graveyard).

▲▲DUNBRODY FAMINE SHIP

Permanently moored on a river in the tiny port of New Ross, this ship is a full-scale reconstruction of a 19th-century three-masted bark built in Quebec in 1845. It's typical of the trading vessels that originally sailed, empty, to America to pick up goods; during the famine, ship owners found that they could make a little money on the westward voyage by transporting countless hungry Irish emigrants. Commonly, boats like this would arrive in America with only 80 percent of their original human cargo. Those who succumbed to "famine fever" (often typhus or cholera) were dumped overboard, and the ships gained their morbid moniker: "coffin ships."

Cost and Hours: €10, daily 9:00-18:00, Oct-March 10:00-17:00, 45-minute tours go 2/hour, last tour starts one hour before closing, upstairs café handy for lunch with nice views of the ship, tel. 051/425-239, www.dunbrody.com.

Getting There: The *Dunbrody* is in New Ross, a 30-minute drive southeast from Jerpoint Abbey via highway R700.

Visiting the Ship: Your visit starts with an audiovisual presentation on the life Irish emigrants were leaving behind, followed by coverage about the building of the vessel. Then you'll follow an excellent guide on board the ship, encountering a couple of passengers (one traveling first class, the other second) who tell vivid tales about life onboard. At the end, you'll get a glimpse of the new life Irish immigrants would encounter in New York.

Crystal cutting at Waterford

Roots seekers are welcome to peruse the computerized file of the names of the million immigrants who sailed on these ships from 1846 through 1865.

▲▲WATERFORD CRYSTAL VISITOR CENTRE

With a tradition dating back to 1783, Waterford was once the largest—and still is the most respected—glassworks in the world. While 70 percent of Waterford Crystal is now manufactured by cheaper labor in Poland, Slovenia, and the Czech Republic, the finest glass craftsmen still reside here, where they create "prestige pieces" for special-order customers. The one-hour tour of this hardworking little factory is a joy. It's more intimate than the old, larger factory, and you're encouraged to interact with the craftsmen. Large tour groups descend midday, so try to visit before 10:00 or after 15:30.

Cost and Hours: Tours cost €13.50 and depart every 30 minutes; Mon-Sat 9:00-17:00 (last tour at 16:30), Sun from 9:30, shorter hours Nov-March, call to confirm; shop open longer hours; on The Mall, one block south of Reginald's Tower; tel. 051/317-000, www.waterfordvisitorcentre.com.

ROCK OF CASHEL

Rising high above the fertile Plain of Tipperary, the Rock of Cashel is one of Ireland's most historic and evocative sights. Seat of the ancient kings of Munster (c. A.D. 300-1100), this is where St. Patrick baptized King Aengus in about A.D. 450. Strategically located and perfect for fortification, the Rock was fought over by local clans for hundreds of years. Finally, in 1101, clever Murtagh O'Brien gave the Rock to the Church. His seemingly benevolent donation increased his influence with the Church, while preventing his rivals, the powerful McCarthy clan, from regaining possession of the Rock. As Cashel evolved into an ecclesiastical center, its Iron Age ring forts and thatch dwellings gave way to the majestic stone church buildings enjoyed by visitors today.

Rick's Tip: Dress warmly. *Bring a coat—while the parking lot can be sheltered, the Rock is exposed and often cold and windy.*

Sights

▲▲▲ROCK OF CASHEL

From the parking lot, it's a steep 100-yard walk up to the Rock itself. On this 200-foot-high outcrop of limestone, the first building you'll enter is the 15th-century Hall of the Vicars Choral, housing the ticket desk, a tiny museum (with a stunted original 12th-century high cross dedicated to St. Patrick and a few replica artifacts), and a 20-minute video (2/hour, shown in the hall's former dormitory). From there you'll explore the following: a round tower, an early Christian cross, a delightful Romanesque chapel, and a ruined Gothic cathedral, all surrounded by my favorite Celtic-cross graveyard with views for miles.

Cost and Hours: €8, families-€20, ticket includes guided tour—see below; open daily 9:00-19:00, mid-March-early June and mid-Sept-mid-Oct until 17:00,

winter until 16:30, last entry 45 minutes before closing; tel. 062/61437, www.heritageireland.ie.

Tours: Guided walks are included with your entrance (2/hour, about 45 minutes). Otherwise, set your own pace with my self-guided tour.

Parking: Pay the €4.50 fee at the machine (under the Plexiglas shelter to the left of the exit) before returning to your car.

WCs: Use the basic ones at the base of the Rock next to the parking lot (there are none up on the Rock).

Rick's Tip: Crowds are worst *June-Aug 11:00-15:00. Plan your visit for early or late in the day. If you're here* **at a peak time, tour the Rock first** *and save the movie, museum, and Hall of the Vicars Choral for the end of your visit.*

⊙ SELF-GUIDED TOUR

Nowhere else in Ireland can you better see the evolution of Irish devotion expressed in stone. This large lump of rock is a pedestal supporting a compact tangle of three dramatic architectural styles: early Christian (round tower and St. Patrick's high cross), Romanesque (Cormac's Chapel), and

The Rock of Cashel looms above the Tipperary countryside.

Rock of Cashel

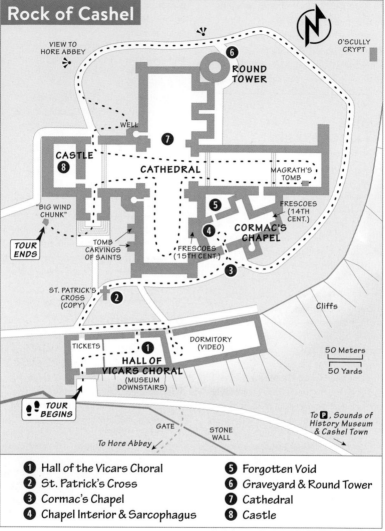

❶ Hall of the Vicars Choral
❷ St. Patrick's Cross
❸ Cormac's Chapel
❹ Chapel Interior & Sarcophagus
❺ Forgotten Void
❻ Graveyard & Round Tower
❼ Cathedral
❽ Castle

Gothic (the main cathedral).

• *Follow this tour counterclockwise around the Rock. Start by descending the indoor stairs opposite the ticket desk into the one-room, vaulted cellar museum.*

❶ Hall of the Vicars Choral: You are in the cellar of the youngest building on the Rock (early 1400s). This would have been the storage room for the vicars (minor clerics) appointed to sing during cathedral services. Today it contains a sparse collection of artifacts (some copies) associated with the religious site. Two glass cases display brooches and primitive axes, while the walls are hung with stone slab carvings. The impressively ornate shrine bell of St. Patrick is a reproduction (the bell would not have been used by him, but rather, dedicated to him, centuries later). But the star of the vault is the **original Cross of**

St. Patrick at the far end. The massive stone base is hollow (see the mirror underneath it). Was it a hiding place for valuable religious objects during raids? Or just too heavy to move otherwise? The cross stood outside for centuries, but hundreds of years of wind and rain slowly buffeted away important detail, scouring it into the stubby shape that remains. On my first visit here, almost 40 years ago, the original cross still stood outside; today, a copy occupies the original location.

• *Climb back up to the ticket desk level and continue up the indoor stairs into the living space of the vicars.*

Walk to the **great hall** with the big brown tapestry. Vicars were granted nearby lands by the archbishop and lived comfortably here, with a large fireplace and white, lime-washed walls (to reflect light and act as a natural disinfectant that discouraged bugs). Window seats gave the blessedly literate vicars the best light to read by. The furniture is original, but the colorfully ornamented oak timber roof is a reconstruction, built to medieval specifications using wooden dowels instead of nails. The large wall tapestry shows King Solomon with the Queen of Sheba.

The vicars, who formed a sort of corporate body to assist the bishop with local administration, used a special seal to authorize documents such as land leases. You can see an enlarged wooden copy of the seal (hanging above the fireplace), depicting eight vicars surrounding a seated organist. It was a good system—until some of the greedier vicars duplicated the seal for their own less holy purposes, forcing the archbishop to curtail its use.

• *Go outside the hall into the grassy space, veer left about 30 feet, and find...*

❼ **St. Patrick's Cross:** St. Patrick baptized King Aengus on the Rock of Cashel in about A.D. 450. This 12th-century cross, a stub of its former glory, was carved to celebrate the handing over of the Rock to the Church 650 years after St. Patrick's visit (the cross that stands here is a copy; the original is in the museum in the Hall of the Vicars Choral, described earlier). Typical Irish high crosses use a ring around the cross' head to support its arms and to symbolize the sun (making Christianity more appealing to the sun-worshipping Celts). But instead, this cross uses the Latin design: The weight of the arms is supported by two vertical beams on each side of the main shaft, representing the two criminals who were crucified beside Christ (today only one of these supports remains).

• *Walk about 100 feet slightly uphill along the gravel path beside the cathedral. Roughly opposite the far end of the Hall of the Vicars Choral is the entry (a glass door) to the chapel.*

❽ **Cormac's Chapel (Exterior):** As the wild Celtic Christian church was reined in and reorganized by Rome 850 years ago, new architectural influences from continental Europe began to emerge on the remote Irish landscape. This small chapel—Ireland's first and finest Romanesque church, constructed in 1134 by King Cormac MacCarthy—reflects this evolution. Imagine being here in the 12th century, when this chapel and the tall round tower were the only stone structures sprouting from the Rock (among a few long-gone, humble wooden structures).

The "new" Romanesque style reflected the ancient Roman basilica floor plan. Its columns and rounded arches created an overall effect of massiveness and strength. Romanesque churches were like dark fortresses, with thick walls, squat towers, and few windows. Irish stone churches of this period (like the one at Glendalough in the Wicklow Mountains) were simple rectangular buildings emphasizing function.

The two square towers resemble those in Regensburg, Germany, further suggesting that well-traveled medieval Irish monks brought back new ideas from the Continent.

Before stepping inside, notice the

weathered tympanum above the door. The carved "hippo" is actually an ox, representing Gospel author St. Luke.

• *The modern, dark-glass chapel door is a recent addition to keep out nesting birds. Enter the chapel and let your eyes adjust to the low light.*

❹ **Chapel Interior:** Just inside, on your left, is an empty stone sarcophagus. Nobody knows for sure whose body once lay here (possibly the brother of King Cormac MacCarthy). The damaged front relief is carved in a Viking style. Vikings had been raiding Ireland for more than 200 years by the time this was carved; they had already intermarried with the Irish, and were seeping into Irish society. Some scholars interpret the relief design (a tangle of snakes and beasts) as a figure-eight lying on its side, looping back and forth forever, symbolizing the eternity of the afterlife.

You're standing in the **nave,** dimly lit by three small windows. Overhead is a round vaulted ceiling with support ribs. The strong, round arches support not only the heavy stone roof, but also the unseen second-story scriptorium chamber, where monks once carefully copied manuscripts by candlelight (considering the poor light, their work was amazingly skillful).

The big main arch overhead, studded with fist-size heads, framed the altar (now gone). Walk into the chancel and look up at the ceiling, examining the faint **frescoes,** a labor of love from 850 years ago. Frescoes are rare in Ireland because of the perpetually moist climate. (Mixing pigments into wet plaster worked better in dry climates like Italy's.) Once vividly colorful, then fading over time, these frescoes were further damaged during and after the Reformation, when Protestants piously whitewashed them. These surviving frescoes were discovered under multiple layers of whitewash during painstaking modern restoration. Take a moment to imagine the majesty of this chapel before its fine ornamentation was destroyed by those Reformation iconoclasts.

• *Walk through the other modern, dark-glass doorway, opposite the door you used to enter the chapel. You'll find yourself in a...*

❺ **Forgotten Void:** This enclosed little space was created when the newer cathedral was wedged between the older chapel and the round tower. Once the main entrance into the chapel, this forgotten doorway is crowned by a finely carved tympanum that decorates the arch above it. It's perfectly preserved because the huge cathedral shielded it from the wind and rain. The large lion (symbol of St. Mark's gospel) is being hunted by a centaur (half-man, half-horse) archer wearing a Norman helmet.

• *Exit the chapel, turning left, and tiptoe through the tombstones around the east end of the cathedral to the base of the round tower.*

❻ **Graveyard and Round Tower:** This graveyard is full. The 20-foot-tall stone shaft at the edge of the graveyard, marking the O'Scully family crypt, was once crowned by an elaborately carved Irish high cross—destroyed during a lightning storm in 1976. The fortified wall dates from the 15th century, when the riches of this outpost merited a little extra protection.

Look out over the **Plain of Tipperary.** Called the "Golden Vale," its rich soil makes it Ireland's most fertile farmland. In St. Patrick's time, it was covered with oak forests. From the corner of the church, beyond the fortified wall on the left, you can see the ruined 13th-century **Hore Abbey** dominating the fields below (free, always open and peaceful).

Gaze up at the **round tower,** the first stone structure built on the Rock after the Church took over in 1101. The shape of these towers is unique to Ireland. Though you might think towers like this were chiefly intended as a place to hide in case of invasion, they were instead used primarily as bell towers and lookout posts. The tower stands 92 feet tall, with walls more than three feet thick. The doorway, which once had a rope ladder, was built high up not only for security, but also because having it at ground level would have weakened the foundation of the top-heavy structure. The interior once contained wooden floors connected by ladders, and served as safe storage for the monks' precious sacramental treasures. The tower's stability is impressive when you consider its age, the winds it has endured, and the shallowness of its foundation (only five feet below present ground level).

Continue walking around the cathedral's north transept, noticing the square "put-log" holes in the exterior walls. During construction, wooden scaffolding was anchored into these holes. After the structure was completed, the builders simply sawed off the scaffolding, leaving small blocks of wood embedded in the walls. With time, the blocks rotted away, and the holes became favorite spots for birds to build their nests.

On your way to the cathedral entrance find the small **well** (in the corner on the left, built into the wall). Its stone lip is groovy from ropes after centuries of use. Without this essential water source, the Rock could never have withstood a siege and would not have been as valuable to clans and clergy. In 1848, a chalice was dredged from the well, likely thrown there by fleeing medieval monks intending to survive a raid. They didn't make it. (If they had, they would have retrieved the chalice.)

• Now enter the...

❼ Cathedral: Traditionally, churches face east toward Jerusalem and the rising sun. Because this cathedral was squeezed between the preexisting chapel, round tower, and drinking well, to make it face east the builders were forced to improvise by giving it a cramped nave and an extra-long choir (where the clergy gathered to celebrate Mass).

Built between 1230 and 1290, the church's pointed arches and high, narrow windows proclaim the Gothic style of the period (and let in more light than earlier Romanesque churches). Walk under the central bell tower and look up at the rib-vaulted **ceiling.** The hole in the middle was for a rope used to ring the church bells. The wooden roof is long gone. When the Protestant Lord Inchiquin (who became one of Oliver Cromwell's generals) attacked the Catholic town of Cashel in 1647, hundreds of townsfolk fled to the sanctuary of this cathedral. Inchiquin packed turf around the exterior and burned the cathedral down, massacring those inside.

Ascend the terraces at the choir end of the cathedral, where the main altar once stood. Stand on the gravestones (of the 16th-century rich and famous) with your back to the east wall (where the narrow windows have crumbled away) and look back down toward the nave. The right wall of the choir is filled with graceful Gothic windows, while the solid left wall hides Cormac's Chapel (which would have blocked most sunlight). The line of stone

Ornate tomb at cathedral

Graveyard and round tower

supports on the left wall once held the long, wooden balcony where the vicars sang. Closer to the altar, high on the same wall (directly above the pointed doorway), is a small, rectangular window called the "leper's squint"—which allowed unsightly lepers to view the altar during Mass without offending the congregation.

The grand **wall tomb** on the left contains the remains of archbishop Miler Magrath, the "scoundrel of Cashel," who lived to be 100. From 1570 to 1622, Magrath was the Protestant archbishop of Cashel who simultaneously profited from his previous position as Catholic bishop of Down. He married twice, had lots of kids, confiscated the ornate tomb lid here from another bishop's grave, and converted back to Catholicism on his deathbed.

• *Walk back down the nave and turn left into the south transept.*

Peek into the modern-roofed wooden structure against the wall on your left. It's protecting 15th-century **frescoes** of the Crucifixion of Christ that were rediscovered during renovations in 2005. They're as patchy and hard to make out (and just as rare for Ireland) as the century-older frescoes in the ceiling of Cormac's Chapel.

On the opposite side of this transept, in alcoves built into the wall, enjoy the wonderful **carvings** of early Christian saints lining the outside walls of tombs (look down at shin level).

• *Exit the cathedral opposite where you entered.*

❽ Castle (or Tower): Back outside, stand beside the huge chunk of wall debris. (This is not "the rock" of Cashel.) Try to picture where it might have perched in the ragged puzzle of ruins above. This end of the cathedral was converted into an archbishop's castle in the 1400s (shortening the nave even more). Looking high into the castle's damaged top floors, you can see the bishop's residence chamber and the secret passageways that were once hidden inside the

thick walls. Lord Inchiquin's cannons weakened the structure during the 1647 massacre, and in 1848, a massive storm (known as "Night of the Big Wind" in Irish lore) flung the huge chunk next to you from the ruins above.

In the mid-1700s, the Anglican Church transferred cathedral status to St. John's in town, and the archbishop abandoned the drafty Rock for a more comfortable residence, leaving the ruins that you see today.

SOUNDS OF HISTORY MUSEUM

In the Brú Ború Cultural Centre (below the Rock of Cashel parking lot, below the statue of the three blissful dancers) is a small museum dedicated to the story of Ireland's ancient and traditional music. The exhibit starts with a video display tracing the physical evolution of Cashel from ancient ring fort to grand religious complex. Then come displays about ancient wind instruments. To wrap it up, there's a small theater where you'll enjoy a 15-minute film introduction to Ireland's beloved traditional music scene.

Cost and Hours: €5, Mon-Sat 9:00-17:00, closed Sun, tel. 062/61122, www.bruboru.ie.

Performances: If overnighting in Cashel in the summer, consider taking in a performance of the Brú Ború musical dance troupe in the center's theater (€20, €50 with dinner, Tue-Sat in late-June-mid-Aug, dinner at 19:00, 75-minute performance at 21:00, informal music session in the café/bar after).

TOWN OF CASHEL

The huggable town at the base of the Rock affords a good break on the long drive from Dublin to Dingle (**TI** open daily 9:30-17:30 in season, tel. 062/61333). The Heritage Centre, next door to the TI, presents a modest six-minute audio explanation of Cashel's history around a walled town model. Parking requires a pay-and-display ticket (€1, enforced Mon-Sat 9:00-18:00, free Sun).

Eating

Near the Rock: **$ Granny's Kitchen** is a tiny, violet-colored place with basic soup-and-sandwich lunches (daily 11:00-16:00, just past parking lot at the base of the Rock). **$$ Café Hans** has the best lunch selection and biggest crowds (Tue-Sat 12:00-17:30, closed Sun-Mon, 75 yards down the road from the parking lot). **$$$$ Chez Hans,** filling an old stone church, is good for a splurge dinner (Tue-Sat 18:00-21:30, closed Sun-Mon, a block below the Rock, tel. 062/61177, www.chezhans.net).

In Town: Next door to the TI, **$ Feehan's Bar** is a convenient stop for a pub grub lunch (daily 12:00-16:00, tel. 062/61929). A couple of blocks farther into town, the **$$ Cellar Pub** hides beneath Bailey's Hotel and serves satisfying dishes (daily 12:00-21:30, tel. 062/61937). Super Valu is the town's supermarket (Mon-Sat 7:00-22:00, Sun 8:00-21:00, 30 Main Street).

Sleeping

If you spend the night in Cashel, you'll be treated to beautifully illuminated views of the ruins. The first listing is a classy hotel in the center of town (a 15-minute walk from the Rock). The rest are cozy, old-fashioned, and closer to the Rock.

$$ Bailey's Hotel is Cashel's best boutique hotel, housed in a fine Georgian townhouse (1709). Its 19 refurbished rooms are large, inviting, and well-appointed, perched above a great cellar-pub restaurant (parking, 42 Main Street, tel. 062/61937, www.baileyshotelcashel.com, info@baileyshotelcashel.com).

$$ Joy's Rockside House B&B is clos-

est to the Rock, resting on its lower slopes. With four large, fresh rooms (three with views of the Rock), it's the best value in Cashel (family room, cash only, parking, Rock Villas Street, parking, tel. 062/63813, mobile 087-222-1676, www.joyrockside.com, joyrocksidehouse@eircom.net, Joan and Rem Joy).

$ Cashel Lodge is a well-kept rural oasis housed in an old stone grain warehouse, a 10-minute walk from the Rock near the Hore Abbey ruins. Its seven comfortable rooms combine unpretentious practicality with Irish country charm. Guests have a ringside seat for beautiful views of the Rock lit up at night (camping spots, parking, Dundrum Road R-505, tel. 062/61003, www.cashel-lodge.com, info@cashel-lodge.com, Tom and Brid O'Brien).

$ Rockville House, 100 yards from the Rock, is a traditional place run by gentleman owner Patrick Hayes. The house itself has six fine rooms, and its old stablehouse, lovingly converted by Patrick, has five more (family room, cash only, 10 Dominic Street, tel. 062/61760, rockvillehse@eircom.net).

$ Wattie's B&B has three rooms that feel lived-in and comfy (cash only, parking, 14 Dominic Street, tel. 062/61923, www.wattiesbandb.ie, wattiesbandbcashel@gmail.com, Maria Dunne).

Transportation

Cashel has no train station; the closest one is 13 miles away in the town of Thurles.

From Cashel by Bus to: Dublin (4/day, 3 hours), **Kilkenny** (3/day, 2.5 hours), **Waterford** (6/day, 2 hours). Bus info: www.buseireann.ie.

Kinsale

County Cork, on Ireland's south coast, is fringed with historic port towns and scenic peninsulas. The typical tour-bus route here includes Blarney Castle and Killarney—places where most tourists wear nametags. Avoid the mistake many travelers make—allowing destinations into their itineraries simply because they're famous from a song or as part of a relative's big-bus-tour memory. If you have the misfortune to spend the night in Killarney town (next door in County Kerry), you'll understand what I mean. The town is a sprawling line of chain hotels and outlet malls littered with pushy shoppers looking for plastic shamrocks.

Rather than kissing the spit-slathered Blarney Stone, spend your time enjoying the bustling, historic maritime town of Kinsale, which makes a great home base (the easy-to-visit historic port of Cobh is nearby). And if you can't go home without saying you kissed the Blarney Stone, it's a convenient stop when connecting to the Ring of Kerry or Dingle.

KINSALE IN 1 DAY

Kinsale is worth two nights and a day. Spend the morning checking out one or two of the town's sights, and taking Don and Barry's excellent Kinsale walking tour (9:15 or 11:15 most days). After lunch, head out to Charles Fort for great bay views and insights into British military life in colonial Ireland. (You can drive, or take a taxi out and walk back.) On your return, stop for a pint at the Bulman Bar. Finish the day with a good dinner and live music in a pub.

With extra time, fit in a visit to Cobh. If you have Irish roots, your ancestors likely sailed from here. Coming from Kilkenny or the Rock of Cashel, you could visit Cobh on your way to Kinsale.

ORIENTATION

Pint-sized and friendly, Kinsale is delightful to visit. Thanks to the naturally sheltered bay barbed by a massive 17th-century star fort, you can submerge yourself in maritime history, from the Spanish Armada to the sailor who inspired Daniel Defoe's *Robinson Crusoe* to the *Lusitania* (torpedoed by the Germans just off the point in 1915). Apart from all the history, Kinsale has a laid-back feel with a touch of wine-sipping class.

Kinsale has a great natural harbor and while the town is prettier than the actual harbor, the harbor was its reason for being. Today, Kinsale is a vibrant bustle of about 5,000 residents. Its population swells to 9,000 with the many "blow-ins" who live here each summer. The town's long and skinny old center is part modern

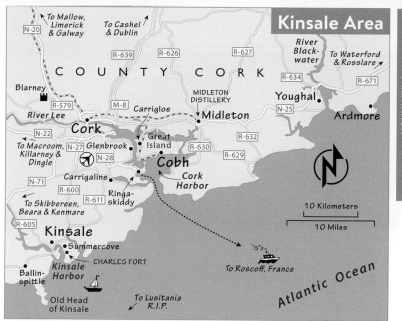

marina (attracting wealthy yachters) and part pedestrian-friendly medieval town (attracting scalawags like us). It's an easy 20 minute stroll from end to end.

Tourist Information: The TI is at the head of the harbor across from the bus stop (Mon-Sat 9:00-17:00, closed Sun, shorter hours Dec-Feb; tel. 021/477-2234, www.kinsale.ie).

Market: Check out the lively open-air market on Wednesdays (June-Sept 9:00-14:00) in the town square on Market Quay.

Laundry: Elite Laundry does an average-sized load for about €12 (Mon-Fri 9:00-17:30, Sat 10:00-17:00, closed Sun, The Glen, tel. 021/477-7345).

Bike Rental: Mylie Murphy's rents bikes from a handy spot near the Centra supermarket. They can recommend paths good for biking or walking that stretch around the harbor (€15/day, includes lock and helmet; Mon-Sat 9:30-18:00 year-round, Sun 11:00-17:00 May-Aug only, shorter hours in winter; arrangements can be made for pickup or drop-off; tel. 021/477-2703).

Taxi: Tom Canty can drive you where you need to go, including Cork Airport for €25 or Cork city for €30 (mobile 087-237-1022).

Rick's Tip: *On the* **first weekend in May, the Kinsale Rugby Sevens Tournament draws hundreds** *of loud, proud, and rowdy rugby fans. If you're not up for the scrum, then scram.*

Tours

▲▲Don & Barry's Kinsale Historic Stroll: To understand the important role Kinsale played in Irish, English, and Spanish history, join gentlemen Don Herlihy or Barry Moloney on a fascinating 1.5-hour walking tour (€8, daily mid-March–mid-Oct at 11:15, also Mon-Sat at 9:15 in May-Sept, no reservation necessary, meet outside the TI, private tours possible, tel. 021/477-2873 or 087/250-0731, www.historicstrollkinsale.com). Both guides are a joy, creatively bringing to life Kinsale's past, placing its story in the wider sweep

KINSALE AT A GLANCE

In Kinsale

▲▲**Don & Barry's Kinsale Historic Stroll** Duo of fascinating guides weave through town revealing the pivotal role Kinsale played in the history of the British Empire. **Hours:** Daily tours mid-March-mid-Oct. See page 123.

▲▲**Charles Fort** Stout 17th-century fortress guarding harbor with great tour explaining British military life and featuring fine views; also the starting point of Scilly Walk—a fine harborside walk back into town. **Hours:** Daily 10:00-18:00, Nov-mid-March until 17:00. See page 129.

▲**Desmond Castle** Compact former customs house and prison housing the Museum of Wine, highlighting the thriving trade that existed for Irish wooden casks. **Hours:** Easter-Sept daily 10:00-18:00, closed Oct-Easter. See page 130.

▲**Kinsale Regional Museum** Grab-bag of domestic and maritime knickknacks, starring *Lusitania* debris beachcombed after the famous sinking. **Hours:** Tue-Sat 10:30-13:30, closed Sun-Mon. See page 130.

Nearby

▲**Cobh** Historic port with two worthwhile sights (both open daily): Titanic Experience (simulation of the last day the ill-fated ship picked up passengers here) and Queenstown Story (exhibit on Cobh's history as Ireland's busiest emigration port). See page 134.

Blarney Castle Commercial, touristy castle featuring the stone that visitors kiss to gain the gift of gab, surrounded by beautifully lush parkland. **Hours:** Mon-Sat 9:00-18:30, Sun until 18:00, later in peak season, shorter hours in winter. See page 137.

of history, and making the stony sights more than just buildings. They collect payment at the end, giving anyone disappointed in the talk an easy escape midway through. Don't get hijacked by imitation tours—ask for Don or Barry. This walk is Kinsale's single best attraction.

Ghost Walk Tour: This is not just any ghost tour; it's more Monty Python-style slapstick comedy than horror. Two high-energy actors—Brian and David—weave funny stunts and stories into a loose history of the town, offering 75 minutes of entertainment on Kinsale's after-dark streets (€10, April-Oct Sun-Fri at 21:00, no tours Sat, leaves from The Tap Tavern, call ahead to confirm, mobile 087-948-0910). You'll spend the first 15 minutes in the back of The Tap Tavern—time to finish your drink and get to know some of the group. This tour doesn't overlap with the more serious historic town walk described above.

◐ Kinsale Town Wander

• *Start on the harbor (just below the TI and across from Dinos Fish & Chips). To trace the route, see the map on the next page.*

Harborfront: The medieval walled town's economy was fueled by its harbor, where ships came to be stocked. The old walls defined the original town and created a fortified zone that facilitated the taxation of goods. In the 17th and 18th centuries, this small and easily defended harbor was busy with rich and hungry tall ships. Kinsale was the last stop for ships making the two-month trip to America. Ships gathered here to take on provisions and to assemble into convoys that made the crossing safer.

Look for the **memorial** shaped like the mast of a tall ship, farther out toward the marina. It's a reminder that this was also a port of military consequence. Dozens of ships from the Spanish Armada could moor here, threatening England.

Clear-cutting of the once-plentiful oak forest upriver (for shipbuilding and barrel-making) hastened erosion and silted up the harbor. By the early 1800s—when British ships needed lots of restocking for the Napoleonic Wars—ships were bigger, Kinsale's port was slowly dying, and nearby Cobh's deep-water port took over the lion's share of shipping. Kinsale settled into a quieter existence as a fishing port.

Wandering through colorful Kinsale

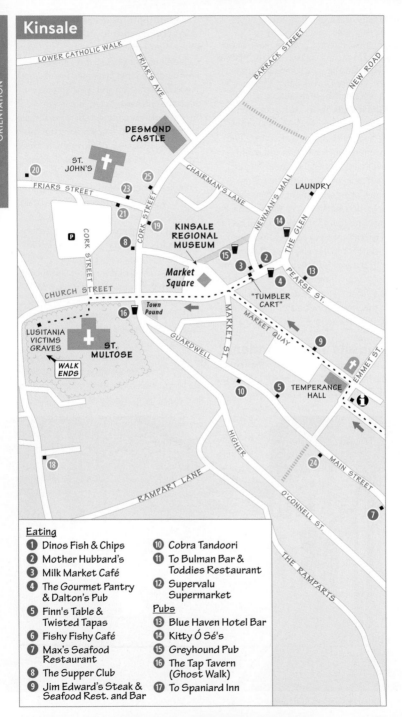

Kinsale

LOWER CATHOLIC WALK

FRIAR'S AVE.

BARRACK STREET

NEW ROAD

DESMOND CASTLE

ST. JOHN'S

20

FRIARS STREET

CHAIRMAN'S LANE

LAUNDRY

25

23

21

19

8

CORK STREET

P

CORK STREET

KINSALE REGIONAL MUSEUM

NEWMAN'S MALL

THE GLEN

14

15

3

2

13

Market Square

4

PEARSE ST.

CHURCH STREET

"TUMBLER CART"

Town Pound

16

9

LUSITANIA VICTIMS GRAVES

ST. MULTOSE

MARKET ST.

MARKET QUAY

EMMET ST.

WALK ENDS

GUARDWELL

10

5

TEMPERANCE HALL

HIGHER

24

MAIN STREET

18

RAMPART LANE

O'CONNELL ST.

THE RAMPARTS

7

Eating
1. Dinos Fish & Chips
2. Mother Hubbard's
3. Milk Market Café
4. The Gourmet Pantry & Dalton's Pub
5. Finn's Table & Twisted Tapas
6. Fishy Fishy Café
7. Max's Seafood Restaurant
8. The Supper Club
9. Jim Edward's Steak & Seafood Rest. and Bar
10. Cobra Tandoori
11. To Bulman Bar & Toddies Restaurant
12. Supervalu Supermarket

Pubs
13. Blue Haven Hotel Bar
14. Kitty Ó Sé's
15. Greyhound Pub
16. The Tap Tavern (Ghost Walk)
17. To Spaniard Inn

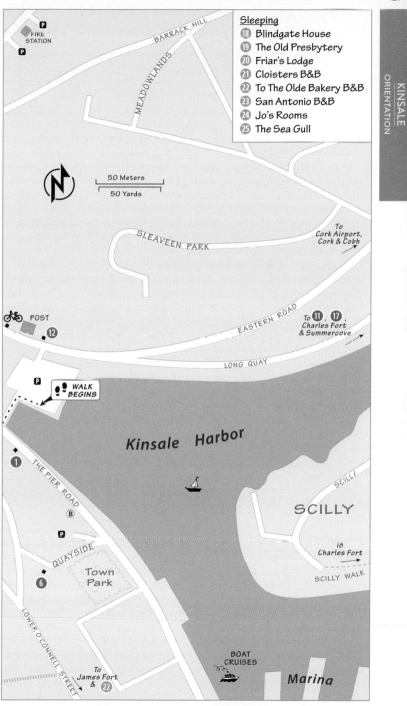

Sleeping
18 Blindgate House
19 The Old Presbytery
20 Friar's Lodge
21 Cloisters B&B
22 To The Olde Bakery B&B
23 San Antonio B&B
24 Jo's Rooms
25 The Sea Gull

Kinsale is Key

Kinsale's perfect natural harbor has made this an important port since prehistoric times. Its importance peaked during the 16th, 17th, and 18th centuries, when it was the gateway to Spain and France—potentially providing a base for either of these two powers in cutting off English shipping.

In about 1500, the pope divided newly discovered lands outside Europe between Spain and Portugal. With the Reformation breaking Rome's lock on Europe, maritime powers such as England were ignoring the pope's grant. England threatened Spain's New World piñata, and Ireland was Catholic. Spain had an economic and a religious reason to defend the pope and Catholicism. The showdown between Spain and England was in Ireland. The excuse: to rescue the dear Catholics of Ireland from the terrible treachery of Protestant England.

So the Irish disaster unfolded. The Ulster chieftains Hugh O'Neill and Red Hugh O'Donnell and their clans had been waging guerilla battles against the English. With Spanish aid, they figured they could actually drive the English out of Ireland. In 1601, a Spanish fleet dropped off 3,000 soldiers, who established a beachhead in Kinsale. After the ships left, the Spaniards were pinned down in Kinsale by the English commander. In harsh winter conditions, virtually the entire Irish-clan fighting force left the north and marched to the south coast, thinking they could liberate their Spanish allies and win freedom from England.

The numbers seemed reasonable (8,000 Englishmen versus 3,000 Spaniards with 7,000 Irish clansmen). The Irish attacked on Christmas Eve in 1601. But, holding the high ground around fortified and Spanish-occupied Kinsale, a relatively small English force kept the Spaniards hemmed in, leaving the bulk of the English troops to rout the Irish, who were adept at ambushes but not at open-field warfare.

The Irish resistance was broken, and its leaders fled to Europe (the "flight of the Earls"). England made peace with Spain and began the "plantation" of mostly Scottish Protestants in Ireland (the seeds of today's Troubles in Ulster). England ruled the waves, and it ruled Ireland. The lesson: Kinsale is key. England eventually built two huge, star-shaped fortresses here to ensure control of the narrow waterway.

• From the TI, walk inland (between the Temperance Hall and the old Methodist church) up Market Quay. Take your first right on Market Street and find an old vehicle on big wheels at the Milk Market Café, across from Dalton's Pub.

Town Center: Study the green metal medieval **Kinsale model** (circa 1381) and the information panel on the wall with another map. It shows the narrow confines of the town, hiding behind its once-proud walls, before much of the bay was reclaimed. You can see how the wall lined the main street along the tidal flats. The subtle curves of Main Street trace the original coastline. (Walking this street, you'll see tiny lanes leading to today's harbor. These originated as piers—just wide enough to roll a barrel down to an awaiting ship.)

Find **Dalton's Pub**—one of 25 pubs in this small-but-never-thirsty town. This is one of many inviting local pubs famous for live folk and trad music.

• *Backtrack to cross Market Square, pass the old courthouse (now the Regional Museum), and take Church Street to a vacant little lot across from The Tap Tavern.*

Town Pound: This small enclosure was where goods and livestock used to be impounded until the owner could pay the associated tax. After the town wall became obsolete, the townspeople used its ready-cut stones for town building projects like this.

• *Walk uphill past The Tap Tavern to the church.*

St. Multose Church: This Anglican church (open after noon) comes with a fortress-like tower. While rebuilt in recent centuries, it goes back to the Middle Ages. In its very proper Anglican interior, you'll see a list of vicars going back to 1377. The humble base of the baptismal font dates from the 6th century.

• *Leaving the church, walk 20 paces, veering left and uphill to two gray concrete gravelly graves (near the gate to the street).*

Lusitania Victims Graves: This remembers "Victims of the *Lusitania* Outrage 1915." Nine months into World War I, just off the coast of Kinsale, the Germans torpedoed the *Lusitania* with many Americans on board. It sank within 20 minutes, and more than half of the 2,000 passengers drowned. This tragedy led to the United States going "over there" and joining what was called "The Great War."

SIGHTS

▲▲CHARLES FORT

Strategically set to be the gatekeeper for this critical harbor, Kinsale's star-shaped Charles Fort is a testimony to the importance of this little town in the 17th century.

Cost and Hours: €5, daily 10:00-18:00, Nov-mid-March until 17:00, last entry one hour before closing, a half-mile south of town, tel. 021/477-2263. Free, guided walks are included (45 minutes, generally on the hour). A little coffee-and-pastry café stands inside the walls.

Visiting the Fort: When built, Charles Fort was Britain's biggest star-shaped fort—a state-of-the-art defense when artillery made the traditional castle obsolete (low, thick walls were tougher for cannons to breach than the tall, thinner walls of older castles). The star design made defending any attack on its walls safer and more effective. Notice how the strongest walls face the sea and how the oldest buildings are crouched

Charles Fort guards Kinsale harbor.

down below the potential cannon fire of attacking ships.

The British occupied this fort until Irish independence in 1922. Its interior buildings were torched in 1923 by antitreaty IRA forces to keep it from being used by Free State troops during the Irish Civil War.

While most of the fort is just ruined buildings with nice views, there is an important exhibit filling two floors of the Barracks Stores building (the tall intact building, just below and to the right of the entry).

After Your Visit: For a beer or meal nearby, try Bulman Bar (with small parking lot) in Summercove, where the road runs low near the water on the way back to town. And to see how easily the forts could bottle up this key harbor, pull over at the grand harbor viewpoint at the high point on the road back into town (between Summercove and The Spaniard pub).

Scilly Walk: The 45-minute walk between Kinsale and Charles Fort offers a delightful chance to connect the town with its leading attraction. Along the way you'll pass great harbor views, quaint cottages, dry stone walls, and the recommended Bulman Bar. While the couple of hundred yards at the beginning and end are along roads (without sidewalks), the middle 80 percent of the walk is along a peaceful, pedestrian-only trail through lush vegetation. Look for *Scilly Walk* signs on the left when walking toward town (near top of hill, 100 yards beyond Bulman Bar).

▲DESMOND CASTLE

This 15th-century fortified customs house has had a long and varied history. It was the Spanish armory during Spain's 1601 occupation of Kinsale. Nicknamed "Frenchman's Prison," it served as a British prison and once housed 600 cramped prisoners of the Napoleonic Wars (not to mention earlier American Revolutionary War prisoners captured at sea—who were treated as rebels, not prisoners, and chained to the

outside of the building as a warning to any rebellion-minded Irish). In the late 1840s, it was a famine-relief center.

Today, the evocative little tower comes with a scant display of its colorful history, as well as the modest two-room Museum of Wine, highlighting Ireland's little-known connection to the international wine trade. In the late Middle Ages, Kinsale was renowned for its top-quality wooden casks. Developing strong trade links with Bordeaux and Jerez, local merchants traded their dependable, empty casks for casks full of wine. Later, Kinsale became a "designated wine port" for tax-collection purposes.

Cost and Hours: €5, daily 10:00-18:00, closed Oct-Easter, last entry at 17:15; tours generally at 10:15, 12:00, 14:15, and 16:00; Cork Street, tel. 021/477-4855.

▲KINSALE REGIONAL MUSEUM

In the center of the old town, traffic circles the market, which later became a courthouse and is now the Regional Museum. Its Dutch architecture reflects the influence of Dutch-born King William of Orange at the end of the 1600s. The modest museum is worth a quick visit for its fun mishmash

Desmond Castle

of domestic and maritime bygones. It also gives a good perspective on the controversial *Lusitania* tragedy. Drop by at least to read the fun 1788 tax code for all Kinsale commercial transactions (outside at the front door).

Cost and Hours: Free, Tue-Sat 10:30-13:30, closed Sun-Mon, staffed by volunteers—hours can be erratic, Market Square, tel. 021/477-7930.

EATING

Back in the 1990s, when Ireland was just getting its cuisine act together, Kinsale was the island's self-proclaimed gourmet capital. While good restaurants are commonplace in Irish towns today, Kinsale still has an edge at mealtime. Local competition is fierce, and restaurants offer creative and tempting menus. Seafood is king. With so many options in the ever-changing scene, it's worth a short stroll to assess your options. Reservations are smart, especially if eating late or on a weekend. Restaurant connoisseurs can check the menu details of Kinsale's top restaurants at www.kinsalerestaurants.com.

Picnickers seek out the **SuperValu** supermarket (daily 8:00-22:00, Pearse Street).

Cheap and Cheery

$ Dinos Fish & Chips, with big windows overlooking the harbor, is a fun and family-friendly chain for budget fish-and-chips (daily 9:00-21:30, across from the TI facing the harbor, tel. 021/477-4561). **$ Mother Hubbard's,** tiny with six tables near Market Square, serves all-day breakfast, toasties, sandwiches, and salads (daily 8:30-14:00, 1 Market Street, tel. 021/477-2440). **$ Milk Market Café**—right next door—is a hit with kids, offering burgers, pizza, and fish-and-chips (daily 10:00-18:00, 3 Market Street). **$ The Gourmet Pantry** is an above-average takeout option (Mon-Sat 9:00-17:30, Sun from 10:00, 4 Market Street, tel. 021/470-9215).

Good Dinners in the Old Center

$$$$ Finn's Table is dressy, refined, and romantic, with white tablecloths, candles, and elegant service. John Finn cooks and Julie Finn serves enticing dinner plates ranging from lamb to lobster. Meat is their passion—John comes from a long line of butchers and still gets the best cuts from his dad's butcher shop. Their three-course early-bird menu, served until 18:30, makes this pricey place more affordable (Thu-Tue 18:00-22:00, closed Wed; Nov-April Thu-Sat only, if open at all; 6 Main Street, tel. 021/470-9636, www.finnstable.com).

$$$ Fishy Fishy Café, a high-energy destination seafood restaurant with spacious seating (indoor, balcony, and terrace) and a wonderful menu, is run by Martin and Maria Shanahan. When I asked, "What's your secret?" they pointed to the portraits of fishermen on the wall and said, "Local, local, local." It's a good lunch or early dinner option for those on a tighter budget. Martin's culinary prowess has led him to host a weekly cooking show on Irish TV (daily 12:00-21:00, reservations recommended, Pier Road, tel. 021/470-0415, www.fishyfishy.ie).

$$$ Max's Seafood Restaurant is spacious and stylish, though not overly romantic. There's no pretense—the focus is simply on great seafood. Chef Olivier

Queva from France offers a fresh, classic selection and a French flair (nice wine by the glass), while his wife Anne Marie serves. This place can get expensive, but there's a good early-bird special until 19:15 (daily 18:00-21:30, 48 Main Street, tel. 021/477-2443).

$$$ The Supper Club is a linen-and-leather upmarket joint with a meat smoker, strong cocktails, and creative desserts (Tue-Sat 18:30-22:00, closed Sun-Mon, 3 Cork Street, tel. 021/477-2847).

$$$ Jim Edward's Steak & Seafood Restaurant and Bar is an energetic place that's clearly a local favorite for its steaks, seafood, and vegetables. Choose between the restaurant's maritime setting or the more intimate, pub-like bar (same menu, bar open daily 12:00-22:00, restaurant from 18:00, Market Quay, tel. 021/477-2541).

Ethnic Food: $$ Twisted Tapas is hip and youthful, serving Spanish tapas and lighter fare "with a twist" (Wed-Sun 18:00-21:00, closed Mon-Tue, 5 Main Street, tel. 021/477-4218). **$$ Cobra Tandoori** is good for tasty Punjabi/Indian cuisine (€11-16 plates, daily 16:00-23:30, 69 Main Street, tel. 021/477-7911).

Near Charles Fort

$$$ Bulman Bar and Toddies Restaurant serves seafood with seasonal produce. The mussels are especially tasty; on a balmy day or evening, diners take a bucket and a beer out to the seawall. This is the only way to eat on the water in Kinsale. Their **$$ pub,** sporting fun decor and a big fireplace, is also good for a coffee or beer after your visit to the fort (pub open daily 12:30-21:00, restaurant open Tue-Sat from 18:30, 200 yards toward Kinsale from Charles Fort in hamlet of Summercove, tel. 021/477-2131).

Pubs: Musical or Mellow

In the Town Center: Kinsale's town pubs are packed with atmosphere and live music (more likely folk, but plenty of tra-

ditional Irish, too). Rather than targeting a certain place, simply walk the area between Guardwell, Pearse Street, and the Market Square. Music starts up after 21:00—you'll hear it as you wander. Pop into each pub that has live music and then settle in to your favorite. **Dalton's Pub** hosts informal amateur sessions with locals after 21:00 (grab a seat by 20:30). The **Blue Haven Hotel Bar** and **Kitty Ó Sé's** are also good bets.

For conversation or an introspective pint, I like the **Greyhound** (off Newman's Mall, behind the Milk Market Café)—no live music, just a scruffy, multi-chambered throwback with no pretenses. Another joint filled with characters who haven't changed in decades is **The Tap Tavern** (corner of Church Street and Guardwell). It's presided over by Mary O'Neill, the unofficial godmother of Kinsale, and her slyly humorous son Brian, who runs the town's recommended ghost tours. Check out the ancient holy well that came to light when they built their appealing back patio.

Outside of Town: Irish music purists will be rewarded if they take the five-minute taxi ride (€10 one-way) out to the **Bulman Bar** near the base of Charles Fort. This is one of Kinsale's two best pubs for traditional Irish music sessions (Thu-Sat at 21:30, Sun at 17:00, get there early to ensure a seat, tel. 021/477-2131). Otherwise, get your trad fix at the charmingly claustrophobic **Spaniard Inn,** a 10-minute walk out to the Scilly peninsula across the harbor from town. It fills the center of a hairpin turn on the crest of the peninsula. The darkly atmospheric interior is about the size of a rail car, with the long bar taking up half the space, so only about 10 seats get an actual view of the musicians (most nights at 21:30, you'll stand all night unless you arrive before 20:30, tel. 021/477-2436).

SLEEPING

Kinsale is a popular place in summer for yachters and golfers (who don't flinch at paying $300 for 18 holes out on the exotic Old Head of Kinsale Golf Course). It's wise to book your room in advance. I've listed peak-season prices. These places are all within a 10-minute walk of the town center.

$$$ Blindgate House, high up on the fringe of town behind St. Multose Church, offers 11 pristine rooms in fine modern comfort (tel. 021/477-7858, mobile 087-237-6676, www.blindgatehouse.com, info@blindgatehouse.com, Maeve Coakley).

$$ The Old Presbytery is a fine, quiet house a block outside the commercial district, with a meandering floor plan, plush lounge, and nine pleasant rooms. Listed in most guidebooks, it has lots of American guests. The breakfasts are a delight, the rooms are stocking-feet cozy, and Noreen McEvoy runs the place with a passion for excellence. Join the other guests for a complimentary wine-and-cheese happy hour every afternoon (RS%, 10 percent discount with cash, family rooms, private parking, 43 Cork Street, tel. 021/477-2027, www.oldpres.com, info@oldpres.com).

$$ Friar's Lodge is a slate-shingled hotel, perched up the hill past St. John's Catholic Church. What its 18 spacious rooms lack in Old World character, they make up for in dependable quality (family rooms, private parking, Friar Street, tel. 021/477-7384, www.friars-lodge.com, mtierney@indigo.ie).

$$ Cloisters B&B has four snug but bright and inviting rooms with a friendly atmosphere fostered by Orla Kenneally and Aileen Healy (2 Friars Street, tel. 021/470-0680, www.cloisterskinsale.com, info@cloisterskinsale.com).

$ The Olde Bakery B&B makes you feel at home, with six quilt-bedded rooms, Lilly the loveable mute mutt, and charmingly chatty hostess Chrissie Quigley (cash only, 56 Lower O'Connell Street, tel. 021/477-3012, www.theoldebakerykinsale.com, oldebakery@gmail.com).

$ San Antonio B&B is a 200-year-old house with five rooms and a funky budget feel, lovingly looked after by gentleman Jimmie Conron (cash only, 1 Friar Street, tel. 021/477-2341, mobile 086-878-9800, jimmiesan@yahoo.ie).

$ Jo's Rooms is a good value, offering five fresh, practical rooms in the center of town (breakfast extra, cash only, small rooms with smaller double beds, 55 Main Street, mobile 087-948-1026, www.joskinsale.com, joskinsale@gmail.com).

$ The Sea Gull, perched up the hill right next to Desmond Castle, offers six retro-homey rooms. It's run by Mary O'Neill, who also runs The Tap Tavern down the hill (RS%, cash only, Cork Street, tel. 021/477-2240, mobile 087-241-6592, marytap@iol.ie).

TRANSPORTATION

Arriving and Departing
By Bus

The nearest train station is in Cork, 15 miles north. But buses run frequently between Kinsale (on Pier Road, behind TI, at south end of town) and Cork's bus station (14/day Mon-Sat, fewer on Sun, 50 minutes).

In **Cork,** the bus station and train station are a 10-minute walk apart. The bus station (corner of Merchant's Quay and Parnell Place) is on the south bank of the River Lee, just over the nearest bridge from the train station (north of the river on Lower Glanmire Road).

From Cork by Train to: Dublin (hourly, 3 hours, www.Irishrail.ie).

From Cork by Bus to: Dublin (every 2 hours, 3.5 hours), **Galway** (hourly, 4.5 hours), **Tralee** (hourly, 2.5 hours), **Kilkenny** (4/day, 2 direct, 3.5 hours). Bus info: tel. 021/450-8188 or www.buseireann.ie.

By Car

Drivers should park and walk. While Kinsale's windy medieval lanes are narrow and congested, parking is easy. The most central lot is at the head of the harbor behind the TI (€1.50/hour, 2-hour maximum, use pay-and-display machine, exact coins required, enforced Mon-Sat 10:30-18:00, free on Sun). A big, safe, free parking lot is across the street from St. Multose Church at the top of town, a five-minute walk from most recommended hotels and restaurants. Parking on the street is pay-and-display. Outlying streets, a 10-minute stroll from the action, have wide-open parking.

By Plane

Cork Airport is handy for travelers starting or ending their trip in southern Ireland (located four miles south of Cork city, on N-27/R-600 to Kinsale, a 30-minute drive away, tel. 021/431-3131, airport code: ORK, www.corkairport.com). Citylink airport buses run to Kinsale (hourly Mon-Sat, fewer on Sunday) and less frequently to other destinations, including Galway (6/day, 4 hours).

NEAR KINSALE

COBH

If your ancestry is Irish, there's a good chance that Cobh, rated ▲, was the last Irish soil your ancestors had under their feet. Cobh (pronounced "cove") was the major port of Irish emigration in the 19th century. Of the six million Irish who have emigrated to America, Canada, and Australia since 1815, nearly half left from Cobh.

The first steam-powered ship to make a transatlantic crossing departed from Cobh in 1838—cutting the journey time from 50 days to 18. When Queen Victoria came to Ireland for the first time in 1849, Cobh was the first Irish ground she set foot on. Giddy, the town renamed itself "Queenstown" in her honor. It was still going by that name in 1912, when the *Titanic* made its final fateful stop here before heading out on its maiden (and only) voyage...just over 100 years ago. To celebrate their new independence from British royalty in 1922, locals changed the town's name back to its original Irish moniker. Today the town's deep harbor attracts dozens of cruise ships per year (with their large packs of eager visitors, though many pass through the town quickly).

Orientation

Cobh sits on a large island in Cork Harbor, connected to the mainland via a short bridge (on the north shore) and a handy drive-on ferry (on the west shore). The town's inviting waterfront is colorful yet salty, with a playful promenade. The butcher's advertisement reads, "Always pleased to meet you and always with meat to please you." A large *Lusitania* memorial is on Casement Square and a modest *Titanic* memorial is nearby on Pearse Square.

A hike up the hill to the towering Neo-

St. Colman's Cathedral is a Cobh landmark.

Cobh

To Cork

To Cuskinny →
East Ferry

BISHOP STREET

PARK RD.

LAUNDRY HILL

JOHN O'CONNELL ST.

100 Meters
100 Yards

WEST VIEW

LAKE ROAD

OLD STREET

CASEMENT

WOLFE TONE ST.

ROCHE'S TERR.

ST. COLMAN'S
CATHEDRAL

CATHEDRAL PL.

CHURCH ST.

HARBOUR HILL

RAHILLY ST.

SPY HILL

BURMA
STEPS

LUSITANIA
MEMORIAL →

Pearse
Square

TITANIC
MEM.

Casement
Square

WEST BEACH

EAST BEACH

LYNCH'S QUAY

To
Carrigloe
& Cork

SPY HILL

WESTBOURNE PLACE

BUS
TERMINUS

TITANIC
EXPERIENCE

KENNEDY
PIER

QUEENSTOWN STORY
MUSEUM &
HERITAGE CENTRE

Cork Harbor

TRAIN
STATION

Eating & Sleeping
1. Trade Winds Rest.
2. Titanic Bar & Grill
3. Centra Market
4. Commodore Hotel
5. Waters Edge Hotel
   & Jacob's Ladder
6. Ard na Laoi B&B

Gothic St. Colman's Cathedral rewards you with a fine view of the port. To get to the cathedral, walk behind the *Lusitania* memorial, go under the stone arch, and strut up steep Westview Street, passing the photogenic row of colorful houses on your right (nicknamed the "deck of cards" by locals). After panting your way to the top, turn right—you can't miss the cathedral steeple.

Arrival in Cobh: If you're driving into Cobh, follow the Heritage Centre signs to The Queenstown Story, where you'll find easy parking at the museum. There's a two-hour parking maximum anywhere in town (first hour free, second hour is €1, pay at machines on street).

Cork's Kent Station has frequent train service to Cobh (usually departs on the hour, returns on the half-hour, www.irish rail.ie).

Tourist Information: The TI is in the old library right at the base of Westview Street (Mon-Fri 9:00-17:30, Sat-Sun 10:30-16:30, tel. 021/481-3301, www.cobh harbourchamber.ie).

Tours

Michael Martin and his staff lead one-hour Titanic Trail walking tours that give you unexpected insights into the tragic *Titanic* and *Lusitania* voyages, Spike Island, and Cobh's maritime history (€9.50, ask for Rick Steves discount and show this book when you pay, daily at 11:00, also 14:00 in summer with required pre-booking, call ahead to confirm tour times in winter, private tours available, meet in lobby of Commodore Hotel, tel. 021/481-5211, mobile 087-276-7218, www.titanic. ie, info@titanic.ie). Seriously interested travelers should look for his book, *RMS Lusitania: It Wasn't and It Didn't*.

Sights

▲THE *TITANIC* EXPERIENCE

It's stirring to think that this modest port town was the ship's final anchorage—and the last chance to get off. Occupying the former White Star Line building where the *Titanic's* final passengers boarded, this compact museum packs a decent punch as it recounts the story of the ship and its final moments.

Cost and Hours: €9.50, daily 9:00-18:00, Oct-April until 17:30, last entry 45 minutes before closing, Casement Square, tel. 021/481-4412, www.titanicexperience cobh.ie.

Visiting the Museum: As you look off the back balcony into the harbor, note the decayed pilings in front of you. These once supported the old pier and represent the passengers' last chance to turn back. One lucky surviving crewman with a premonition did.

Inside the museum, you travel room to room with your host, the ship's fourth mate, in audiovisual form. He meets you at the boarding dock, full of pride in the new vessel. He joins you in replicas of a posh first-class cabin and a no-frills third-class cabin before his commentary is interrupted by the sound of ice tearing at the hull. You then enter an exhibition room featuring an animation that silently depicts the ship sinking in its steel-twisting, slow-motion ballet to the bottom (settling as two crunched hulls 600 yards apart and 12,000 feet deep).

The last stop is a room highlighting the luxurious ship's innovative firsts. It was one of the first equipped with a wireless "Marconi room" to send messages from sea to shore—or to other ships. *Titanic* was the first ever to issue an SOS message by Morse code. Another wall explains in grim detail the effects of hypothermia on the human body.

Before you leave, check out the list of 123 passengers who boarded the *Titanic* in Cobh. Your entry ticket has one of these passengers' names on it. See if you survived (you've got a 30 percent chance).

▲THE QUEENSTOWN STORY

Filling a harborside Victorian train station, this museum is an earnest attempt to make the city's history come to life. The topics—the famine, Irish emigration, Australia-bound prison ships, the sinking of the *Lusitania*, and the ill-fated voyage of the *Titanic*—are interesting enough to make it a worthwhile stop.

Cost and Hours: €9.50; Mon-Sat 9:30-18:00, Sun 11:00-18:00; Nov-April until 17:00; last entry one hour before closing, handy café, Cobh Heritage Centre, tel. 021/481-3591, www.cobhheritage.com.

Visiting the Museum: Coverage of the *Titanic* and the *Lusitania* was beefed up for the centennials of these famous ships' sinking (2012 and 2015, respectively). You'll learn about one priest who got off the *Titanic* at Cobh. His photos of the early legs of the voyage are a priceless historical reference. But in general, the museum itself, while kid-friendly and engaging, is weak on actual historical artifacts. It reminds me of a big, interesting history picture book with the pages expanded and tacked on the wall.

Before departing, walk over to the Annie Moore statue next to the water, 25 yards from the front door. She emigrated from Cobh to the US and was the first person to be processed through Ellis Island when it opened on January 1, 1892.

Nearby: Those with Irish roots to trace can use the Heritage Centre's **genealogy search service,** located right across from the Queenstown Story ticket booth. Since Cobh was the primary Irish emigration port, this can be a great place to start your search (€50/hour consultation and research assistance by appointment only, email ahead to book—genealogy@cobhheritage.com). See the sidebar on page 331 for more tips on researching your Irish heritage.

Eating

The nicest place in town is **Trade Winds,** with both a **$$$ pub** (downstairs) and **$$$$ restaurant** (upstairs). It's near the Commodore Hotel, facing the waterfront at 16 Casement Square. **$$$ Titanic Bar & Grill** is sunken under the Titanic Experience, with fun outdoor seating on fine days. **$$$ Jacob's Ladder** restaurant in the Waters Edge Hotel is also good. For picnic fixings, head to **Centra Market,** facing the water on West Beach Street.

Sleeping

These hotels are all centrally located near the harbor, less than a five-minute walk from the Queenstown Story. **$$$ Commodore Hotel** is a grand 170-year-old historic landmark with 40 rooms (Westbourne Place, tel. 021/481-1277, www. commodorehotel.ie, commodorehotel@ eircom.net). **$$$ Waters Edge Hotel** has 19 bright, modern rooms and a pleasant harbor-view restaurant (Yacht Club Quay, tel. 021/481-5566, www.watersedgehotel. ie, info@watersedgehotel.ie). **$ Ard na Laoi B&B** is a friendly place with five fresh rooms (cash only, 15 Westbourne Place, tel. 021/481-2742, www.ardnalaoi.ie, info@ ardnalaoi.ie, Michael O'Shea).

BLARNEY CASTLE

If you're driving between Kinsale and the Ring of Kerry, it's easy to stop here, though many find it a tourist trap. It's only famous as the place of tourist pilgrimage, where busloads line up to kiss a stone on its top rampart and get "the gift of gab." The stone's origin is shrouded in myth (perhaps brought back from the Holy Land by crusaders). The best thing about this overrated sight is the opportunity to watch a cranky man lower lemming tourists over the edge, belly up and head back, to kiss the stone (covered with spit and lipstick) while an automated camera snaps a photo—which will be available for purchase by the parking lot.

The tradition goes back to the late 16th century, when Queen Elizabeth I was trying to plant loyal English settlers in Ireland to tighten her grip on the rebellious island. She demanded that the Irish clan chiefs recognize the Crown as the legitimate titleholder of all lands. One of those chiefs was Cormac MacCarthy, Lord of Blarney Castle (who was supposedly loyal to the queen). He was smart enough never to disagree with the queen—instead, he would cleverly avoid acquiescing to her demands by sending a never-ending stream of lengthy and deceptive excuses, disguised with liberal doses of flattery (while subtly maintaining his native Gaelic loyalties). In her frustration, the queen declared his endless words nothing but "blarney."

While the 15th-century Blarney Castle is a shell, the surrounding grounds are beautiful and well-kept. There are even some hints of Ireland's pre-Christian past on the grounds; you can see dolmens beside the trail in the forested Rock Close.

Cost and Hours: €15, Mon-Sat 9:00-18:30, Sun until 18:00, later in peak season, shorter hours in winter, free parking, helpful TI, tel. 021/438-5252.

Getting There: It's 5 miles northwest of Cork, 20 miles northwest of Cobh, and 24 miles north of Kinsale.

Kissing the Blarney Stone

Kenmare
& the
Ring of Kerry

It's no wonder that, since Victorian times, visitors have been attracted to this dramatic chunk of Ireland. Mysterious ancient ring forts stand sentinel on mossy hillsides. Beloved Irish statesman Daniel O'Connor maintained his ancestral estate here, far from 19th-century politics. And early Christian hermit-monks left a lonely imprint of their devotion, in the form of simple stone dwellings atop an isolated rock crag far from shore...a holy retreat on the edge of the then-known world.

Today, it seems like every tour bus in Ireland makes the ritual loop around the scenic Ring of Kerry, using the bustling and famous tourist town of Killarney as a springboard. Killarney National Park is gorgeous and well worth driving through. But I prefer to skip Killarney town (useful only for its transportation connections). Instead, make the tidy town of Kenmare your home base, and use my suggestions to cleverly circle the much-loved peninsula—entirely missing the convoy of tour buses.

If you only have time for one peninsula tour, I recommend Dingle (see comparison on page 155), but with more time, you could do both (see below for the most efficient way to do it).

KENMARE & THE RING OF KERRY IN 1 DAY

All you need in compact Kenmare is one night and an early start the next day to drive the Ring of Kerry. The Ring is best driven clockwise, leaving Kenmare by 8:30; for route specifics, see page 151.

Without a car, you can take a minibus tour from Kenmare, though it's not as enjoyable as driving the loop yourself.

Here's a good strategy for your visit: Whether you're coming to Kenmare from Kinsale or elsewhere, you'll likely drive through the town of Killarney. After Killarney, you can see any of these sights on your way to Kenmare: Muckross House, Killarney National Park, and the Kissane Sheep Farm.

Ideally, arrive in Kenmare by late afternoon and see the town's sights, then get an early start on the Ring of Kerry in the morning. After driving the Ring, head to Dingle for the night.

Hardy hikers might consider adding another day here to visit the rugged island of Skellig Michael, which requires an overnight in Portmagee or St. Finian's Bay. Be aware that island access is unpredictable—boats can book up weeks in advance and then are only able to make the crossing about five days out of seven due to rough seas, even in summer.

KENMARE

Cradled in a lush valley, this charming little town (known as Neidín, or "Little Nest," in Irish) hooks you with its rows of vividly colored shop fronts and go-for-a-stroll atmosphere. The nearby finger of the gentle sea feels more like a large lake, called the Kenmare River, just to confuse things. Far from the assembly-line tourism of Killarney town, Kenmare (rhymes with "been there") also makes a great launch-pad for enjoying the sights along the road around the Iveragh (eev-er-AH) Peninsula—known to shamrock lovers everywhere as the Ring of Kerry.

Orientation

Carefully planned Kenmare is shaped like an "X," forming two triangles. The upper (northern) triangle contains the town square—where fairs and markets have been held for centuries (colorful market Wed in summer), the adjacent TI and Heritage Centre, and a cozy park. The lower (southern) triangle contains three one-way streets busy with shops, lodgings, and restaurants. Use the tall Holy Cross Church spire to get your bearings (next to the northeast parking lot, handy public WC across the street).

Tourist Information: The helpful TI is on the town square (Mon-Sat 9:30-13:30 & 14:00-17:15, closed Thu in spring and fall, Sun year-round, and all of Nov-March; tel. 064/664-1233). The TI also sporadically offers a 1.5-hour, €10 guided town walk (get details and book at the TI).

Laundry: O'Shea's Cleaners and Launderette is across from the Lansdowne Arms Hotel, hidden in the back recesses of O'Shea's photography shop (Mon-Sat 9:00-20:00, Sun 12:00-18:00, tel. 064/664-0808).

Bike Rental: Finnegan's Corner rents bikes and has route maps (standard bike-€15/day, €20/24 hours, beefed-up road bike-€30/day; Mon-Sat 9:30-18:30, Sun 12:00-18:00; leave ID for deposit, office in gift shop at 37 Henry Street, across from post office, tel. 064/664-1083, www.finneganscycles.com).

Taxi: Try **Murnane Cabs** (mobile 087-236-4353) or **Kenmare Coach and Cab** (mobile 087-248-0800).

Parking: The town's two largest public

Welcome to Kenmare.

In Kenmare

Ancient Stone Circle One of Ireland's most intact and easily accessible stone circles, over 3,000 years old. See page 143.

Kenmare Lace and Design Centre Modest cubbyhole with lovingly displayed examples of the lacemaking craftsmanship that put Kenmare on the map. **Hours:** Mon-Sat 10:15-17:30, closed mid-Oct-Easter and Sun year-round. See page 143.

The Ring of Kerry

▲▲▲**Driving the Ring of Kerry** Famous, scenic 135-mile loop road, featuring Iron Age ring forts, Daniel O'Connell's Derrynane estate, and grand views of the rugged coast and islands. See page 151.

▲▲**Kissane Sheep Farm** Working sheep farm on scenic hillside, with demonstrations of sheep shearing and dog herding. **Hours:** Most afternoons April-Sept by appointment only (minimum 15 people), closed Oct-March. See page 150.

▲**Muckross House and** ▲**Muckross Farms** Fine lakeside manor house surrounded by lush gardens, adjacent to folk park devoted to rural farm life over the past 200 years. **Hours:** House—daily 9:00-17:30, July-Aug until 18:30, shorter hours in winter. Farms—daily June-Aug 10:00-18:00, shorter hours rest of year and closed Nov-mid-March. See page 148.

▲**Killarney National Park** Ireland's best national park, laced with hiking trails, waterfalls, and drives through old-growth forests dotted with postcard views of the lakes of Killarney. See page 149.

Side-trip

▲▲▲**Skellig Michael** A craggy pinnacle of an island, topped with monks' huts, reachable by a boat from Portmagee, then a steep hike—an excursion for hardy hikers with extra time. See page 161.

parking lots (behind the TI and across from the church, free overnight) cling to the two main roads departing town to the north. Street parking is free for two hours.

Tours: Finnegan's Tours runs day tours with guides who give a casual, anecdotal narration (route depends on day: Ring of Kerry on Mon, Wed, and Fri; Ring of Beara on Tue; Glengarriff and Garnish Island on Thu; €30 for any tour, reserve a day in advance by phone or three days in advance by email; for Sept-June, call to arrange tours; tel. 064/664-1491, mobile 087-248-0800, www.kenmarecoachandcab.com, info@kenmarecoachandcab.com).

Sights
ANCIENT STONE CIRCLE

Of the approximately 100 stone circles that dot southwest Ireland (Counties Cork and Kerry), Kenmare's is one of the most accessible. More than 3,000 years old, it may have been used both as a primitive calendar and as a focal point for rituals. The circle has a diameter of 50 feet and consists of 15 stones ringing a large center boulder (possibly a burial monument). Experts think this stone circle (like most) functioned as a celestial calendar—it tracked the position of the setting sun to determine the two solstices (in June and December), which mark the longest and shortest days of the year.

Cost and Hours: €2, drop coins into honor box in hut by entry when attendant is away, always open.

Getting There: It's a five-minute walk from the TI. From the city center, face the TI, turn left, and walk 200 yards down Market Street, passing a row of cute 18th-century houses on your right. Beyond the row of houses, veer right through an unmarked modern gate mounted in stone columns, and continue 50 yards down the paved road. You'll pass the entry hut on your right. The stone circle is behind the adjacent hedge.

KENMARE LACE AND DESIGN CENTRE

A single large room (above the TI) displays the delicate lacework that put Kenmare on the modern map. From the 1860s until World War I, the Poor Clare convent at Kenmare was the center of excellence

Kenmare's ancient stone circle

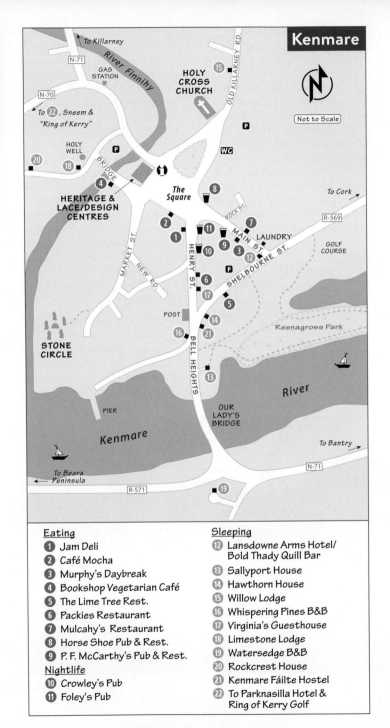

Kenmare

To Killarney
N-71
River Finnihy
GAS STATION
N-70
To 22, Sneem & "Ring of Kerry"
HOLY WELL
20
18
BRIDGE
4
HERITAGE & LACE/DESIGN CENTRES
MARKET ST.
NEW RD.
HENRY ST.
STONE CIRCLE
PIER
Kenmare

HOLY CROSS CHURCH
15
OLD KILLARNEY RD.
Not to Scale
The Square
8
2
11
1
10
9
ROCK ST.
MAIN ST.
7
LAUNDRY
3
12
SHELBOURNE ST.
6
17
5
POST
16
14
21
13
BELL HEIGHTS
OUR LADY'S BRIDGE
Reenagross Park
River
To Cork
R-569
GOLF COURSE

WC

To Bantry
N-71
R-571
19
To Beara Peninsula

Eating
1. Jam Deli
2. Café Mocha
3. Murphy's Daybreak
4. Bookshop Vegetarian Café
5. The Lime Tree Rest.
6. Packies Restaurant
7. Mulcahy's Restaurant
8. Horse Shoe Pub & Rest.
9. P. F. McCarthy's Pub & Rest.

Nightlife
10. Crowley's Pub
11. Foley's Pub

Sleeping
12. Lansdowne Arms Hotel/ Bold Thady Quill Bar
13. Sallyport House
14. Hawthorn House
15. Willow Lodge
16. Whispering Pines B&B
17. Virginia's Guesthouse
18. Limestone Lodge
19. Watersedge B&B
20. Rockcrest House
21. Kenmare Fáilte Hostel
22. To Parknasilla Hotel & Ring of Kerry Golf

Nuns' Lace

Sister Margaret Cusack, a.k.a. Sister Mary Francis Clare, lived in the town from 1862 to 1881, becoming the famous Nun of Kenmare. Her controversial religious life began when she decided to become an Anglican nun after her fiancé's sudden death. Failing to be accepted as one of Florence Nightingale's nurses during the Crimean War, she converted to Catholicism, joined the Poor Clare order as Sister Mary Francis Clare, and moved with the order to Kenmare. She became an outspoken writer who favored women's rights and lambasted the tyranny of the landlords during the Great Potato Famine (1845-1849). She eventually took church funds and attempted to set herself up as abbess of a convent in Knock. Her renegade behavior led to her leaving the Catholic faith, converting back to Protestantism, writing an autobiography, and lecturing about the "sinister influence of the Roman Church."

After the devastation of the famine, an industrial school was founded in Kenmare to teach trades to destitute youngsters. The school, run by the Poor Clare sisters, excelled in teaching young girls the art of lacemaking. Inspired by lace created in Italy, Kenmare lace caught the eye of Queen Victoria and became much coveted by Victorian society. Examples of it are now on display in the Victoria and Albert Museum (London), the Irish National Museum (Dublin), and the US National Gallery (Washington, DC).

for Irish lacemaking. Inspired by antique Venetian lace, but creating their own unique designs, nuns taught needlepoint lacemaking as a trade to girls in a region struggling to get back on its feet in the wake of the catastrophic famine. Queen Victoria commissioned five pieces of lace in 1885, and by the end of the century tourists began visiting Kenmare on their way to Killarney just for a peek at the lace. Nora Finnegan, who runs the center, usually has a work in progress to demonstrate the complexity of fine lacemaking to visitors.

Cost and Hours: Free, Mon-Sat 10:15-17:30, closed mid-Oct-Easter and Sun year-round, tel. 064/664-2978, www.kenmarelace.ie.

Experiences

Horseback Riding

River Valley Riding Stables offers day treks for all levels of experience through beautiful hill scenery in the Roughty River Valley (adults-€20/hour, kids-€15/hour, group discounts, long hours, based at Sheen Falls Lodge 1.5 miles southeast of Kenmare—cross Our Lady's Bridge and turn left on N-71, mobile 087-958-5895, rivervalleystables@hotmail.com).

Boating and Hiking

Star Sailing rents boats, gives sailing lessons, and organizes hill walks. Hop on a small two-person sailboat (€45 for 1 hour, €35/additional hour) or a six-person boat (€65 for 1 hour, €55/additional hour).

Or kick around in a kayak (single–€20/hour, double–€36/hour). Phone ahead to reserve boats (daily 10:00-17:00, located 5 miles southwest of Kenmare on R-571 on Beara Peninsula, courtesy shuttle can pick you up in Kenmare, tel. 064/664-1222, www.staroutdoors.ie; adjacent Con's Restaurant is open daily 12:00-20:00).

Golfing

Another way to experience Ireland's 40 shades of green is to splurge on a scenic day on the links. The **Kenmare Golf Club** is right on the edge of town (€40 greens fee, €30 Oct-April, on R-569 toward Cork, tel. 064/664-1291, www.kenmaregolfclub.com). Or try the **Ring of Kerry Golf and Country Club** (weekdays–€55 greens fee, weekends–€65, prebook on weekends, 4 miles west of town on N-70, tel. 064/664-2000, www.ringofkerrygolf.com).

Nightlife

Wander the compact Kenmare town triangle and stick your head in wherever you hear something you like. Music usually starts at 21:30 (although some pubs have early 18:30 sessions—ask at the TI) and ranges from Irish traditional sessions to sing-along strummers. **Crowley's** is an atmospheric shoebox of a pub with an unpretentious clientele. **Foley's** whiskey tube collection adorns its window, inviting you in for a folksy songfest. The Lansdowne Arms Hotel sponsors live traditional sessions in their **Bold Thady Quill Bar.**

Eating

If dining, make a reservation or get a table early, as many finer places book up later in the evening during the summer. Pub dinners are a good value and easier on the budget, but pub kitchens close earlier than restaurants.

Lunch

Soup-and-sandwich lunch options abound. **$ Jam** is an inviting place with seating inside and out, and soups, salads, and sandwiches on the menu. They make sandwiches or wraps to go for picnics (daily 8:00-17:00, Henry Street, tel. 064/664-1591). **$ Café Mocha** is a basic sandwich shop (daily 9:00-17:30, on the town square, tel. 064/664-2133). **Murphy's Daybreak** supermarket is a good place to stock up for a Ring of Kerry picnic (Mon-Sat 8:00-22:00, Sun 9:00-21:00, Main Street). **$ The Bookshop Vegetarian Café** is delightful for a healthy, peaceful lunch or some coffee, cakes, and pastries (daily, on Bridge Street just around the corner from the TI, tel. 064/667-9911).

Dinner

$$$ The Lime Tree Restaurant occupies the former Lansdowne Estate office, which gave more than 4,000 people free passage to America in the 1840s. These days, it serves delicious, locally caught seafood dishes in a modern yet cozy dining hall (reservations smart, daily 18:30-21:30, closed Nov-March, Shelbourne Street, tel. 064/664-1225, www.limetreerestaurant.com).

$$$$ Packies is a popular bistro that has a leafy, low-light interior and cottage ambience, and serves traditional cuisine with French influence. Their seafood gets rave reviews (Mon-Sat 18:00-22:00, closed Sun, reservations wise, Henry Street, tel. 064/664-1508).

$$$$ Mulcahy's Restaurant has a jazz-mellowed, elegant ambience and creatively presented gourmet dishes. Given the Indian, Japanese, and American influences, there's always a good vegetarian entrée (Thu-Tue 17:00-22:00, closed Wed, reservations smart, Main Street, tel. 064/664-2383).

$$$ Horse Shoe Pub and Restaurant, specializing in steak and spareribs, somehow turns rustic farm-tool decor into a romantic candlelit sanctuary (daily 17:00-22:00, Main Street, tel. 064/664-1553).

$$ P. F. McCarthy's Pub and Restaurant feels like a sloppy saloon, serving reasonable salad or sandwich lunches and filling dinner fare (daily 12:00–21:00, 14 Main Street, tel. 064/664-1516).

Sleeping

$$$ Lansdowne Arms Hotel is the town's venerable grand hotel, with generous public spaces. This centrally located, 200-year-old historic landmark rents 25 large, crisp rooms (music in pub until late on Fri-Sat, parking, corner of Main and Shelbourne Streets, tel. 064/664-1368, www.lansdownearms.com, info@lansdownearms.com).

$$$ Sallyport House, an elegant, quiet house with five rooms filled with antique furniture, has been in Helen Arthur's family for generations. Ask her to point out the foot-worn doorstep that was salvaged from the local workhouse and built into her stone chimney (cash only, no kids, parking, closed Nov-mid-March, 5-minute walk south of town before crossing Our Lady's Bridge, tel. 064/664-2066, www.sallyporthouse.com, port@iol.ie).

$$ Hawthorn House is a fine, modern, freestanding house with a lounge, warm and friendly hostess Mary O'Brien, and 10 comfy rooms. Mary's front parlor is a homage to her son Stephen's hard-won success as a player for the dominant County Kerry Irish football team. The house is set in a quiet residential location just a block from all the pub and restaurant action (family rooms, parking, Shelbourne Street, tel. 064/664-1035, www.hawthornhousekenmare.com, hawthorn@eircom.net). Mary's modern, self-catering apartment next door works well for those wanting to linger (weekly rentals).

$$ Willow Lodge, on the main road at the edge of town, feels American-suburban, with friendly hosts and seven comfortable rooms (cash only, family rooms, parking, 100 yards beyond Holy Cross Church, tel. 064/664-2301, www.willowlodgekenmare.com, willowlodgekenmare@yahoo.com, jovial Paul and talkative Gretta Gleeson-O'Byrne).

$ Whispering Pines B&B offers five rooms with sincere, traditional Irish hospitality in a spacious house warmed by the presence of hostesses Mary Fitzgerald and daughter Kathleen (cash only, closed Oct-March, at the edge of town on Bell Height, tel. 064/664-1194, www.whisperingpineskenmare.com, wpines@eircom.net).

$ Virginia's Guesthouse, ideally located near the best restaurants, is well kept by Neil and Noreen. Its nine rooms are fresh, roomy, and appealing (breakfast extra, 36 Henry Street, mobile 086-306-5291, www.virginias-kenmare.com, virginias.guesthouse@gmail.com).

$ Limestone Lodge stands rock-solid beside a holy well, with five comfy rooms in a quiet location. Friendly hosts Sinead and Siobhan Thomas are experts on Kenmare's famous lace, and Casey, their wiggly Jack Russell terrier, is an expert at being cute (cash only, family rooms, parking, tel. 064/664-2231, mobile 087-757-4411, www.limestonelodgekenmare.com, info@limestonelodgekenmare.com).

$ Watersedge B&B is a mile south of town, serenely isolated on a forested hillside and overlooking the estuary. The modern house has four clean, colorful rooms and a kid-pleasing backyard (cash only, parking, tel. 064/664-1707, mobile 087-413-4235, www.watersedgekenmare.com, watersedgekenmare@gmail.com, Noreen and Vincent O'Shea). To get here, drive south over Our Lady's Bridge, bear left, immediately look for the B&B sign, and take the first right onto the road heading uphill. Go 100 yards up the paved road, then—at the end of the white cinder-block wall (on left)—turn right onto the private lane and drive 100 yards to the dead-end. It's worth it.

$ Rockcrest House is secluded down a quiet, leafy lane, with six large rooms and a fine front-porch view (cash only; as you pass the TI heading north out of town, take the first left after crossing the bridge; tel. 064/664-1248, mobile 087-904-3788, www.visit-kenmare.com, info@visit-kenmare.

com, Marian and David O'Dwyer). Ask about their two self-catering cottage rentals.

¢ **Kenmare Fáilte Hostel** (fawl-chuh) maintains 34 budget beds in a well-kept, centrally located building with more charm than most hostels (private rooms available, closed mid-Oct-April, Shelbourne Street, tel. 064/664-2333, mobile 087-711-6092, run by Finnegan's Corner bike rental folks directly across street, www.kenmare hostel.com, info@kenmarehostel.com).

$$$$ **Parknasilla Hotel** is a 19th-century luxury hotel (82 rooms) lost in 500 plush acres of a subtropical park overlooking the wild Atlantic Ocean. The tranquility, combined with old-fashioned service and Victorian elegance, makes this a good stop for anyone interested in luxuriating on the Ring of Kerry. Originally an old railroad hotel for Romantic Age tourists, in recent decades it has been a ritual splurge for Irish families and wedding groups (highest rates July-Aug, 19th-century diversions, park walks, tel. 064/667-5600, www.parknasillahotel.ie, reservations@ parknasillahotel.ie).

Transportation

Kenmare has no train station (the nearest is in Killarney, 20 miles away) and only a few bus connections (www.buseireann. ie). Most buses transfer in Killarney.

From Kenmare by Bus to: Killarney (3/day, 45 minutes), **Tralee** (3/day, 2 hours), **Dingle** (3-4/day, 3 hours, change in Killarney), **Kinsale** (3/day, 4 hours, 2 changes), **Dublin** (4/day, 7.5 hours, change in Killarney and Limerick).

KILLARNEY

Killarney's value is its location. For most tour organizers, it's the logical jumping-off point for excursions around the famous Ring of Kerry peninsula. If you're approaching the region from Kinsale, drive through Killarney and hop on the Ring to visit Muckross House, Killarney National Park, and Kissane Sheep Farm (in the mountains) en route to Kenmare. By taking a bite out of the Ring the day before you sleep in Kenmare, you'll be better situated to drive most of the remainder of the Ring of Kerry loop the next day.

Killarney is a household word among American tourists. Springing from the bus and train station are a few colorful streets lined with tourist-friendly shops and restaurants. If you're traveling in the region without a car, you'll have to stop here. The Killarney bus and train stations flank the big, modern Killarney Outlet Centre mall. If you have a layover between connections, walk five minutes straight out from the front of the mall, and check out Killarney's shop-lined High Street and New Street. The TI is a 15-minute walk from the train station, on Beech Street.

Sights near Killarney
▲MUCKROSS HOUSE AND FARMS

Perhaps the best stately Victorian home you'll see in the Republic of Ireland, Muckross House (built in 1843) is magnificently set at the edge of Killarney National Park. It's adjacent to Muckross Farms, a fascinating open-air farm museum that shows rural life in the 1930s. Besides the mansion and farms, this regular stop on the tour-bus circuit also includes a fine garden idyllically set on a lake and an information center for the national park. The poignant juxtaposition of the magnificent mansion and the humble farmhouses illustrates in a thought-provoking way the vast gap that once separated rich and poor in Ireland.

Cost and Hours: House-€9, farms-€9, €15 combo-ticket includes both (Heritage Cards not accepted for farms). House open daily 9:00-17:30, July-Aug until 19:00, last entry one hour before closing. Farms open daily June-Aug 10:00-18:00, May and Sept daily 13:00-18:00, March-April and Oct Sat-Sun only 13:00-18:00, closed Nov-Feb, tel. 064/667-0144, www. muckross-house.ie.

Getting There: Muckross House is

conveniently located for a break on the long ride from Kinsale or Cashel to Dingle or Kenmare. From Killarney, follow signs to Kenmare, where you'll find Muckross House three miles (5 km) south of town. As you approach from Killarney, you'll see a small parking lot two miles before the actual parking lot. This is used by horse-and-buggy bandits to hoodwink tourists into thinking they have to pay to clip-clop to the house. Giddy-up on by to find a big, safe, and free parking lot right at the mansion.

Tours: The only way to see the interior of the house is with the 45-minute guided tour, which gives meaning to your visit (included with admission, offered frequently throughout the day). Book your tour as soon as you arrive; they can fill up. Then enjoy a walk in the gardens or lunch in their better-than-average cafeteria until your tour begins.

Visiting the House and Farms: A visit to **Muckross House** takes you back to the Victorian period—the 19th-century boom time, when the sun never set on the British Empire and the Industrial Revolution (born in England) was chugging the world into the modern age. Of course, Ireland was a colony back then, with big-shot English landlords. During the Great

Muckross House

Potato Famine of 1845-1849, most English gentry lived very well—profiting off the export of their handsome crops to lands with greater buying power—while a third of Ireland's population starved.

Muckross House feels lived-in (and it was, until 1933). Its fine Victorian furniture is arranged around the fireplace under Waterford crystal chandeliers and lots of antlers. You'll see Queen Victoria's bedroom (ground floor, since she was afraid of house fires). The owners of the house spent a couple of years preparing for the royal visit in 1861, eager to gain coveted titles and nearly bankrupting themselves in the process. The queen stayed only three nights and her beloved Prince Albert died soon after the visit. The depressed queen never granted the titles for which the grand house's owners had so hoped.

The house exit takes you through an **information center** for Killarney National Park, with a relaxing 15-minute video on "Ireland's premier national park," featuring lots of geology, flora, and fauna (free, shown on request).

The **Muckross Traditional Farms** consists of six different vintage farmhouses. The farms are strung along a mile-long road, with an old bus shuttling those who don't want to hike (free, 4/hour). For those interested in Irish farm life from the 1920s until electricity arrived in 1955, this is a great experience—but only if you engage the attendants in conversation. Each farm is staffed by a Kerry local who enjoys telling tales of life on the farm in the old days.

▲KILLARNEY NATIONAL PARK

As you drive from Killarney to Kenmare, heading south on N-71, you'll sweep through scenic Killarney National Park (just south of Killarney town) on the most mountainous stretch of the Ring of Kerry. This 25,000-acre park is Ireland's oldest, established in 1932. Glacially sculpted rock ridges cradle three large lakes teeming with trout and salmon, making them popular for sport fishing.

Hikers enjoy an easy 10-minute stroll along a mossy trail from the roadside up to **Torc Waterfall** (look for small parking lot beside N-71, 2 miles—3 km—south of Muckross House), then lace up their boots to take on more strenuous trails beyond. If you go early or late in the day, keep an eye out for Ireland's only native herd of red deer. The park's old-growth oak, yew, and alder groves are the best-preserved in Ireland, and rhododendrons explode beside the road in late May and June.

Take a quiet moment to contemplate your lush surroundings. This is what the majority of Ireland looked like 8,000 years ago, before Neolithic man settled and began rudimentary slash-and-burn farming. Later English colonial harvesting of timber exacerbated the deforestation process. Today, Ireland has the smallest proportion of forested land—just 10.5 percent—of any EU nation.

Enjoy expansive lake views from **Ladies View,** right beside the N-71 road, half a mile (1 km) from the park's southern exit. Just south of the park exit, you'll pass long, thin Looscaunagh Lough (beside the road on the left). A few hundred yards farther, the Black Valley opens up beneath you on the right. This remote valley was the last chunk of Ireland to get electricity—in 1978. The highest bump on the distant ridge across the Black Valley to the west is Carrauntoohil, Ireland's tallest mountain at 3,400 feet.

▲KISSANE SHEEP FARM

Call ahead to arrange an hour's visit to this hardworking 2,500-acre Irish farm, perched on a scenic slope above the Black Valley. John Kissane, whose family has raised sheep here for five generations, gives hands-on demonstrations of sheep shearing. John (or his brother Noel) explains the process and invites you to touch the pile of fresh wool afterward. You can feel the lanolin, which acts as natural waterproofing for the sheep and is extracted from the wool to sell to pharmaceutical firms (synthetic manufacturing has driven the price of wool so low, it's not worth selling otherwise). But the highlight of any visit is the demonstration of sheepherding by the highly alert family dogs (border collies trained here since puppyhood). John commands the dogs from afar using an array of verbal calls and hand signals. Little Sean is at his dad's side, learning the trade, though these days the farm makes more money from visiting tourists than it does in the traditional sheep-and-wool trade.

Cost and Hours: €7, by appointment only most afternoons April-Sept (minimum 15 people)—call ahead and coordinate your visit with a visiting big bus tour as they don't do private demonstrations; closed Oct-March, on N-71 between Ladies View and Moll's Gap, tel. 064/663-4791, mobile 087-260-0410, www.kissanesheepfarm.com, noel@kissanesheepfarm.com.

Torc Waterfall in Killarney National Park

Kissane Sheep Farm

From Kissane Sheep Farm to Kenmare: Continue driving south on N-71. Going over Moll's Gap (WCs and Avoca Café beside parking lot), you'll descend into Kenmare. The rugged, bare rock on either side of the road was rounded and smoothed by the grinding action of glaciers over thousands of years. In the distance to the north (on your right) you can see the Gap of Dunloe, a perfect example of a U-shaped glacial valley notch.

RING OF KERRY

The Ring of Kerry (the Iveragh Peninsula) has been the perennial breadwinner of Irish tourism for decades now. Lassoed by a winding coastal road (the Ring), this mountainous, lake-splattered region comes with breathtaking scenery and the highest peak in Ireland. While a veritable fleet of tourist buses circles it each day, they generally stay together and stop at the same handful of attractions. Therefore, if you avoid those places at rush hour, the Ring feels dramatic, isolated, and unspoiled.

Armed with a good map and a reliable alarm clock, you can avoid the crowds and enjoy one of the most rewarding days in Ireland. To include a boat trip out to the remote, evocative island of Skellig Michael, add another day and plan an overnight in the Portmagee area. (Note that there aren't lots of ATMs throughout the Ring; bring sufficient cash with you from Kenmare.)

Without a car, take a one-day minibus tour of the Ring of Kerry from Kenmare; see page 143.

▲▲▲Driving the Ring of Kerry

The entire Ring of Kerry loop is 135 miles and takes 4.5 hours to drive without making any stops. Drive counterclockwise around the Ring to entirely miss the chain of tour buses. Be sure to factor in time to stop for lunch and to see the sights. Tank up before leaving, as gas in Kenmare is cheaper than out on the Ring.

On a one-day visit to the Ring, I'd leave Kenmare by 8:30 and head clockwise (against the prevailing tour-bus traffic). Allow time for stops at Staigue Ring Fort (45 minutes) and Derrynane House (1 hour), and get to Waterville before noon. Shortly after Waterville, leave the main Ring for the Skellig Ring (a road that's too narrow for big buses). Plan to have lunch out on the Skellig Ring, either as a picnic on the lovely beach at St. Finian's Bay, or in Portmagee. On the last half of the route, there are two more hour-long stops: the Skellig Experience Centre (near Portmagee) and two additional big ring forts (near Cahersiveen).

For me, the two most photogenic coastal stretches are out near the tip of the peninsula: between Caherdaniel and Waterville (on the Ring of Kerry), and from Ballinskelligs to Portmagee (on the Skellig Ring).

The only downside of going against all the bus traffic is that, on the narrow parts of the Ring road, buses always have the right-of-way. If there's a bottleneck, it's up to you to back up to the nearest wide spot in the road to let a less nimble bus get through a tight curve. With an early start, you can avoid these hassles: On my last circuit, I got to Waterville by 11:30, from where I slipped happily into the bus-free

Ring of Kerry Loop Trip

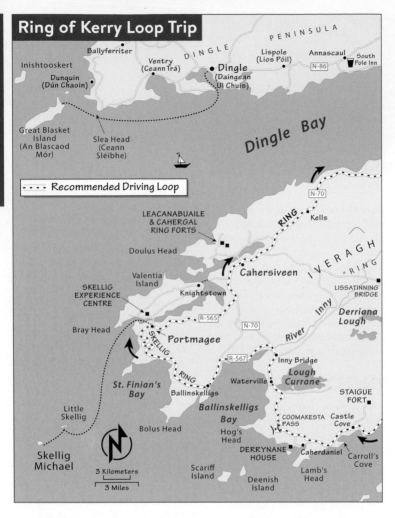

DINGLE PENINSULA

Inishtooskert

Ballyferriter

Ventry (Ceann Trá)

Dunquin (Dún Chaoin)

Dingle (Daingean Uí Chuis)

Lispole (Lios Póil)

Annascaul
South Pole Inn
N-86

Great Blasket Island (An Blascaod Mór)

Slea Head (Ceann Sléibhe)

Dingle Bay

---- Recommended Driving Loop

LEACANABUAILE & CAHERGAL RING FORTS

Doulus Head

Valentia Island

SKELLIG EXPERIENCE CENTRE

Bray Head

Knightstown

RING

Kells

N-70

Cahersiveen

IVERAGH

"RING

LISSATINNING BRIDGE

Derriana Lough

Inny

R-565

N-70

River

SKELLIG

Portmagee

RING

R-567

Inny Bridge

Lough Currane

St. Finian's Bay

Ballinskelligs

Waterville

Little Skellig

Bolus Head

Ballinskelligs Bay

Hog's Head

STAIGUE FORT

COOMAKESTA PASS

Castle Cove

Skellig Michael

N

3 Kilometers

3 Miles

Scariff Island

Deenish Island

DERRYNANE HOUSE

Lamb's Head

Caherdaniel

Carroll's Cove

Skellig Ring...and didn't encounter a single bus the rest of the day.

Smart drivers equip themselves with a good map before driving the Ring of Kerry loop. If you don't have one already, pick up the *Complete Road Atlas of Ireland* by Ordnance Survey (sold in most TIs and bookstores in Ireland). The *Fir Tree Aerial* series provides a useful map that covers both the Iveragh (Ring of Kerry) and Dingle peninsulas, giving you a bird's-eye feel for the terrain (sold in many TIs and bookstores in County Kerry).

Rick's Tip: *The flat, inland, northeastern section of the Ring, from Killorglin to Killarney on N-72, is* **skippable***.*

◑ Self-Guided Tour

Here's a self-guided sightseeing tip sheet for my preferred clockwise route, kilometer by kilometer. If you do any exploring, you'll likely get hopelessly off pace, but the kilometer references still help—just do the arithmetic to figure out how far various

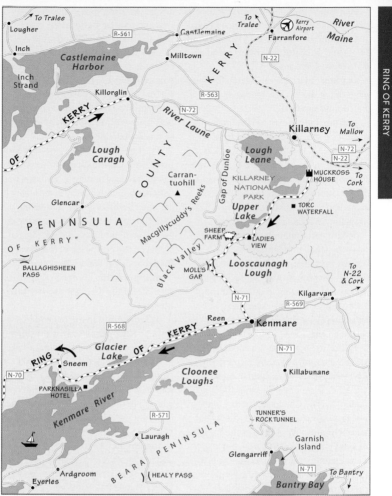

stops are from each other. Several of these stops are explained in far greater detail later in this chapter, in the same order in which they're listed here. To understand your options, read the rest of this chapter before you start on your tour.

0 km: Leave Kenmare.

17.6 km: Glacier Lake has a long, smooth limestone "banister" carved by a glacier 10,000 years ago.

22.8 km: The posh 19th-century Parknasilla Hotel is a great stop for tea and scones.

26 km: Visit the town of Sneem.

40.4 km: Turn off for the Staigue Fort.

41.5 km: Enjoy great views across the bay of the Beara Peninsula beyond a ruined hospital with IRA ties. No one wants to touch these ruins today out of fear of "kicking up a beehive."

43.5 km: Carroll's Cove has a fine beach with some of the warmest water in Ireland, grand views of Kenmare Bay, a trailer park, and "Ireland's only beachside bar."

46.4 km: Take the turnoff for Derrynane House (home of Daniel O'Connell).

50.4 km: Enjoy brilliant views for the next two kilometers to Coomakesta Pass.

52.4 km: The Coomakesta Pass lookout point (700-foot altitude) offers grand vistas in both directions.

54.5 km: On a clear day, watch for fine views of the distant Skellig Islands with their pointy summits.

59.6 km: In the town of Waterville, you'll see a sculpture of Charlie Chaplin standing on the waterfront. Waterville is also home to the Butler Arms Hotel—a fine stop for tea and scones in its Charlie Chaplin room (with lots of photos of the silent-film icon and his young wife frolicking as they lived well in Ireland).

65 km: After rejoining the main road, cross the small bridge that's locally famous for salmon fly-fishing. Take the first left (R-567) for the Skellig Ring loop (follow brown *Skellig Ring* signs through Ballinskelligs, and then scenically to Portmagee). At this point, you've left the big-bus route.

75 km: St. Finian's Bay lies about halfway around, with a pleasant picnic-friendly beach that's been discovered by surfers (no WCs). Just before the bay is the small, modern Skelligs Chocolate Factory, with free, tasty samples as well as a café for coffee and muffins. This stop is especially fun for kids (Mon-Fri 10:00-17:00—but longer hours in summer, Sat-Sun 12:00-17:00, tel. 066/947-9119, www.skelligschocolate.com).

80 km: Photographers and walkers will want to turn left into the driveway that advertises "Best View in County Kerry." Park and pay the €4 fee at the hut. Then walk 10 minutes straight up the gravel road, where you'll be confronted by a dramatic coastal cliff that opens up onto dramatic coastal views. The beehive huts nearby are replicas, but true to the originals.

83 km: You reach Portmagee, a small port town and jumping-off point for boats to the Skellig Islands.

83.2 km: Cross the bridge to the Skellig Experience Centre. You're now on Valentia Island, its name hinting at medieval trading connections with nearby Spain—which lies due south. Dinosaur hunters may want to detour and follow the signs to the modest but ancient tetrapod tracks, frozen in stone, on the north side of the island (ask for directions at the visitors center).

91.2 km: At the church in Knightstown, turn left for the Knightstown Heritage Museum.

93 km: Return to the main road and go through Knightstown to the tiny ferry (€6/car, runs constantly 8:00-21:00, 1-km trip).

95 km: Leaving the ferry, rejoin N-70 (the main Ring of Kerry route), turning left for the town of Cahersiveen. From here, you can detour a few kilometers to two impressive stone ring forts, Cahergal and Leacanabuaile.

100 km: Return to N-70 at Cahersiveen and follow signs for *Glenbeigh* and *Killorglin*. Enjoy views of the Dingle Peninsula across Dingle Bay. Eagle eyes can spot stumpy Eask Tower and Inch Beach.

Lakes of Killarney

St. Finian's Bay

The Ring of Kerry vs. the Dingle Peninsula

If I had to choose one spot to enjoy the small-town charm of traditional Ireland, it would be Dingle and its history-laden scenic peninsula. But the Ring of Kerry—a much bigger, more famous, and more touristed peninsula just to its south—is also great to visit. If you go to Ireland and don't see the famous Ring of Kerry, your Uncle Pat will never forgive you. Here's a comparison to help with your itinerary planning.

Both peninsulas come with a scenic loop drive. Dingle's is 30 miles. The Ring of Kerry is 120 miles. Both loops come with lots of megalithic wonder. Dingle's prehistory is more intimate, with numerous evocative stony structures. The Ring of Kerry's prehistory shows itself in three massive ring forts—far bigger than anything on Dingle.

Dingle town is the perfect little Irish burg—alive with traditional music pubs, an active fishing harbor, and the sturdy cultural atmosphere of an Irish-speaking Gaeltacht region. You can easily spend three fun nights here. In comparison, Kenmare (the best base for the Ring of Kerry loop) is pleasant but forgettable. Those spending a night on the west end of the Ring of Kerry find a rustic atmosphere in Portmagee (the base for a cruise to magical Skellig Michael).

Both regions are beyond the reach of the Irish train system and require a car or spotty bus service to access. Both offer memorable scenery, great restaurants, warm B&B hospitality, and similar prices. The bottom line: With limited time, choose Dingle. If you have a day or two to spare, the Ring of Kerry is also a delight.

The rest of the loop is less scenic. At Killorglin, you've seen the best of it. From here, go either to Dingle (left) or to Kenmare/Killarney/Kinsale (right).

Sneem

Although it's inundated by tour buses daily from 14:00 to 16:00, Sneem is peaceful and laid-back the rest of the day. This humble town has two entertaining squares. The Irish joke, "Since we're in Kerry, the square on the east side is called South Square and the one on the west is called North Square." On the first (South) square, you'll see a statue of Steve "Crusher" Casey, the local boy who reigned as world champion heavyweight wrestler (1938-1947). A sweet peat-toned rapid gurgles under the one-lane bridge connecting the two Sneem squares. The North Square features a memorial to former French president Charles de Gaulle's visit. (Irish on his mother's side, de Gaulle came here for two weeks of R&R after his final retirement from office in 1969.) Locals call the memorial "da gallstone."

Statue of Steve "Crusher" Casey

The Ring Forts of Kerry

The Ring of Kerry comes with three awe-inspiring prehistoric ring forts—among the largest and best preserved in all of Ireland. Staigue Fort (near the beginning of my recommended clockwise Ring route) is most impressive and in a desolate setting. The two others—Cahergal and Leacanabuaile, 200 yards apart just north of Cahersiveen (closer to the end of the Ring, after Valentia Island)—are easier to visit and plenty evocative. Each ring fort is about a 2.5-mile (4-km) side-trip off the main drag. If you're trying to beat the tour-bus convoy, Staigue Fort is problematic because it eats up morning time before the buses have passed you. The Cahersiveen ring forts are your last stop in the Ring of Kerry, once bus traffic is of no concern.

All of these ring forts are roughly the same age and have the similar basic features. The circular drystone walls were built sometime between 500 B.C. and A.D. 300 without the aid of mortar or cement. About 80 feet across, with walls 12 feet thick at the base and up to 25 feet high, these brutish structures would have taken 100 men six months to complete.

Expert opinion is divided on the reason they were built. Civilization was morphing from nomadic hunter-gatherers to settled farmers, so herders used these forts to gather their valuable cattle inside and protect them from ancient rustlers. Other experts see the round design as a kind of amphitheater, where local clan chieftains would have gathered for important meetings or rituals. However, the ditch surrounding the outer walls of Staigue Fort suggests a defensive, rather than ceremonial, function. Without written records, we can only imagine the part these magnificent piles of finely stacked stones played in ancient dramas.

Between Sneem and Portmagee

▲STAIGUE FORT

This impressive ring fort is worth a stop on your way around the Ring (always open, drop €1 in the gray donation box beside the gate). While viewing the imposing pile of stone, read "The Ring Forts of Kerry" sidebar.

Getting There: The fort is 2.5 miles (4 km) off the main N-70 road up a narrow rural access lane (look for signs just after the hamlet of Castle Cove). Honk on blind corners to warn oncoming traffic as you drive up the hedge-lined lane.

▲DERRYNANE HOUSE

This is the home of Daniel O'Connell, Ireland's most influential 19th-century politician, whose tireless nonviolent agitation gained equality for Catholics 185 years ago. The coastal lands of the O'Connell estate that surround Derrynane (rhymes with MaryAnn) House are now a national historic park. A visit here is a window into the life of a man who not only liberated Ireland from the last oppressive anti-Catholic penal laws, but also first developed the idea of a grassroots movement—organizing on a massive scale to achieve political ends without bloodshed (see sidebar, later).

Cost and Hours: €5; May-Sept daily 10:30-18:00; mid-March-April and Oct Wed-Sun 10:30-17:00, closed Mon-Tue; open weekends only in Nov, closed Dec-mid-March; last entry 45 minutes before closing, tel. 066/947-5113.

Getting There: Just outside the town of Derrynane, pick up a handy free regional map from the private TI inside the brown Wave Crest market, which is a great place to buy picnic food (TI open daily May-Sept 9:00-18:00, closed Oct-April, tel. 066/947-5188). One mile after the market, take a left and follow the signs into Derrynane National Historic Park.

Visiting the House: The house has a quirky floor plan. Ask about the next scheduled 20-minute audiovisual show, which fleshes out the highlights of O'Connell's turbulent life and makes the contents of the house more interesting.

Downstairs in the study, look for the glass case containing the pistols used in O'Connell's famous duel. Beside them are his black gloves, one of which he always wore on his right hand when he went to Mass (out of remorse for the part it played in taking a man's life). The dining room is lined with family portraits. Upstairs in the drawing room, you'll find his ornately carved chair with tiny harp strings and wolfhound collars made of gold. In a drawer in an upstairs bedroom is a copy of O'Connell's celebrated speech imploring the Irish not to riot when he was arrested. And in another upstairs

room is his deathbed, brought back from Genoa.

The coach house (out back) shows off the enormous grand chariot that carried O'Connell through throngs of joyous Dubliners after his release from prison in 1844. He added the small chapel wing to the house in gratitude to God for his prison release.

Portmagee

Just a short row of snoozy buildings lining the bay, Portmagee is the best harbor for boat excursions out to the Skellig Islands (see "Getting There" on page 162). It's a quiet village with a handful of B&Bs, two pubs, a bakery, a market, and no ATMs—the closest ATM is 6 miles (10 km) east in Cahersiveen. On the rough harborfront, a slate memorial to sailors lost at sea from here reads, "In the nets of God may we be gathered."

A 100-yard-long bridge connects Portmagee to gentle Valentia Island, where you'll find the Skellig Experience Centre (on the left at the Valentia end of the bridge). A public parking lot is at the Portmagee end of the bridge, with award-winning WCs (no kidding: look for the proudly displayed "Irish Toilet of the Year 2002 runner-up" plaque).

EATING

These options all line the waterfront (between the pier and the bridge to Valentia Island). **$$$ The Moorings** is a nice restaurant with great seafood caught literally just outside its front door (March-Oct Tue-Sun 18:00-22:00, closed Mon and in winter, reservations a good idea, tel. 066/947-7108, www.moorings.ie). The **$$ Bridge Bar,** next door, does traditional pub grub. Call ahead to check on their traditional music and dance schedule (daily 12:00-22:00, live music Fri and Sun nights, tel. 066/947-7108). The **$$ Fisherman's Bar** is less flashy, with more locals and cheaper prices (daily 10:00-21:00, tel. 066/947-7103).

For picnic supplies, **O'Connell's Market**

Portmagee's harbor

is the only grocery (Mon-Sat 9:00-19:00, Sun 9:30-12:30). **Skellig Mist Bakery** can make basic lunch sandwiches to take on Skellig boat excursions (daily 9:00-17:30, tel. 066/947-7250).

SLEEPING

The first two listings are in town. The last listing is south of Portmagee, on St. Finian's Bay.

$$$ Moorings Guesthouse feels like a small hotel, with 17 rooms, a pub and a fine restaurant downstairs, and the most convenient location in town, 50 yards from the end of the pier (family rooms, tel. 066/947-7108, www.moorings.ie, moorings@iol.ie, Gerard and Patricia Kennedy).

$$$ Portmagee Heights B&B is a modern, solid slate home up above town, renting eight fine rooms (cash only, family rooms, on the road into town, tel. 066/947-7251, www.portmageeheights. com, portmageeheights@gmail.com, hostess Monica Hussey can arrange Skellig boat trips).

$$ Beach Cove B&B offers three comfortable, fresh, and lovingly decorated rooms in splendid isolation four miles south of Portmagee, over lofty Coomanaspic ridge, beside the pretty beach at St. Finian's Bay (100 yards from the Skelligs Chocolate Factory). Charming Bridie O'Connor will arrange a boat trip out to the Skelligs for you. Her adjacent cottage out back has two double rooms, making it ideal for families (sleeps four but no breakfast, tel. 066/947-9301, mobile 087-139-0224, www.stayatbeachcove.com, beachcove@ eircom.net). Bridie's husband, Jack, was the head coach of the Kerry football team until he retired in 2012...making him a very important person in this part of Ireland (Kerry has won more football titles than any other Irish county, three of them with Jack at the helm).

Valentia Island

These two sights are on Valentia Island, across the bridge from Portmagee.

SKELLIG EXPERIENCE CENTRE

Whether or not you're actually sailing to Skellig Michael (described later), this little center (with basic exhibits and a fine 15-minute film) explains it well—both

Daniel O'Connell (1775-1847)

Born in Cahersiveen and elected from Ennis as the first Catholic member of the British Parliament, O'Connell was the hero of Catholic emancipation in Ireland. Educated in France at a time when punitive anti-Catholic laws limited schooling for Irish Catholics at home, he witnessed the carnage of the French Revolution. Upon his return to Ireland, he saw more bloodshed during the futile Rebellion of 1798.

Abhorring all this violence, O'Connell dedicated himself to peacefully gaining equal rights for Catholics in an Ireland dominated by a wealthy Protestant minority. He formed the Catholic Association with a one-penny-per-month membership fee and quickly gained a huge following. Although Catholics weren't allowed to hold office, he ran for election to Parliament anyway and won a seat in 1828. His unwillingness to take the anti-Catholic Oath of Supremacy initially kept him out of Westminster, but the moral force of his victory caused the government to concede Catholic emancipation the following year.

Known as "the Liberator," O'Connell began working toward his next goal—repealing the Act of Union with Britain. When his massive "monster meeting" rallies attracted thousands, his popularity spooked the British authorities, who threw him in jail on trumped-up charges of seditious conspiracy in 1844. He was soon released because his trial was deemed unfair, and perhaps partly because the authorities feared that his incarceration could provoke further unrest. When the Great Potato Famine hit in 1845, some Irish protesters advocated for violent action against the British, which O'Connell had long opposed. He died two years later in Genoa on his way to Rome, but his ideals lived on: His Catholic Association was the model of grassroots organization for the Irish, both in their homeland and in America.

the story of the monks and the natural environment.

Cost and Hours: €5, daily July-Aug 10:00-19:00, May-June and Sept until 18:00, March-April and Oct-Nov until 17:00, closed Dec-Feb, last entry one hour before closing, call ahead outside of peak season as hours may vary, on Valentia Island beside bridge linking it to Portmagee, tel. 066/947-6306, www.skelligexperience.com.

Boat Trips: The Skellig Experience Centre arranges two-hour boat trips, circling both Skellig Michael and Little Skellig (without actually bringing people ashore)—perfect for those who want a close look without the stair climb and vertigo that go with a visit to the island (€30, sailing daily about 14:45 and returning by

17:00, weather permitting, depart from Valentia Island pier, 50 yards below the Skellig Experience Centre).

VALENTIA HERITAGE MUSEUM

The humble Knightstown schoolhouse, built in 1861, houses an equally humble but interesting little museum. You'll learn about tetrapods (those first fish to climb onto land—which locals claim happened here). You'll also follow the long story of the expensive, frustrating, and heroic battle to lay telegraph cable across the Atlantic, which—after some false starts—finally succeeded in 1866, when the largest ship in the world connected this tiny island of Valentia with Newfoundland.

Cost and Hours: €3.50, daily 10:30-17:00, closed Oct-March, tel. 066/947-6985, www.valentiaisland.ie.

Evolution in Ireland: Tetrapods to Telegraphs

Evolution, literacy, communication—Ireland has played a starring role in all three.

Many Irish paleontologists believe that the fossilized tetrapod tracks preserved on Valentia Island are the oldest in Europe. It was here that some of the first fish slithered out of the water on four stubby legs 385 million years ago, onto what would become the Isle of Saints and Scholars. Over time, those tetrapods evolved into the ancestors of today's amphibians, reptiles, birds, mammals...and humans, with the desire to record their thoughts and history, and communicate with others across the miles.

Irish scribes—living in remote outposts like the Skellig Islands just off this coast—kept literate life alive in Europe through the darkest depths of the so-called Dark Ages. In fact, in about the year 800, Charlemagne imported monks from this part of Ireland to be his scribes.

Just more than a thousand years later, in the mid-19th century, Paul Julius Reuter—who provided a financial news service in Europe—knew his pigeons couldn't fly across the Atlantic. So he relied on ships coming from America to drop a news capsule overboard as they rounded this southwest corner of Ireland. His boys would wait in boats with nets to "get the scoop." They say Europe learned of Lincoln's assassination (1865) from a capsule tossed out of a boat here.

The first permanent telegraph cables were laid across the Atlantic from here to Newfoundland, giving the two hemispheres instantaneous electronic communication. Queen Victoria was the first to send a message—greeting American president James Buchanan in 1858. The cable broke more than once, but it was finally permanently secured in 1866. Radio inventor Guglielmo Marconi achieved the first wireless transatlantic communication from this corner of Ireland to America in 1901.

Today, driving under the 21st-century mobile-phone and satellite tower that crowns a hilltop above Valentia Island, while gazing out at the Skellig Islands, a traveler has to marvel at humanity's progress—and the part this remote corner of Ireland played in it.

Rick's Tip: *If you're interested in* **tetrapods,** *the actual "***first footprints***" are a 15-minute drive from the Valentia Heritage Museum, on a bit of rocky shoreline, a 10-minute hike below a parking lot. Get details locally.*

Cahergal and Leacanabuaile Ring Forts

Crowning bluffs in farm country, 2.5 miles (4 km) off the main road at Cahersiveen, these two windy and desolate forts are each different and worth a look. Just beyond the Cahersiveen town church at the tourist office, turn left, cross the narrow bridge, turn left again, and follow signs to the ancient forts—you'll see the huge stone structures in the distance. You'll hike 10 minutes from the tiny parking lot (free, always open, no museum). Both forts are roughly 100 yards off the road (uphill on the right) and are 200 yards from each other. For details, see "The Ring Forts of Kerry" sidebar, earlier.

Leacanabuaile ring fort

SKELLIG MICHAEL

A trip to this jagged, isolated pyramid—the Holy Grail of Irish monastic island settlements—rates as a truly memorable ▲▲▲ experience. After visiting Skellig Michael a hundred years ago, Nobel Prize-winning Irish playwright George Bernard Shaw called it "the most fantastic and impossible rock in the world."

Rising seven miles offshore, the Skelligs (Irish for "splinter") are two gigantic slate-and-sandstone rocks crouched aggressively on the ocean horizon. The larger of the two, Skellig Michael, is more than 700 feet tall and a mile around, with a tiny cluster of abandoned beehive huts clinging near its summit like stubborn barnacles. The smaller island, Little Skellig, is home to a huge colony of gannet birds (like large, graceful seagulls with six-foot wingspans), protected by law from visitors setting foot onshore.

Skellig Michael (dedicated to the archangel) was first inhabited by sixth-century Christian monks. Inspired by earlier hermit-monks in the Egyptian desert, they sought the purity of isolation to get closer to God. Neither Viking raids nor winter storms could dislodge them, as they patiently built a half-dozen small, stone, igloo-like dwellings and a couple of tiny oratories. Their remote cliff terrace perch is still connected to the sea 600 feet below by an amazing series of rock stairs. Viking Olav Trygvasson, who later became king of Norway and introduced Christianity to his country, was baptized here in 993.

Chiseling the most rudimentary life from solid rock, the monks lived a harsh, lonely, disciplined existence here, their colony surviving for more than 500 years. They collected rainwater in cisterns and lived off fish and birds. To supplement their meager existence, they traded bird eggs and feathers with passing boats for cereals, candles, and animal hides (used for clothing and for copying scripture). They finally moved their holy community ashore to Ballinskelligs in the early 1100s. But Christian pilgrims continued to visit Skellig Michael for centuries as penance...edging out onto a ledge to kiss a stone cross that has since toppled into the ocean.

In 2014, the ruggedly exotic Skellig Michael was used as a filming location for the final scenes of *Star Wars: The Force Awakens.* Controversy soon arose: Environmental groups voiced concerns about the impact on the island's fragile ecosystem, especially native seabirds who nested here. Disney scrapped plans for filming the next installment, *Star Wars VIII,* on the island. Instead it built its own version of the location at Sybil Head on the Dingle Peninsula. Expect a steady stream of *Star Wars* tourists at both filming locations. *Go mbeidh an Fórsa leat!* (May the Force be with you!)

Getting There

Boat trips cost €60 and officially run to Skellig Michael daily from mid-May to September, but the schedule is heavily dependent on weather conditions.

Boats normally depart Portmagee at 10:00 (depending on tides), sail for an hour, leave you on the island from roughly 11:00 until 13:30, and get you back into Portmagee by 14:30 (with plenty of time to drive on to Dingle). Fifteen small boats have permits to land on Skellig Michael. Each boat can carry a dozen passengers. This limits the number of daily visitors and minimizes the impact on the sensitive island ecosystem.

To book a trip, call as soon as you know your dates—these trips can fill up weeks in advance. Contact Patrick Murphy (tel. 066/947-7156, mobile 087-234-2168, www.esatclear.ie/~skelligsrock, murphy seacruise@esatclear.ie), Joe Roddy (mobile 087-284-4460), or Brendan Casey (tel. 066/947-2437, mobile 087-228-7519).

Bring your camera, a sandwich lunch (easy to buy at the recommended Skellig Mist Bakery in Portmagee), water, sunscreen, rain gear, hiking shoes, and your sense of wonder.

Planning Tips: Your best bet is to reserve a room near Portmagee or St. Finian's Bay—whichever best fits your

Skellig Michael

itinerary. Then call a few days in advance to make a boat reservation. Keep your fingers crossed for good weather, then contact the boat operator on the morning of departure to get the final word.

Visiting Skellig Michael

Since you'll have only 2.5 hours to explore the island, begin by climbing the seemingly unending series of stone stairs to the monastic ruins (600 vertical feet of uneven steps with no handrails). Save most of your photographing for the way down. Photo-bugs who linger too long below risk missing the enlightening 20-minute free talk among the beehive huts, given by guides who camp on the island from April through October. Afterward, poke your head into some of the huts and try to imagine the dark, damp, and devoted life of a monk here more than 1,000 years ago. After rambling through the ruins, you can give in to the puffin-spotting photo frenzy as you wander back down the stairs.

The two lighthouses on the far side of the island are now automated, and access to them has been blocked off. There are no WCs or modern shelters of any kind on Skellig Michael.

If you visit between May and early August, you'll be surrounded by fearless rainbow-beaked puffins, which nest here in underground burrows. Their bizarre swallowed cooing sounds like a distant chainsaw. These portly little birds live off fish, and divers have reported seeing them 20 feet underwater in pursuit of their prey.

Your return boat journey usually includes a pass near Little Skellig, which looms like an iceberg with a white coat of guano—courtesy of the 20,000 gannets that circle overhead like feathered confetti. These large birds suddenly morph into sleek darts when pursuing a fish, piercing the water from more than 100 feet above. You're also likely to get a glimpse of gray seals lazing on rocks near the water's edge.

Dingle Town
& Peninsula

For over 35 years, my Irish dreams have been set here on the sparse but lush Dingle Peninsula. This westernmost tip of Ireland offers just the right mix of far-and-away beauty, isolated wanders, and ancient wonders—all within convenient reach of its main town. Dingle town is just large enough to have all the necessary tourist services and the steady nocturnal beat of Ireland's best traditional music scene.

Locals are fond of saying, "The next parish over is Boston." When I asked a local if he was born here, he thought for a second and said, "No, it was about six miles down the road." I asked his friend if he'd lived here all his life. He said, "Not yet."

Dingle feels so traditionally Irish because it's part of the Gaeltacht, a region where the government subsidizes the survival of the Irish language and culture. While English is always there, the signs, chitchat, and songs come in Irish Gaelic. Children carry Gaelic footballs to class and the local preschool brags it's "ALL Gaelic."

Despite growing more touristy over the years, Dingle's charms are resilient. As the older generation slows down, a new generation of entrepreneurs is giving Dingle fresh vitality.

DINGLE TOWN & PENINSULA IN 2 DAYS

Take one day to sightsee and relax in Dingle town. Take my self-guided walks (through town and to the harbor), marvel at the chapel's stained-glass windows, have an excellent dinner, and enjoy trad music in the pubs.

On your second day, explore the 30-mile loop around the peninsula by bike or car (see route specifics on page 188). By spending at least two nights, you'll feel more like a local on your second evening in the pubs. It's not uncommon to find Americans slowing way down in Dingle.

DINGLE TOWN

Of the peninsula's 10,000 residents, about 2,000 live in Dingle town (Daingean Ui Chuis). Its few streets, lined with ramshackle but gaily painted shops and pubs, run up from a rain-stung harbor sheltering fishing boats and leisure sailboats. Traditionally, the buildings were drab gray or whitewashed, but Ireland's "Tidy Town" competition a few decades back prompted everyone to paint their buildings in playful pastels.

The courthouse (1832) is open one day per month. The judge does his best to wrap up business within a few hours. During the day, you'll see teenagers—already working on ruddy, beer-glow

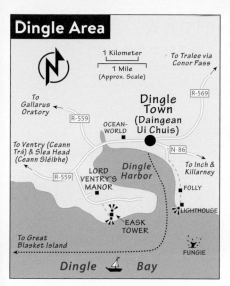

Dingle Area

1 Kilometer

1 Mile
(Approx. Scale)

To Tralee via
Conor Pass

R-569

To
Gallarus
Oratory

R-559

**Dingle
Town
(Daingean
Ui Chuis)**

OCEAN-
WORLD

N-86

To Ventry (Ceann
Trá) & Slea Head
(Ceann Sléibhe)

R-559

LORD
VENTRY'S
MANOR

*Dingle
Harbor*

To Inch &
Killarney

FOLLY

LIGHTHOUSE

EASK
TOWER

To Great
Blasket Island

FUNGIE

Dingle ⛵ *Bay*

cheeks—roll kegs up the streets and into the pubs in preparation for another night of music and *craic* (fun conversation and atmosphere). It's a friendly town.

Rick's Tip: *Dingle's activity level ramps up in late April, peaks through July and August, and slows by late September. It's smart to* **book your lodging** *as soon as you know your dates.*

Orientation

Dingle—extremely comfortable on foot—hangs on a medieval grid of streets between the harbor (where the bus to Tralee, with the nearest train station, stops) and Main Street (three blocks inland). Nothing in town is more than a 10-minute walk away. Street numbers are rarely used. Everyone knows each other, and people on the street are fine sources of information.

Tourist Information: The TI has a great town map (free) and a staff who know the town, but less about the rest of the peninsula (Mon-Sat 9:00-13:00 & 13:30-17:00, generally closed Sun, shorter hours off-season, on Strand Street by the water, tel. 066/915-1188).

The Mountain Man, a hiking shop run by local guide Adrian Curran, is a clearing-house for information on outdoor activities, recreation, and peninsula tours (daily 9:00-18:00, June-mid-Sept until 21:00, just off harbor at Strand Street, tel. 066/915-2400, www.themountainmanshop.com).

Farmers Market: On Fridays, vendors sell their fresh produce, homemade marmalade, and homespun crafts (mid-April-mid-Oct 9:00-15:00, in a small parking lot across the street from SuperValu grocery store).

Money: Two banks with ATMs are staggered across from each other on Main Street. Expect to use cash (rather than credit cards) to pay for most peninsula activities.

Laundry: Dingle Cleaners is convenient (Mon-Sat 9:00-18:00, closed Sun, beside Moran's Market and gas station, tel. 066/915-0680); there's no self-service laundry in Dingle.

Bike Rental: Try **Paddy's Bike Hire,** with reliably maintained 21-speed hybrids (€15/day, includes helmet and lock, daily 9:00-19:00, must leave driver's license, directly across Dykegate from An Café Liteartha, tel. 066/915-2311). **Dingle Electric Bike Experience** rents less-tiring electric bikes as well as 24-speed hybrid bikes, and can deliver them to your hotel and pick them up later (electric-€40/day, hybrid-€20/day, tel. 086/084-8378, www.dinglebikes.com).

Taxi: Try **Diarmuid Begley** (mobile 087-250-4767), Sean with **S.O.L. Cabs** in Dingle (mobile 087-660-2323), or

DINGLE TOWN & PENINSULA AT A GLANCE

In Dingle Town

▲▲**Harry Clark Windows at Díseart Institute** Glorious display of Art Nouveau-style stained glass craftsmanship, adorning a former convent chapel. **Hours:** Mon-Fri 9:00-17:00, Sat and Sun 10:00-15:00. See page 175.

▲**Fungie** Friendly, honest-to-goodness dolphin in the harbor and the star of one-hour sightseeing cruises. **Hours:** Cruises run daily, depending on demand. See page 177.

▲**Oceanworld** Earnest presentation of mostly local sea life that makes a good, kid-friendly, rainy-day retreat. **Hours:** Daily 10:00-18:00, shorter hours off-season. See page 177.

▲**Bike and Hike to Eask Tower** Moderate bike ride followed by steep schlep up to remote Eask Tower and stunning 360-degree views. See page 178.

The Dingle Peninsula

▲▲▲**Dingle Driving Tour** A compact 30-mile road takes the better part of a day to link the most intimate historic sites and memorable coastal views in Ireland. See page 188.

▲▲**Great Blasket Centre** Insightful tribute to the storytelling skill and hardscrabble fishing life of a lost culture that inhabited the Blasket Islands up until the early 1950s. **Hours:** Daily 10:00-18:00, closed Nov-Easter. See page 198.

What's in a Name?

Linguistic politics have stirred up a controversy over the name of this town and peninsula. As a Gaeltacht, the entire region gets subsidies from the government, which supports the survival of the traditional Irish culture and language. A precondition of this financial support is that towns use their Irish Gaelic name. In 2005, well-meaning government officials in Dublin dictated that Dingle convert its name to the Irish Gaelic "An Daingean" ("on DANG-un"). But as it turns out, four separate Irish towns are named Daingean ("fortress"), so in 2012 Dingle's name was changed again—to Daingean Ui Chuis ("Fortress of the Husseys," a Norman founding family back in the late Middle Ages).

The town has resisted these dictates from Dublin. Dingle has become so wealthy from the tourist trade that it sees its famous name as a trademark, and doesn't want to become "the cute tourist town with the unpronounceable name, formerly known as Dingle." While official road signs identify the town only as *Daingean Ui Chuis*, you'll notice that many have been modified by a crude *DINGLE*, stenciled by stubborn locals. In town, most businesses, all tourist information, and nearly all people—locals and tourists alike—refer to it as Dingle.

For the sake of clarity, in this book I follow the predominant convention: Dingle instead of Daingean Ui Chuis. But for ease of navigation, I've also generally included the place's Irish name in parentheses. For a list of these bilingual place names, see the sidebar on page 187.

Tom Kearney out in Dunquin (mobile 087-933-2264).

Tours: Sciúird Archaeology Tours, worth ▲▲▲, are offered by a father-son team with passion for sharing the long history of Dingle Peninsula. Stops include beehive huts, the Reasc Monastery, the Gallarus Oratory, and Kilmalkedar Church—but not the Great Blasket Centre (€30, 3 hours, minibus departs daily at 10:00 from the Fungie statue at the TI or at your B&B by request, book by email as soon as you know your dates, tel. 066/915-1606, www.collinskirrary.com/#sciuird, collinskirrary@eircom.net).

Dingle Slea Head Tours does single- and multiday private driving tours of the region from Dingle (www.dinglesleahead tours.com for details). They also run Slea Head tours daily at 10:00 and 14:00 (3 hours, €30, minimum 4 people).

Claire Galvin & Kevin O'Shea take fit hikers (with proper footwear) into the scenic back country of the Dingle Peninsula. Routes can be tailored to your interests (tel. 087/624-7230 or 087/790-3950, www.celticnature.com).

Boat Tours: Dingle Dolphin Boat Tours offers a one-hour bay cruise with a guarantee to see Fungie the dolphin (€16, at least 4 times daily in summer), a 2.5-hour "Sea Safari" focusing on coastal wildlife (€45, daily at 12:30), and a day trip to Great Blasket Island (€55, must book ahead, schedules vary with weather and tides, office in back corner of TI beside Fungie sculpture, tel. 066/915-6422, www. dingledolphin.com).

Dingle Bay Charters covers a similar line-up at competitive prices. Their office is at base of the large Dingle Marina jetty—not to be confused with the shorter commercial fishing pier (tel. 066/915-1344, mobile 087/672-6100, https:// dingleboattours.com).

Blasket Island Ferry shuttles visitors from Dunquin Pier at the far west end of the peninsula to Great Blasket Island

Dingle Town Walk

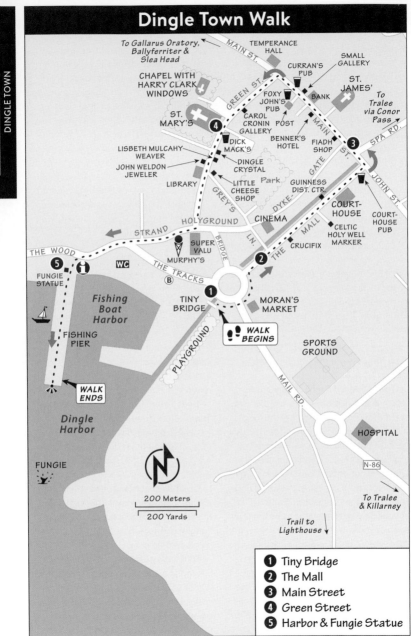

To Gallarus Oratory,
Ballyferriter &
Slea Head

MAIN ST.

TEMPERANCE
HALL

SMALL
GALLERY

CURRAN'S
PUB

GREEN ST.

CHAPEL WITH
HARRY CLARK
WINDOWS

ST.
JAMES'

FOXY
JOHN'S
PUB

BANK

To
Tralee
via Conor
Pass

ST.
MARY'S

CAROL
CRONIN
GALLERY

POST

4

BENNER'S
HOTEL

MAIN ST.

SPA RD.

3

DICK
MACK'S

FIADH
SHOP

LISBETH MULCAHY
WEAVER

DINGLE
CRYSTAL

GATE

JOHN ST.

JOHN WELDON
JEWELER

Park

GUINNESS
DIST. CTR.

LIBRARY

LITTLE
CHEESE
SHOP

GREY'S

HOLYGROUND

CINEMA

DYKE LN.

COURT-
HOUSE

COURT-
HOUSE
PUB

STRAND

THE MALL

CELTIC
HOLY WELL
MARKER

CRUCIFIX

THE WOOD

SUPER
VALU

MURPHY'S

BRIDGE

2

FUNGIE
STATUE

5

WC

THE TRACKS

B

1

MORAN'S
MARKET

Fishing
Boat
Harbor

TINY
BRIDGE

WALK
BEGINS

SPORTS
GROUND

FISHING
PIER

PLAYGROUND

WALK
ENDS

Dingle
Harbor

MAIL RD.

HOSPITAL

FUNGIE

N

N-86

200 Meters

200 Yards

To Tralee
& Killarney

Trail to
Lighthouse

1 Tiny Bridge
2 The Mall
3 Main Street
4 Green Street
5 Harbor & Fungie Statue

(€30, kids–€15, hourly starting at 10:00, weather permitting, advanced booking recommended, tel. 066/915-6422, mobile 085/775-1045, www.blasketisland.com).

● Dingle Town Walk

• *Start just beyond the "old roundabout" and beside the playground at the...*

❶ **Tiny Bridge:** This pedestrian bridge, with its black-and-gold wrought-iron railing, was part of the original train line coming into Dingle. The train once picked up fish in Dingle; its operators boasted that the cargo would be in London markets within 24 hours. The narrow-gauge tracks ran right along the harborfront.

All the land beyond the old buildings you see today has been reclaimed from the sea. Look inland and find the building on the left with the slate siding (the back wall of O'Flaherty's pub), facing the worst storms coming in from the sea. This was the typical design for 19th-century weatherproofing.

• *From here, cross the roundabout and walk up the big street called...*

❷ **The Mall:** After about 20 yards, two stubby red-brick pillars mark the entry to the police station. These pillars are all that remain of the 19th-century British Constabulary, which afforded a kind of Green Zone for British troops when they tried to subdue the local insurgents here. It was burned down in 1922, during the Civil War; the present building dates from 1938. Today, in a small peaceful town like Dingle, the police department is virtually unarmed.

The big white crucifix across the street and 50 yards up The Mall is a memorial to heroes who died in the 1916 Rising. Note that it says in the people's language, "For honor and glory of Ireland, 1916 to 19___." The date is unfinished until Ireland is united and free.

• *On the same side of the street, just past the* Russels B&B *sign, take 15 paces up the B&B's driveway to see an old stone etched with a cross sitting atop the wall (on the right).*

This marks the site of a former Celtic holy well, a sacred spot for people here 2,000 years ago. Now, cross over the street, and continue walking uphill along the delightful gurgling stream.

Fifty yards farther up is another much-honored spot: the distribution center for Guinness (unmarked). From this warehouse with its rusty, red, corrugated second-floor, pubs throughout the peninsula are stocked with beer.

Across the street is the blocky, riot-resistant 19th-century courthouse, made of gray stone. Once a symbol of British oppression, today it's a laid-back place where the roving County Kerry judge drops by to adjudicate cases on the last Friday of each month (mostly domestic disputes and drunken disorderliness). Next door, with the blue walls, is the popular Court House Pub (recommended for trad music).

• *Continue to the big intersection and pause at the small bridge over a little stream.*

Notice the colors. A century ago, all these buildings were just shades of black and white. Their exteriors were originally exposed stonework (like the houses upstream). Then in the 1920s came the plaster (notice the bumps on the yellow Small Bridge Pub), and in the 1970s— cheery pastels (along with modern tourism). Now head left into the commercial heart of the town on...

❸ **Main Street:** First, find the little Fiadh Handwoven Design Shop, on the left just past the first little corner, across from Ashes Bar. Fiadh (pronounced Fia) Durham creates locally inspired contemporary designs at her loom and welcomes curious visitors (check out her fine scarves).

A few steps farther up on the left is Benner's Hotel. This was Dingle's first hotel, where the old Tralee stagecoach route ended. Note the surviving Georgian facade and door.

Across the street, up a short gravel alley, is St. James' Church. Since the 13th century, a church has stood here (just inside the medieval wall, closed to public during the day). Today, it's Anglican on Sundays and filled with great traditional music several nights a week.

• *Farther uphill on the same side is a co-op gallery.*

The Small Gallery (An Gailearai Beagg) is the cute little showroom of the West Kerry Craft Guild, a collective of 14 local artists and artisans who each staff the shop two days a month to show off their work.

Facing each other just uphill are two of Dingle's most unapologetically traditional drinking holes, Curran's and Foxy John's. You're welcome to pop in and look around, though you'll feel a little more welcome if you order a drink (a small beer is "a glass" or half-pint).

James Curran runs Curran's Pub out of what was once his grandma's general store. On the last Saturday of every month—when farm families were in town for the market—the wives would pick up their basics here, ordering butter, tea, sugar, jams, and salted meat through the little window. (Just about everything else they consumed was home-grown.) The same shelves grandma used for jams

and socks today stock beer and whiskey. Notice the "snug" in front. Until the 1950s, women weren't really welcome to drink in Irish pubs, but they could discreetly nurse a sherry in the "snug" while their men enjoyed the main room.

Foxy John's Pub, across the street, is still a working hardware store. Any time of day, you can order a bag of nails with your pint. Notice the back room; while pubs historically have had a legal "last call" at 11:30, the action would often migrate to the back room after the front door was locked.

• *Walk uphill to the Green Street intersection.*

On your right, notice the big Temperance Hall, which dates back to a 19th century church-promoted movement that attempted to cut down the consumption of alcohol. To this day Ireland has a serious alcohol problem behind the happy veneer of all this pub fun. You'll see pickled old timers who spend every morning of their last years on the same barstool. Today the Temperance Hall is a meeting place for AA groups, youth clubs, scouts, and other various social and support groups.

• *Now head downhill opposite the Temperance Hall to discover...*

Courthouse Pub

Harry Clark windows

Medieval Dingle

The wet sod of Dingle is soaked with medieval history. In the dimmest depths of the Dark Ages, peace-loving, bookish monks fled the chaos of the Continent and its barbarian raids. They sailed to the drizzly fringe of the known world—to places like Dingle. These monks kept literacy alive in Europe, and later provided scribes to Charlemagne, who ruled much of central Europe in the year 800.

It was from this peninsula that the semi-mythical explorer-monk St. Brendan is said to have set sail in the sixth century in search of a legendary western paradise. Some think he beat Columbus to North America by almost a thousand years.

Dingle was a busy seaport in the late Middle Ages. Dingle and Tralee were the only walled towns in Kerry. Castles stood at the low and high ends of Dingle's Main Street, protecting the Normans from the angry and dispossessed Irish outside. Dingle was a gateway to northern Spain—a three-day sail due south. Many 14th- and 15th-century pilgrims left from Dingle for the revered Spanish church in Santiago de Compostela, thought to house the bones of St. James.

❹ **Green Street:** Green Street is a reminder that 16th-century Dingle traded with Spain and was a port of embarkation for pilgrims on their way to Santiago de Compostela. A few steps down Green Street on the left, look above Kanon's Korner Fish shop to find a stone carved with the year "1586"—perhaps a remnant of that Spanish influence.

Farther along on the left, look for the Carol Cronin Gallery, an art gallery that clearly loves the sea. Popping in, you're likely to meet Carol at work.

Down the street on the right, pop into the beautiful, modern St. Mary's Church.

The former convent behind it shows off its delightful Harry Clark stained-glass windows—the single most important cultural sight in Dingle. Don't miss them (described later, under "Sights in Dingle"). Then, wander in the backyard to check out the tranquil nuns' cemetery, with its white-painted iron crosses huddling peacefully together under a big copper beech tree.

Across from St. Mary's (hence the nickname "the last pew") is Dick Mack's Pub, another traditional pub well worth a peek, even for nondrinkers. This was once a tiny leather shop that expanded into a pub at night. The pub was established in 1899 by great-grandpa Mack (master of the westernmost train station in Europe), whose mission was to provide "liquid replenishment" to travelers. Today, Dick Mack retains its old leather-shop ambience. In fact it's popular for hand-crafted belts. (Their motto: "Step up and get waisted.")

Green Street continues downhill past inviting boutiques, cafés, and estate agents (showing the current price of houses here). Many fine Dingle shops show off work by local artisans.

Dingle Crystal features Sean Daly and his Waterford-trained crystal-cutting skills. Sean prides himself on the deep, sharp cuts in his designs—see the video of him at work.

A few steps farther on is the shop of Lisbeth Mulcahy Weaver, filled with traditional but stylish woven woolen wear. It's also the Dingle sales outlet of her husband, a well-known potter from Slea Head. Across the street is John Weldon Jewellers—ideal for those interested in hand-crafted gold and silver with Celtic designs.
• *At the corner of Green Street and Grey's Lane, turn left and follow your nose.*

The little cheese shop is a foodie shrine playfully governed by Maja Binder, a German who trained in Switzerland. Poke your head inside, even if only for a whiff of her various traditional handmade cheeses.

Back on Green Street you'll see Dingle's library, a gift from the Carnegie Foundation, with a small exhibit about local

Dingle Peninsula

Atlantic Ocean

3 Kilometers
3 Miles

The Seven Hogs

Rough Point

Brandon Head

Brandon Bay

Mt. Brandon

See Dingle Peninsula Loop Drive map

Tiduff

Castlegregory

Cloghane   Ballyduff

CONOR PASS

Three Sisters

GALLARUS ORATORY

D I N G L E   P E N I N S U L A
(A N   D A I N G E A N)

Sybil Head

Ballyferriter
(Baile an Fheirtearaigh)

See Dingle Area map

Dingle
(Daingean Uí Chuis)

Lispole
(Lios Póil)

Annascaul

N-86   South Pole Inn

Clogher Head

Ventry
(Ceann Trá)

PUICIN
WEDGE
TOMB

Inishtooskert

Dunquin
(Dún Chaoin)

MINARD CASTLE

Slea Head
(Ceann Sléibhe)

Dingle Bay

Great Blasket Island
(An Blascaod Mór)

---

patriot Thomas Ashe and the Blasket Island writers. The best historic photos you'll find in town decorate the library's walls with images of 19th-century Dingle.

• *At the bottom of Green Street, take a right and head (past the best ice cream in town—at recommended Murphy's) to...*

❺ The Harbor and the Fungie Statue: The harbor was built in 1992 on reclaimed land. The string of old stone shops facing the harbor was the loading station for the railway that hauled the fish from Dingle until 1953. Dingle's fishing industry survives, but it's an international endeavor. Most fishing boats that now ply these waters are Spanish, French, and Basque. Rather than going home with their catch, they offload their fish (mackerel, tuna, cod, herring, and prawns) onto trucks that lumber directly to their homelands.

Enjoy the kid-friendly scene around the bronze statue of Dingle's beloved dolphin, Fungie. From the Fungie statue, look straight out. Dead ahead on the dis-

tant hill is the Eask Tower. Farther to the right, the big, yellow 18th-century manor house across the harbor was owned by Lord Ventry, the dominant English landlord of the time, and is now a school. Even farther to the right, the pyramid in the distance is Mount Eagle, marking Slea Head at the end of Dingle Peninsula. The building to the left with two big basement doors is a boathouse. At high tide, boats would float in, and be dry-docked at low

Dingle's harbor

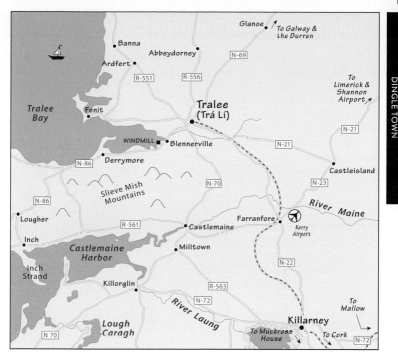

tide for repairs. Beyond the boathouse and the harbor wall is the mouth of Dingle Harbor, playful Fungie, and the open sea.

Sights

▲▲HARRY CLARK WINDOWS AT THE DÍSEART INSTITUTE

Just behind Dingle's St. Mary's Church stands the former Presentation Sisters' convent, now home to the Díseart (dee-SHIRT, rhymes with "T-shirt") Institute of Education and Celtic Culture. The sisters of this order, who came to Dingle in 1829 to educate local girls, worked heroically during the famine. The convent contains the beautiful Neo-Gothic Chapel of the Sacred Heart, built in 1884. During Mass in the chapel, the Mother Superior would sit in the covered stall in the rear, while the sisters—filling the carved stalls—chanted in response.

The chapel was graced in 1922 with 12 windows—the work of Ireland's top stained-glass man, Harry Clark. Long

appreciated only by the sisters, these special windows, which show six scenes from the life of Christ, are now open to the public. The convent has become a center for sharing Christian Celtic culture and spirituality.

Cost and Hours: €3, Mon-Fri 9:00-17:00, Sat and Sun 10:00-15:00, tel. 066/915-2476, www.diseart.ie.

Visiting the Chapel: Stop at the reception room to pay and pick up a loaner description with a self-guided walk. While Harry Clark's windows are the big draw, it's also worth noting the recently painted, charming art of Coloradan Eleanor Yates, especially her *Last Supper,* which pictures Dingle Harbor out the window. Upstairs is the chapel with the beloved stained glass of Harry Clark. While the windows behind the altar are Victorian, Clark's early-20th-century windows ring the chapel with six easy-to-read scenes. Clockwise from the back entrance, they are the visit of the Magi, the Baptism of Jesus, "Let the

Tom Crean, Unsung Antarctic Explorer

Kerrymen are a hardy lot, and probably none more so than Antarctic explorer Thomas Crean. In 1901, Crean volunteered to join the crew of the RSS *Discovery*. Onboard were Captain Robert Falcon Scott and other soon-to-be famous explorers, including Ernest Shackleton. Their mission: to be the first men to reach the South Pole.

The effort required pulling sleds laden with supplies across miles of ice in extreme conditions. Crean quickly gained his mates' respect for his hard work, calm presence, and cheerful (if tuneless) singing. The *Discovery* Expedition pushed the boundaries of Antarctic exploration, but didn't reach the pole (Britain's second attempt, in 1909 under Shackleton, got much closer before also turning back).

Determined to try again, Scott handpicked Crean for the crew for the *Terra Nova* Expedition (1910-1913). Early on, Crean saved some expedition members stranded on a drifting ice floe—encircled by orcas—by leaping between floating chunks of ice, then scaling an ice wall to get help. Later, Crean and two others were the last support team ordered to turn back as Scott made the final push to the pole. Having come so close, the otherwise unshakable Crean wept at the news. Near the end of the 730-mile return trip, Crean's two mates, sick and freezing, could go no farther. Exhausted and provisioned with only three cookies and two sticks of chocolate, Crean made a nonstop, solo, 35-mile march through a blizzard to reach help, saving his mates' lives. (Though Scott's party did reach the pole, a Norwegian team led by Roald Amundsen beat them to it—by a month; Scott and his men didn't survive the trip back.)

Crean's most famous act of heroism took place on his third and final polar expedition (1914-1917), led by Shackleton. Their ship, the *Endurance*, was crushed by ice, marooning the crew on Elephant Island. Hoping to find help at a whaling station, Shackleton, Crean, and four others sailed a modified open lifeboat 800 miles in 17 days to South Georgia Island. There they were forced to hike across the rugged, unexplored interior to reach the station on the other side. A ship was sent to rescue the exhausted and malnourished crew, all of whom had miraculously survived the 18-month ordeal.

Crean never did reach the South Pole himself, turning down Shackleton's request to join him on his next (and final) trek. But Crean distinguished himself as a hero among explorers—who named both a mountain and a glacier after him in Antarctica—and was honored by King George V. In 1920, he retired from the navy, returned to County Kerry. He married, bought a pub, and stashed his medals away, never again speaking of his experiences.

Fungie, Dingle's resident dolphin

little children come to me," the Sermon on the Mount, the Agony in the Garden, and Jesus appearing to Mary Magdalene. Each face is lively and animated in the imaginative, devout, neo-medieval, and fun-loving style of Harry Clark.

▲FUNGIE

In 1983, a bottlenose dolphin moved into Dingle Harbor and became a local celebrity. Fungie (FOON-ghee) is now the darling of the town's tourist trade and one reason you'll find so many tour buses parked along the harbor. A recent study theorizes that he may be one of a half-dozen dolphins released from "Dolphinariums" (under pressure from animal rights activists) on the southern coast of Britain. This would account for Fungie's loner ways and comfort around humans.

Hardy little tour boats thrive by baiting passengers with the chance of an up-close Fungie encounter, then motoring out to the mouth of the harbor, where they troll around looking for him (see page 169). You don't pay unless you see the dolphin. Fungie is slowing down a bit as he ages and locals are gearing up for a day

when tour boats will have to settle for puffins. Still, if there's a group of boats at the mouth of the harbor, Fungie always comes out to play.

▲OCEANWORLD

This aquarium offers a little peninsula history, 300 different species of fish in thoughtfully described tanks, and the easiest way to see Fungie the dolphin: on video. The aquarium's mission is to teach, and you're welcome to ask questions.

Cost and Hours: €14, €38-44 for families with children (4-6 people), daily 10:00-18:00, shorter hours off-season, cafeteria, just past harbor on west edge of town, tel. 066/915-2111, www.dingle-oceanworld.ie.

DINGLE DISTILLERY TOUR

The hometown distillery offers one-hour tours of their operation that include two sample hard drinks—a whiskey and a gin or vodka. This informal tour, competing with loud warehouse machinery, is a possible rainy-day option of interest to die-hard connoisseurs unable to visit more established Irish distilleries. The distillery is a 20-minute walk from town, just over the bridge on the Slea Head Drive

(€15, tours run daily in season at 12:00, 14:00 and 16:00, tel. 086/777-5551, www. dingledistillery.ie).

Experiences
▲Bike and Hike to Eask Tower

The bike-and-hike trek to Eask Tower, totaling about 10 miles round-trip, is a good compromise for those wanting more exercise than a mellow harbor walk. (Or you can skip the bike and drive to the trailhead.)

Rent a bike in town and pedal west past the aquarium, going left at the round-about that takes you over the bridge onto R-559 toward Slea Head. After almost two miles, turn left at the brown sign to *Holden's Leather Workshop*. A narrow leafy lane leads another two miles or so to a hut on the right marked *Eask Tower* (the tower looms on the bare hill above). Pay the €2 trail fee at the hut (if unattended, feed the honor box) and hike about a mile straight up the hill. It's a steep trail. You'll zigzag around sheep and tiptoe over their droppings. You'll also need to navigate through (possibly climb) a couple of waist-high, metal-rung gates. After 45 minutes, you'll

reach the stone signal tower on the crown of the hill. Enjoy fantastic views of Dingle town (to the north) and Dingle Bay with the Iveragh Peninsula (home of the Ring of Kerry to the south). Spot the two jagged Skellig Islands off the distant tip of the Iveragh Peninsula.

Horseback Riding

Dingle Horse Riding takes out beginners for a 1.5-hour trail ride and more experienced riders on longer excursions (call ahead to book, follow Main Street out of Dingle, turn right at sign, tel. 066/915-2199, www.dinglehorseriding.com). Long's Horseriding Centre is farther out on the peninsula just past Ventry (sign on right)—an easy stop for drivers doing the Slea Head Loop (beach rides and beach-and-mountain trail rides, call to book, tel. 066/915-9034, www.longsriding.com). In either case, mountain rides are only for advanced riders, and all horses come with English-style saddles (no horn to hang on to).

Golf

Dingle Pitch & Putt's scenic 18 holes offer a relaxing diversion for average duffers on

Biking outside Dingle Town

Eask Tower

a green headland overlooking the harbor. They also have a "crazy course"—miniature golf (€7, includes gear, daily 10:00-19:00, closed Nov-March; located behind Milltown House about a 25-minute walk out of town—after crossing over the bridge, take the first left and then the first right; tel. 066/915-2020).

Located nine miles west of Dingle town, near the wildly scenic tip of the Dingle Peninsula and the town of Ballyferriter, Ceann Sibéal/Dingle Links offers a round of golf in a hard-to-beat setting (€70-85 July-Aug, fee reduced rest of year, open daily till dusk, Ballyferriter, tel. 066/915-6255, www.dinglelinks.com).

Nightlife

▲▲▲MUSIC IN DINGLE PUBS

Traditional pub music is Dingle town's best experience. Even if you're not into pubs, take an afternoon nap and then give these an evening whirl. Dingle is renowned among traditional musicians as an ideal place to perform. The town has piles of pubs that feature music most nights, and there's never a cover charge—just buy a beer. The scene is a decent mix of locals, Americans, Brits, and Germans. Music normally starts at 21:30-ish, and the last call for drinks is at "half eleven" (23:30), sometimes later on weekends. For a seat near the music, arrive early. If the place is chockablock with people, power in and find breathing room in the back. By midnight, the door is usually closed and the chairs are stacked.

Make a point to wander the town and follow your ear. Smaller pubs may feel a bit foreboding to a tourist, but rest assured that people—locals as well as travelers—are out for the *craic*. Irish culture is very accessible in the pubs; they're like highly interactive museums waiting to be explored. If you sit at a table, you'll be left alone. But stand or sit at the bar and you'll be engulfed in conversation with new friends. Have a glass in an empty, no-name pub and chat up the publican. Pubs are no longer smoky, but can be stuffy and hot, so leave your coat at home. I know it's going to be a great trad music session when my eyeglasses steam up as I enter.

Enjoying the pub experience

Dick Mack's Pub

Dingle Pub Crawl: The best place to start a pub crawl is at **O'Flaherty's,** the first music pub in Dingle, located on Holy-ground street. Quietly intense owner Fergus O'Flaherty sings and plays a half-dozen different instruments during almost nightly traditional-music sessions. His domain is dripping in old-time photos and town memorabilia—it's unpretentious, cluttered fun.

Moving up Strand Street, find **John Benny's.** Its dependably good tradition-al-music sessions come with John him-self joining in on accordion when he's not pouring pints. **Paddy Bawn Brosnan's Pub** (also on the Strand) brags no music and no food—just beer and sports. If any game's on TV—especially Gaelic football or hurling—you can watch it here with the locals.

Then head up Green Street. **Dick Mack's,** across from the church, is nick-named "the last pew." Once a leather shop, today the pub sells only drinks, with several rooms, a fine snug, ample beer choices, and a fascinating ambience.

Green Street climbs to Main Street, where two more Dick Mack-type places are filled with locals deep in conversation (but no music): **Foxy John's** and **Curran's.** For more on each of these (and Dick Mack), see the town walk, earlier.

Wander down Main Street. The **Din-gle Pub** seems designed for John Den-ver and Irish Rovers fans. It's well estab-lished as *the* place for folk-ballad singing rather than the churning traditional beat of an Irish folk session. Just downhill, **The Mighty Session** is the roughest scene in town—it may not offer the warm welcome you've come to expect in Irish pubs. At the bottom of Main Street, **Small Bridge Bar** offers live music nightly.

I'd finish my night at the **Court House Pub** (on The Mall, next to the old gray courthouse). This is a steamy little hide-away with low ceilings and high-caliber musicians who perform nightly at 21:00, and my favorite men's room in Ireland—with kegs for urinals.

Off-Season: From October through April, the music hibernates for the most part. But on weekends, your best bets are the Small Bridge Bar, O'Flaherty's, the Court House Pub, and John Benny's.

▲▲Folk Concerts

If you're not a night owl, these are your best opportunities to hear Irish traditional music in a more controlled, early-evening environment. (In these settings, many of the musicians find flash photography to be an irritating distraction.)

St. James' Church: Top local musicians offer a quality evening of live, acoustic, traditional Irish music in the fine little St. James' Church (100 seats), just off Main Street. These concerts are organized by local piper Eoin Duignan, whose command of the melodic *uileann* bagpipes is a highlight most nights (€13 in advance, €15 at the door; Mon, Wed, and Fri at 19:30, May-Oct only; mobile 087-284-9656; see sign on church gate or, for more details or to book a ticket, drop by Paul Geaneys Pub, Leac a Ré craft shop, or Siopa Ceoil music shop).

Siopa Ceoil Trad Concert: The Siopa Ceoil music shop hosts intimate traditional Irish music sessions in its cozily cramped, 35-seat space (€15, includes a tasty Irish decaf during break between sets; May-Sept Tue, Thu, Sat, and Sun at

19:00; 2 The Colony, tel. 066/915-2618, mobile 087-914-5826, www.siopaceoil.ie).

Cinema

Dingle's little theater is **The Phoenix** on Dykegate. Its film club (50-60 locals) meets here Tuesdays year-round at 20:45 for coffee and cookies, followed by a film at 21:00 (€8 for film, anyone is welcome). The regular film schedule for the week is posted on the door.

Eating

Remember that while seafood is a treat here, so is the lamb. Some pricier restaurants serve good-value, early-bird specials from 17:30 to 19:00. Many cheap and cheery lunch places close at 18:00. Most pubs stop serving food at about 21:00 (to make room for their beer drinkers and musicians).

Dining in Dingle

$$$$ Out of the Blue Seafood-Only Restaurant is the locals' choice for just plain great fresh fish. The interior is bright and elegantly simple. The chalkboard menu is dictated by what the fishermen caught that morning. If they're closed, there's been a storm and the fishermen couldn't go out (Mon-Sat 17:00-21:30, Sun 12:30-15:00, some outdoor picnic-table seating, reservations smart, just past the TI, facing the harbor on The Waterside, tel. 066/915-0811, www.outoftheblue.ie).

$$$$ James G. Ashe Pub and Restaurant, an old-fashioned joint, is popular with locals for its nicely presented, top-quality, traditional Irish food and seafood at good prices. Check out the photos of Gregory Peck, who was related to the Ashe family and visited the pub often. I like their beef-and-Guinness stew (daily 12:00-15:00 & 17:30-21:30, Main Street, tel. 066/915-0989).

$$$$ Global Village Restaurant is where Nuala Cassidy and Martin Bealin concoct their favorite dishes. Martin has a passion for making things from scratch

Music performance at St. James' Church

Dingle Center Restaurants & Pubs

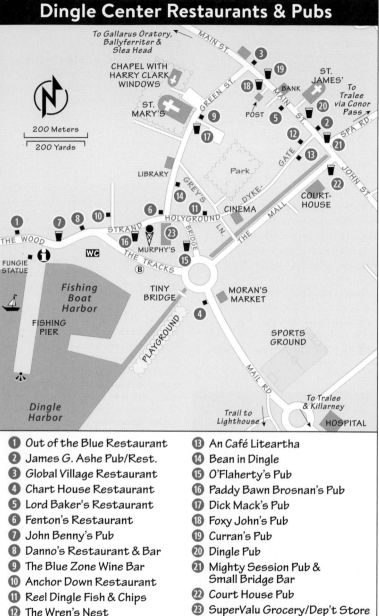

To Gallarus Oratory,
Ballyferriter &
Slea Head

MAIN ST.

CHAPEL WITH
HARRY CLARK
WINDOWS

GREEN ST.

BANK

ST.
JAMES'

To
Tralee
via Conor
Pass

MAIN ST.

POST

ST.
MARY'S

SPA RD.

GATE ST.

LIBRARY

Park

JOHN ST.

GREY'S LN.

DYKE LN.

CINEMA

THE MALL

COURT-
HOUSE

200 Meters

200 Yards

STRAND

HOLYGROUND

THE WOOD

THE TRACKS

MURPHY'S

BRIDGE ST.

FUNGIE
STATUE

WC

B

Fishing
Boat
Harbor

TINY
BRIDGE

MORAN'S
MARKET

FISHING
PIER

PLAYGROUND

SPORTS
GROUND

MAIL RD.

Dingle
Harbor

Trail to
Lighthouse

To Tralee
& Killarney

HOSPITAL

❶ Out of the Blue Restaurant	⓭ An Café Liteartha
❷ James G. Ashe Pub/Rest.	⓮ Bean in Dingle
❸ Global Village Restaurant	⓯ O'Flaherty's Pub
❹ Chart House Restaurant	⓰ Paddy Bawn Brosnan's Pub
❺ Lord Baker's Restaurant	⓱ Dick Mack's Pub
❻ Fenton's Restaurant	⓲ Foxy John's Pub
❼ John Benny's Pub	⓳ Curran's Pub
❽ Danno's Restaurant & Bar	⓴ Dingle Pub
❾ The Blue Zone Wine Bar	㉑ Mighty Session Pub & Small Bridge Bar
❿ Anchor Down Restaurant	
⓫ Reel Dingle Fish & Chips	㉒ Court House Pub
⓬ The Wren's Nest	㉓ SuperValu Grocery/Dep't Store

and giving dishes a creative twist with inspiration gleaned from his world travels. No chips, no deep-fat-fried anything. It's an eclectic, healthy, fresh seafood-eaters' place (good salads, daily 17:30-22:00, Nov-Feb open Fri-Sun only, top of Main Street, tel. 066/915-2325, mobile 087-917-5920).

$$$$ Chart House Restaurant serves contemporary cuisine in a sleek, well-varnished dining room. Settle back into the shipshape, lantern-lit space. The menu is shaped by what's fresh and seasonal, and the chef is committed to always offering a good vegetarian entrée (daily 18:00-22:00 except closed Mon Oct-May, at roundabout at base of town, reservations wise, tel. 066/915-2255, www.thecharthousedingle.com, Jim McCarthy).

$$$$ Lord Baker's is the venerable elder among fine Dingle dining options. John Moriarty and his family concoct quality dishes served in a friendly yet refined atmosphere. The seafood soup is a memorable specialty (Fri-Wed 18:00-21:30, closed Thu, reservations smart, Main Street, tel. 066/915-1277 or 066/915-1141, www.lordbakers.ie).

$$$$ Fenton's is good for seafood meals with a memorable apple-and-berry-crumble dessert (Tue-Sun 18:00-21:30, closed Mon, reservations smart, on Green Street down the hill below the church, tel. 066/915-2172, mobile 087-248-2487, www.fentonsrestaurantdingle.com).

Less Expensive Dingle Meals

$$ John Bonny's Pub is a waterfront pub dishing up traditional Irish fare. John, the proprietor, hopes people will come here for dinner, and stay for a drink and to enjoy his nightly live music (food daily 12:30-21:30, music after 21:30, The Pier).

$$ Danno's Restaurant and Bar is a sprawling and fun-loving eatery for inexpensive burgers, fish-and-chips, and pub grub. Danno's interior is a mix of railroad and rugby memorabilia. He offers some of the best outdoor seating in town (closed

Mon, Strand Street, tel. 086/236-4404).

$$ The Blue Zone is a hip jazz wine bar offering pizza, salad, and an international cosmopolitan vibe. Tight, busy, and family-friendly, it's a tasty alternative to Dingle's pub grub and fish-dominated fare (Thu-Tue 17:30-11:30, closed Wed, Green Street across from St. Mary's Church, tel. 066/915-0303).

$$ Anchor Down is another fresh fish option that is much easier on the wallet. The Sheehy family, who are local fishermen, supply their simple little cottage up the lane with a variety of fresh fish—and chips if you want them (daily 11:30-21:30, closed Dec-Feb, up the lane behind Out of the Blue, 3 The Colony, tel. 066/915-1545).

$ Reel Dingle Fish & Chips is the best chippie in town, serving mostly takeout, but with a few stools. They serve generous portions—consider splitting—and are also good for burgers (daily 13:00-22:00, near SuperValu grocery store on Holyground, tel. 066/915-1713).

$ The Wren's Nest is a mellow coffeehouse, reflecting musician-owner John Ryan's philosophical demeanor. This lunch-only refuge, with an ultra-appealing back garden, serves wholesome omelets, sandwiches, cakes, and tea. A small corner stage hosts occasional open-mic acoustic music gigs; you can also check out the schedule of *bodhrán* and music lessons (daily 11:00-17:00, Dykegate Street, mobile 086-177-3119).

$ An Café Liteartha, a simple refuge hidden behind a wonderfully cluttered bookstore, serves soup and sandwiches to a good-natured crowd of Irish speakers (daily 10:00-18:00, Oct-April until 17:00 and closed Sun, Dykegate Street, tel. 066/915-2204).

$ Bean in Dingle is an inviting and hip coffee shop run by Justin and Luke Burgess. They serve baked goodies and fresh sandwiches along with good coffee drinks (daily 8:30-18:00, Green Street).

Ice Cream: For two decades **Murphy's ice cream** has been a Dingle favorite. Their

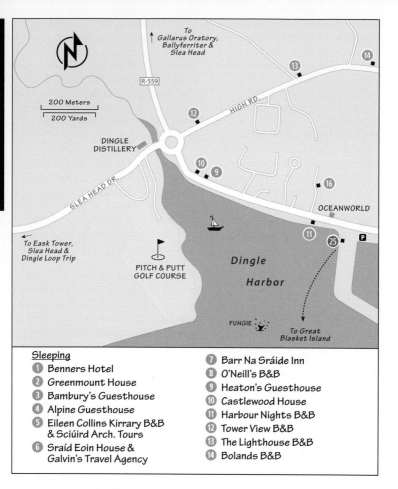

Sleeping

1. Benners Hotel
2. Greenmount House
3. Bambury's Guesthouse
4. Alpine Guesthouse
5. Eileen Collins Kirrary B&B & Sciúird Arch. Tours
6. Sraíd Eoin House & Galvin's Travel Agency
7. Barr Na Sráide Inn
8. O'Neill's B&B
9. Heaton's Guesthouse
10. Castlewood House
11. Harbour Nights B&B
12. Tower View B&B
13. The Lighthouse B&B
14. Bolands B&B

famously adventurous flavors include lavender, candied chili pepper, rosewater, clove, and even gin (daily 11:00-22:00, shorter hours off-season, two locations on Strand Street).

Picnics

The **SuperValu** supermarket/department store, at the base of town, has everything and stays open late (daily until 21:00 or 22:00). Smaller groceries, such as **Centra,** are scattered throughout the town (daily 8:00-21:00, on Main Street). Consider a grand-view picnic out on the end of the newer pier (as you face the harbor, it's the pleasure-boat pier on your right). You'll find picnic tables on the harbor side of the roundabout and benches along the busy harborfront.

Sleeping
In or near the Town Center

$$$$ Benners Hotel was the only hotel in town a hundred years ago. It stands bewildered by the modern world on Main Street, with sprawling public spaces and 52 abundant, overpriced rooms (tel. 066/915-1638, www.dinglebenners.com, info@dinglebenners.com).

$$$ Greenmount House sits among chilly palm trees at the top of town. A five-minute hike up from the town

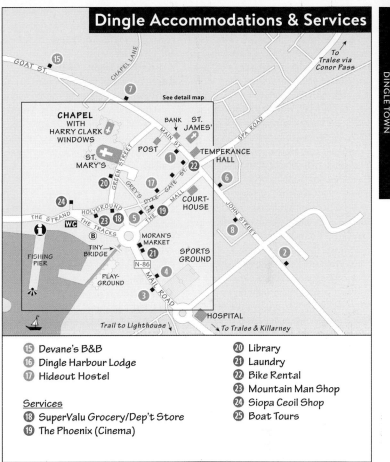

Dingle Accommodations & Services

Ⓘ Devane's B&B
Ⓘ Dingle Harbour Lodge
Ⓘ Hideout Hostel

Services
Ⓘ SuperValu Grocery/Dep't Store
Ⓘ The Phoenix (Cinema)

Ⓘ Library
Ⓘ Laundry
Ⓘ Bike Rental
Ⓘ Mountain Man Shop
Ⓘ Siopa Ceoil Shop
Ⓘ Boat Tours

center, this guesthouse commands a fine view of the bay and mountains. Gary Curran runs one of Ireland's best B&Bs, with two fine rooms, three superb rooms, and nine sprawling suites in a modern building with lavish public areas and wonderful breakfasts (parking, top of John Street, tel. 066/915-1414, www. greenmounthouse.ie, info@greenmounthouse.ie). Seek out the hot tub in their back-garden cabin.

$$ Bambury's Guesthouse, hosted by cheerful Bernie Bambury, is big and modern with views of grazing sheep and the harbor. The 12 rooms are airy and comfy (coming in from Tralee it's on your left on Mail Road, 2 blocks before Esso station; tel. 066/915-1244, www.bamburysguesthouse. com, info@bamburysguesthouse.com).

$$ Alpine Guesthouse looks like a Monopoly hotel, and is fittingly comfortable and efficient. Its 14 bright and fresh rooms come with pastoral views, a cozy lounge, and friendly owner Paul O'Shea (RS%, family rooms, easy parking, Mail Road, tel. 066/915-1250, www. alpineguesthouse.com, alpinedingle@ gmail.com). Driving into town from Tralee, this will be the first lodging on your right, next to the sports field and a block uphill from the Dingle Esso station.

$ Eileen Collins Kirrary B&B, which

takes up a quiet corner in the town center, is run by the same Collins family that does archaeological tours of the peninsula (see page 169). They offer five pleasant rooms, great prices, a large garden, and a homey friendliness (cash only, tel. 066/915-1606 or mobile 087-150-0017, Kirrary House, just off The Mall on Avondale at Dykegate and Grey's Lane, www.collinskirrary.com, collinskirrary@eircom.net, Eileen Collins).

$$ Sraíd Eoin House offers five pleasant, top-floor rooms above Galvin's Travel Agency (RS%, cash only family rooms, John Street, tel. 066/915-1409, www.sraideoinbnb.com, sraideoinhouse@ hotmail.com, friendly Kathleen and Maurice O'Connor).

$$ Barr Na Sráide Inn, central and hotel-like, has 29 basic rooms (family deals, self-service laundry, bar, parking, past McCarthy's pub on Upper Main Street, tel. 066/915-1331, www.barrnas-raide.com, barrnasraide@eircom.net).

$ O'Neill's B&B is homey and friendly, with six decent rooms on a quiet street at the top of town (cash only, parking, John Street, tel. 066/915-1639, www. oneillsbedandbreakfast.com, info@ oneillsbedandbreakfast.com, Mary and Stephen O'Neill).

Beyond the Pier

These accommodations are a 10-15-minute walk from Dingle's town center. They tend to be quieter, since they are farther from the late-night pub scene.

$$$ Heaton's Guesthouse, big, peaceful, and comfortable, is on the water just west of town at the end of Dingle Bay—a five-minute walk past Oceanworld on The Wood. The 16 thoughtfully appointed rooms come with all the amenities (creative breakfasts, parking, The Wood, tel. 066/915-2288, www.heatonsdingle.com, info@heatonsdingle.com, David Heaton).

$$$ Castlewood House is a palatial refuge with 12 tasteful rooms, classy furnishings, and delicious breakfasts. The breakfast room and patio have a wonderful view of Dingle Harbor (parking, The Wood, tel. 066/915-2788, www.castlewooddingle. com, info@castlewooddingle.com, Brian and Helen Heaton).

$ Harbour Nights B&B weaves together a line of old row houses to create a 14-room guesthouse facing the harbor (just past the aquarium on The Wood, parking, tel. 066/915-2499, mobile 087-686-8190, www.dinglebandb.com, info@ dinglebandb.com, Seán and Kathleen Lynch).

Above Town

$ Tower View B&B is a big, bright-yellow modern home just outside of town on a lovely quiet lot. This kid-friendly mini farm rents eight fine rooms (family rooms, High Road, tel. 066/915-2990, www.towerview dingle.com, info@towerviewdingle.com, Aiden & Helen Murphy).

$$ The Lighthouse B&B is a cozy place, with six prim rooms, wonderful views near the crest of the hill, and Lucky the fluff-ball mutt (family rooms, High Road, tel. 066/915-1829, www.lighthousedingle.com, info@lighthousedingle.com, Denis & Mary Murphy).

$$ Bolands B&B is family-run with a traditional, welcoming atmosphere and six comfortable rooms (family rooms, Goat Street, tel. 066/915-1426, http://bolands dingle.ie, bolanddingle@eircom.net, Breda & Michael Boland).

$ Devane's B&B caters to the active bike-and-hike crowd, with six clean and practical rooms that are a good value given their close proximity to town (cash only, Goat Street, tel. 066/915-1193, www. devanesdingle.com, devanesdingle@ eircom.net, Kevin & Geraldine Devane).

Hostels and Dorms

$$ Dingle Harbour Lodge is a former hostel, pleasantly refurbished and morphing into a hotel hybrid with 29 rooms on the edge of town. You have the feeling of being a guest in a comfy hotel without the fancy prices (family

All Roads Lead to Daingean Ui Chuis

The western half of the Dingle Peninsula is part of the Gaeltacht, where locals speak the Irish Gaelic language. In an effort to ward off English-language encroachment, all place names on road signs were controversially changed to Irish-only in the past decade. As you travel around the Dingle Peninsula, refer to this cheat sheet of the most useful destination names. A complete translation of all Irish place names is included in the Gazetteer section at the back of the *Complete Road Atlas of Ireland* by Ordnance Survey.

English Name	Irish Gaelic Name
Dingle	*Daingean Ui Chuis* (DANG-un e koosh)
Ventry	*Ceann Trá* (k'yown—rhymes with "crown" traw)
Slea Head	*Ceann Sléibhe* (k'yown SHLAY-veh)
Dunquin	*Dún Chaoin* (doon qween)
Blasket Islands	*Na Blascaodaí* (nuh BLAS-kud-ee)
Great Blasket Island	*An Blascaod Mór* (on BLAS-kade moor)
Ballyferriter	*Baile an Fheirtearaigh* (BALL-yuh on ERR-ter-ee)
Reasc Monastery	*Mainistir Riaisc* (MON-ish-ter REE-isk)
Gallarus	*Gallaras* (GAHL-russ)
Kilmalkedar	*Cill Mhaoil-cheadair* (kill moyle-KAY-dir)
Annascaul	*Abhainn an Scáil* (ow'en on skahl)
Lispole	*Lios Póil* (leesh pohl)
Tralee	*Trá Lí* (tra-LEE)

rooms, up a long driveway off The Wood past the aquarium, tel. 066/915-1577, www.dingleharbourlodge.com, info@dingleharbourlodge.com).

¢ **Hideout Hostel** is friendly and central, just across the lane from the movie theater. Michael (ME-hall) grew up on this street and manages a relaxed, fun atmosphere (private rooms available, Dykegate Street, tel. 066/915-0559, www.thehideouthostel.com, info@thehideouthostel.com).

Transportation
Arriving and Departing

Tralee (Trá Lí), 30 miles from Dingle, is the region's transportation hub, with the nearest train station to Dingle. Most bus trips also make connections in Tralee. For more info, see Tralee's "Transportation" section at the end of this chapter.

BY BUS

Dingle has no bus station and only one bus stop, on the waterfront behind the Super-Valu supermarket; look for the bus shelter with the roof made from an overturned traditional black-tarred boat (bus info toll tel 1850-836-611, www.buseireann.ie).

From Dingle by Bus to: Galway (5/day, 6.5 hours), **Dublin** (4/day, 8-9 hours, transfer in Tralee and Limerick), **Rosslare** (3/day, 9 hours), **Tralee** (5/day, fewer off-season and Sun, 1.5 hours).

BY CAR

Drivers choose two roads into Dingle town: the narrow, but very exciting, Conor Pass road; or the faster, easier, N-86 through Lougher and Annascaul (Abhainn an Scáil).

On a clear day, Conor Pass comes with incredible views over Tralee Bay and Brandon Bay. On the north slope approaching the pass, pull out at the waterfall. From here, there's a fun five-minute scramble to a dramatic little glacier-created lake. Pause also at the summit viewpoint to look down on Dingle town and harbor. If you're not staying overnight (i.e., parking at your B&B), use the waterfront parking lot extending west from the TI (pay-and-display, daily 8:00-18:00).

Ferry Shortcut: If you're driving from Dingle, heading north straight to Galway, the inland Limerick route is fastest and cheapest (roughly €2 in tolls). But if you're going to the Cliffs of Moher and the Burren, the 20-minute Killimer-Tarbert ferry connection allows you to avoid the 80-mile detour around the River Shannon and is more scenic (€19/ carload, departs hourly, June-Sept every 30 minutes; generally departs :30 past the hour going north and on the hour going south—check timetables online; no need to reserve, tel. 065/905-3124, www. shannonferries.com).

BY PLANE

Kerry Airport, halfway between Tralee and Killarney, is a one-hour drive from Dingle. Short puddle-jumper flights connect the region to Dublin and make a visit to Dingle possible even for travelers with limited time. For more on Kerry Airport, see the end of this chapter.

DINGLE PENINSULA LOOP

The gloriously green Dingle Peninsula is 10 miles wide and runs 40 miles from Tralee to Slea Head. The top of its mountainous spine is Mount Brandon—at 3,130 feet, it's the second-tallest mountain in Ireland. While only a few tiny villages lie west of Dingle town, the peninsula is home to 50,000 sheep.

A loop trip around the peninsula, worth ▲▲▲, is about 30 miles (45 km) long and must be driven (or biked) in a clockwise direction. It's easy by car, or a demanding five hours by bike. Remember that minibus tours are offered, too (see page 169).

Along the way, you'll see lots of grass-fed Friesian (or Holstein) cows and the belted Galloway breed from Scotland (looking like they have a white blanket tossed over them). The only wild animal you'll encounter is a rabbit. In spring or summer, you'll likely enjoy a festival of flowers all along the way as you follow the blue signs with white squiggles—a stylized "WAW"—reminding you that this is "The Wild Atlantic Way."

Dingle Driving Tour

To get the most out of your trip, read through this entire section before departing.

Set your odometer to zero (if possible) at Oceanworld, as you leave Dingle. Even if you get off track, the kilometers listed below let you judge the distance from one sight to the next. Then go step-by-step (staying on R-559 the entire way and following the brown *Slea Head Drive* signs most of the way—through kilometer 37). The road is narrow and can be congested mid-July to late August.

❂ *Self-Guided Tour*

0.0 km: Leave Dingle town west along the waterfront (0.0 km at Oceanworld). Driving out of town, on the left you'll see a row of humble "two up and two down" cottages from a 1908 affordable-housing government initiative.

0.5 km: Dingle Harbor has an eight-foot tide. The seaweed was used to make formerly worthless land arable. (Seaweed is a natural source of potash—organic farming, before it was trendy.) Across the River Milltown estuary, the white **Milltown House** was Robert Mitchum's home during the 1969 filming of *Ryan's Daughter*. (Behind that is Dingle's pitch-and-putt golf course.) Look for the narrow

Dingle Peninsula Loop Drive

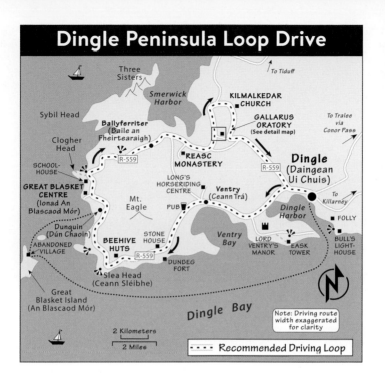

To Tiduff

Three Sisters

Smerwick Harbor

KILMALKEDAR CHURCH

Sybil Head

GALLARUS ORATORY
(See detail map)

To Tralee via Conor Pass

Ballyferriter
(Baile an Fheirtearaigh)

Clogher Head

R-559

REASC MONASTERY

Dingle
(Daingean Ui Chuis)

R-559

SCHOOL-HOUSE

LONG'S HORSERIDING CENTRE

GREAT BLASKET CENTRE
(Ionad An Blascaod Mór)

Mt. Eagle

Ventry
(Ceann Trá)

PUB

To Killarney

Dingle Harbor

FOLLY

Dunquin
(Dún Chaoin)

BEEHIVE HUTS

STONE HOUSE

Ventry Bay

LORD VENTRY'S MANOR

EASK TOWER

BULL'S LIGHT-HOUSE

ABANDONED VILLAGE

R-559

DUNBEG FORT

Slea Head
(Ceann Sléibhe)

Great Blasket Island
(An Blascaod Mór)

Dingle Bay

Note: Driving route width exaggerated for clarity

2 Kilometers

2 Miles

···· Recommended Driving Loop

mouth of this blind harbor (behind you, in the distance at the opposite end of the harbor) and the Ring of Kerry beyond that. Dingle Harbor is so hidden that ships needed the Eask Tower to find its mouth. If a group of small boats are gathered at the mouth of the harbor, Fungie has come out to play.

0.7 km: At the roundabout, turn left over the bridge. On the far side, the blue building on the right was the site of a corn-grinding mill in the 18th century (with a ghostly black waterwheel hiding behind it). Today it's a modern warehouse that shelters the **Dingle Distillery** (tours daily—see page 177). Just beyond that on the right, you'll pass the junction where you'll complete this loop trip 30 miles from now. The gas station on your left is the westernmost on the peninsula (you won't see another on this drive).

1.3 km: The Milestone B&B is named for the stone **pillar** (*gallaun* in Irish) in its front yard. This pillar may have

been a prehistoric grave or a boundary marker between two tribes. Half of the stone's length is buried underground. This peninsula, literally an open-air archaeological museum, is dotted with more than 2,000 such monuments dating from the Neolithic Age (roughly 3000 B.C.) through early Christian times.

The land ahead on the left holds the estate and mansion of Lord Ventry, whose family came to Dingle as post-Cromwellian War landlords in 1666. Today his mansion (built in 1750, out of view and closed to the public) houses an all-Irish-language girls boarding school.

As you drive past the **Ventry estate** (at 2.8 km, on the right, is Ventry's slate-roofed blacksmith shop), you'll pass palms, magnolias, and exotic flora, which were introduced to Dingle by Lord Ventry. The Gulf Stream is the source of the mild climate, which supports subtropical plants (it rarely snows here). Fuchsias—imported from Chile and spreading like

Dingle Peninsula loop drive

weeds—line the roads all over the peninsula and redden the countryside from June through September. More than 100 inches of rain a year gives this area its "40 shades of green."

4.6 km: Stay off the "soft margin" as you enjoy views of Ventry Harbor, its long beach (to your right as you face the water), and distant Skellig Michael, which you'll see all along this part of the route. **Skellig Michael**—the pyramid-shaped island in the distance—holds the rocky remains of a sixth-century monastic settlement. Mount Eagle (1,660 feet), rising across the bay, marks the end of Ireland—and that's where you're heading.

6.6 km: In the town of **Ventry**—a.k.a. Ceann Trá (translated roughly as "beach head")—Irish is the first language. Ventry is little more than a bungalow holiday village today. Urban Irish families love to come here in the summer to immerse their kids in the traditional culture and wild nature. A large hall at the edge of the village is used as a classroom where big-city students come to learn the Irish language.

Just past town, a lane leads left to a fine beach and mobile-home vacation community. An information board explains the history, geology, and bird life of the harbor. The humble trailer park has no running water or electricity. Locals like it for its economy and proximity to the beach. From here, a lane leads inland to **Long's Horseriding Centre.**

7.3 km: The bamboo-like **rushes** on either side of the road are the kind used to make the local thatched roofs. Thatching, which nearly died out because of fire danger, is more popular now that anti-flame treatments are available. It's expensive, as few qualified thatchers remain in Ireland. Black-and-white magpies fly overhead.

8.5 km: This intersection has the "Three Gs"—God (a church), groceries, and Guinness. The pub just past the church is **Páidí Ó Sé's.** The Irish football star Páidí Ó Sé was a household name in Ireland. He won eight all-Ireland football titles for Kerry as a player from 1970 to 1988. He then trained the Kerry team for many years before further endearing himself to his fans by running this pub. A heroic **statue** remembers Paddy, who died in 2012.

10.7 km: *Taisteal go Mall* means "go slowly"; the building on the right, surrounded by a tall net to keep the balls in, is the village schoolhouse. In summer

Horseback riding on the beach

it's used for Irish Gaelic courses for kids from the big cities. On the left is the small Celtic and Prehistoric Museum, a quirky private collection of prehistoric artifacts, including arrowheads and ancient jewelry, collected by a retired musician named Harris (€5, daily 10:00-17:00).

11.1 km: The circular mound (which looks like a big round hedge) on the right is a late-Stone Age **ring fort.** It was a petty Celtic chieftain's headquarters—a stone-and-earth stockade filled with little thatched dwellings. Such mysterious sites survived untouched through the centuries because of superstitious beliefs that they were "fairy forts." While this site is unexcavated, archaeologists have found evidence that people have lived on this peninsula since about 4000 B.C.

11.7 km: Look ahead up Mount Eagle at the patchwork of stone-fenced fields. In the distance on the left is another view of Skellig Michael.

12.5 km: Dunbeg Fort (50 yards downhill on the left) is made up of a series of defensive ramparts and ditches around a central *clochan* (€3, May-Sept 9:00-18:00, July-Aug until 19:00). A third of the fort fell into the sea during a violent storm in 2014. Forts like this are the most important relics left from Ireland's Iron Age (500 B.C.-A.D. 500).

The modern stone-roofed dwelling across the street is the welcoming and recommended **Stone House Restaurant,** with an adjacent visitors center, where you can check out a 10-minute video that gives a bigger picture of the prehistory of the peninsula (included with Dunbeg Fort ticket). A traditional *currach* boat is permanently dry-docked in the parking lot.

Roughly 50 yards up the road and 100 yards off the road to the right is a thatched cottage abandoned by a family named Kavanaugh during the famine (around 1848). With a few rusty and chipped old artifacts and good descriptions, it offers an evocative peek into the simple lifestyles of the area in the 19th century (€3, daily 10:00-18:00, closed Nov-April). The owner, Gabriel, also runs working sheep dog demonstrations (in Irish for the dogs, English for tourists; €5/person, must book ahead by phone, mobile 087-762-2617, www.dinglesheepdogs.com).

13.2 km: A group of **beehive huts** (*clochans*) is a short walk uphill (€3, daily 9:00-19:00, WC). While reconstructed, these mysterious stone igloos, which cluster together within a circular wall, are a better sight than the similar group of beehive huts down the road.

Farther on (at 14.0 km), you'll ford a stream. There's never been a bridge here; this bit of road—nicknamed the "upside-down bridge"—was designed as a ford.

14.7 km: Pull off to the left at this second group of beehive huts. (Aedan runs this family enterprise where you can see more *clochans,* hold a baby lamb, and use the WC for €3.) Look downhill at the rocky field. In the movie *Far and Away,* that's where Lord Ventry evicted (read: torched) peasants from their cottages. Even without Hollywood, this is a bleak and godforsaken land. Look across the bay at the Ring of Kerry in the distance and ahead at the Blasket Islands.

16 km: At **Slea Head** (Ceann Sléibhe)—marked by a crucifix, a pullout, and great views of the Blasket Islands—you turn the corner on this tour. On stormy days, the waves are "racing in like white horses."

16.7 km: Pull into the little parking lot (at *Dún Chaoin* sign) for views of **Great Blasket Island and Dunmore Head** (the westernmost point in Europe) and to review the roadside map (which traces your route) posted in the parking lot.

Great Blasket Island is an icon of traditional Irish culture. Because the islanders subsisted off the sea, rather than on potatoes, they survived the famine. The most traditional of Irish communities, about 100 people lived there until 1953, when the government evacuated the island. While the island is uninhabited today, small tour boats shuttle visitors from Dingle and from Dunquin Harbor (just ahead). To learn more, visit the Blasket Island Centre (a few miles farther down the road).

As you drive on, notice the ruined stone houses (and the sheep oblivious to the amazing views). The scattered village just down the road was abandoned during the famine. Some homes are now fixed up, as this is a popular place these days for

Building a Rock Fence

The Emerald Isle is as rocky as it is green. When the English took the best land, they told the Irish to "go to hell or go to Connaught" (the rugged western part of Ireland where the soil was particularly poor and rocky). Every spring, farmers "harvest" rocks driven up by the winter frost in order to plant more edible fare. Over generations, Irish farmers stacked these rocks into fences, which still divide so much of the land.

The fences generally have no visible gates. But upon closer look, you'll see a "V" built into the wall by larger rocks, which are then filled in with smaller rocks. When a farmer needs to move some cattle, he slowly unstacks the smaller rocks, moves the cattle through, and then restacks them. Flying low over western Ireland, the fields—alligatored by these rock fences—seem to stretch forever. And nearly all have these labor-intensive V-shaped gates built in.

summer vacationers. You can see more good examples of land reclamation, patch by patch, climbing up the hillside. Mount Eagle was the first bit of land that Charles Lindbergh saw after crossing the Atlantic on his way to Paris in 1927. Villagers here were as excited as he was—they had never seen anything so big in the air.

Look above, at the patches of land slowly made into farmland by the inhabitants of this westernmost piece of Europe. Rocks were cleared and piled into fences. Sand and seaweed were laid on the clay, and in time it was good for grass. The created land, if at all tillable, was generally used for growing potatoes; otherwise, it

View from Slea Head

was only good for grazing. Much of this farmland has now fallen out of use.

About a kilometer down a road on the left, a plaque celebrates the 30th anniversary of the filming of *Ryan's Daughter*. From here, a trail leads down to a wild beach.

19 km: The Blasket Islands' residents had no church or cemetery on the island. On the left stretches their **cemetery.** The famous Blascaod storyteller Peig Sayers (1873-1958) is buried at its center. Just off this coast is the 1588 shipwreck of the *Santa María de la Rosa*, of the Spanish Armada. And ahead is the often-tempestuous Dunquin Harbor. Blasket Island farmers—who on a calm day could row across in 30 minutes—would dock here and hike over the saddle and 12 miles into Dingle to sell their produce.

Hey! There's a dead man floating out at sea. Oh, it's just an island. (While its official name is The Sleeping Giant, that island has always been known to Blasket Islanders as "The Dead Man.")

21.3 km: From here a lane leads a kilometer to the **Great Blasket Centre,** described on page 198. This excellent modern cultural museum offers the best look at the island culture.

23.1 km: Grab the scenic **Clogher Head pullout.** The view from here is spectacular. Ahead is Mount Brandon, Ireland's second highest peak (at 3,123 feet). Working to the left you'll see Butter Harbor (the name believed to originate from times when Vikings stopped here to grease up their hulls). Then spot the three swoopy peaks—the Three Sisters. Left of that is Sybil Head (where scenes from *Star Wars: The Force Awakens* were shot). On the summit of Sybil Head, the tiny black square is a watchtower from the days when Britain feared an invasion from Napoleon. The entire coast was lined with these, all within sight of each other to relay a warning signal if under attack by the bloody French. And under the Three Sisters is the popular Dingle Links golf course.

Ahead, on the right, study the top fields, untouched since the planting of 1845, when the potatoes didn't grow, but rotted in the ground. The faint vertical ridges of the potato beds can still be seen—a reminder of the famine. Before the famine, 40,000 people inhabited this peninsula. After the famine, the population was so small that there was never again a need to farm so high up. Today, only 10,000 people live on the peninsula.

From this pull-out, a breezy 15-minute walk leads out to Clogher Head. The dirt road stretches off to the left and peters out after 200 yards. But it's all open ground and easy to navigate. There you'll be rewarded with postcard-worthy panoramic views.

28 km: The town of **Ballyferriter,** established by a Norman family in the 12th century, is the largest on this side of Dingle Peninsula. The pubs serve grub, the fine old church dates to the 1860s, and the old schoolhouse (on the left) is a museum with modest exhibits that provide the best coverage of this very historic peninsula (€3, generally daily 10:00–17:00, closed Oct-May, tel. 066/915-6333, www.west kerrymuseum.com).

Keep on Slea Head Drive (R-559), following signs to *Dingle.*

30 km: The road bends over a tiny yellow bridge, past a pub and microbrewery (on the right); 50 yards after that watch for a tiny unmarked paved road going uphill on the right. Detour right up this lane, where you'll find the scant remains

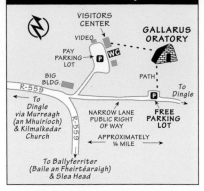

of **Reasc Monastery** about 300 yards up (no sign).

This is the stony footprint of a monastic settlement dating from the 6th to 12th century (free, always open). The inner wall divided the community into sections for prayer and business (cottage industries helped support the monastery). In 1975, only the stone pillar was visible, as the entire site was buried. The layer of black tar paper (near the base of the walls) marks where the original rocks stop and the excavators' reconstruction begins. The stone pillar is Celtic (c. 500 B.C.). When Christians arrived in the fifth century, they didn't throw out the Celtic society. Instead, they carved a Maltese-type cross over the Celtic scrollwork.

One of the cottage industries operated by the monastery was a double-duty kiln. Just outside the wall (opposite the oratory, past the duplex *clochan,* at the bottom end), find a stone hole with a passage facing the southwest wind. This was the kiln—fanned by the wind, it was used for cooking and drying grain. Locals would bring their grain to be dried and ground, and the monks would keep a tithe (their 10 percent cut). With the arrival of the Normans in the 12th century, these small religious communities were pushed aside by a militaristic feudal system.

Return to the main road and continue on.

Reasc standing stone

Gallarus Oratory

32 km: Go left at the big Dingle Peninsula Hotel, following *Gallarus* signs and staying on Slea Head Drive.

33 km: Turn right up the narrow lane. The "free" car park is a private enterprise on private land (with a short video, WC, and shop), where you'll be charged €3 to see the site. To park for free, go farther up the lane (at 33.4 km) to a tiny five-car pull-out on the left, where a path leads through a gate 200 yards to the amazing **Gallarus Oratory** (free, always open).

Built about 1,300 years ago, the Gallarus Oratory is one of Ireland's best-preserved early Christian churches. Shaped like an upturned boat, its finely fitted drystone walls are still waterproof. As you step in, notice how thick the walls are. A simple, small arched window offers scant daylight over where the altar would have stood. Picture the interior lit by candles during medieval monastic services. It would have been tough to fit more than about a dozen monks inside. Notice the holes once used to secure covering at the door, and the fine alternating stonework on the corners.

From the oratory, return to the main road and continue, following the brown *Slea Head Drive* signs. (To skip the Kilmalkedar Church—last stop on this tour—and go directly back to Dingle, continue up the narrow lane and turn right when you hit the bigger road.)

35.5 km: At the junction in the center of the next village, leave Slea Head Drive by taking a right on R-559 (signed Dingle, 10 km). For an optional stop (your own private mini Gallarus Oratory), pull off at 37.1 km at the cemetery, cross the road, and hike 200 yards to St. Brandon's Oratory, which dates to the sixth century (even older than Gallarus).

37.3 km: The ruined 12th-century **church of Kilmalkedar** (Cill Mhaoil-cheadair, on the left at the yellow hiker sign) has a classic Romanesque arch and a well-worn cross atop its roof. It's surrounded by a densely populated graveyard (which has risen noticeably above the surrounding fields over the centuries). In front of the church, you'll find the oldest (late medieval) tombs, a stately early Christian cross (substantially buried by the rising graveyard and therefore

Ruined church of Kilmalkedar

oddly proportioned), and a much older ogham stone. This stone, which had already stood here 900 years when the church was built, is notched with the mysterious Morse code-type ogham script used from the third to seventh centuries. It may have marked a grave or a clan border, indicating this was an important pre-Christian gathering place. The hole was drilled through the top of the stone centuries ago as a place where people would come to seal a deal by touching thumbs through this stone. The church fell into ruin during the Reformation.

38 km: Continue uphill, overlooking the water. You'll pass another ancient "fairy fort" on the right. The bay stretched out below you is Smerwick Harbor. In 1580 a force of 600 Italian and Spanish troops (sent by the pope to aid a rebellion against the Protestant English) surrendered at this bay to the English. All 600 were beheaded by the English forces, which included Sir Walter Raleigh.

41.7 km: At the crest of the hill you may see the belted Galloway beef cattle with their white blankets. The spruce forest on the right was planted with government supplements (to meet EU forest

standards for minimizing Ireland's carbon footprint). From here, enjoy a long coast back into Dingle town (sighting, as old-time mariners did, on the Eask Tower).

44 km: Take a left past the Dingle Distillery, go over the bridge, and head back into Dingle. At 45 km, you're back at the Oceanarium where you started. Well done!

BLASKET ISLANDS

This rugged group of six islands off the tip of the Dingle Peninsula seems particularly close to the soul of Ireland. Life here was hard, but the sea provided for all, and no one went hungry. Each family had a cow, a few sheep, and a plot of potatoes. They cut their peat from the high ridge and harvested fish from the sea. There was no priest, pub, or doctor. Because they were not entirely dependent upon the potato, island inhabitants survived the famine relatively unscathed. These people formed the most traditional Irish community of the 20th century—the symbol of ancient Gaelic culture.

From this simple but proud fishing/farming community came three writers of

Blasket Islands

international repute whose Gaelic works—basically tales of life on Great Blasket Island—have been translated into many languages. You'll find *Peig* (by Peig Sayers) and *The Islandman* (Thomas O'Crohan) in shops everywhere. But the most readable and upbeat is *Twenty Years A-Growing* (Maurice O'Sullivan), a somewhat-true, Huck Finn-esque account of the author's childhood and adolescence and of island life as it was a hundred years ago.

The population of Great Blasket Island, once home to as many as 160 people, dwindled until the government moved the last handful of residents to the mainland in 1953. The island's café closed down some time ago, but the simple hostel reopened several years ago on a seasonal basis. Today Great Blasket is little more than a ghost town overrun with rabbits on a peaceful, grassy, three-mile-long poem. There are often free guided walks on the island in season (for details ask at the Great Blasket Centre).

If you visit, you can explore the ghost town, and take the easy hike along the ridge running down the center of the island over spongy moss terrain. Bring everything you need (picnic lunch, water, rain gear), and plan on having no shelter if a squall blows in.

Getting to the Blasket Islands

In summer, various boats run between **Dingle town** and the Blasket Islands, with a 3.5-hour stop to explore the Great Blasket Island. The ride (which may include a quick look at Fungie the dolphin) traces the spectacular coastline all the way to Slea Head. Competing boats offer similar services from Dingle town and operate when there's enough demand. The tricky landing at Great Blasket Island's primitive and slippery little boat ramp makes getting off a challenge and landing virtually impossible in wet weather. Boats generally depart from the marina pier in Dingle at 11:00 and return from Great Blasket at 17:30. For details, see the boat tour listings on page 169. These boats also do three-hour eco-tours for those interested in puffins, dolphins, and seals.

Boats also go from **Dunquin Harbor** to the Blasket Islands (book ahead; see Blasket Island Ferry listing on page 169).

Sights

▲▲GREAT BLASKET CENTRE

This sight isn't on the Blasket Islands, but on the mainland facing them. It's an essential stop before visiting the islands—or a good place to learn about them without making the crossing. It fits neatly into the Dingle Peninsula Loop Trip.

This state-of-the-art Blascaod and Gaelic heritage center gives visitors the best look possible at the language, literature, and way of life of Blasket Islanders. The building's award-winning design mixes interpretation and the surrounding countryside. Its spine, a sloping village lane, leads to an almost sacred view of the actual island. Don't miss the exceptional 20-minute video, a virtual visit to the island back when it was inhabited (shows on the half-hour), then hear the sounds, read the poems, browse through old photos, and gaze out the big windows at those rugged islands...and imagine. Even if you never got past limericks, the poetry of these people—so pure and close to each other and nature—will have you dipping your pen into the cry of the birds.

Cost and Hours: €5, daily 10:00-18:00, closed Nov-Easter, fine cafeteria run by friendly Christy, well-signposted on the Slea Head Drive near Dunquin/Dún Chaoin, tel. 066/915-6444, www.blasket.ie.

TRALEE

Tralee (traw-LEE) is County Kerry's transit hub. Many travelers will pass through, whether by car, train, or bus. Some stay an hour to see the sights.

This amiable town, near the base of the Dingle Peninsula, comes alive for the famous Rose of Tralee International Festival, usually held in mid-August. It's a celebration of arts and music, culminating in the election of the Rose of Tralee—the most beautiful woman at the festival (no matter which country she was born in, as long as she has Irish heritage).

Sights

▲KERRY COUNTY MUSEUM

Easily the best place to learn about life in Kerry, this museum (located in Ashe Memorial Hall in the center of town) has three parts: Kerry slide show, museum, and medieval-town walk.

Cost and Hours: €5; daily 9:30-17:30, Oct-May until 17:00 and closed Sun-Mon; tel. 066/712-7777, www.kerrymuseum.ie.

Visiting the Museum: Get in the mood by relaxing for 10 minutes through the Enya-style continuous slide show of Kerry's spectacular scenery. Then wander through 7,000 years of Kerry history in the museum (well-described, no need for free headphones). The Irish joke that when a

Great Blasket Centre

Tralee

particularly stupid guy moved from Cork to Kerry, he raised the average IQ in both counties—but this museum is pretty well done. It starts with good background info on the archaeological sites of Dingle, progresses through Viking artifacts found in the area, and goes right up to a video showing highlights of the Kerry football team (a fun look at Irish football, which is more like rugby than soccer). Good coverage is given to adventurous Kerryman Tom Crean, who survived three Antarctic expeditions with Scott and Shackleton (see page 176). The lame finale is a stroll back in time on a re-creation of Tralee's circa-1450 Main Street. Before leaving, horticulture enthusiasts will want to ramble through the rose garden in the adjacent park.

BLENNERVILLE WINDMILL

On the western edge of Tralee, just off the N-86 Dingle road, spins a restored mill originally built in 1780. Its eight-minute video tells the story of the windmill, which ground grain to feed Britain as that country steamed into the Industrial Age. In the 19th century, Blennerville was a major port for America-bound emigrants. It was also the home port where the *Jeanie Johnston* was built. This modern-day replica of a 19th-century ship tours Atlantic ports, explaining the Irish emigrant experience. Most of the time, it's docked and available to tour in Dublin, on the north shore of the River Liffey (see page 67).

Cost and Hours: €5 gets you a one-room emigration exhibit, the video, and a peek at the spartan interior of the working windmill; daily June-Aug 9:00-18:00, April-May and Sept-Oct 9:30-17:30, closed Nov-March, last entry 45 minutes before closing, tel. 066/712-1064.

Transportation
Arriving and Departing

BY TRAIN AND BUS

Travelers headed to or from Dingle will likely go through Tralee. The town's bus station (bus info tel. 066/716-4700, www.buseireann.ie) is across the parking lot from the train station (train info tel. 066/712-3522, www.irishrail.ie).

From Tralee by Train to: Dublin (every 2 hours, 6/day on Sun, 1 direct in morning, otherwise change in mellow Mallow, 4 hours), **Killarney** (8/day, 35 minutes).

By Bus to: Dingle (5/day, fewer off-season and on Sun, 1.5 hours), **Galway** (8/day, 4 hours), **Doolin/Cliffs of Moher** (2/day, 5 hours), **Ennis** (6/day, 3.5 hours, change in Limerick), **Rosslare** (2/day, 7 hours), **Shannon** (7/day, 3 hours), **Dublin** (7/day, 6 hours).

BY PLANE

Kerry Airport is a 20-minute drive from Tralee and a one-hour drive from Dingle. It's just off the main N-22 road, halfway between Killarney and Tralee (airport code: KIR, tel. 066/976-4644, www.kerryairport. ie). Dingle Shuttle Bus is your best connection to Dingle town, but you must reserve in advance (€25/person one-way, minimum 3 passengers, mobile 087-250-4767, www.dingleshuttlebus.com). You can also connect to the airport via taxi (€30 from Tralee, €80 from Dingle) or bus (3/day to Dingle via Tralee).

Blennerville Windmill

County
Clare

Those connecting Dingle in the south with Galway up the coast to the north can entertain themselves along the way by joyriding through the fascinating landscape and tidy villages of County Clare.

Overlooking the Atlantic, the dramatic Cliffs of Moher offer tenderfeet a thrilling hike. The Burren is a unique, windblown limestone moonscape that hides an abundance of flora, fauna, caves, and history.

Ennis is a workaday Irish place with a medieval history, a great traditional Irish music scene, and a market bustle—ideal for anyone tired of the tourist crowds. If you stick around long enough to enjoy evening entertainment, join a tour-bus group for a medieval banquet in a castle in Kinvarra or meet up with trad music enthusiasts from around Europe for tin-whistling in Doolin.

COUNTY CLARE IN 1 DAY

A car is the best way to experience County Clare and the Burren. The region can be an enjoyable daylong drive-through or a destination itself. None of the sights take much time. But do get out and walk a bit.

If you have more time, you could take a walking tour (of the Cliffs of Moher or the Burren) or a cruise from Doolin (to see the Cliffs of Moher and the Aran Island of Inisheer). For an overnight stay, good choices are Doolin and Ennis.

If you're driving from Dingle to Galway, I'd recommend the following day plan: Rather than taking the main N-21 road via Limerick, drive north from Tralee on N-69 via Listowel to catch the Tarbert-Killimer car ferry (avoiding Limerick's rush-hour traffic). Even though the ferry is slower and more expensive, it's more direct to the Burren (for specifics, see page 188).

From Killimer, drive north on N-67 via Kilkee and Milltown Malbay. The little surfer-and-golfer village of Lahinch makes a good lunch stop. Then drive the coastal route to the Cliffs of Moher for an hour-long break. (You could wait to eat at the cafeteria at the cliffs, but big-bus tour groups can clog it at midday in summer.) The scenic drive from the cliffs through the Burren, with a couple of stops, takes about two hours. Consider partaking in the 17:30 medieval banquet at Dunguaire Castle (reservations required) near Kinvarra, one hour south of Galway.

By Train or Bus: Using public transportation, your gateways to this region are Ennis from the south and Galway from the north. Linking the smaller sights within County Clare and the Burren by bus is difficult: Book a tour instead (see page 215).

Rick's Tip: Visit an **ATM in Ennis, Galway, or Lahinch** before you enter this region. There are no ATMs in Doolin, Kilfenora, or Ballyvaughan.

▲▲▲**Cliffs of Moher** Steep cliffs bordered by a bluff-top trail—offering breathtaking coastal views—perched precariously 600 feet above the churning Atlantic. **Hours:** Visitors center—Daily 9:00-19:30, gradually later closing times toward midsummer—as late as 21:00 July-Aug; Oct-April until 17:00. See page 210.

▲▲**The Burren** Desolate but botanically diverse, a limestone wonderland for hikers, sheltering evocative 4,000-year-old burial structures that witnessed man's transition from hunter-gatherer to farmer-herder. See page 214.

▲**Doolin** A friendly crossroads town drawing great musicians to its pubs and serving as an easy base for cruising along the Cliffs of Moher and day-tripping to the Aran Island of Inisheer. See page 212.

▲**Ennis** County's main market town (a great overnight base for nearby Shannon Airport) sporting fun trad music pubs, historic abbey ruins, and nearby Craggaunowen open-air folk park. See page 204.

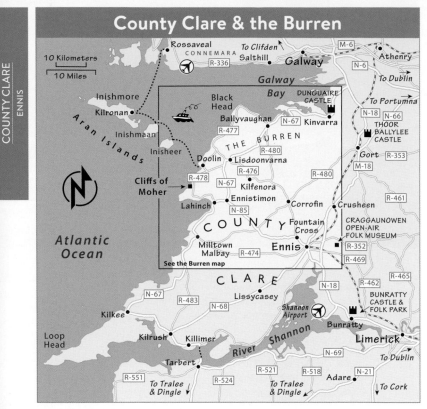

County Clare & the Burren

ENNIS

This pleasant market town (pop. 25,000), rated ▲, is a handy transportation hub, with good rail connections to Limerick, Dublin, and Galway. Ennis is 15 miles from Shannon Airport and makes a good first- or last-night base in Ireland for travelers who aren't locked into Dublin flights. It also offers a chance to wander around an Irish town that is not reliant upon the tourist dollar (although not shunning it either).

Muhammad Ali visited the town in 2008 after discovering that one of his great-grandfathers had been born in Ennis. Locals credit his success to his fightin' Irish side.

Orientation

The center of Ennis is a tangle of contorted streets (often one-way). Use the steeple of Saints Peter and Paul Cathedral and the Daniel O'Connell monument column (at either end of the main shopping drag, O'Connell Street) as landmarks.

Tourist Information: The TI is just off O'Connell Street Square (Mon-Sat 9:30-17:30, closed Sun year-round and Mon Oct-May, some lunchtime closures, tel. 065/682-8366).

Laundry: Fergus launderette is opposite the Parnell Street parking lot (Mon-Sat 8:30-18:00, closed Sun, tel. 065/682-3122).

Taxi: A good local bet is **Burren Taxis** (tel. 065/682-3456).

Walking Tours: Jane O'Brien leads 1.5-hour walking tours of Ennis departing from the TI (€10, mid-May-mid-Sept Mon-Tue and Thu-Sat at 11:00, available for private tours, mobile 087-648-3714, www.enniswalkingtours.com).

Bus Tours: Barratt Tours runs bus tours of the Cliffs of Moher and the Burren (€27, April-Oct daily, departs from TI at 10:30 and returns by 17:30, call to confirm schedule, tel. 061/333-100, mobile 087-237-5986, www.4tours.biz).

Sights

CLARE MUSEUM

This small but worthwhile museum, housed in the large TI building, has eclectic displays about ancient ax heads, submarine development, and local boys who made good—from 10th-century High King Brian Ború to 20th-century statesman Éamon de Valera. Coverage includes the Battle of Dysert O'Dea in 1318. One of the few Irish victories over the invading Normans, it delayed English domination of most of County Clare for another 200 years.

Cost and Hours: Free, Mon-Sat 9:30-12:30 & 14:00-17:00, closed Sun year-round and Mon Oct-May, tel. 065/682-3382, www.clarelibrary.ie.

ENNIS FRIARY

The Franciscan monks arrived here in the 13th century, and the town grew up around their friary (which is like a monastery). Today, it's still worth a look for its 15th-century limestone carvings (now protected by a modern roof to keep their details from further deterioration).

Cost and Hours: €5, sometimes includes tour—depends on staffing, daily 10:00-18:00, closed Nov-March, tel. 065/682-9100.

Visiting the Friary: If more than one guide is on duty, ask for a brief introduction to the five carvings taken from the McMahon family tomb. The last one, of Christ rising on the third day, has a banner with a tiny swastika. But look

closely: It's rotating as the rising sun would. Despite the swastika's detestable WWII association, it's actually a centuries-old symbol of good luck (the word "swastika" comes from Sanskrit and means "well-being"). Postwar visitors, unaware of the symbol's older meaning, misunderstood it and tried to rub it out of the carving, thus its very faint presence today.

Near Ennis

▲CRAGGAUNOWEN

This open-air folk museum nestles in a pretty forest, an easy 20-minute drive east of Ennis. All the structures are replicas, except for the small 16th-century castle (tower house), which the park was built around. A friendly weaver, spinning her wool on the castle's ground floor, is glad to tell you the tricks of her trade. A highlight is the Crannog, a fortified Iron Age thatch-roofed dwelling built on a small man-made island, which gives you a grubby idea of how clans lived 2,000 years ago. A modern surprise hides in a corner of the park under a large glass teepee: the *Brendan*, the original humble boat that

Craggaunowen tower house

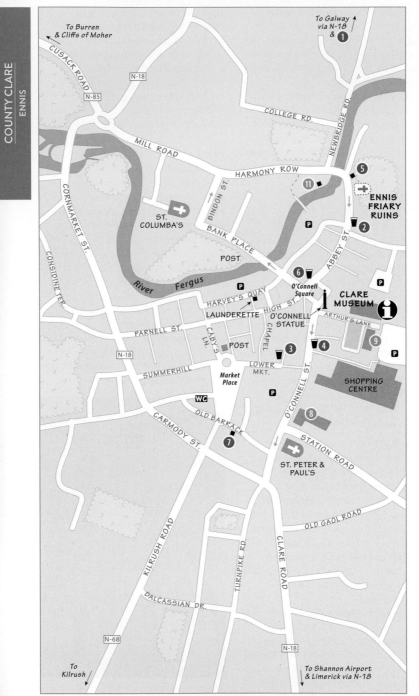

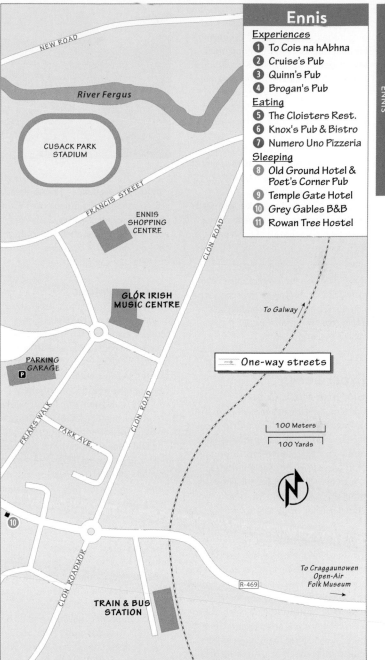

Ennis

Experiences
1. To Cois na hAbhna
2. Cruise's Pub
3. Quinn's Pub
4. Brogan's Pub

Eating
5. The Cloisters Rest.
6. Knox's Pub & Bistro
7. Numero Uno Pizzeria

Sleeping
8. Old Ground Hotel & Poet's Corner Pub
9. Temple Gate Hotel
10. Grey Gables B&B
11. Rowan Tree Hostel

scholar Tim Severin sailed from Ireland to North America in 1976 (via frosty stepping stones like Iceland and Greenland). He built this boat out of tanned hides, sewn together using primitive methods, to prove that Ireland's St. Brendan may indeed have been the first to discover America on his legendary voyage, 900 years before Columbus and 500 years before the Vikings.

Cost and Hours: €10, daily 10:00-17:00, shorter hours off-season, last entry one hour before closing, tel. 061/360-788, www.shannonheritage.com.

Getting There: The park is well-signposted nine miles (15 km) east of Ennis off R-469, which leads out of town past the train station.

Craggaunowen

famous Irish set dances. Phone ahead to see if a *ceilidh* is scheduled on off nights (€10-15, sporadically May-Sept Wed and Fri at 20:30, call ahead to confirm, at edge of Ennis on N-18 Galway road, tel. 065/682-4276, www.coisnahabhna.ie).

Rick's Tip: *Skip the commercialized Bunratty Castle and Folk Park, near the Shannon Airport, past Limerick on the road to Ennis. Leave it to the jet-lagged, big-bus American tour groups.*

Experiences
Glór Irish Music Centre

Ennis' modern theater center (*glór* is Irish for "sound") connects you with Irish culture. It's worth considering for traditional music, dance, or storytelling performances (€10-25, year-round usually at 20:00, 5-minute walk behind TI on Friar's Walk, ticket office open Mon-Sat 10:00-17:00, closed Sun, tel. 065/684-3103, www.glor.ie).

Cois na hAbhna

This original stage show, housed in the local Cois na hAbhna Hall, is a fine way to spend an evening. Sponsored by Comhaltas, a nonprofit organization focused on Irish traditional music, it's a celebration of Irish performing arts presented in two parts. The first half features great Irish music, song, and dance. After the break, you're invited to kick up your heels and take the floor as the dancers teach some

Traditional Music

Live music begins in the pubs at about 21:30. The best is **Cruise's** on Abbey Street, with music nightly year-round and good food (bar is cheaper than restaurant, tel. 065/682-8963). Other pubs offering weekly traditional music nights (generally on weekends, but schedules vary) are **Quinn's** on Lower Market Street (tel. 065/682-8148) and **Brogan's** on O'Connell Street (tel. 065/682-9480). The **Old Ground Hotel** hosts live music year-round in its pub (Tue-Sun, open to anyone); although tour groups stay at the hotel, the pub is low-key and feels real, not staged.

Eating

The Cloisters, next door to Ennis Friary, inhabits equally historic 800-year-old walls. Its steak, lamb, and fish dishes are the best in town and are served in a tasteful atmosphere, either in the upstairs **$$$$ restaurant** (Tue-Sun 17:30-21:00) or the downstairs **$$$ pub** (Tue-Sun 12:00-17:30, both sections closed Mon, Abbey Street, tel. 065/686-8198).

The **Old Ground Hotel** serves up hearty meals in its **$$$ Poet's Corner Pub**

The Voyage of St. Brendan

It has long been part of Irish lore that St. Brendan the Navigator (A.D. 484-577) and 12 followers sailed from the southwest of Ireland to the "Land of Promise" (what is now North America) in a *currach*—a wood-frame boat covered with ox hide and tar. According to a 10th-century monk who poetically wrote of the journey, St. Brendan and his crew encountered a paradise of birds, were attacked by a whale, and suffered the smoke of a smelly island in the north before finally reaching their Land of Promise.

The legend and its precisely described locations still fascinate modern readers. Parts of the tale hold up: The smelly island could well be the sulfuric volcanoes of Iceland. Other parts seem like devoted delirium: The holy monks claimed to have come upon Judas, chained to a rock in the middle of the ocean for all eternity.

A British scholar of navigation, Tim Severin, re-created the entire journey in 1976-1977. He and his crew set out from Brendan Creek in County Kerry in a *currach*. The prevailing winds blew them to the Hebrides, the Faroe Islands, Iceland, and finally to Newfoundland. While this didn't successfully prove that St. Brendan sailed to North America, it did prove that he could have. (You can visit Tim Severin's boat at the Craggaunowen open-air folk museum.)

According to his 10th-century biographer, "St. Brendan sailed from the Land of Promise home to Ireland. And from that time on, Brendan acted as if he did not belong to this world at all. His mind and his joy were in the delight of heaven."

(Mon-Sat 12:00-21:00, Sun 16:00-21:00).

For better than average pub grub, I like **$ Knox's Pub** on Abbey Street (daily 12:00-21:00, tel. 065/682-287). Or try one of the places mentioned under "Nightlife in Ennis," earlier.

The simple **$ Numero Uno Pizzeria** is good for an easy pub-free dinner (Mon-Sat 12:00-23:00, Sun from 15:00, on Old Barrack Street off Market Place, tel. 065/684-1740).

Sleeping

$$$$ Old Ground Hotel is a stately, ivy-covered 18th-century manse (minister's residence) with 105 rooms and a family feel. Pan Am clipper pilots stayed here during the early days of transatlantic seaplane flights (four blocks from station at intersection of Station Road and O'Connell Street, tel. 065/682-8127, www.flynnhotels.com, reservations@oldgroundhotel.ie).

$$$ Temple Gate Hotel's 70 rooms are more modern and less personal (breakfast extra, just off O'Connell Street, in courtyard with TI, tel. 065/682-3300, www.templegatehotel.com, info@templegatehotel.com).

$ Grey Gables B&B has 12 tastefully decorated rooms (cash only, wheelchair access, family rooms, parking, on Station Road 5 minutes from train station toward town center, tel. 065/682-4487, www.bed-n-breakfast-ireland.com, marykeane.ennis@eircom.net, Mary Keane).

¢ Rowan Tree Hostel is a well-run budget option, centrally located beside the gurgling River Fergus. It incorporates a grand old gentleman's club into its modern additions with better-than-expected private rooms and tidy dorm rooms. A pleasant café/bar rounds out the complex (on Harmony Row next to the bridge, tel. 065/686-8687, www.rowantreehostel.ie, info@rowantreehostel.ie).

Transportation
Arriving and Departing

BY CAR

If you're not spending the night (i.e., stowing your car at your B&B), parking is best in one of several pay-and-display lots (enforced Mon-Sat 9:30-17:30, free on Sun). The centrally located multistory lot on Market Place Square charges €5 per day (Mon-Sat 7:30-19:30, closed Sun).

BY TRAIN OR BUS

The train and bus station is located southeast of town, a 15-minute walk from the town center. To reach town, exit the station parking lot and turn left on Station Road, passing through a roundabout and past the recommended Grey Gables B&B. Turn right after the Old Ground Hotel onto O'Connell Street.

From Ennis by Train to: Galway (5/day, 1.5 hours), **Limerick** (9/day, 40 minutes), **Dublin** (9/day, 3-4 hours, change in Limerick, Limerick Junction, or Athenry). Train info: Tel. 065/684-0444, www.irishrail.ie.

By Ennis by Bus to: Galway (hourly, 1.5 hours), **Dublin** (almost hourly, 4-5.5 hours), **Limerick** (hourly, 1 hour), **Ballyvaughan** (1/day, 2.5 hours), **Tralee** (6/day, 3.5 hours, change in Limerick), **Doolin** (5/day, 2 hours). Bus info: Tel. 065/682-4177, www.buseireann.ie.

BY PLANE

Shannon Airport is about 15 miles south of Ennis. The major airport in western Ireland comes with far less stress than Dublin's overcrowded airport (airport code: SNN, airport tel. 061/712-000, www.shannonairport.ie). It has a TI, ATMs, and a baggage storage desk.

From Shannon Airport by Bus to: Ennis (bus #51 runs between the airport and the Ennis train station hourly, 20 minutes after the hour starting at 8:20, 30 minutes), **Galway** (bus #51, hourly, 1.5 hours), **Limerick** (hourly, 1 hour, can continue to Tralee—2 hours more, and Dingle—4/day, another 2 hours; bus tel. 061/313-333, www.buseireann.ie).

Sleeping near Shannon Airport: Consider **$$ Park Inn by Radisson Shannon Airport** (tel. 061/471-122, www.parkinn.com).

CLIFFS OF MOHER

A visit to the Cliffs of Moher (pronounced MO-hur)—a ▲▲▲ sight—is one of Ireland's great natural thrills. For five miles, the dramatic cliffs soar as high as 650 feet above the Atlantic.

Getting There

The Cliffs of Moher are located on R-478, south of Doolin. The parking lot across the road from the visitors center is for the general public; pay the attendant as you drive in. The lot next to the visitors center is for tour buses and disabled visitors.

If you're without wheels, it's easiest to get here on a bus tour out of Galway or Ennis; check the companies listed on page 215 (tours generally include the Burren). Or—to see (but not visit) the cliffs—you can take a boat from Doolin; see page 213.

Orientation

Cost: €6, includes parking and admission to the visitors center and its exhibit. It costs €2 to climb O'Brien's Tower (not worth it).

Hours: Daily 9:00-19:30, gradually later closing times toward midsummer—as late as 21:00 July-Aug; Oct-April until 17:00.

The Cliffs of Moher

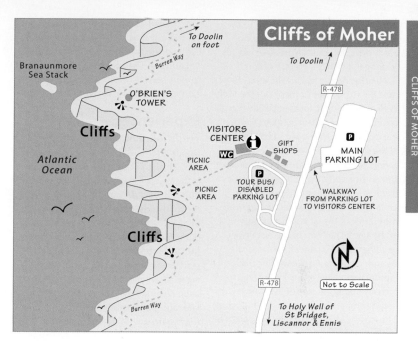

Information: Tel. 065/708-6141, www. cliffsofmoher.ie.

Services: You'll find an information desk and ATM in the visitors center—the Tolkienesque labyrinth tucked under the grassy hillside—flanked by six hobbit garages housing gift shops (across the street from the parking lot). **Cliffs View Café,** upstairs in the visitors center, serves coffee and substantial cafeteria-style hot meals until 16:30. There's also the **Puffin's Nest,** a small sandwich café downstairs.

● Self-Guided Tour

The visitors center is designed smartly to orient you to the cliffs experience, spiraling up and finally out onto the cliffs themselves in this order: entry (TI, shop, café); nature exhibit; short film in theater; main restaurant and WC; and outside to the cliffs. (While this is ideal, if the weather seems iffy and you see a sun break, you could do the cliff walk first.)

Visitors Center: The Atlantic Edge exhibit (downstairs) focuses mainly on natural and geological history, native bird and marine life, and virtual interactive exhibits aimed at children. You may even learn why the cliffs are always windy. A small theater shows *The Ledge Experience,* a film following a gannet as he flies along the cliffs and then dives underwater, encountering puffins, seals, and even a humpback whale along the way. (The film is on a five-minute loop with the start-time clock ticking down above the theater door.)

The Cliffs: After leaving the visitors center, walk 200 yards to the **cliff** edge. A protective wall of the local Liscannor slate (notice the squiggles made by worms, eels, and snails long ago when the slate was still mud on the seafloor) keeps visitors safely back from the cliff. You can walk behind the protective wall in either direction. The trail to the right (north, toward the castle-like tower) is more rewarding.

O'Brien's Tower, built in 1835, marks the highest point of the cliffs (but isn't worth the fee to climb...30 feet up doesn't improve the views much). Hike five minutes up to the tower and look to the north (your right). In the distance, on windy days, you can see the Aran Islands wearing their white necklace of surf.

Nearby: Before leaving the area, drivers can take 10 minutes to check out the **Holy Well of St. Bridget,** located beside the tall column about a half-mile (1 km) south of the cliffs on the main road to Liscannor. In the short hall leading into the hillside spring, you'll find a treasury of personal and religious offerings left behind by devoted visitors seeking cures and blessings. A trickle of water springs from the hillside at the far end. To the right of the simple hall entrance is a stairway heading up into a peaceful graveyard. Be sure to check out the wishing tree (sometimes called a fairy bush or rag tree) halfway up the left side of the stairway. It's usually draped in ribbons tied to branches. These were offerings to saints as part of a healing ritual.

DOOLIN

Rated ▲, Doolin had long been a mecca for Irish musicians, who came together here to play before a few lucky aficionados. Many music lovers would come here directly from Paris or Munich, as the town was on the tourist map for its traditional music. But now crowds have overwhelmed the musicians, and I prefer Dingle's richer music scene. Still, as Irish and European fans crowd the pubs, the *bodhrán* beat goes on.

Orientation

The "town" is just a few homes and shops strung out along a valley road from the tiny harbor. Residents generally divide the town into an Upper Village and Lower Village. The Lower Village is the closest thing to a commercial center (it has a couple of pubs and a couple of music shops).

Tourist Information: The privately owned TI at Hotel Doolin in the Upper Village books rooms and Aran Islands boat

trips (daily 8:30-19:00, closed off-season, tel. 065/707-5642). You'll find a similar boat-booking outfit in the Lower Village.

Laundry: The Lodge Doolin offers laundry service (drop-off only, pick up clothes in 8 hours, daily 8:00-20:00).

Experiences
Traditional Music

Doolin is famous for three pubs, all featuring Irish folk music: Nearest the harbor, in the Lower Village, is **Gus O'Connor's Pub** (tel. 065/707-4168). A mile farther up the road, the Upper Village—straddling a bridge—is home to two other destination pubs: **McGann's** (tel. 065/707-4133) and **McDermott's** (tel. 065/707-4328). Music starts between 21:30 and 22:00, finishing at about midnight. Get there before 21:00 if you want a place to sit, or pop in later and plan on standing. The *craic* is fine regardless. Pubs serve decent dinners before the music starts.

Cliffs of Moher Walks, Shuttle Bus, and Cruises

From Doolin, you can hike up the Burren Way along the coast to the Cliffs of Moher. Local guide and farmer Pat Sweeny operates **Doolin Cliff Walk,** leading walking tours that depart daily at 10:00 from O'Connor's Pub. The five-mile walk to the cliffs takes three hours and is not safe for kids under age 10; you catch the 13:30 bus back to Doolin (€10, May-Sept, mobile 086-822-9913, www.doolincliffwalk.com; phone ahead to reserve and check weather

Doolin pub

and trail conditions).

Alternatively, the **Hop-on, Hop-off Coastal Shuttle Bus** (16 seats) stops throughout Doolin, along the Cliffs of Moher coastal walk, and in the town of Liscannor (€6, departs every 90 minutes starting at 9:00 from Doolin Park & Ride lot—next to R-478, down the hill halfway between N-67 and Doolin Pier, tel. 065/707-5599, mobile 087-775-5098, www.cliffsofmohercoastalwalk.ie).

Two companies offer boat cruises along the Cliffs of Moher: **Doolin2Aran Ferries** (tel. 065/707-5949, mobile 087-245-3239, www.doolin2aranferries.com) and **O'Brien Line** (tel. 065/707-5618, www.obrienline.com). Boats depart from the pier in Doolin (same dock as Aran Islands boat, €20, runs daily April-Oct, 3/day, weather and tides permitting, call or go online for sailing schedule and to reserve).

Eating

Doolin's only gourmet option is **$$$ Cullinans,** facing the T-intersection as you come down the hill into the Upper Village (Mon-Tue and Thu-Sat 18:00-21:00, closed Sept-Easter and Wed and Sun year-round, reservations smart in summer, tel. 065/707-4183, www.cullinansdoolin.com, info@cullinansdoolin.com).

The **$$ Ivy Cottage** in the Lower Village, just past the bridge, has a pleasant, leafy tea garden out front. They do a dish of the day as well as simple sandwiches, quiche, or chowder (daily 10:00-18:00). You can order fish-and-chips to take away.

$$ The Cliff Coast Café, across the bridge in the Doolin Inn, serves dependable dishes (daily 11:00-21:00, shorter hours off-season).

Doolin has earned a reputation for consistently good pub grub. In the Lower Village, try **$$ Gus O'Connor's Pub,** and in the Upper Village, give **$$ McGann's** a spin. **Mac's Daybreak** is the town market and gas station (daily 7:30-21:00, on R-478 above town next to Harbour View B&B).

Sleeping

$$ Harbour View B&B offers six rooms in a fine modern house overlooking the coast a mile from the Doolin fiddles. Amy Lindner keeps the place immaculate (on main road halfway between Lisdoonvarna and Cliffs of Moher, next to Aran View Market and gas station, tel. 065/707-4154, www.harbourviewdoolin.com, clarebb@eircom.net).

$$ Half Door B&B is the coziest place around, with six woody rooms and a pleasant sun porch. It's just a short walk from the best pubs in the Upper Village (cash only, family rooms, a keg's roll from McDermott's pub, tel. 065/707-5959, www.halfdoordoolin.com, ann@halfdoordoolin.com).

$ The Lodge Doolin is a modern compound of four stone buildings with 21 bright, airy, good-value rooms (located halfway between Upper and Lower Villages, tel. 065/707-4888, www.doolinlodge.com, info@doolinlodge.com). The lodge offers laundry service.

¢ Doolin Inn & Hostel, right in Doolin's Lower Village, caters creatively to the needs of backpackers in town for the music. Friendly Anthony and Dierdre are on top of the local scene. The upper house has the Inn, which offers good-value double rooms and a café. The lower house across the road is the hostel (mobile 087-282-0587, www.doolinhostel.ie, reservationsanthony@doolinhostel.ie).

Transportation

From Doolin by Bus to: Galway (5/day, 1.5 hours), **Ennis** (5/day, 2 hours). Buses depart from Doolin's hostel.

From Doolin by Ferry to the Aran Islands: Doolin2Aran Ferries or O'Brien Line both take you to the closest island, Inisheer (with time to explore), then back along the Cliffs of Moher (they also go to Inishmore, the farthest island; if you're doing that, it's best to spend the night). For the full rundown on ferries from Doolin, see page 260.

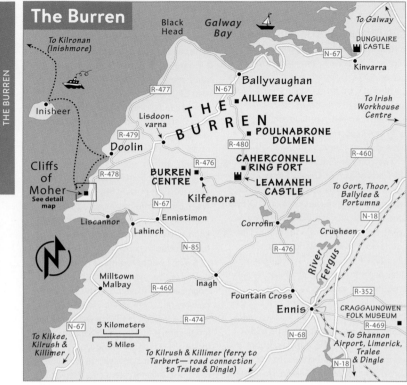

THE BURREN

Literally the "rocky place," the Burren is just that. This 10-square-mile limestone plateau, a ▲▲ sight, is so barren that a disappointed Cromwellian surveyor of the 1650s described it as "a savage land, yielding neither water enough to drown a man, nor a tree to hang him, nor soil enough to bury him." But he wasn't much of a botanist, because the Burren is in fact a unique ecosystem, with flora that has managed to adapt since the last Ice Age, 10,000 years ago. It's also rich in prehistoric and early Christian sites. This limestone land is littered with hundreds of historic stone structures, including dozens of Iron Age stone forts. When the first human inhabitants of the Burren came about 6,000 years ago, they cut down its trees with shortsighted slash-and-burn methods, which accelerated erosion of the topsoil (already scoured

to a thin layer by glaciers)—making those ancient people partially responsible for the stark landscape we see today.

You can either get a quick overview using my self-guided driving tour, or take your time and really get a feel for the land with one of the walking tours below. Travelers without a car can see the Burren with a bus tour.

Tours
Walking Tours

Most travelers zip through the seemingly barren Burren without stopping, grateful for the soft soil they garden back home. But healthy hikers and armchair naturalists may want to slow down and take a closer look. Be sure to wear comfortable shoes for the wet, uneven, rocky bedrock. These guides can bring the harsh landscape to life.

Cloudgazing in the Burren

From Ballyvaughan (at the northern entrance to the Burren): **Shane Connolly** leads in-depth, three-hour guided walking tours, explaining the region's history, geology, and diverse flora, and the role humans have played in shaping this landscape. This proud farmer really knows his stuff (€15, daily at 10:00 and 15:00, call to book and confirm meeting place in Ballyvaughan, tel. 065/707-7168, http://homepage.eircom. net/~burrenhillwalks).

From Kilfenora (at the southern entrance to the Burren): **Tony Kirby** leads regularly scheduled two-hour "Heart of Burren Walks" during the summer, and the rest of the year by appointment. His expertise peels back the rocky surface to reveal the surprisingly fascinating natural and human history that has created this unique region (€20, June-Aug Tue-Thu at 10:30, Fri-Sun at 14:15, meet at Burren Centre in Kilfenora, tel. 065/682-7707, mobile 087-292-5487, www.heartofburrenwalks. com, info@heartofburrenwalks.com).

Bus Tours

From Galway: Galway Tour Company's standard all-day bus tour of the Burren covers Kinvarra, Aillwee Cave, Poulnabrone Dolmen, and the Cliffs of Moher (€30, discounts if you book online, departs at 9:00, returns about 17:30, confirm schedule ahead). For €15 more, you can add a boat ride out from nearby Doolin to the Aran Island of Inisheer. **Lally Tours** and **Healy Tours** run similar day trips (see page 224 for contact information for all three companies).

From Ennis: Barratt Tours has a bus tour combining the Burren and Cliffs of Moher (see page 205).

⊘ Burren Driving Tour

This drive from Kilfenora to Kinvarra offers the best quick swing through the historic Burren and covers about 30 miles from start to finish.
• *Begin in the town of Kilfenora, 8 kilometers (5 miles) southeast of Lisdoonvarna, at the T-intersection where R-476 meets R-481.*

Kilfenora

This town's hardworking, community-run **Burren Centre** shows an informative 10-minute video explaining the geology and botany of the region, and then ushers you into its enlightening museum exhibits (€6, daily June-Aug 9:30-17:30, mid-

Leamaneh Castle

March-May and Sept-Oct 10:00-17:00, closed in winter, tel. 065/708-8030, www. theburrencentre.ie). You'll also see copies of a fine eighth-century golden collar and ninth-century silver brooch (originals in Dublin's National Museum).

The ruined **church** next door has a couple of 12th-century crosses, but there isn't much to see. Mass is still held in the church, which claims the pope as its bishop by papal dictate. As the smallest and poorest diocese in Ireland, Kilfenora was almost unable to function after the Great Potato Famine, so in 1866 Pope Pius IX supported the town as best he could—by personally declaring himself its bishop.

For lunch in Kilfenora, consider the cheap and cheery **Burren Centre Tea Room** (daily 9:30-17:30, located at far back of building) or the more atmospheric **Vaughan's Pub.** If you're spending the night in County Clare, make a real effort to join the locals at the fun set-dancing get-togethers run by the Vaughans in the **Barn Pub,** adjacent to their regular pub. This dance scene is a memorable treat (€5, Sun at 21:30, also Thu in July-Aug, call to confirm schedule, tel. 065/708-8004).

• *To continue from Kilfenora into the heart of the Burren, head east out of town on R-476. After about 5 kilometers (3 miles), you'll come to the junction with northbound R-480. Take the sharp left turn onto R-480, and slow down to gaze up (on the left) at the ruins of...*

Leamaneh Castle

This ruined shell of a fortified house is closed to everyone except the female ghost that supposedly haunts it. From the outside, you can see how the 15th-century fortified tower house (the right quarter of the remaining ruin) was expanded 150 years later (the left three-quarters of the ruin). The castle evolved from a refuge into a manor, and windows were widened to allow for better views as defense became less of a priority.

• *From the castle, continue north on R-480 (direction: Ballyvaughan). After about 8 kilometers (5 miles), you'll hit the start of the real barren Burren. Keep an eye out for the next stop.*

Caherconnell (Cahercommaun) Ring Fort

Of the many ring forts in the area, this one is the most accessible. You can see the

Poulnabrone Dolmen

low stone profile of Caherconnell to the left on the crest of a hill just off the road. You can park in the gravel lot and walk up to the small visitors center and handy café for an informative 20-minute film followed by a quick wander through the small fort. The fort sometimes features a sheepherding demo with dogs (generally at 12:00 and 15:00—call to confirm).

Cost and Hours: €7, €9.60 with sheepherding demo, daily July-Aug 10:00-18:00, Easter-June and Sept-Oct 10:30-17:30, closed in winter, tel. 065/708-9999, www.caherconnell.com.

• *The stretch from the ring fort north to Ballyvaughan offers the starkest scenery. Soon you'll see a 10-foot-high stone structure a hundred yards off the road to the right (east, toward an ugly gray metal barn). Pull over for a closer look.*

Poulnabrone Dolmen

While it looks like a stone table, this is a portal tomb. Two hundred years ago, locals called this a "druids' altar." Five thousand years ago, it was a grave chamber in a cairn of stacked stones. Amble over for a look (It's crowded with tour buses at midday, but it's all yours early or late.)

Wander about for some quiet time with the wildflowers and try to think like a geologist. You're walking across a former seabed, dating from 250 million years ago when Ireland was at the equator (before continental drift nudged it north). Look for white smudges of fossils. Stones embedded in the belly of an advancing glacier ground the scratches you see in the rocks. The rounded boulders came south from Connemara, carried on a giant conveyor belt of ice, and then were left behind when the melting glaciers retreated north.

• *As you drive away from the dolmen (continuing north), look for the 30-foot-deep sinkhole beside the road on the right (a collapsed cave). From here, R-480 winds slowly downhill for about 6 kilometers (4 miles), eventually leaving the rocky landscape behind and entering a comparatively lush green valley. Eventually, on the right, you'll find the turn up to...*

Aillwee Cave

As this is touted as "Ireland's premier show cave," I couldn't resist a look. While fairly touristy and not worth the time or money if you've seen a lot of caves, it's

Botany of the Burren in Brief

The Burren is a story of water, rock, geological force, and time. It supports the greatest diversity of plants in Ireland. Like nowhere else, Mediterranean and Arctic wildflowers bloom side by side in the Burren. It's an orgy of cross-pollination that attracts more insects than Doolin does music lovers—even beetles help out. Limestone, created from layers of coral, seashells, and mud, is the bedrock of the Burren. (The same formation resurfaces 10 miles or so out to sea to form the Aran Islands.)

Geologic forces in the earth's crust heaved up the land, and the glaciers swept it bare and shattered it like glass under their weight—dropping boulders as they receded. Rain, reacting naturally with the limestone to create a mild but determined acid, slowly drilled potholes into the surface. Rainwater cut through the limestone's weak zones, leaving crevices on the surface and one of Europe's most extensive systems of caves below. Algae grew in the puddles, dried into a powder, and combined with bug parts and rabbit turds (bunnies abound in the Burren) to create a very special soil. Plants and flowers fill the cracks in the limestone. Grasses and shrubs don't do well here, and wild goats eat any trees that try to grow, giving tender little blossoms a chance to enjoy the sun. Different blooms appear throughout the months, sharing space rather than competing. The flowers are best in June and July.

the easiest way to sample the massive system of caves that underlies the Burren. Your guide walks you 300 yards into the plain but impressive cave, giving a serious 40-minute geology lesson.

Rick's Tip: *If you take the tour, also take a sweater: The cave is a constant 50°F.*

Just below the cave (and on the same property) is the **Burren Birds of Prey Centre,** which houses owls, eagles, hawks, and falcons (bird demonstrations daily—call for schedule).

Adjacent to the cave, the **Hawk Walk** gets visitors face-to-beak with a Harris hawk, "the world's only social raptor." After a brief training session, an instructor

Dunguaire Castle

leads a small group on a 45-minute hike up a nearby mountain trail. Those paying the stiff €70 fee get to launch and call back the bird to perch on their arm (limited slots, must reserve).

Cost and Hours: Cave-€12, bird center-€10, €18 combo-ticket includes both sights but not Hawk Walk; open daily at 10:00, last tour at 18:30 July-Aug, otherwise 17:30, Dec-Feb call ahead for limited tours; clearly signposted just south of Ballyvaughan, tel. 065/707-7036, www.aillweecave.ie.

• *Continuing on, our final destination is...*

Kinvarra

This tiny town, between Ballyvaughan and Galway, is waiting for something to happen in its minuscule harbor. It faces Dunguaire Castle, a four-story tower house from 1520 that stands a few yards out in the bay.

The touristy but fun **Dunguaire Castle medieval banquet** is the town's most worthy attraction (€57, cheaper if you book online, most evenings at 17:30 and sometimes at 20:30, mid-April–mid-Oct, reservations required, tel. 061/360-788, castle tel. 091/637-108, www.shannonheritage.com).

Warning: This company also operates banquets at two other castles in the region, so be sure that you make your reservation for the correct castle.

The evening is as intimate as a gathering of 55 tourists under one time-stained, barrel-vaulted ceiling can be. You get a decent four-course meal with wine (or mead if you ask sweetly), served amid an entertaining evening of Irish tales and folk songs. Remember that in medieval times, it was considered polite to flirt with wenches. It's a small and multitalented cast: one harpist and three singer/actors who serve the "lords and ladies" between tunes. The highlight is the 40-minute stage show, which features songs and poems by local writers, and comes with dessert.

You can visit the castle itself by day without taking in an evening banquet (€6, daily 10:00-16:30).

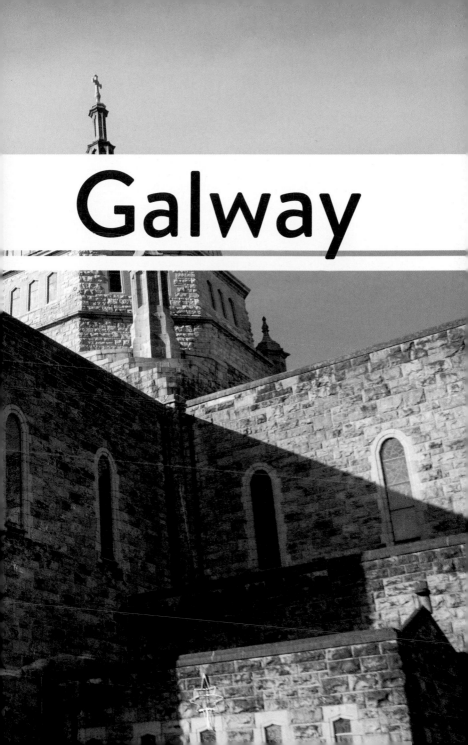

Galway

Galway offers the most easily accessible slice of Ireland's west coast. With 76,000 people, this is Galway County's main city, a lively university town, and the region's industrial and administrative center.

While Galway has a long and interesting history, precious little from old Galway survives. What does remain has the disadvantage of being built in the local limestone, which, even if medieval, looks like modern stone construction.

What Galway lacks in sights it makes up for in ambience. Spend an afternoon just wandering its medieval streets, with their delightful mix of colorful facades, labyrinthine pubs, weather-resistant street musicians, and steamy eateries. After dark, blustery Galway heats up, with a fine theater and a pub scene that attracts even Dubliners. Visitors mix with old-timers and students as the traditional music goes round and round.

Galway is well-connected by train to Dublin. And it's a convenient jumping-off point for visiting the Aran Islands (a Gaelic cultural preserve), the Burren (an area of geologic and prehistoric interest, to the south), and Connemara (a region steeped in Irish history, to the north).

GALWAY IN 1 DAY

The real joy of Galway is in its street scene. Although you could see the town's sights in a couple of hours, the best part of Galway is its nightlife—starring traditional music.

Here are efficient plans:

By Car: Spend two nights in Galway and the day visiting the Aran Islands. For example: If you're driving north from Dingle, visit the Cliffs of Moher and the Burren en route, and spend the night in Galway. In Galway, stroll from Eyre Square to Galway Bay, seeking out a pub with music. On the next day, visit the Aran Islands (Inishmore), then return to Galway to enjoy another music-filled evening. Take off early the following day to drive through the region of Connemara on your way to Northern Ireland.

By Public Transportation and Tour: Arrive in Galway by train or bus. Spend two nights there, and use your full day for a day trip to the Aran Islands (my top choice), the Burren and Cliffs of Moher, or the Connemara region. Tour companies make day trips to all three regions affordable and easy.

GALWAY AT A GLANCE

▲**Medieval Galway's "Latin Quarter"** Half-mile-long pub and shopping zone linking Eyre Square to Galway Bay, dotted with old Norman architecture and weather-proof street musicians. See page 225.

▲**Eyre Square** Grassy fair-weather community gathering spot, location of beloved JFK speech, and haven for Frisbee tossers and dog walkers. See page 225.

▲**Cathedral of St. Nicholas** Town's 50-year-old center of worship with richly appointed Interior and quirky mosaic honoring JFK at the foot of Christ's Ascension. See page 230.

▲**Salthill** Unpretentious suburb with a popular swimming beach and waterfront promenade, fun for strollers, joggers, and cyclists. See page 270.

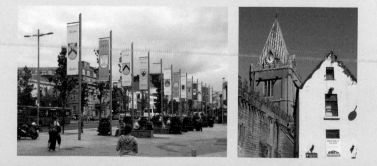

ORIENTATION

The center of Galway is Eyre (pronounced "air") Square. Within three blocks of the square, you'll find the TI, Aran boat offices, a tour pickup point, accommodations (from the best cheap hostel beds to fancy hotels), and the train station. The train and public bus station butt up against Hotel Meyrick, a huge gray railroad hotel that overlooks and dominates Eyre Square. The lively old town lies between Eyre Square and the river. From Eyre Square, Williams Gate leads a pedestrian parade right through the old town (changing street names several times) to Wolfe Tone Bridge. Nearly everything you'll see and do is within a few minutes' walk of this spine.

Tourist Information

The well-organized **TI,** located a block from the bus/train station, has regional as well as local information (Mon-Sat 9:00-17:00, closed Sun, Forster Street, tel. 091/537-700, www.discoverireland.ie).

Tours

In Galway

▲**Hop-on, hop-off city bus tours** compete for your euros. They depart from the northwest end of Eyre Square (opposite end of the square from the huge Hotel Meyrick), have similar schedules and prices, and make the dozen most important stops, including the cathedral, Salthill, and the Spanish Arch. These large coaches can't penetrate some of the winding medieval back streets, but you can get off, explore, and hop back on later. **Galway City** buses are blue (€10, April-Sept daily at 11:00, 12:30, 14:00, and 15:30, tel. 091/770-066, www.galwaybustours.ie). **City Sightseeing** buses are red (€12, April-Sept daily at 10:30, 12:00, 13:30, and 15:00, tel. 091/562-905, www.lallytours.com).

There are many **walking tours** in this town full of stories waiting to be told. Most are flexible in their start time and location (call ahead to confirm). **Galway Walking Tours** are led by Fiona Brennan, who takes her guests on leisurely 1.5-hour explorations of the city (€10, mobile 087-290-3499, www.galwaywalkingtours.com, fiona@galwaywalkingtours.com). **Liam Silke** comes from one of Galway's oldest families and portrays Galway's town crier as he leads 1.5-hour tours (€10, departs at 11:30 from TI, tel. 091/588-897, mobile 086-348-0958, www.walkingtoursgalway.com, info@walkingtoursgalway.com). **Galway Walk and Talk Tours** operate with the motto that "a walker has plenty of stories to tell" (€10, departs at 10:30 from TI, mobile 087-690-1452, www.walkandtalk-tour.com).

Galway Region

Galway Tour Company runs bus tours all over the region, including to the Burren, Cliffs of Moher, Aran Islands, and Connemara (office located just a few doors down Forster Street from TI, toward Eyre Square, tours depart from private coach station on Fairgreen Road—across from TI, tel. 091/566-566, www.galwaytourcompany.com, info@galwaytourcompany.com). If Galway Tour Company's tours are booked, try similar **Lally Tours** (tel. 091/562-905, www.lallytours.com) or **Healy Tours** (tel. 091/770-066, mobile 087-259-0160, www.healytours.ie). Drivers take cash only; to pay with a credit card, book in advance.

Helpful Hints

Markets: On Saturdays year-round and Sundays in summer, a fun market clusters

Galway bus tour

around St. Nicholas' Church (all day, best 9:00–14:00).

Laundry: Galway Dry Cleaners is close to the recommended B&Bs on College Road (drop-off service, Mon-Sat 9:30–17:30, closed Sun, on Bothar Ui Eithir, 2-minute walk uphill from TI, tel. 091/568-393).

Bike Rental: On Yer Bike rents bikes to tool around flat Galway town. Consider a pleasant ride out to the end of Salthill's beachfront promenade and back (€10-15/day, Mon-Sat 9:00–19:00, Sun 12:00–18:00, shorter hours off-season, 42 Prospect Hill, tel. 091/563-393, mobile 087-942-5479, www.onyourbikecycles.com).

Taxi: Give **Big-O-Taxis** a try (tel. 091/585-858).

Rick's Tip: *Expect huge crowds—and much higher prices—during the* **Galway Arts Festival** *(mid to late July, www.galwayartsfestival.com) and Galway Oyster Festival (late Sept, www.galwayoysterfest.com).*

SIGHTS

▲The Medieval "Latin Quarter"

Walking from Eyre Square down the pedestrian (and tourist) spine of old Galway to the River Corrib takes you past the essential sights in town. I've connected these sights in an easy downhill stroll.

▲EYRE SQUARE

Galway is dominated by its main, parklike square. On a sunny day, Eyre Square is filled with people just hanging out. In the Middle Ages, it was a field right outside the town wall. The square is named for the mayor who gave the land to the city in 1710. It now contains John F. Kennedy Park—established in memory of the Irish-American president's visit in 1963, when he filled this space with adoring Irish just a few months before he was assassinated (a JFK bust near the kids' play area commemorates his visit).

Walk to the rust-colored "Hooker" sculpture, built in 1984 to celebrate the 500th anniversary of the incorporation of the city. The sails represent Galway's square-rigged fishing ships ("hookers") and the vessels that made Galway a trading center so long ago. The Browne Doorway, from a 1627 fortified townhouse, is a reminder of the 14 family tribes that once ruled the town (Lynch's Castle, nearby, gives you a feel for an intact townhouse). Each family tribe had a town castle—much like the towers that characterize the towns of Italy, with their feuding noble families. So little survives of medieval Galway that the town makes a huge deal of any remaining window or crest. Each of the 14 colorful flags lining the west end of the square represents a different original Norman founding tribe.

• *From the top of Eyre Square, walk down Williams Gate—a street named for the old main gate of the Norman town wall that once stood here. The spine of medieval Galway, the road changes names several times as it leads downhill to the River Corrib. After about three blocks you'll see a bold limestone "town castle" on your right.*

LYNCH'S CASTLE

Now a bank, this limestone tower, Galway's best late-15th-century fortified townhouse, was the home of the Lynch family—the most powerful of the town's 14 tribes—and the only one of their mansions to survive. More than 80 of the mayors who ruled Galway in the 16th and 17th centuries were from the Lynch family.

• *Continuing another block downhill, you'll veer a half-block to the right off the main pedestrian flow, to the big church.*

COLLEGIATE CHURCH OF ST. NICHOLAS

This church, the finest medieval building in town (1320), is dedicated to St. Nicholas of Myra, the patron saint of sailors. Columbus is said to have worshiped here in 1477, undoubtedly contemplating a scary voyage. Its interior is littered

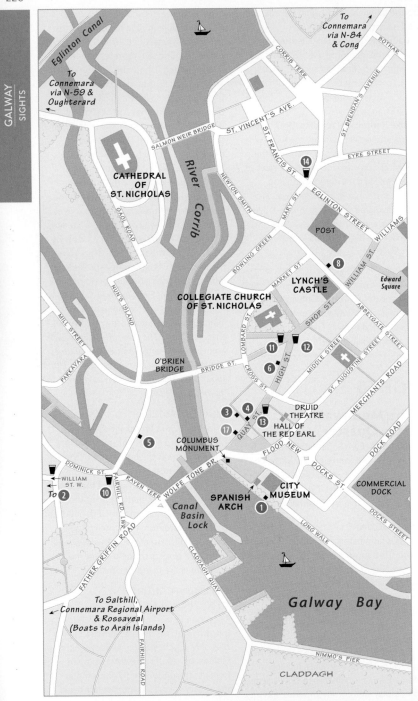

Galway

To
Knock & Sligo
via N-17

ST. BRIDGET'S PLACE

NA MBAN

ROSEMARY ST.

BOTHAR UI EITHIR

PROSPECT HILL

22

23

MAGDALENE
LAUNDRY
MEMORIAL

CITY
HALL

COLLEGE ROAD

To
Galway Airport
& The Burren

19

20

21

BROWNE
DOORWAY

"HOOKER"
SCULPTURE

GATE

7

Eyre
Square

FORSTER STREET

COACH STATION
(PRIVATE BUS TOURS)

FRENCHVILLE LANE

15

STATION RD

PUBLIC BUS
STATION

B

9

EYRE
SQUARE
SHOPPING
CENTRE

18

16

VICTORIA PLACE

TRAIN
STATION

Lough
Atalia

QUEEN STREET

DOCK ROAD

LOUGH ATALIA ROAD

N

100 Meters

100 Yards

Eating
1. Ard Bia at Nimmo's
2. To Kai Café/Rest., The Universal & The Crane
3. The Seafood Bar at Kirwan's
4. McDonagh's Fish-and-Chips
5. Rouge Restaurant
6. Murphy's Ice Cream
7. Galway Bakery Co. (GBC)
8. The Lighthouse Vegetarian Café
9. Supermarket

Nightlife
10. Monroe's Pub
11. Tig Cóilí Pub

Eating (cont.)
12. Taaffe's Pub
13. The Quays Pub
14. Barr An Chaladh

Sleeping
15. Park House Hotel
16. Hotel Meyrick
17. Jurys Inn Galway
18. Kinlay Hostel
19. Petra House
20. Balcony House B&B
21. Asgard Guest House

Other
22. Laundry
23. Bike Rental

Lynch's Castle

with obscure bits of town history. Consider attending an evening concert of traditional Irish music in this atmospheric venue (see "Nightlife," later).

An **open-air market** surrounds the church most Saturdays year-round and also on Sundays in summer.

• *Returning to the pedestrian mall, carry on another block and a half downhill. Look for The Quays pub on your left.*

THE QUAYS

This pub was once owned by "Humanity Dick," an 18th-century Member of Parliament who was the original animal-rights activist. His efforts led to the world's first conviction for cruelty to animals in 1822. It's worth a peek inside for its lively interior.

• *Head down the lane just before the pub, about 50 yards, to the big glass windows on the right...*

HALL OF THE RED EARL

A big glass wall shows the excavation site of the Hall of the Red Earl. Wall diagrams and storyboards explain that these are the dusty foundations of Galway's oldest building,

once the 13th-century hall of the Norman lord Richard de Burgo (free, closed Sun).

Across the lane is the **Druid Theatre.** This 100-seat venue offers top-notch contemporary Irish theater. Although the theater company is away on tour more often than not, it's worth checking their schedule online or dropping by to see if anything's playing (€20-30 tickets, Chapel Lane, tel. 091/568-660, www.druid.ie).

• *Finally, walk to the end of the pedestrian mall, cross the busy street, and follow it to the Wolfe Tone Bridge, where you'll find two gray stone monuments (each about as tall as you are). Above the bridge, a sign says Welcome to Galway's West End. You just walked the tourist gauntlet. (Across the river and to the right is a trendy foodie zone.) Stand between the two stone monuments.*

COLUMBUS MONUMENT

The monument (closest to the bridge) was given to Galway by the people of Genoa, Italy, to celebrate the 1477 visit here of Christopher Columbus—Cristoforo Colombo in Italian. (That acknowledgment, from an Italian town so proud and protective of its favorite son, helps to substantiate the famous explorer's legendary visit.) The other memorial is dedicated to sailors lost at sea.

• *Don't cross the bridge. Instead, stroll left downstream to the old fortified arch.*

SPANISH ARCH

Overlooking the River Corrib, this makes up the best remaining chunk of the old city wall. A reminder of Galway's former

Galway's waterfront at Spanish Arch

Galway Legends and Factoids

Because of the dearth of physical old stuff, the town milks its legends. Here are a few that you'll encounter repeatedly:

- In the 15th century, the mayor, one of the Lynch tribe, condemned his son to death for the murder of a Spaniard. When no one in town could be found to hang the popular boy, the dad—who loved justice more than he loved his son—did it himself.
- Columbus is said to have stopped in Galway in 1477. He may have been inspired by tales of the voyage of St. Brendan, the Irish monk who is thought by some (mostly Irish) to have beaten Columbus to the New World by almost a thousand years.
- On the main drag, you'll find a pub called The King's Head. It was originally given to the man who chopped off the head of King Charles I in 1649. For his safety, he settled in Galway—about as far from London as an Englishman could get back then.
- William Joyce, born in America, spent most of his childhood in Galway and later was seduced by fascist ideology in the 1930s. He moved to Germany and became "Lord Haw-Haw," infamous as the radio voice of Nazi propaganda during World War II. After the war, he was hanged in London for treason. His daughter had him buried in Galway.

importance in trade, the arch (c. 1584) is the place where Spanish ships would unload their cargo (primarily wine).
• *Walk through the arch and take an immediate right. Go past the stone steps to the far corner of the embankment over the river.*

RIVER CORRIB SIGHTS

Enjoy this river scene. On either side is a park—a constant party on sunny days. (It's ideal for a picnic of fish-and-chips from the recommended McDonagh's chipper, near the end of the pedestrian mall.) Across the river is the modern housing project that replaced the original Claddagh in the 1930s. **Claddagh** was a picturesque, Irish-speaking fishing village with a strong tradition of independence—and open sewers. This gaggle of thatched cottages functioned as an independent community with its own "king" until the early 1900s, when it was torn down for health reasons.

The old Claddagh village is gone, but the tradition of its popular ring (sold all over town) lives on. **The Claddagh ring** shows two hands holding a heart that wears a crown. The heart represents love, the crown is loyalty, and the hands are friendship. If the ring is worn with the tip of the heart pointing in, it signifies that the wearer is taken. However, if the tip of the heart points out, it means the wearer is available.

Survey the harbor. A few of Galway's famous square-rigged "hooker" fishing ships are often tied up and on display. Called "hookers" for their method of fishing with multiple hooks on a single line, these sturdy yet graceful boats were later used to transport turf from Connemara, until improved roads and electric heat made them obsolete.

More Sights

GALWAY CITY MUSEUM

Fragments of old Galway are kept in this modern museum. Check out the intact Galway "hooker" fishing boat hanging from the ceiling. The ground floor houses the archaeological exhibits: prehistoric and ancient Galway-related treasures such as medieval pottery, Iron Age axe heads, and Bronze Age thingamajigs. The first floor sheds light on Galway's role in the Irish struggle for independence in the early 1900s. The top floor is devoted to "sea science" (oceanography).

Cost and Hours: Free, Tue-Sat 10:00-17:00, Sun 12:00-17:00, closed Sun Oct-March and Mon year-round, handy café with cheap lunches, on the Spanish Parade near the Spanish Arch, tel. 091/532-460, www.galwaycitymuseum.ie.

▲CATHEDRAL OF ST. NICHOLAS

Opened by American Cardinal Cushing in 1965, this is one of the last great stone churches built in Europe. The interior is a treat and is worth a peek.

Cost and Hours: Free, open to visitors daily 8:30-18:30 as long as you don't interrupt Mass, church bulletins at doorway list upcoming Masses and concerts, located across Salmon Weir Bridge on outskirts of town, tel. 091/563-577.

Visiting the Cathedral: Inside, you'll see mahogany pews set on green Connemara marble floors under a Canadian cedar ceiling. The acoustically correct cedar enhances the church's fine pipe organ. Two thousand worshippers sit on three sides facing the central altar. A Dublin woman carved the 14 larger-than-life Stations of the Cross. The carving above the chapel (left of entry) is from the old St. Nicholas church. Explore the modern stained glass. Find the Irish Holy Family—with Mary knitting and Jesus offering Joseph a cup of tea. The window depicting the Last Supper is particularly creative—find the 12 apostles.

Next, poke your head into the side chapel with a mosaic of Christ's Resurrection (if you're standing in the nave facing the main altar, it's on the left and closest to the front). Take a closer look at the profiled face in a circular frame, below and to the right of Christ—the one looking

up while praying with clasped hands. It's JFK, nearly a saint in Irish eyes at the time this cathedral was built.

Outer Galway

▲SALTHILL

This small resort town packs pubs, discos, a splashy water park, amusement centers, and a fairground up against a fine, mile-long beach promenade (Ireland's longest). Watch for local power walkers "kicking the wall" when they reach the western end of the promenade to emphasize that they've gone the entire distance.

At the **Atlantaquaria Aquarium,** which features native Irish aquatic life and some Amazonian species, kids can help feed the fish at 13:00 (fresh water), 15:00 (big fish), 16:00 (small fish), and 17:00 (naughty kids fed to piranhas). They can cuddle the crustaceans anytime (€12, Mon-Fri 10:00-17:00, Sat-Sun until 18:00, touch tanks, The Promenade, tel. 091/585-100, www.nationalaquarium.ie).

For beach time, a relaxing sunset stroll, late-night traditional music, or later-night disco action, Salthill hops.

The River Corrib glides through Galway.

Magdalene Laundries Memorial

Documentaries and films such as *The Magdalene Sisters* and *Philomena* have highlighted the plight of unmarried, pregnant Irish women who were incarcerated and put to work doing laundry as virtual slaves. Viewing premarital pregnancy as one step short of prostitution, various Catholic orders operated these infamous "Magdalene laundries." (No such stigma applied to the men involved.) Across from the TI (at 47 Forster Street), a modest and easy-to-miss statue stands on the site of one such facility, operated by the Sisters of Mercy, which opened in 1824 with a capacity of 110 young women, and closed in 1984 with 18 inmates remaining. It's estimated that upwards of 10,000 women passed through the Magdalene laundry system. Magdalene survivors claim that they were held against their will, forced to work without pay, and physically abused...and their children were sold for adoption. The Irish government apologized in 2013 for turning a blind eye to the mistreatment of these "fallen women," who were imprisoned out of sight, often with the consent of their shamed families.

Getting There: To get to Salthill, catch bus #401 from Eyre Square in front of the AIB bank, next to Meyrick Hotel (3/hour, €2).

EXPERIENCES

Nightlife

▲ Traditional Irish Music

Galway, like Dingle and Doolin, is a mecca for good Irish music (nightly 21:30-23:30). But unlike Dingle and Doolin, this is a university town, and many pubs are often overrun with noisy students. Still, your chances of landing a seat close to a churning band surrounded by new Irish friends are good any evening of the year.

Across Wolfe Tone Bridge: A good place to start is at **Monroe's,** with its vast, music-filled interior (check website for trad music schedule, Dominick Street, tel. 091/583-397, www.monroes.ie). The **Crane,** near Monroe's, has trad sessions nightly at 21:30 downstairs, a variety of other music upstairs, and Celtic Tales storytelling sessions on Thursdays from April to October (€10 for storytelling at 20:00, other sessions free, 2 Sea Road, tel. 091/587-419, www.thecranebar.com).

On the Main Drag: Pubs known for Irish music include **Tig Cóilí,** featuring Galway's best trad sessions (Mon-Sat at 18:00 and 22:00, Sun at 14:00 and 21:00, intersection of Main Guard Street and High Street, tel. 091/561-294); **Taaffe's** (nightly music sessions at 17:30 and 21:30, Shop Street, across from St. Nicholas Church, tel. 091/564-066); and **The Quays** (trad music most nights at 21:30, sporadic schedule, young scene, Quay Street, tel. 091/568-347). A bit off the main drag, **Barr An Chaladh** is a scruffy little place offering nightly trad or ballad sessions and more locals (3 Daly's Place, tel. 091/895-762).

Performances

Instead of a pub, you can also attend a concert or performance.

Trad on the Prom: This fine, traditional, music-and-dance troupe was started by Galway-born performers, who returned home after years of touring with *Riverdance* and the Chieftains. Their show—so popular that it has lasted for more than a decade—is a great way to enjoy live step dancing and accomplished musicians in a fairly intimate venue (€30, mid-May–Sept only, shows at 20:30 on Tue, Thu, and Sun—call to confirm, and best to reserve ahead online; at Leisureland Theatre beside Salthill Park, 30-minute walk west of town along the Salthill promenade or short

Trad music in Galway

ride on bus #401 from Eyre Square; tel. 091/582-860, mobile 087-674-1877, www. tradontheprom.com).

Tunes in the Church: The Collegiate Church of St. Nicholas is a mellow, medieval venue with great acoustics, hosting a rotating lineup of accomplished trad musicians. The 1.5-hour concerts are fun for early birds who don't want to stay up to catch the same great players in a local pub later that night (€15; June-July Mon-Fri at 20:00, daily in Aug; where High Street and Shop Street intersect, mobile 087-962-5425, www.tunesinthechurch.com).

EATING

Near the Bottom of the Old Town

$$$ Ard Bia at Nimmo's fills an old stone warehouse behind the Spanish Arch. It's rustically elegant, with beautifully presented dishes from a farm-to-table menu. If parsnip crisps, pickled rhubarb, beetroot risotto, and pan-roasted baby squid sound good, you'll enjoy this place (open daily, café lunches 12:00-15:30, finer dinners 18:00-21:30, Long Walk Street, tel.

091/561-114 or 091/539-897, run by Aoibheann—pronounced aye-von).

$$$ Kai Café and Restaurant is a stylish little place with a candlelit, stone-and-hardwood ambience. A café at lunch and a restaurant at dinner, it serves local foodies quirky, contemporary Irish cuisine. This is your kind of place if taste treats like Indian red pepper ratatouille, gooseberry chutney, ox tongue press, and stuffed courgette flowers are your thing (daily 12:00-15:00 & 18:30-22:00, reservations required for dinner, 20 Sea Road, tel. 091/526-003, www.kaicaferestaurant.com).

$$$ The Universal gastropub is another hit with Galway foodies. This feels more like a food lover's pub with an open kitchen, stools at the bar, and eight little tables. Choose tapas or full plates of creative, ingredient-driven cuisine, with lots of craft beers on tap (food served Tue-Sat 18:00-22:00, 9 William Street West, tel. 091/728-271).

$$$ The Seafood Bar at Kirwan's is a good place in the touristy center for quality seafood in a romantic setting (Mon-Sat 12:30-14:30 & 18:00-22:00, Sun 17:00-21:00, Kirwan's Lane, tel. 091/568-266, www.kirwanslane.com).

$ McDonagh's Fish-and-Chips is a favorite among residents. It has a fast, cheap, all-day **chipper** on one side and a more expensive sit-and-stay-awhile dinner-only **restaurant** on the other. The restaurant serves the same food, but you'll pay €4 extra to enjoy a nice table setting and a side of mushy peas. Both have a couple of outside tables right in the Quay Street action (chipper open Mon-Sat 12:00-23:00, Sun 14:00-21:00; restaurant open Mon-Sat 17:00-22:00, closed Sun; 22 Quay Street, tel. 091/565-001).

$$$ Rouge is a French splurge with leather couches and live jazz or mellow music almost nightly. Instead of à la carte, you'll choose between two set menus (daily 18:00-24:00, reservations wise, 38 Lower Dominick Street, tel. 091/530-681, www.rougegalway.com).

Dessert: For ice cream, try **Murphy's,** made from locally sourced, homemade ingredients. While you'll pay a premium for even a small cup (€4.50), it's worth it for flavors like Dingle sea salt (hand-harvested) and caramelized brown bread (daily 12:00-20:00, 12 High Street).

Near Eyre Square

$$ Galway Bakery Company (GBC) is a popular, basic place for a quick Irish meal with a self-serve buffet line (daily 8:00-18:00, later in summer, 7 Williams Gate, near Eyre Square, tel. 091/563-087). They have a simple, good-value restaurant upstairs (open later).

Galway's "Latin Quarter"

$$ The Lighthouse Vegetarian Café is a calm and cozy little vegetarian haven (lunch only) with creative, well-presented plates and fresh-baked goods, just steps behind Lynch's Castle (daily 12:00-17:00, 8 Abbeygate Street Upper, mobile 087-352-0198).

Supermarket: Dunnes is tucked in the Eyre Square Shopping Centre (Mon-Sat 9:00-19:00, Thu-Fri until 21:00, Sun 11:00-19:00, supermarket in basement). Lots of smaller grocery shops are scattered throughout town.

SLEEPING

Rick's Tip: With easy train access from Dublin, Galway is a popular weekend destination for rambunctious **"stag" and "hen" parties.** *If you want a good night's sleep on a Friday or Saturday, steer clear of hotels with bars downstairs or nearby.*

Hotels

$$$$ Park House Hotel, a plush, business-class hotel, offers the best value for a fancy place. Ideally located a block from the train station and Eyre Square, it has 84 spacious rooms and all the comforts you'd expect (expensive full Irish breakfast, elevator, pay parking, great restaurant, helpful staff, Forster Street, tel. 091/564-924, www.parkhousehotel.ie, reservations@parkhousehotel.ie).

$$$$ Hotel Meyrick, filled with palatial Old World elegance and 97 rooms, marks the end of the Dublin-Galway train line and the beginning of Galway. Since 1845, it has been Galway's landmark hotel...JFK stayed here in 1963 when it was the Great Southern (at the head of Eyre Square, tel. 091/564-041, www.hotelmeyrick.ie, reshm@hotelmeyrick.ie).

$$$$ Jurys Inn Galway has 130 American-style rooms in a modern hotel, centrally located where the old town hits the river. The big, bright rooms have double beds and huge modern bathrooms (breakfast extra, elevator, lots of tour groups, pay parking, Quay Street, tel. 091/566-444, US tel. 800-423-6953, www.jurysinns.com, jurysinngalway@jurysinns.com).

¢ **Kinlay Hostel** is a no-nonsense place just 100 yards from the train station, with 224 beds in bare, clean, and simple rooms, including 15 doubles/twins. Easygoing people of any age feel welcome here, but if you want a double, book well ahead—several months in advance for weekends (private rooms available, elevator, baggage storage, on Merchants Road just off Eyre Square, tel. 091/565-244, www.kinlaygalway.ie, info@kinlaygalway.ie).

B&Bs

These B&Bs are homey, reasonably priced, and about a 10-minute walk from Eyre Square. All have free parking and include a full "Irish fry" breakfast.

$$ Petra House is Galway's best lodging value. Consistently helpful and attentive owners Frank and Joan Maher maintain a peaceful-feeling brick building with nine fresh rooms. It's homey, lovingly maintained, and topped off by breakfasts I look forward to (family rooms, elegant sitting room, 29 College Road, tel. 091/566-580, mobile 087-451-1711, www.petrahousegalway.net, petrahouse@eircom.net).

$$ Balcony House B&B rents eight pleasant, large rooms (family rooms, 27 College Road, tel. 091/563-438, www.aaabalconyhouse.com, info@aaabalconyhouse.com). Teresa Coyne is the mellow lady of the house.

$$ Asgard Guesthouse offers eight rooms and an appealing glass-atrium breakfast room (family rooms, 21 College Road, tel. 091/566-855, www.galway-cityguesthouse.com, info@galwaycityguesthouse.com, Mary O'Flynn).

TRANSPORTATION

Arriving and Departing
By Train and Bus
Trains and most buses share the same station, virtually on Eyre Square (which has the nearest ATMs). The train station can store your bag (Mon-Fri 8:00-18:00, closed Sat-Sun). To get from the station to the TI, go left on Station Road as you exit the station (toward Eyre Square), and then turn right on Forster Street.

Don't confuse the public bus station (in same building as the train station) with the coach station (a block away, across the street from the TI), which handles only privately owned coaches. Citylink buses from Dublin and Dublin's airport, as well as regional day-tour buses, all use the coach station.

TRAIN AND BUS CONNECTIONS
From Galway by Train to: Dublin (8/day, 3 hours), **Limerick** (4/day, 2 hours), **Ennis** (5/day, 1.5 hours). For **Belfast** and **Tralee,** you'll change in or near Dublin. Train info: Tel. 091/561-444, www.irishrail.ie.

From Galway by Bus to: Dublin (hourly, 3.5 hours; also see Citylink, below), **Kilkenny** (3/day, 5 hours), **Cork** (hourly, 4.5 hours), **Ennis** (hourly, 1.5 hours), **Shannon Airport** (hourly, 2 hours), **Cliffs of Moher** (8/day in summer, some with change in Ennis, 2 hours), **Doolin** (5/day, 1.5 hours), **Limerick** (hourly, 2 hours), **Dingle** (5/day, 6 hours), **Tralee** (8/day, 4 hours), Westport (6/day, 2-4 hours), **Rosslare** (2/day, 8 hours), **Belfast** (every 2 hours, 6 hours, change in Dublin), **Derry** (6/day, 5.5 hours). Bus info: Tel. 091/562-000, www.buseireann.ie.

Citylink buses runs cheap and fast bus service from the coach station near the TI to **Dublin** (arriving at Bachelor's Walk, a block from Tara Street DART station; hourly, 2.5 hours), **Dublin Airport** (hourly, 3 hours), and **Cork Airport** (6/day, 4 hours). Bus info: Tel. 091/564-164, www.citylink.ie.

By Car

Drivers staying overnight at a College Road B&B can park there for free (each has a small lot in front). For daytime parking, the most central and handiest parking garage is under the recommended Jurys Inn Galway in the town center (€2.20/hour, €30/24 hours, Mon-Sat 8:00-1:00 in the morning, Sun 9:00-18:00). Otherwise, you'll have to buy a pay-and-display ticket and put it on your dashboard (€2, 2-hour maximum).

BEST OF THE REST

CONNEMARA

If you have a car, consider spending a day exploring the wild western Irish fringe known as Connemara. Hike the peak of Croagh Patrick, the mountain from which St. Patrick supposedly banished the snakes from Ireland. Pass through the desolate Doo Lough Valley on a road stained with tragic famine history. Bounce on a springy peat bog. Drop in at a Westport pub owned by a member of the Chieftains, the popular traditional Irish music group. This beautiful area also claims a couple of classic Irish towns—Cong and Leenane—as well as the photogenic Kylemore Abbey.

Connemara in 1 Day

By Car: The Connemara area makes a satisfying **day trip from Galway.** I've listed the region's prime towns and sights in a loop that starts and ends in Galway (driving north, then back south).

Drivers who are aiming for **Northern Ireland** from Galway can easily modify the loop route by stopping just in Cong and Westport on the way north, or with more time, visiting the described sights in this order: Cong, then across the Maam Valley to Leenane, and up to Louisburgh and Murrisk on the way to Westport (consider spending the night). From there you'll head northeast to Sligo, Donegal, and across the border into Northern Ireland.

Without a Car: It's most efficient to take a **day tour** from Galway. Three Galway-based organizations—Galway Tour Company, Lally Tours, and Healy Tours—run all-day tours of nearby regions; see page 224 for contact information.

❷ Connemara Driving Tour

With a long and well-organized day, you can loop around from Galway and enjoy the most important sights of Connemara (five hours of driving and 200 miles). You'll be thankful you picked up a good map before departing. For maximum coverage, lace together the sights described in this chapter in a route that goes in this order: Cong, Westport, Murrisk, Louisburgh, through the Doo Lough Valley to Leenane, then on to Clifden (passing Kylemore Abbey and Connemara National Park), along the coast to Roundstone, and finally back to Galway.

Cong

The town of Cong offers a fascinating mix of attractions: a medieval ruined abbey, a modern church with exquisite stained-glass windows, and a falconry experience on the grounds of the extravagant Ashford Castle. Everything is within a short walk of the parking lot in front of the abbey. The **TI,** where you can pick up a handy map, is across from the entrance to Cong Abbey.

Cong Abbey

The ruins of **Cong Abbey** (free and always open) are the main attraction in town. The abbey was built starting in the early 1100s in Romanesque style and then into the Gothic

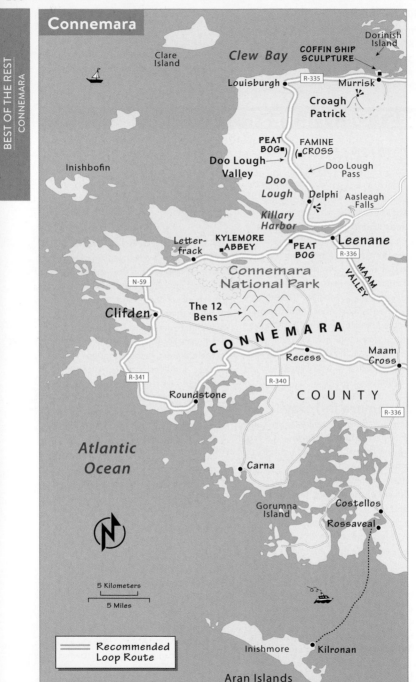

Connemara

Clare
Island

Clew Bay

Dorinish
Island

**COFFIN SHIP
SCULPTURE**

Louisburgh •

R-335

Murrisk •

**Croagh
Patrick**

**PEAT
BOG**■

**FAMINE
CROSS**
■

**Doo Lough
Valley**

*Doo
Lough*

Doo Lough
Pass

Inishbofin

Delphi •

Aasleagh
Falls

*Killary
Harbor*

Letter-
frack •

**KYLEMORE
ABBEY**
■

■ **PEAT
BOG**

• **Leenane**

R-336

*Connemara
National Park*

M
A
A
M

V
A
L
L
E
Y

N-59

The 12
Bens

Clifden •

C O N N E M A R A

Recess •

Maam
Cross •

R-341

R-340

C O U N T Y

R-336

Roundstone •

*Atlantic
Ocean*

• Carna

Gorumna
Island

Costellos •

Rossaveal •

N

5 Kilometers

5 Miles

Inishmore •

Kilronan •

Recommended
Loop Route

Aran Islands

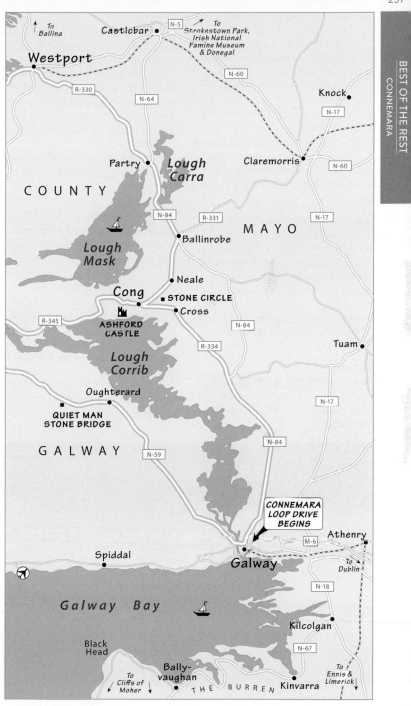

age. Take a walk through the cloister and down the gravel path behind the abbey. From a little bridge you'll see the **monks' stone house.** It was designed so part of the stream would flow directly under it. The monks simply lowered a net through the floor and attached a bell to the rope; whenever a fish was netted, the bell would ring.

Next to the abbey's cemetery is the modern, concrete, bunker-like **Church of St. Mary of the Rosary.** Drop in to marvel at its three exquisite windows, made by Irish artist Harry Clarke in 1933 (free, daily 8:00-22:00).

▲▲IRELAND SCHOOL OF FALCONRY

If you've never experienced falconry, this is a great chance. Animal lovers, aviation engineers, and wannabe medieval hunters will thrill to this hour-long experience. You must reserve ahead (€90 for 1 participant, €70 each for 2, on the grounds of Cong's Ashford Castle, tel. 094/954-6820, mobile 087-297-6092, www.falconry.ie, info@falconry.ie).

EATING

Fuel up at the **$$ Hungry Monk Café** (closed Sun, on Abbey Street) or **$$ The Crowe's Nest** (daily, in Ryan's Hotel on Main Street).

Westport

Westport, with just 9,000 people, is "the big city" in this part of Ireland. While other villages seem organic and grown out of the Middle Ages, this is a planned town. It was built in the late 1700s with a trendy-back-then Georgian flair by celebrated architect James Wyatt, who designed it to support the adjacent estate of the English Lord Browne.

Westport's **TI** (called the "Discover Ireland Centre") is on Bridge Street (closed Sun).

Westport Walk

This little walk—almost a complete loop—will acquaint you with Westport's charms, beginning at the eight-sided main "square" called the Octagon and ending at the clock tower on Bridge Street.

Octagon: Surrounded by 30 townhouses, this was the centerpiece of the planned town back in the 1760s. The big limestone structure with the clock was the old market house, where trade was organized, and taxes and customs paid.

The monument in the center of the Octagon was built in 1843 to remember Lord Browne's banker, George Glenden-

Monks' stone house

Ashford Castle, home of the Ireland School of Falconry

ning. But the statue of the English banker was shot to pieces by Irish patriots in 1922, during the civil war (the column is still pocked by the gunfire). Today St. Patrick perches on top.

James Street: Stroll downhill from the Octagon along James Street. Notice a few things. First, there are no stop signs. That's because traffic is supposed to be so friendly that drivers yield to anyone in a crosswalk without being reminded. Second, there are no chain stores—by popular demand, the town council has allowed no big chains to open up in the town center.

Along the River: At the bottom of James Street, stand at the bridge and notice the fancy Anglican church across the river (wealthy English Protestants). Rather than crossing the bridge, head right, to the more humble Catholic church. In front of the church, by the water, is a bust of Westport-born **Major John MacBride,** one of the more colorful rebels of the 1916 Easter Rising. MacBride joined a band of insurgents marching into position in Dublin at the start of the rebel-

lion, and was among the 14 men executed at Kilmainham Gaol after its failure.

Bridge Street to the Clock Tower: At the next bridge, turn right and go uphill on Westport's main Bridge Street, lined by some of the finest old storefronts in Ireland.

Farther up the street, **Matt Molloy's Pub** is the biggest draw in town—famous because its namesake owner is the flutist for the trad group, the Chieftains. You can hear music here nightly. Explore the pub during the day when it's quiet and empty. The back room is a small theater with photos of celebrated guests on the wall.

At the top of Bridge Street, you'll reach the classic storefront of **Thomas Moran**—so classic it's on an Irish stamp. Tidy flower patches (tended by an army of volunteers) surround the **clock tower,** which dates to 1947. The tower marks the town's second square—and the end of our walk.

EATING

You'll find plenty of **$** budget options along Bridge Street, including **Ring's Bistro** (closed Sun, hidden up Market Lane off

Bridge Street) and **Chilli Restaurant & Coffee Shop.**

These **$$$** places serves contemporary Irish cuisine (dinners only, reservations smart): **Sage Restaurant** (daily, 10 High Street, www.sagewestport.ie) and **The Pantry & Corkscrew** (closed Mon, The Octagon, www.thepantryandcorkscrew. com).

SLEEPING

Westport is the best place along this route to spend a night. Try modern **$$$ Clew Bay Hotel** (www.clewbayhotel.com), good-value **$ Boulevard Guesthouse** (www.boulevard-guesthouse.com), or budget **¢ Old Mill Hostel** (www.oldmill hostel.com).

Murrisk, Croagh Patrick, and a Coffin Ship Sculpture

In the tiny town of Murrisk you'll find the trailhead for the long hike up Croagh Patrick and a monument remembering the famine.

Croagh Patrick

This fabled mountain pilgrimage destination rises 2,500 feet above the bay from Murrisk. In the fifth century, St. Patrick is said to have fasted on its summit for the 40 days of Lent. It's from here that he supposedly rang his bell, driving all the snakes from Ireland.

From the trailhead at Murrisk (where you'll find a big pay-and-display parking lot and a visitors center), you can see the ruddy trail worn by a thousand years of pilgrims heading up the hill and along the north ridge to the summit.

Hikers should allow three hours to reach the top and two hours to get back down (wear solid boots if you have them, and bring plenty of water, sunscreen, and rain gear). There is a primitive WC on the summit. The trail is easy to follow, but the upper half of the mountain is a steep slope of loose, shifting scree. I'd advise buying (or renting) a walking stick in nearby Westport.

Coffin Ship Sculpture

Across the street from the Croagh Patrick trailhead is a modern bronze ship sculpture. A memorial to the famine, it depicts a "coffin ship," like those of the late 1840s that carried the sick and starving famine

Coffin ship sculpture

survivors across the ocean in hope of a new life. But many of the ships contracted to take the desperate emigrants were worn out and barely seaworthy. The poor were weak from starvation and vulnerable to "famine fever," which they spread to others in the putrid, cramped holds of these ships. Pause a moment to look at the silent skeletons swirling around the ship's masts.

Doo Lough Valley and a Famine Cross

The Doo Lough Valley, stretching between Louisburgh and Delphi (on R-335), is some of the most desolate country in Ireland. Signs of human habitation vanish from the bogland, and it seems ghosts might appear beside the road. Stop at the summit (north end of the valley, about 13 kilometers south of Louisburgh) when you see a simple gray stone cross. The lake below is Doo Lough (Irish for "Black Lake").

County Mayo's rural folk were the hardest hit when the Great Potato Famine came in 1845. In the winter of 1849, about 600 starving Irish walked 12 miles from Louisburgh over this summit and south to Delphi Lodge, hoping to get food from their landlord. But they were turned away. Almost 200 of them died along the side of this road. Today an annual walk commemorates the tragedy.

Killary Harbor and Aasleagh Falls

As you drive toward the town of Leenane, you'll skirt along Killary Harbor. The rows of blue floats in the harbor mark mussel farms, with the molluscs growing on hanging nets in the cold seawater.

At the east end of Killary Harbor, stop to enjoy the scenic Aasleagh Falls. In late May, the banks below the falls explode with lush, wild, purple rhododendron blossoms.

Leenane

The "town" of Leenane (actually just a crossroads) is a good place for a break. Drop into the Leenane Sheep and Wool Centre to see interesting wool-spinning and weaving demonstrations (€5, daily 9:30-18:00, closed Nov-March; demos run June-Aug at 10:00, 11:30, 14:00, and 15:30; café, tel. 095/42323, www. sheepandwoolcentre.com).

Doo Lough Valley

Kylemore Abbey, a Connemara landmark

Bog Fun

About eight kilometers west of Leenane, you'll find some areas on the south side of N-59 that offer a good, close look at a turf cut in a peat bog. Be sure to get out and frolic in the peat fields...with decent footwear and an eagle eye for mushy spots.

Walk a few yards onto the spongy green carpet. Find a dry spot and jump up and down to get a feel for it. Have your companion jump; you'll feel the vibrations 30 feet away.

These bogs once covered almost 20 percent of Ireland. As the climate got warmer at the end of the last Ice Age, plants began growing along the sides of the many shallow lakes and ponds. When the plants died in these waterlogged areas, there wasn't enough oxygen for them to fully decompose. Over the centuries, the moss built up, layer after dead layer, helping to slowly fill in the lakes.

It's this wet, oxygen-starved ecosystem that has preserved ancient artifacts so well, many of which can be seen in Dublin's National Museum. Most bizarre are the wrinkled bog mummies that are occasionally unearthed. These human remains (many over 2,000 years old) are so incredibly intact that their eyelashes, hairstyles, and the last meal in their stomachs can be identified. They were likely sacrificial offerings to the pagan gods of Celtic times.

People have been cutting, drying, and burning peat as a fuel source for more than a thousand years. The cutting usually begins in April or May, when drier weather approaches. You'll probably see stacks of "turf" piled up to dry along recent cuts. In the past few decades, bogs have been recognized as a rare habitat, and conservation efforts have been encouraged. These days, the sweet, nostalgic smell of burning peat is becoming increasingly rare.

Kylemore Abbey

This Neo-Gothic country house was built by the wealthy English businessman Mitchell Henry in the 1860s, after he and his wife had honeymooned in the area. After World War I, refugee Benedictine nuns from Ypres, Belgium, took it over and ran it as an exclusive girls' boarding school. The nuns still live upstairs, but you can visit the half-dozen open rooms down-

Coastal Connemara

stairs that display the Henry family's cushy lifestyle. Hourly tours of the abbey and gardens are so so; it's best just to enjoy the setting (€13 combo-ticket for abbey and gardens; daily 9:00-18:00, July-Aug until 19:00, www.kylemoreabbeytourism.ie).

Connemara National Park

This park encompasses almost 5,000 acres of wild bog and mountain scenery. The visitors center (just outside Letter-frack) displays worthwhile exhibits of local flora and fauna, which are well-explained in the 15-minute Man and the Landscape film that runs every half-hour (free; park open daily year-round; visitors center open daily 9:00-17:30, closed Nov-Feb; tel. 095/41054, www.connemaranation-alpark.ie). For a quick visit, take a nature walk along the boardwalk raised above the bog. Nature lovers may want to enjoy a two-hour walking tour with a park naturalist (July-Aug, Wed and Fri at 11:00, departs from visitors center). Call ahead to con-

firm walking tour schedules, and bring rain gear and hiking shoes.

Coastal Connemara

If you're short on time, you can connect Clifden and Galway with the fast main road (N-59). But the slower coastal loop along R-341 rewards drivers with great scenery. The essence of scenic Connemara—rocky yet seductive—is captured in this neat little 38-kilometer stretch. The 12 Bens (peaks) of Connemara loom deeper inland. In the foreground, broad shelves of bare bedrock are netted with stone walls, which interlock through the landscape. The ocean slaps the hard-scrabble shore. Fishermen cast into their favorite little lakes, and ponies trot in windswept fields. Abandoned, roofless stone cottages stand mute. While the loop is pretty desolate, Roundstone is a perfect place to stop for a cup of coffee to fuel your ride back to Galway.

Aran
Islands

Strewn like limestone chips hammered off the jagged west coast, the three Aran Islands—Inishmore, Inishmaan, and Inisheer—confront the wild Atlantic with stubborn grit. Craggy, vertical cliffs fortify the southern flanks of each island. Windswept rocky fields, stitched together by stone walls, blanket the interiors. And the island's precious few sandy beaches hide in coves that dimple the northern shores. During the winter, severe gales sweep through; because of this, most of the settlements on the islands are found on the more sheltered northeastern side.

There's a stark beauty about the Aran Islands and the simple lives their inhabitants eke out of a mean sea and less than six inches of topsoil. In the past, people made a precarious living here from fishing and farming. The scoured bedrock offered little in the way of soil, so it was created by the islanders—the result of centuries of layering seaweed with limestone sand and animal dung. Fields are small, divided by several thousand miles of "drystone" wall (made without mortar).

Nowadays, tourism boosts the islands' economy. The islands are a Gaeltacht area—a Gaelic cultural preserve. While the islanders speak Irish among themselves, they happily speak English for their visitors.

I cover two of the three islands. The largest island, Inishmore (9 miles by 2 miles), is the most populated, popular, and interesting—starring Dun Aengus, the must-see Iron Age fort. The 800 people of Inishmore greet as many as 2,000 visitors a day. The vast majority of these are day-trippers, washing ashore with the docking of each ferry. Inishmore is easy to visit when you're in Galway, near the mainland port of Rossaveal, from where you sail to Inishmore. And flights from Connemara Airport (18 miles west of Galway) take you to any of the islands.

For most, the big island is quiet enough. But less touristy Inisheer is a good alternative if you're staying in Doolin, a 35-minute ferry ride away.

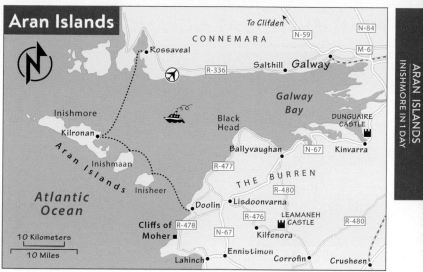

Aran Islands

INISHMORE IN 1 DAY

Most travelers visit Inishmore (Inis Mór) as a day trip by boat from Galway. Here's a good framework: Leave Galway at 9:00 on the shuttle bus to Rossaveal, where you'll catch the 10:30 boat. You'll step off the boat in Kilronan at about 11:15.

Arrange minivan transport or rent a bike, visit Dun Aengus, and grab a bite at one of the two simple cafés near the base of the Dun Aengus fort trail (or bring a picnic). Explore the island during low tide, and depart on the boat when high tides return between 16:00 and 18:00. You can squeeze an extra three to four hours out of your day trip by booking an early flight

Inishmore (best reached from Galway)

▲▲▲**Dun Aengus** Remote 2,000-year-old Iron Age ring fort, perched on a cliff with breathtaking coastal views and surrounded by a defensive ring of sharp stones. **Hours:** Daily March-Oct 9:00-18:00, off-season 9:30-16:00, closed Mon-Tue in Jan-Feb. See page 251.

▲▲**Island Minivan Tours** Dependable, weather-proof transport between the island's sights, driven by gift-of-gab locals who contribute random, humorous, and occasionally factual commentary en route. See page 251.

Seven Churches and St. Enda's Church Ruins of two separate early Christian communities at opposite ends of the island, both reachable by minivan, bike, or pony trap. See pages 252, 253.

Black Fort, St. Benen's Church, and the Worm Hole Three separate, isolated ancient sites scattered across the island, offering dramatically windswept vistas reachable only by rocky and rewarding hikes. See pages 254, 253, 252.

Inisheer (best reached from Doolin)

Small, quiet-island alternative to Inishmore's hectic day-tripper scene, featuring modest sights that include the ruins of O'Brien's Castle, the sand-sunken St. Cavan's Church, and the beached *An Plassy* shipwreck. See page 256.

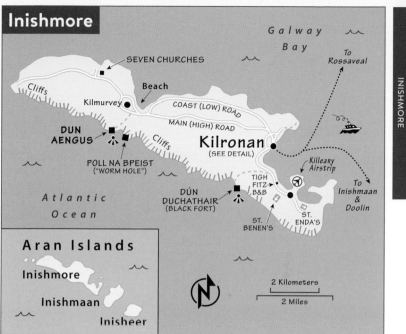

over and a late flight back from Connemara Regional Airport, near Rossaveal.

Staying Overnight: Travelers spending the night can savor the quiet time before and after the day-trip crowds. Here's how I'd suggest you spend your arrival day: Since most day-trippers make a beeline straight off the boat to Dun Aengus, head in the opposite direction to check out the subtle charms of the less-visited eastern end of the island. Buy a picnic at the Spar supermarket in Kilronan. Then walk to either the ruins of tiny St. Benen's Church (an easy 45-minute hike one way from Kilronan) or the rugged Black Fort ruins (a rocky 1-hour scramble one way from Kilronan). Save Dun Aengus for later in the afternoon, after the midday crowds have subsided. Enjoy an evening in the pubs and take a no-rush midmorning boat trip or flight back to the mainland the next day.

INISHMORE

The largest of the Aran Islands has a blockbuster sight: the striking Dun Aengus fort, set on a sheer cliff. Everyone arrives at Kilronan, the Aran Islands' biggest town, though it's just a village. Groups of backpackers wash ashore with the docking of each ferry. Minivans, bike shops, and a few men in pony carts sop up the tourists.

Orientation

Your first stop on Inishmore is the town of Kilronan, huddling around the ferry pier. There are about a dozen shops and B&Bs, about half as many restaurants, and a couple of **bike-rental huts** (regular 21-speed bikes about €10/day plus €10 deposit, electric bikes €25/day plus €20 deposit).

A few blocks inland up the high road, you'll find the best folk-music **pub** (Joe Watty's), a **post office,** and a tiny **bank**

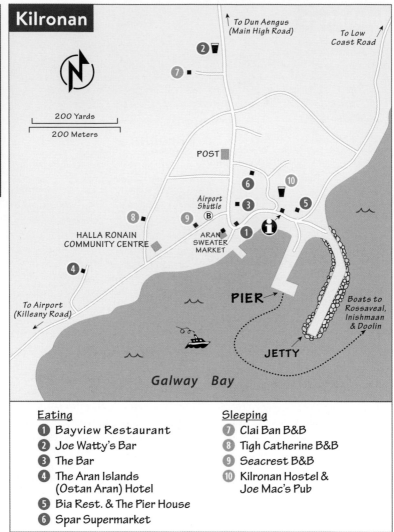

Kilronan

To Dun Aengus
(Main High Road)

To Low
Coast Road

200 Yards

200 Meters

POST

Airport
Shuttle

HALLA RONAIN
COMMUNITY CENTRE

ARAN
SWEATER
MARKET

To Airport
(Killeany Road)

PIER

Boats to
Rossaveal,
Inishmaan
& Doolin

JETTY

Galway Bay

Eating
1 Bayview Restaurant
2 Joe Watty's Bar
3 The Bar
4 The Aran Islands
(Ostan Aran) Hotel
5 Bia Rest. & The Pier House
6 Spar Supermarket

Sleeping
7 Clai Ban B&B
8 Tigh Catherine B&B
9 Seacrest B&B
10 Kilronan Hostel &
Joe Mac's Pub

across from the roofless Anglican church ruins.

A friendly **café/shop** with free Wi-Fi lurks on the back side of the stony Aran Sweater Market building, across from the high cross (daily 10:00-20:00, shorter hours off-season; also has Irish lessons for tourists, a detailed map for hikers, and shows the 1934 documentary *Man of Aran*). Public **WC**s are 100 yards beyond the TI (see below) on the harbor road.

The huge Spar **supermarket,** two blocks inland from the harbor, has the island's only **ATM.**

Rick's Tip: *Bring cash or get it when you arrive. Most B&Bs and quite a few other businesses don't accept credit cards.*

Tourist Information: Kilronan's TI is helpful (daily 10:00-17:00, July-Aug until

18:00, may close during lunch, shorter hours in winter, faces the harbor, tel. 099/61263). The free map given out by the TI or ferry operator is all the average day-tripper or leisure biker will need to navigate. But serious hikers who plan on scampering out to the island's craggy fringes will want to invest in the detailed black-and-white *Oileáin Árann* map and companion book by Tim Robinson (€16, sold at Man of Aran Coffee & Craft Shop behind Aran Sweater Market, and at some bookstores in Galway).

Tours

Fewer than 100 vehicles roam the island, and most of them seem to be minivans, offering ▲▲ tours. A line of vans (seating 8-18 passengers) awaits the arrival of each ferry, offering €15 island tours. They're basically a shared taxi service that will take you to the various sights, drop you off, and return at an agreed time to take you to the next attraction.

Chat with a few drivers to find one who likes to talk. On my tour, I learned that 800 islanders live in 14 villages (actually just crossroads), with three elementary schools and three churches. Most islanders own a small detached field where they keep a couple of cows (sheep are too much trouble). When pressed for more information, my guide explained that there are 400 types of flowers and 19 types of bees on the island. Then he pointed to the 2,000-year-old ring fort on the hilltop and grinned, saying, "It's so popular with visitors that we plan to build another 2,000-year-old ring fort next year."

The tour, a convenient time-saver, zips you to the end of the island for a quick stroll in the desolate fields, gives you 15 minutes to wander through the historic but visually unimpressive Seven Churches, and then drops you off for two hours at Dun Aengus (30 minutes to hike up, 30 minutes at the fort, 20-minute hike back down, 40 minutes in café for lunch

or shopping at drop-off point) before running you back to Kilronan. These sights can be linked together in various sequences, but the trailhead crossroads below Dun Aengus—with two cafés—makes the best lunch stop. Ask your driver to take you back along the smaller coastal road (scenic beaches and sunbathing seals at low tide).

Sights

▲▲▲DUN AENGUS (DÚN AONGHASA)

The stone fortress hangs spectacularly and precariously on the edge of a cliff 200 feet above the Atlantic. The crashing waves seem to say, "You've come to the end of the world." Gaze out to sea and consider this: Off this coast, Hy-Brasil—a phantom island cloaked in mist—was said to pop into view once every seven years. This mythical place appeared on maps as late as the mid-1800s.

Little is known about this 2,000-year-old Iron Age fort. Its concentric walls are 13 feet thick and 10 feet high. As an added defense, the fort is ringed with a commotion of spiky stones, sticking up like lances, called *chevaux-de-frise* (literally, "Frisian horses," named for the

Dun Aenghus

Frisian soldiers who used pikes to stop charging cavalry). Slowly, as the cliff erodes, hunks of the fort fall into the sea.

Dun Aengus doesn't get crowded until after 11:00; if you can, get there early or late. A small visitors center (housing the ticket office and controlling access to the trail) displays aerial views of the fort and tells the story of its inhabitants. Trail access to the fort is open and free when the visitors center is closed.

Cost and Hours: €5; daily March-Oct 9:00-18:00, off-season 9:30-16:00, closed Mon-Tue in Jan-Feb; last entry one hour before closing, during June-Aug guides at the trailhead answer questions and can sometimes give free tours up at the fort if you call ahead, 5.5 miles from Kilronan, tel. 099/61008.

Warnings: Rangers advise visitors to wear sturdy walking shoes and watch kids closely; there's no fence between you and a crumbling 200-foot cliff overlooking the sea. Also, be very careful about unexpected gusts of wind and uncertain footing near the edge. The Irish don't believe in litigation, just natural selection.

SEVEN CHURCHES
(NA SEACHT TEAMPAILL)

Close to the western tip of the island, this gathering of ruined chapels, monastic houses, and fragments of a high cross dates from the 8th to 11th century. The island is dotted with reminders that Christianity was brought to the islands in the fifth century by St. Enda, who established a monastery here. Many great monks studied under Enda. Among these "Irish apostles" who started Ireland's "Age of Saints and Scholars" (A.D. 450-800) was Columba (Colmcille in Irish), the founder of a monastery on the island of Iona in Scotland—home of the Irish monks who produced the Book of Kells. Check out the ornate gravestones (best detail on sunny days) of the "seven Romans," located in the slightly elevated back corner of the graveyard, farthest from the road. These pilgrims came here from Rome in the ninth century, long after the fall of the Roman Empire.

KILMURVEY

The island's second-largest village nestles below Dun Aengus. More a simple crossroads than a village, it sports two soup-and-sandwich cafés, a gaggle of homes, and a great sheltered swimming beach with a blue flag. Throughout Ireland, "blue flag" beaches proclaim clean water, safe currents, and the color of your toes when you shiver back to your towel.

THE WORM HOLE (POLL NA BPEIST)

Off the beaten path and accessible only by hiking, this site (also called the "Serpent's Lair") takes the "logic" out of geologic. It's a large, perfectly rectangular, 40-by-100-foot seawater-filled pool (60 feet deep) that was cut by nature into the flat coastal bedrock. You'd swear that God used a cake knife to cut out this massive slab—just to mess with us. The Worm Hole was formed when the roof of the hidden cave underneath (cut by tidal action) collapsed just so.

Boulder-hopping your way across the narrowest section of the island, you'll

Seven Churches

Currach *and* Navogue *Boats*

These are the traditional fishing boats of the west coast of Ireland—lightweight and easy to haul. In your coastal travels, you'll see a few actual *currach* or *navogue* boats—generally retired and stacked. The *currach* is native to the Aran Islands, while the *navogue* is native to the Dingle Peninsula. A fisherman would build a boat to suit his needs: a higher bow to deal with more surf, higher sides to lean over when pulling up lobster pots, a flat stern, etc. Few raw materials were needed to make the boats: a wooden frame with canvas (originally cowhide) and paint with tar. A disadvantage was their fragility when hauling anything other than men or fish. When transporting sheep, farmers would lash each sheep's pointy little hooves together and place it carefully upside-down in the *currach*—so it wouldn't puncture the frail little craft's canvas skin.

find the Worm Hole beneath the island's southern cliffs, one mile straight south of Kilmurvey's fine beach. It's signposted from the Main Road as *Pol na bPeist,* but Tim Robinson's detailed map (see "Tourist Information," earlier) is handy for navigating here.

ANCIENT SITES NEAR KILLEANY

The quiet eastern end of Inishmore offers ancient sites in evocative settings for overnight visitors with more time, or for those seeking rocky hikes devoid of crowds. First, get a good hiking map. Then consider assembling a picnic, to fuel up either before or after you spend a couple of hours exploring these sights on foot. Ask the folks in town for directions (almost always a memorable experience in Ireland).

Closest to the road, amid the dunes one mile past the Tigh Fitz B&B and just south of the airport, is the eighth-century **St. Enda's Church** (Teaghlach Einne). Protected from wave erosion by a stubborn breakwater, it sits half-submerged in a sandy graveyard, surrounded by a sea of sawgrass and peppered with tombstones. St. Enda is said to be buried here, along with 125 other saints who flocked to Inishmore in the fifth century to learn from him.

St. Benen's Church (Teampall Bheanáin) perches high on a desolate ridge opposite the Tigh Fitz B&B. Walk up the stone-walled lane, passing a holy well and the stubby remains of a round tower. Then take another visual fix on the church's silhouette on the horizon, and zigzag up the stone terraces to the top. The 30-minute hike up from the B&B pays off with a great view. Dedicated to St. Benen, a young disciple of St. Patrick himself, this tiny (12-by-6-foot) 10th-century oratory is aligned north-south (instead of the usual east-west) to protect the doorway from prevailing winds.

About a five-minute walk past the Tigh Fitz B&B (on your left as you head toward the airport), you'll notice an abandoned stone pier and an adjacent, modest medieval ruin. This was **Arkin Fort,** built by Cromwell's soldiers in 1652 using cut stones taken from the round tower and the monastic ruins that once stood below St. Benen's Church. The fort was used as a prison for outlawed priests before they

St. Benen's Church

were sent by English authorities to the West Indies to be sold into slavery.

Hidden on a remote, ragged headland an hour's walk from Kilronan to the south side of the island, you'll find the **Black Fort** (Dún Duchathair). After Dun Aengus, this is Inishmore's most dramatic fortification. A good map is essential to navigate here. Built on a promontory with cliffs on three sides, its defenders would have held out behind drystone ramparts, facing the island's interior attackers. Watch your step on the uneven ground, be ready to course-correct as you go, and chances are you'll have this windswept ruin all to yourself. Imagine the planning and cooperative effort that went into building these life-saving structures 2,000 years ago, before Gore-Tex and granola bars.

Experiences
Pub Music
Kilronan's pubs offer music sporadically on summer nights. Nothing is dependably scheduled, so ask at your B&B or look for posted notices on the front of the Spar supermarket or post office. **Joe Watty's Bar,** on the high road 100 yards past the post office, is worth the 10-minute walk from the dock. Its appealing front porch goes great with a pint, and Irish folk music warms the interior most nights. The more central **Joe Mac's Pub** (next to the hostel) and **The Bar** (next to the high cross at the base of the high road) are also possibilities.

Events
Late June is when Inishmore shakes off its slumber and kicks up its heels. The **Patrún** is a three-day annual celebration during the last weekend in June (boat races, fun run). June 23 is **St. John's Eve Bonfire Night,** a Christian/pagan tradition held the night before St. John's Day, close to (but not on) the summer solstice. Each community stokes a raging fire around dusk, and dozens are visible not only on the island, but also on the distant shore of Connemara.

Eating
There are few restaurants in Kilronan and none are fancy. Plan on comfort food at reasonable prices.

The island's most central and stylish (a relative term) option is the **Bayview Restaurant,** standing proudly purple beside the high cross (daily 12:00-21:00,

The Black Fort

tel. 086/792-9925). I like the friendly vibe and tasty grub up the hill at **$$ Joe Watty's Bar** (daily April-Oct 12:30-15:30 & 17:00-21:00, tel. 099/20892, pleasant front-porch seating).

The **Aran Islands Hotel** has a modern **$$ pub** serving simple lunches and hot dinners (daily 12:00-21:00, tel. 099/61104). **The Pier House** operates the dependable **$$$ Bia Restaurant** on the ground floor of its guesthouse (daily May-Sept 11:00-21:30, tel. 099/61811).

Supermarket: The **Spar** has all the groceries you'll need (Mon-Sat 9:00-18:00, Sun 10:00-17:00).

Sleeping

All of the following places are in Kilronan. Remember, this is a rustic island. Many rooms are plain, with simple plumbing. Luxury didn't make the leap from the mainland.

$$ The **Aran Islands (Ostan Aran) Hotel** is the most modern option on the island. Its 20 rooms (four with large harbor-facing porches) have the comforts you'd expect. Beware of loud weekend stag/hen parties drawn to their downstairs pub (tel. 099/61104, www.aranislandshotel.com, info@aranislandshotel.com, 10-minute walk east of the dock on the coast road heading toward Killeany).

$$ The Pier House stands solidly, 50 yards from the pier, offering 12 decent rooms, a good restaurant downstairs, and sea views from many of its rooms (tel. 099/61417, www.pierhousearan.com, pierhousearan@gmail.com).

$ Clai Ban, the only really cheery place in town, is run by friendly Marion and Bartley Hernon. Their six rooms and warm hospitality are worth the 10-minute uphill walk from the pier (cash only, family rooms, walk past bank out of town and up the 50-yard-long lane on left, tel. 099/61111, claibanhouse@gmail.com).

$ Tigh Catherine is a well-kept B&B with four homey rooms overlooking the harbor (cash only, on Church Road up behind the Halla Ronain community

center, tel. 099/61464, mobile 087-980-9748, catherineandstiofain@gmail.com, Catherine Mulkerrin).

$ Seacrest B&B offers six uncluttered rooms in a central location behind the Aran Sweater Market (cash only, tel. 099/61292, mobile 087-161-6507, seacrestaran@gmail.com, Geraldine and Tom Faherty).

¢ Kilronan Hostel, overlooking the harbor near the TI, is cheap but noisy above Joe Mac's Pub (tel. 099/61255, www.kilronanhostel.com, kilronanhostel@gmail.com).

Getting Around Inishmore

Just about anything on wheels functions as a **taxi** here. A trip from Kilronan to Dun Aengus to the Seven Churches and back to Kilronan costs €15 per person in a shared minivan. **Pony carts** cost about €50 for two people (€80 for 4) for a trip to Dun Aengus and back.

Biking is great. Before heading out, check that your bike seat is set at the correct height and stable enough so that you can fully extend both legs as you pedal. (The most frequent bike rental complaint is a seat that won't stay in place and slowly slips down...cramping your legs when you're far down the island.) Take it for a short test spin while you're still near the rental shop.

Novice bikers should be aware that the terrain is hilly and there are occasional

Biking outside Kilronan

headwinds and unpredictable showers (figure 30 minutes to ride from Kilronan to start of trailhead up to Dun Aengus). Cyclists should take the high road over and the low road back—fewer hills, scenic shoreline, and at low tide, a dozen seals basking in the sun.

Keep a sharp lookout along the roads for handy, modern limestone signposts (with distances in kilometers) that point the way to important sights. They're in Irish, but you'll be clued in by the small metal depictions of the sights embedded within them.

INISHEER

The island of Inisheer (Inis Oírr), a quick trip from Doolin, offers a vivid glimpse of Aran Island culture and has an engaging smorgasbord of salty but modest sights. The roughly circular little island has less than a quarter of the land area and population of Inishmore. But Inisheer's close proximity to the mainland makes it an easy 35-minute boat journey from Doolin (take an early boat to maximize your

time), and it's a good option for those with limited time who aren't going north to Galway.

Orientation

You'll dock on the north side of the island in its only settlement. Facing inland with your back to the pier, you'll be able to see nearly all of the island's landmarks. Although some pony carts and minivan drivers meet you at the pier, I'd rely on them only on a rainy day (€10).

For me, the joy of compact Inisheer is seeing it on a bike ride or a long breezy walk. The bike-rental outfit is right at the base of the pier (€10/2 hours, €12/day, tel. 099/75049, www.rothai-inisoirr. com, no deposit necessary "unless you look suspicious"). Any of the boat operators in Doolin can give you a free map of the island showing Inisheer's primitive road network. That's all you'll need to navigate.

There are three pubs on the island, one small grocery store, and no ATMs. All the sights, with the exception of the lonely lighthouse on the southern coast, are

Sleepy Inisheer

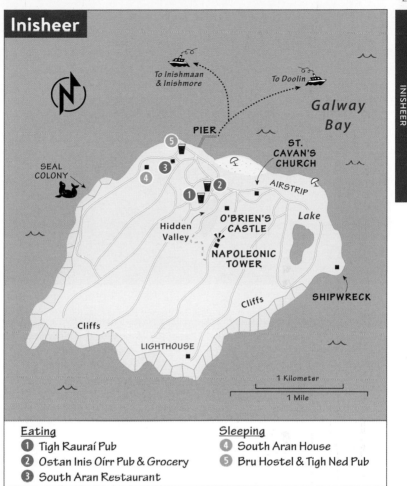

Inisheer

To Inishmaan & Inishmore

To Doolin

Galway Bay

PIER

ST. CAVAN'S CHURCH

AIRSTRIP

SEAL COLONY

Hidden Valley

O'BRIEN'S CASTLE

Lake

NAPOLEONIC TOWER

SHIPWRECK

Cliffs

Cliffs

LIGHTHOUSE

1 Kilometer

1 Mile

Eating
1 Tigh Rauraí Pub
2 Ostan Inis Oírr Pub & Grocery
3 South Aran Restaurant

Sleeping
4 South Aran House
5 Bru Hostel & Tigh Ned Pub

concentrated on the northern half.

Inisheer lacks the dramatic (and much higher) coastal cliffs of Inishmore, but has its own unique photogenic charms.

◉ Inisheer Tour

The sights on this self-guided tour are free, open all the time, and marked on your free boat company map. See them in the order listed, from west to east, across the northern half of the island. If you bike rather than hike, be prepared to walk the bike up (or down) short, steep hills.

O'BRIEN'S CASTLE (CAISLEAN UI BHRIAIN)

The ruins of this castle dominate the hill-top and are visible from almost anywhere on the northern half of the island. It's a steep 20-minute walk from the pier up to the castle ruins. The small castle was built as a tower house refuge around 1400 by the O'Brien clan from nearby County Clare. It sits inside a low wall of a much older Iron Age ring fort. Cromwell's troops destroyed the castle in 1652, leaving the evocative ruins you see today.

O'Brien's Castle

If you've huffed your way up to O'Brien's Castle, then go another easy five minutes to the **Napoleonic Tower** (An Tur Faire), which was built in the early 1800s to watch for a feared French invasion that never took place. The views from this highest point on the island are worth it.

• *Consult your map and continue walking (south) on the paved road into the heart of the island. Take your first right turn, roughly 100 yards after the Napoleonic Tower, onto a rocky, grassy cow lane that zigzags downhill into a lush hidden valley, displaying the prettiest mosaic of ivy-tangled rock walls and small green fields I've seen anywhere on the Aran Islands.*

Once you've wound your way back down to the main north-shore road again, turn right and continue east with the airstrip on your left. On your right, you'll soon see a time-passed graveyard up atop a sandy hill. Hike the 50 yards up into the graveyard to find...

ST. CAVAN'S CHURCH (TEAMPALL CHAOMHAIN)
St. Cavan was the brother of St. Kevin, who founded the monastery at Glen-dalough in the Wicklow Mountains (see page 98). In the middle of the graveyard is a sunken sandpit holding the rugged, roofless remains of an 11th-century church. The shifting sand dunes almost buried it before sawgrass stabilized the hill. St. Cavan's reputed gravesite is protected by a tiny modern structure worth poking your head into for its candlelit atmosphere. Local folklore held that if you spent a night sleeping on the tomb lid, your particular illness would be cured.

• *Walk back down to the north-shore road and head out on the coast road (to the southeast) 30 minutes to the remote...*

SHIPWRECK OF THE *AN PLASSY*
This freighter was wrecked offshore on Finn's Rock in 1960. But islanders worked with the coastal patrol to help rescue the crew with no loss of life. A couple of weeks later the unmanned ship was washed high up onto the rocky shore, where it still sits today, a rusty but fairly intact ghost ship with a broken back. The fierce winter winds and record-breaking waves of 2013 shifted the wreck, further weakening it, and discussions are under

The wreck of the An Plassy

way to remove it as it deteriorates. A local told me, "We may have to go out some night with lanterns to bring in a new shipwreck." Beware of unstable footing on the rounded cobbles thrown up by the surf near the wreck.

• *With more time, consult your map and seek out the remaining intimate little church ruins and holy wells that the island has to offer. Or head back to town for a beverage while you await the return ferry.*

Eating

Inisheer's three main pubs offer decent pub grub (usually 12:30-20:30). **$$ Tigh Rauraí Pub** (House of Rory) is the epi-center of island social life (from the pier, head east to the edge of the beach and turn right—inland—up a narrow lane for 100 yards). Just below it, closer to the beach, **$$ Ostan Inis Oírr Pub** (Hotel Inisheer) sports a colorful collage of international flags draping the pub's ceiling and stag/hen parties on weekends. **$$$ Tigh Ned Pub** (House of Ned) is right next door to the hostel, near the pier on the north-shore road. Life could be worse

than to sit outside at their appealing front tables on a summer evening, enjoying a pint in the salt air.

For a mellow evening meal, try the **$$ South Aran Restaurant,** a five-minute walk west of the pier on the north-shore road (daily 18:00-21:00, tel. 099/75073, mobile 087-340-5687).

Picnic lovers flock to the island's small **grocery,** Siopa XL, behind Ostan Inis Oírr Pub and below Tigh Rauraí Pub (Mon-Sat 9:00-18:00, Sun 10:00-14:00).

Sleeping

A scattering of B&Bs dots the northern half of the island. Here are two good options:

$ South Aran House is a quiet, well-run place with five spic-and-span, black-and-white rooms. Humorous Enda and friendly Maria Conneely are generous with local tips and also run the nearby South Aran Restaurant, where you'll have breakfast (easy 10-minute walk west of pier on north-shore road, call ahead with your ferry arrival time so they can meet you with keys, tel. 099/75073, mobile 087-340-5687, www.southaran.com, info@southaran.com). Their small rental cottage sleeps two.

¢ **Bru Hostel Radharc na Mara** is a simple, economical, 40-bed option just 100 yards west of the pier, next to Tigh Ned Pub. They also offer five basic doubles in their adjacent B&B directly behind (includes continental breakfast, open mid-March-Oct, tel. 099/75024, radharcnamara@hotmail.com).

TRANSPORTATION

Arriving and Departing
By Ferry

FROM ROSSAVEAL (NEAR GALWAY)
Island Ferries sails to Inishmore from the port of Rossaveal, 20 miles west of Galway. The company runs a shuttle bus from Galway to the Rossaveal dock (3/day April-Oct, 2/day Nov-March, bus ride and ferry crossing each takes 45 minutes; coming from Galway, allow 2 hours in transit one-way; €25 round-trip boat crossing plus €7 round-trip for shuttle bus, 10 percent discount if you book online, WCs on board). Catch shuttle buses from Galway on Queen Street, a block behind the Kinlay Hostel (check-in 1.5 hours before sailing); shuttles return to Galway immediately after each boat arrives. Ferry schedule for April-Oct: from Rossaveal at 10:30, 13:00, and 18:30; from Inishmore at 8:15, 12:00, 16:00, and 17:00 (plus 18:30 July-Aug). Island Ferries has two offices in Galway: on Forster Street across from the TI and at 19 Eyre Square (tel. 091/568-903, after-hours tel. 091/572-273, www.aranislandferries.com).

Note: The boat you take out to the islands may not be the same as the one you come back on. And sometimes you'll board by walking up the gangplank of one boat and walking across its deck to another boat docked beside or behind it. Make sure to ask.

Driving to Rossaveal: Drivers should go straight to the ferry landing in Rossaveal, passing several ticket agencies and pay parking lots. At the boat dock, you'll find a convenient €8/day lot and an office that sells tickets for Island Ferries (with better WCs than on the ferry). Check to see what's going when and for how much.

FROM DOOLIN
Boats from Doolin sail to all three Aran Islands. However, service is patchier and less reliable than the bigger boats out of Rossaveal—though recent completion of a second, deeper-water pier at Doolin has improved things, as boats are less at the mercy of the tides that bedeviled crossings from the original port.

While it's possible to travel from Doolin to Inishmore and back in one day, keep in mind that it's a long trip to distant Inishmore (1.25 hours compared with 45 minutes from Rossaveal), leaving less time ashore. Instead, consider an overnight stay on Inishmore, or opt for a day trip to the nearby, though less spectacular, smaller island of Inisheer.

For details on staying in Doolin, see page 213.

Parking in Doolin: With a car, Doolin is easy to reach; without one, it's better to get to Inishmore from Rossaveal. Parking at the Doolin dock is pay-and-display (€1/2 hours, €5 overnight). Give yourself enough time to deal with parking and the line to pay at the machine.

Buying Tickets: The scene at the Doolin ferry dock is a confusing mosh pit of competition. Two ferry companies operate from three ticket huts with one thing in mind: snaring your business. They have similar schedules and prices.

No matter which company you choose, it's smart to check online for discounts. It's also important to double-check schedules, arrive at least 15 minutes early, be alert, and be patient. Boats can be 30 minutes late...or 10 minutes early. You're on Irish time.

Doolin2Aran Ferries is run by the Garrihy family (to Inishmore: €25 round-trip, 1.25 hours, generally departs Doolin at 10:00 and 13:00, departs Inishmore at 11:30 and 16:00; to Inisheer: €20 same-day round-trip, 30 minutes, departs Doolin at 10:00, 11:00, 13:00, and 17:30, departs Inisheer at 8:30, 12:15, 14:00, and 16:45. They also offer a fun €30 triangular day trip that takes you from Doolin to Inisheer, drops you off on Inisheer for about 3.5 hours, then sails along the base of the Cliffs of Moher before docking back in Doolin (departs at 10:00 and 11:00, has you back in Doolin by 16:45, runs April-Oct, tel. 065/707-5949, mobile 087-245-3239, www.doolin2aranferries.com).

Doolin Ferry/O'Brien Line, run by Bill O'Brien, has been at it the longest, with similar schedules and occasionally cheaper prices. They also offer a cruise along the base of the Cliffs of Moher that includes a stop at Inisheer (tel. 065/707-5618, www.obrienline.com).

By Plane

Aer Arann Islands, a friendly and flexible little airline, flies daily from Connemara Regional Airport, serving all three islands (3/day, up to 11/day in peak season, €25 one-way, €49 round-trip, groups of 4 or more pay €44 each, 10-minute flight, tel. 091/593-034, www.aerarannislands.ie,

info@aerarannislands.ie). These eight-seat planes get booked up—reserve as soon as you are sure of your dates (by email, with a credit card). Note that the baggage weight limit is 50 pounds total, so pack an overnight bag and leave your remaining clothes (but not your valuables) locked in the trunk of your car or stored in your Galway hotel.

From May through September, a sight-seeing-only Aer Arann flight leaves from the same airport at 12:00 each day. Cruising at 500 feet, you'll fly above all three Aran Islands with an extra swoop past the Cliffs of Moher (€60, 40 minutes, may not go if not enough people sign up).

Getting to and from the Airports: Connemara Regional Airport is 20 slow miles west of Galway—allow 45 minutes for the drive, plus 30 minutes to check in before the scheduled departure. A mini-bus shuttle (€5 one-way) runs from Victoria Hotel off Eyre Square in Galway an hour before each flight. Be sure to reserve a space on the shuttle bus at the same time you book your flight. The Kilronan airport on Inishmore is minuscule. A mini-bus shuttle (€3 one-way, €5 round-trip) travels the two miles between the airport and Kilronan (stop is behind the Aran Sweater Market).

Northern

Northern Ireland is a different country from the Republic—both politically (it's part of the United Kingdom) and culturally (a combination of Irish, Scottish, and English influences). Occupying the northern one-sixth of the island of Ireland, it's only about 13 miles from Scotland at the narrowest point of the North Channel, and bordered on the south and west by the Republic.

That border is almost invisible. But when you leave the Republic of Ireland and enter Northern Ireland, you *are* crossing an international border (although you don't have to flash your passport). The 2016 British referendum vote to leave the EU may change the way this border crossing is handled in the future, but for now it's business as usual.

You won't use euros here; Northern Ireland issues its own Ulster pound, which, like the Scottish pound, is interchangeable with the English pound. Price differences create a lively daily shopping trade for those living near the border. Some establishments near the border may take euros, but at a lousy exchange rate. Keep any euros for your return to the Republic, and get pounds from an ATM inside Northern Ireland instead. And if you're heading to Britain next, it's best to change your Ulster

Ireland

pounds into English ones (free at any bank in Northern Ireland, England, Wales, or Scotland).

It's important for visitors to Northern Ireland to understand the ways its population is segregated along political, religious, and cultural lines. Roughly speaking, the eastern seaboard is more Unionist, Protestant, and of English-Scottish heritage, while the south and west (bordering the Republic of Ireland) are Nationalist, Catholic, and of indigenous Irish descent. Cities are often clearly divided between neighborhoods of one group or the other. Early in life, locals learn to identify the highly symbolic (and highly charged) colors, jewelry, music, names, accents, and vocabulary that distinguish the cultural groups.

Over the last century, the conflict between these two groups has been not about faith, but about politics: Will Northern Ireland stay part of the United Kingdom (as the Unionists want), or become part of the Republic of Ireland (the goal of Nationalists)?

The roots of Protestant and Catholic differences date back to the time when Ireland was a colony of Great Britain. Four hundred years ago, Protestant settlers from England and Scotland were strategically "planted" in Catholic Ireland to help assimilate the island into the British economy. In 1620, the dominant

Northern Ireland Almanac

Official Name: Since Northern Ireland (pronounced "Norn Iron" by locals) is not an independent state, there is no official country name. Some call it Ulster (although historically that has included three counties that today lie on the Republic's side of the border), while others label it the Six Counties.

Size: 5,400 square miles (about the size of Connecticut), constituting a sixth of the island.

Population: With 1.8 million people, it's the smallest of the four United Kingdom countries (the others are England, Wales, and Scotland).

Geography: Northern Ireland is shaped roughly like a doughnut, with the UK's largest lake in the middle (Lough Neagh, 150 square miles and a prime eel fishery). Gently rolling hills of green grass rise to the 2,800-foot Slieve Donard. The weather is temperate, cloudy, moist, windy, and hard to predict.

Latitude and Longitude: 54°N and 5°W (as far north as parts of the Alaskan panhandle).

Biggest Cities: Belfast, the capital, has 300,000 residents. Half a million people—nearly one in three Northern Irish—inhabit the greater Belfast area. Derry (called Londonderry by Unionists) has 95,000 people.

Economy: Northern Ireland's economy is more closely tied to the UK than to the Republic of Ireland, and is subsidized by the UK and EU. Traditional agriculture (potatoes and grain) is fading fast, though modern techniques and abundant grassland make Northern Ireland a major producer of sheep, cows, and grass seed. Modern software and communications companies are replacing traditional manufacturing. Shipyards are rusty relics, and the linen industry is now threadbare (both victims of cheaper labor in Asia).

Government: Northern Ireland is not a self-governing nation, but is part of the UK, ruled from London by Queen Elizabeth II and Prime Minister Theresa May, and represented by 18 elected Members of Parliament. For 50 years (1922-1972), Northern Ireland was granted a great deal of autonomy and self-governance, known as "Home Rule." The current National Assembly (108-seat Parliament)—after an ineffective decade of political logjams—has recently begun to show signs of rejuvenation.

English powerbase in London felt entitled to call both islands—Ireland as well as Britain—the "British Isles" on maps (a geographic label that irritates Irish Nationalists to this day). These Protestant settlers established their own cultural toehold on the island, laying claim to the most fertile land. Might made right, and God was on their side. Meanwhile, the underdog Catholic Irish held strong to their Gaelic culture on their ever-diminishing, boggy, rocky farms.

By the beginning of the 20th century, the sparse Protestant population could no longer control the entire island. When Ireland won its independence in 1921 (after a bloody guerrilla war against British rule), 26 of the island's 32 counties became the Irish Free State, ruled from Dublin with dominion status in the British Commonwealth—similar to Canada's level of sovereignty. In 1949, these 26 counties left the Commonwealth altogether and became the Republic of Ireland, severing all political ties with Britain. Meanwhile, the six remaining northeastern counties—the only ones

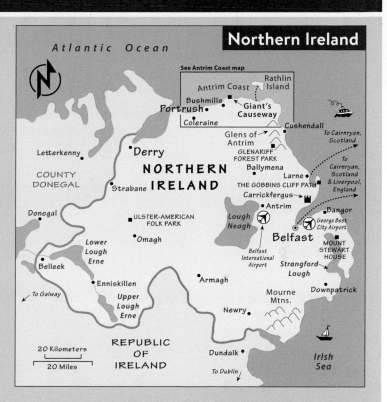

Flag: The official flag of Northern Ireland is the Union flag of the UK. But you'll also see the green, white, and orange Irish tricolor favored by Nationalists, and the Northern Irish flag (white with a red cross and a red hand at its center) used by Unionists (see "The Red Hand of Ulster" sidebar on page 290).

with a Protestant majority who considered themselves British—chose not to join the Irish Free State and remained part of the UK.

But within these six counties—now joined as the political entity called Northern Ireland—was a large, disaffected Irish (mostly Catholic) minority who felt marginalized by the drawing of the new international border. This sentiment was represented by the Irish Republican Army (IRA), who wanted all 32 of Ireland's counties to be united in one Irish nation—

their political goals were Nationalist. Their political opponents were the Unionists—Protestant British eager to defend the union with Britain, who were primarily led by two groups: the long-established Orange Order, and the military muscle of the newly mobilized Ulster Volunteer Force (UVF).

In World War II, the Republic stayed neutral while the North enthusiastically supported the Allied cause—winning a spot close to London's heart. Derry (a.k.a. Londonderry) became an essential Allied convoy port, while Belfast lost more than 800 civilians during four Luftwaffe bombing raids in 1941. After the war, the split between North and South seemed permanent, and Britain invested heavily in Northern Ireland to bring it solidly into the UK fold.

In the Republic of Ireland (the South), where 94 percent of the population was Catholic and only 6 percent Protestant, there was a clearly dominant majority. But in the North, at the time it was formed, Catholics were a sizable 35 percent of the population—enough to demand attention when they complained about anti-Catholic discrimination on the part of the Protestant government. It was this discrimination that led to the Troubles, the conflict that filled headlines from the late 1960s to the late 1990s.

In the 1960s, the Catholic minority in Northern Ireland was inspired—partly by Martin Luther King Jr. and the civil rights movement in America, beamed into Irish living rooms by the new magic

Nationalist mural in Belfast

of television news—to begin a nonviolent struggle to end discrimination and advocate for better jobs and housing. Extremists polarized issues, and once-peaceful demonstrations—also broadcast on TV news—became violent.

Unionists were afraid that if the island became one nation, the relatively poor Republic of Ireland would drag down the comparatively affluent North, and feared losing political power to a Catholic majority. As the two sides clashed in 1969, the British Army entered the fray. Their role, initially a peacekeeping one, gradually evolved into acting as muscle for the Unionist government. In 1972, a tragic watershed year, more than 500 people died as combatants moved from petrol bombs to guns, and a new, more violent IRA emerged. In the 30-year (1968-1998) chapter of the struggle for an independent and united Ireland, more than 3,000 people died.

In the 1990s—with the UK (and Ireland's) membership in the EU, the growth of its economy, and the weakening of the Catholic Church's authority—the influence of the Republic of Ireland became less threatening to the Unionists. Optimists hailed the signing of a breakthrough peace plan in 1998, called the "Good Friday Peace Accord" by Nationalists, or the "Belfast Agreement" by Unionists. This led to the release of political prisoners on both sides in 2000—a highly emotional event.

British Army surveillance towers in Northern Ireland cities were dismantled in 2006, and the army formally ended its 38-year-long Operation Banner campaign in 2007. In 2010, the peace process was jolted forward by a surprisingly forthright apology offered by then British Prime Minister David Cameron, who expressed regret for the British Army's offenses on Bloody Sunday. The apology was prompted by the Saville Report—the results of an investigation conducted by the UK government as part of the Good Friday Accord. It found that the

Northern Ireland Terminology

You may hear Northern Ireland referred to as **Ulster**—the traditional name of Ireland's ancient northernmost province. When the Republic of Ireland became independent in 1922, six of the nine counties of Ulster elected to form Northern Ireland, while three counties joined the Republic.

The mostly Protestant **Unionist** majority—and the more hardline, working-class **Loyalists**—want the North to remain in the UK. The **Ulster Unionist Party** (UUP) is the political party representing moderate Unionist views (Nobel Peace Prize co-winner David Trimble led the UUP from 1995 to 2005). The **Democratic Unionist Party** (DUP) takes a harder stance in defense of Unionism. The **Ulster Volunteer Force** (UVF), the **Ulster Freedom Fighters** (UFF), and the **Ulster Defense Association** (UDA) are Loyalist paramilitary organizations: All three are labeled "proscribed groups" by the UK's 2000 Terrorism Act.

The mostly Catholic **Nationalist** minority—and the more hardline, working-class **Republicans**—want a united and independent Ireland ruled by Dublin. The **Social Democratic Labor Party** (SDLP), founded by Nobel Peace Prize co-winner John Hume, is the moderate political party representing Nationalist views. **Sinn Fein** takes a harder stance in defense of Nationalism. The **Irish Republican Army** (IRA) is the now-disarmed Nationalist paramilitary organization formerly linked with Sinn Fein. The **Alliance Party** wants to bridge the gap between Unionists and Nationalists.

The long-simmering struggle to settle Northern Ireland's national identity precipitated the **Troubles,** the violent, 30-year conflict (1968-1998) between Unionist and Nationalist factions. To gain more insight into the complexity of the Troubles, the 90-minute documentary *Voices from the Grave* provides an excellent overview (easy to find on YouTube). Also check out the University of Ulster's informative and evenhanded Conflict Archive at http://cain.ulst.ac.uk/index.html.

1972 shootings of Nationalist civil-rights marchers on Bloody Sunday by British soldiers was unjustified and the victims innocent (vindication for the victims' families, who had fought since 1972 to clear their loved ones' names).

Major hurdles to a lasting peace persist, but downtown checkpoints and "bomb-damage clearance sales" have been gone for decades. Replacing them are a forest of construction cranes, especially in rejuvenated Belfast. Tourists in Northern Ireland were once considered courageous (or reckless). Today, more tourists than ever are venturing north to Belfast and Derry, and cruise-ship crowds disembark in Belfast to board charter buses that fan out to visit the Giant's Causeway and Old Bushmills Distillery.

When locals spot you with a map and a lost look on your face, they're likely to ask, "Wot yer lookin fer?" in their distinctive Northern accent. They're not suspicious of you, but trying to help you find your way. They may even "giggle" (Google) it for you. You're safer in Belfast than in many UK cities—and far safer, statistically, than in most major US cities. You'd have to look for trouble to find it here. Just don't seek out spit-and-sawdust pubs in working-class neighborhoods and spew simplistic

Visitors are drawn by the geologic formations of the Giant's Causeway.

opinions about sensitive local topics. Tourists notice lingering tension mainly during the "marching season" (Easter-Aug, peaking in early July). July 12—"the Twelfth"—is traditionally the most confrontational day of the year in the North, when proud Protestant Unionist Orangemen march to celebrate their Britishness (often through staunchly Nationalist Catholic neighborhoods—it's still good advice to lie low if you stumble onto any big Orange parades).

As the less-fractured Northern Ireland enters the 21st century, one of its most valuable assets is its industrious people—and their legendary work ethic. When they emigrated to the US, they became known as the Scots-Irish and played a crucial role in our nation's founding. They were signers of our Declaration of Independence, a dozen of our presidents, and the ancestors of Davy Crockett and Mark Twain.

Northern Irish workers have a proclivity for making things that go. They've produced far-reaching inventions like Dunlop's first inflatable tire. The Shorts aircraft factory (in Belfast) built the Wright Brothers' first six aircraft for commercial sale and the world's first vertical takeoff jet. The Titanic was the only flop of Northern Ireland's otherwise successful shipbuilding industry. The once-futuristic DeLorean sports car was made in Belfast.

Notable people from Northern Ireland include musicians Van Morrison and James Galway, and actors Liam Neeson, Roma Downey, Ciarán Hinds, and Kenneth Branagh. The North also produced Christian intellectual and writer C. S. Lewis, Victorian physicist Lord Kelvin, engineer Harry Ferguson (inventor of the modern farm tractor and first four-wheel drive Formula One car), and soccer-star playboy George Best—who once famously remarked, "I spent most of my money on liquor and women...and the rest I wasted."

As in the Republic, sports are big in

the North. Northern-born golfers Rory McIlroy, Graeme McDowell, and Darren Clarke have won a fistful of majors over the past decade, filling local hearts with pride. With close ties to Scotland, many Northern Irish fans follow the exploits of Glasgow soccer teams—but which team you root for betrays which side of the tracks you come from. Those who cheer for Glasgow Celtic are Nationalist and Catholic; those waving banners for the Glasgow Rangers are Unionist and Protestant. To maintain peace, some pubs post signs on their doors banning patrons from wearing sports jerseys. Luckily, sports with no sectarian history are now being introduced, such as the Belfast Giants ice hockey team—a hit with both communities.

Northern Ireland seems poised to do great things. In your travels, you'll encounter a fascinating country with a complicated, often tragic history—and a brightening future.

Belfast

Seventeenth-century Belfast was just a village. With the influx of English and Scottish settlers—and the subjugation of the Irish—the character of the place changed. Spurred by the success of the local linen, rope-making, and especially shipbuilding industries, Belfast blossomed. The Industrial Revolution took root here with a vengeance, earning the city its nickname ("Old Smoke").

Belfast is the birthplace of the *Titanic* (and many other ships that didn't sink). In 2012, to mark the 100th anniversary of the *Titanic* disaster, a modern new attraction was launched in Belfast's shipyard, telling the ill-fated ship's fascinating and tragic story. Nearby, two huge, mustard-colored cranes (nicknamed Samson and Goliath) stand idle now, but serve as a reminder of this town's former shipbuilding might...strategic enough to be the target of Luftwaffe bombing raids in World War II.

At the beginning of the 21st century, the peace process began to take root, and today, it feels like a new morning in Belfast. It's hard to believe that the bright and bustling pedestrian center was once a subdued, traffic-free security zone. These days, both Catholics and Protestants root for the Belfast Giants ice hockey team.

Still, it's a fragile peace, and pubs with security gates are reminders that the island is still split.

BELFAST IN 1 DAY

Belfast makes a pleasant overnight stop, with plenty of inexpensive accommodations, weekend hotel deals, and a relaxed neighborhood with B&Bs 30 minutes away in Bangor.

With one day in Belfast, browse the pedestrian zones around City Hall, take the City Hall tour (11:00, 12:00 on Sat-Sun), have lunch, and ride a shared black taxi up Falls Road. Visit the Titanic Belfast after midday crowds subside. Stroll the Golden Mile.

In the evening, choose among these options: Make reservations for a memorable splurge meal at the Merchant Hotel, have dinner at a pub, or rub elbows with the locals in the historic Crown Liquor Saloon. See what's on at the Opera House or Lyric Theatre.

With extra time: With a second day, take the City Sightseeing bus tour in the morning, then visit Carrickfergus Castle in the afternoon, or check out more of Belfast's sights, such as the Ulster Folk Park and Transport Museum.

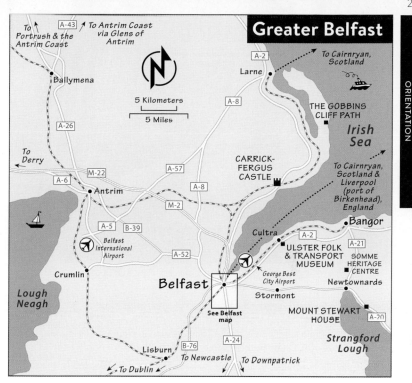

Greater Belfast

To Portrush & the Antrim Coast

A-43 ↗ To Antrim Coast via Glens of Antrim

Ballymena

5 Kilometers

5 Miles

A-26

To Derry

M-22

A-6

A-57

Antrim

A-8

M-2

A-5 B-39

Belfast International Airport

A-52

Crumlin

Lough Neagh

Belfast

See Belfast map

Lisburn B-76

To Dublin

To Newcastle

A-24

To Downpatrick

Larne

A-2

To Cairnryan, Scotland

A-8

THE GOBBINS CLIFF PATH

Irish Sea

CARRICK-FERGUS CASTLE

To Cairnryan, Scotland & Liverpool (port of Birkenhead), England

Bangor

Cultra

A-2

ULSTER FOLK & TRANSPORT MUSEUM

A-21

SOMME HERITAGE CENTRE

George Best City Airport

Newtownards

Stormont

MOUNT STEWART HOUSE

A-20

Strangford Lough

If day-tripping from Dublin: Using the handy, two-hour Dublin-Belfast train (get "day return" tickets), you could make Belfast a day trip (this plan works any day but Sunday):

Catch the 7:35 train from Dublin's Connolly Station (arriving in Belfast's Central Station at 9:45). Take the City Hall tour at 11:00, browse the pedestrian zone, have lunch, ride a black taxi up Falls Road, and visit Titanic Belfast (or the Ulster Folk Park and Transport Museum). Return to Dublin in the evening (last train departs Belfast Mon-Sat at 21:30).

ORIENTATION

Belfast is flat and spread out, with the following zones of interest: **Titanic Quarter** (northeast of city center; docklands with Odyssey entertainment complex and Titanic Belfast), **western Belfast** (work-ing-class sectarian neighborhoods west of A-12 freeway), **city center** (Donegall Square, City Hall, pedestrian shopping, and TI), **Cathedral Quarter** (north of City Hall; Ulster-Scots Centre, Northern Ireland War Memorial, and lively nightlife), and **southern Belfast** (Botanic Gardens, Queen's University, and Ulster Museum).

The eastern part of Belfast is more affluent and residential, with little of interest to the average sightseer, except perhaps for Stormont (the seat of government in Northern Ireland).

The modern bookends of sightseeing interest are the Titanic Belfast attraction (in the Titanic Quarter to the north) and the Lyric Theatre (near the university district to the south). Their contemporary angularities contrast sharply with the red-brick uniformity of old Belfast. But the core of your city navigating will hinge on four more central landmarks (listed from

BELFAST AT A GLANCE

▲▲▲**Titanic Belfast** Excellent but crowded high-tech exhibit covering the famously infamous ship and local shipbuilding, housed in a stunning structure on the site where the *Titanic* was built. **Hours:** Daily April-Sept 9:00-18:00, June-Aug until 19:00; Oct-March 10:00-17:00. See page 280.

▲▲**Sectarian Neighborhoods Taxi Tours** Local cabbies drive visitors through West Belfast's Falls Road and Shankill Road neighborhoods, offering personal perspectives on the slowly fading Troubles. See page 277.

▲▲**City Hall** Central Belfast's polished and majestic celebration of Victorian-era pride built with industrial wealth. **Hours:** Daily 8:30-17:00. See page 284.

▲**Ulster Museum** Mixed bag of local artifacts, natural history, and coverage of political events; a good rainy-day option near Queen's University. **Hours:** Tue-Sun 10:00-17:00, closed Mon. See page 287.

▲**Botanic Gardens** Belfast's best green space, featuring the Palm House loaded with delicate tropical vegetation. **Hours:** Daily 8:00 until dusk; Palm House open daily 10:00-17:00, Oct-March until 16:00. See page 287.

Near Belfast

▲▲**Ulster Folk Park and Transport Museum** A glimpse into Northern Ireland's hardworking heritage, split between a charming re-creation of past rural life and halls of innovative vehicular advances (8 miles east of Belfast). **Hours:** March-Sept Tue-Sun 10:00-17:00; Oct-Feb Tue-Fri 10:00-16:00, Sat-Sun 11:00-16:00; closed Mon year-round. See page 287.

▲**Carrickfergus Castle** Northern Ireland's first and most important fortified refuge for invading 12th century Normans (14 miles northeast of Belfast). **Hours:** Daily 10:00-17:00, Oct-March until 16:00. See page 289.

▲**The Gobbins** Rugged, unique, wave-splashed hiking trail cut into coastal rock, accessible by guided tour (34 miles northeast of Belfast). **Hours:** Visitors center daily 9:30-17:30, guided hikes about every hour in good weather. See page 289.

Near Bangor
▲**Mount Stewart House** Fine 18th-century manor house displaying ruling-class affluence, surrounded by lush and calming gardens (18 miles east of Belfast). **Hours:** Daily 10:00-16:30, closed Nov-Feb. See page 295.

north to south): St. Anne's Cathedral, City Hall, Shaftesbury Square, and Queen's University. Find them on your map, and use them to navigate as you stroll the town.

Belfast's "Golden Mile" commercial drag—stretching from Hotel Europa to the university district—connects the central and southern zones with some of the best dinner and entertainment spots.

Tourist Information

The modern TI (look for *Visit Belfast* sign) has a courteous staff and baggage storage (Mon-Sat 9:00-17:30, June-Sept until 19:00, Sun 11:00-16:00 year-round; a couple of doors down from Linen Hall Library, just across Chichester Street, north of City Hall at 9 Donegall Square North, tel. 028/9024-6609, http://visitbelfast.com). City **walking tours** depart from the TI (see "Tours," later).

Sightseeing Pass

The **Belfast Visitor Pass** combines iLink smartcards for free bus and rail travel, with sightseeing discounts, for one day or two or three consecutive days within the Belfast Visitor Pass Zone (all of downtown Belfast as far out as the Ulster Folk and Transport Museum in Cultra, but not as far as Carrickfergus Castle or Bangor). The handy one-day pass saves money for anyone visiting Titanic Belfast (10 percent discount) and the Ulster Folk and Transport Museum (30 percent discount) while connecting them by train or bus (free with pass). Buy it at the TI, any train station, either airport, Europa Bus station, or online (£6.50 for 1-day pass, multiday passes available, tel. 028/9066-6630, www.translink.co.uk).

Tours
In Belfast

On Foot: Belfast Compass Tours introduces you to the city's 300-year history on a balanced two-hour stroll. Highlights include City Hall, St. George's Market, Albert Clock, and the opulent Merchant

Hotel (£7, must book in advance, mobile 079-4425-6560 or 079-3440-7751, www. belfastcompasstours.com).

Belfast Trad Trail Tours hosts this musical pub crawl. Led by two local musicians, it's a great intro to Irish music and the pulsing evening scene of the Cathedral Quarter. It starts at 16:00 and lasts about 2.5 hours, allowing you time afterward to dine and explore the neighborhood (£15, mid-May-Aug daily at 16:00, meet at Dirty Onion Pub, 3 Hill Street, tel. 028/9028-8818, www.tradtrail.com).

Sectarian Neighborhoods Walking Tours, led by two different companies, offer opposite viewpoints on the Troubles and local culture; it's best to book ahead for either one. **Coiste Irish Political Tours** offers the Nationalist/Republican perspective on extended, two-hour walks along Falls Road (£10; Tue, Thu, and Sat at 11:00, Sun at 14:00; tel. 028/9020-0770, www.coiste.ie). **Sandy Row Walking Tours** provides the Unionist/Loyalist point of view during its 1.5-hour walks centering

Tour guide in Belfast

on Sandy Row, Belfast's oldest residential neighborhood (£7.50; daily at 10:00, 14:00, and 17:00; mobile 079-0925-4849, www.historicsandyrow.co.uk).

By Bus: City Sightseeing offers the best quick introduction to the city's political and social history. Their open-top, double-decker buses link major sights and landmarks. Pay cash on bus or book online in advance (£12.50 for 48 hours, 2/hour, fewer in winter, daily 10:00-16:00, 20 stops, 1.5-hour loop; departs from Castle Place on High Street, 2 blocks west of Albert Clock Tower; tel. 028/9032-1321, http://belfastcitysightseeing.com). A similar service is offered by City Tours. Its route, with more than 20 stops, starts on High Street (near Albert Clock), then veers westward to take in Falls and Shankill roads (£10 for 48 hours, runs 2/hour 9:45-16:45, pay cash on bus or book in advance, tel. 028/9032-1912, www.citytoursbelfast.com).

By Taxi: Sectarian Taxi Tours are the easiest way to view the evolving murals of the Catholic and Protestant communities with a local. Taxi Trax Black Taxi Tours—from a Nationalist Catholic area—gives 90-minute Falls Road-based tours(£35/1-3 people, £12/additional person, tel. 028/9031-5777 or mobile 078-9271-6660, www.taxitrax.com). NI Black Taxi Tours—from a Unionist Protestant area—takes you on 90-minute tours around Shankill Road (£30/1-3 people, £10/additional person, book in advance, mobile 077-2968-3104, www.niblacktaxi-tours.com).

By Boat: The **Lagan Boat Company** shows you shipyards on this one-hour cruise, narrated by a member of the Belfast Titanic Society (£10; April-Oct daily sailings at 12:30, 14:00, and 15:30; fewer off-season, tel. 028/9024-0124, www.laganboatcompany.com). Tours depart from the Lagan Pedestrian Bridge and Weir on Donegall Quay. The quay is located just past the leaning Albert Clock Tower, a 10-minute walk from the TI.

To Antrim Coast

By Bus: McComb's Giant's Causeway tour visits Carrickfergus Castle, the Giant's Causeway, Dunluce Castle (photo stop only), Carrick-a-Rede Rope Bridge, and Old Bushmills Distillery (£25, doesn't include distillery admission, daily depending on demand, book through and depart from Belfast International City Hostel, pickup around 9:00, back to Belfast by 19:00). Their Game of Thrones tour visits many of the sites where the hit fantasy TV series was filmed (£35, starts around 8:30, back to Belfast by 19:00). They also have private guides (book in advance, tel. 028/9031-5333, www.mccombscoaches.com).

Helpful Hints

Markets: On Friday, Saturday, and Sunday, the Victorian confines of St. George's Market is a commotion of commerce and a people-watching delight. Friday is a variety market (6:00-14:00), Saturday blooms with food and garden items (9:00-15:00), and Sunday creaks with crafts and antiques (10:00-16:00). It's located at the corner of Oxford and East Bridge streets, five blocks east of Donegall Square (tel. 028/9043-5704, www.belfastcity.gov.uk/markets).

Shopping Mall: Victoria Square is a glitzy American-style mall. Its huge glass dome reflects Belfast's economic rejuvenation. For fine city views, ride the free elevator to the observation platform high up inside the dome (Mon-Sat 9:30-18:00, Wed-Fri until 21:00, Sun 13:00-18:00, 3 blocks east of City Hall—bordered by Chichester, Victoria, Ann, and Montgomery streets; www.victoriasquare.com).

Services: Located directly across University Road from the red-brick university building, **Queen's University Student Union** is just as handy for tourists as it is for college students. Inside you'll find an ATM, WCs, a minimarket, and Wi-Fi. Grab a quick and cheap sandwich and coffee at **Clement's Coffee Shop** (long hours Mon-Sat, closed Sun).

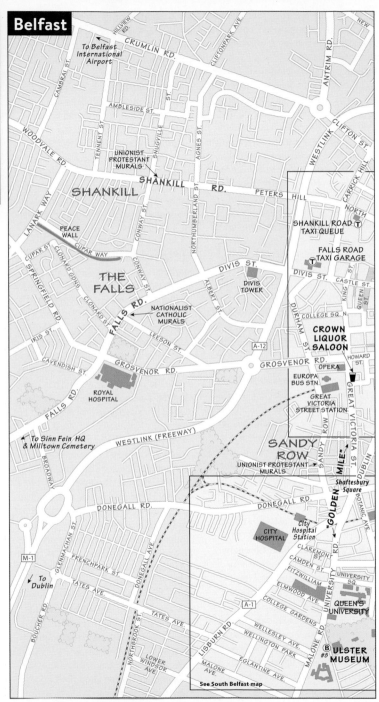

Belfast

HILLVIEW RD.

CRUMLIN RD.

To Belfast
International
Airport

CLIFTONPARK AVE.

NEW

ANTRIM RD.

CAMBRAI ST.

AMBLESIDE ST.

WOODVALE RD.

TENNENT ST.

SNUGVILLE ST.

AGNES ST.

ST.

WESTLINK

CLIFTON ST.

UNIONIST
PROTESTANT
MURALS

SHANKILL RD.

PETERS HILL

CARRICK HILL

SHANKILL

CONWAY ST.

NORTHUMBERLAND ST.

SHANKILL ROAD
TAXI QUEUE T

NORTH

LANARK WAY

PEACE
WALL

CUPAR WAY

FALLS ROAD
TAXI GARAGE T

CUPAR ST.

CLONARD GDNS.

CONWAY ST.

CRUMLIN ST.

DIVIS ST.

DIVIS ST.

CASTLE ST.

SPRINGFIELD RD.

THE
FALLS

CLONARD ST.

ALBERT ST.

DIVIS
TOWER

KING ST.

QUEEN ST.

FALLS RD.

NATIONALIST
CATHOLIC
MURALS

LEESON ST.

COLLEGE SQ. N

CROWN
LIQUOR
SALOON

IRIS ST.

DURHAM ST.

A-12

HOWARD ST.

CAVENDISH ST.

GROSVENOR RD.

GROSVENOR RD.

OPERA

GREAT VICTORIA ST.

FALLS RD.

ROYAL
HOSPITAL

EUROPA
BUS STN.

To Sinn Fein HQ
& Milltown Cemetery

WESTLINK (FREEWAY)

GREAT
VICTORIA
STREET STATION

DUBLIN RD.

BROADWAY

SANDY
ROW

SANDY ROW

"GOLDEN MILE"

UNIONIST PROTESTANT
MURALS

Shaftesbury
Square

BOTANIC AVE.

M-1

DONEGALL RD.

DONEGALL RD.

CITY
HOSPITAL

City
Hospital
Station

GLENMACHAN ST.

FRENCHPARK ST.

DONEGALL AVE.

CLAREMONT ST.

UNIVERSITY RD.

To
Dublin

TATES AVE.

CAMDEN ST.

FITZWILLIAM ST.

UNIVERSITY
SQ.

BOUCHER RD.

TATES AVE.

ELMWOOD AVE.

COLLEGE GARDENS

QUEEN'S
UNIVERSITY

NORTHBROOK ST.

LISBURN RD.

A-1

WELLESLEY AVE.

MALONE RD.

B
#8

ULSTER
MUSEUM

LOWER
WINDSOR
AVE.

WELLINGTON PARK

MALONE AVE.

EGLANTINE AVE.

See South Belfast map

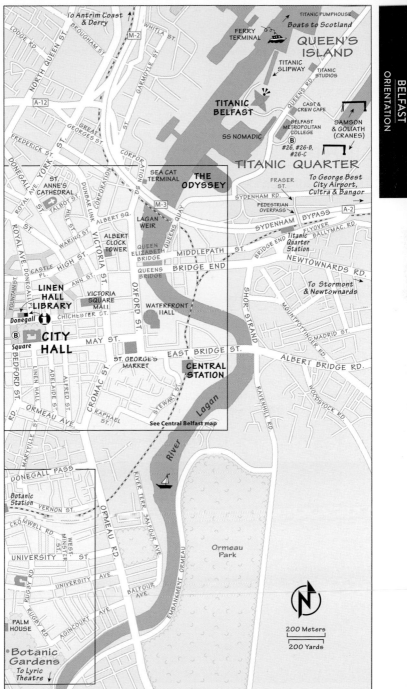

To Antrim Coast & Derry

M-2

TITANIC PUMPHOUSE

Boats to Scotland

FERRY TERMINAL

QUEEN'S ISLAND

TITANIC SLIPWAY

TITANIC STUDIOS

QUEENS RD.

TITANIC BELFAST

CAST & CREW CAFE

BELFAST METROPOLITAN COLLEGE

SAMSON & GOLIATH (CRANES)

SS NOMADIC

B

#26, #26-B, #26-C

TITANIC QUARTER

SEA CAT TERMINAL

THE ODYSSEY

FRASER ST.

To George Best City Airport, Cultra & Bangor

SYDENHAM RD.

PEDESTRIAN OVERPASS

A-2

M-3

LAGAN WEIR

SYDENHAM BYPASS

BRIDGE END

Titanic FLYOVER

BALLYMAC. RD.

ALBERT CLOCK TOWER

QUEEN ELIZABETH BRIDGE

MIDDLEPATH

ST.

Titanic Quarter Station

QUEENS BRIDGE

BRIDGE END

NEWTOWNARDS RD.

ST. ANNE'S CATHEDRAL

LINEN HALL LIBRARY

VICTORIA SQUARE MALL

WATERFRONT HALL

SHORT STRAND

To Stormont & Newtownards

Donegall

CHICHESTER ST.

CITY HALL

B

Square

MAY ST.

ALBERT BRIDGE RD.

EAST BRIDGE ST.

ST. GEORGE'S MARKET

CENTRAL STATION

River Lagan

See Central Belfast map

DONEGALL PASS

Botanic Station

VERNON ST.

ORMEAU RD.

Ormeau Park

UNIVERSITY ST.

UNIVERSITY AVE.

BALFOUR AVE.

PALM HOUSE

Botanic Gardens

To Lyric Theatre

N

200 Meters
200 Yards

Laundry: Globe Launderers has both self-serve and drop-off service (daily, 37 Botanic Avenue, tel. 028/9024-3956).

Bike Rental: Belfast Bike Tours rents bikes only if reserved in advance (£15/day, daily but no set hours, off Wellington Park behind Wellington Park Hotel, mobile 078-1211-4235, www.belfastbike-tours.com).

SIGHTS

Titanic Quarter

Up until the mid-1990s, this district was a barren wasteland of cement slabs and rusting industrial relics. But during the Celtic Tiger boom years (which spilled over into the North), shrewd investors saw the real-estate potential and began building posh, high-rise condos.

The first landmark project to be completed was the Odyssey entertainment complex (in 2000). To draw more visitors and commemorate the proud shipbuilding industry of the Victorian and Edwardian Ages, another flagship attraction was needed. The 100th anniversary of the *Titanic* disaster in 2012 provided the perfect opportunity, and the result is Titanic Belfast.

THE ODYSSEY

This huge millennium-project complex offers a food pavilion, bowling alley, and science center with interactive, educational exhibits for youngsters. Where else can a kid play a harp with laser-light strings? (£9.80, kids-£6.50, Mon-Fri 10:00-17:00, Sat until 18:00, Sun 12:00-18:00, last entry one hour before closing, 2 Queen's Quay, 10-minute walk north of Belfast's Central Station, tel. 028/9046-7790, www.w5online.co.uk).

▲▲▲TITANIC BELFAST

This £97 million attraction stands right next to the original slipways where the *Titanic* was built. Creative displays tell the tale of the famous ocean liner, proudly heralded as the largest man-made moving object of its time. The sight has no actual artifacts from the underwater wreck (out of respect for the fact that it's a mass grave). The artifacts on display are from local shipbuilding offices and personal collections.

Cost and Hours: £18; daily April-Sept 9:00-18:00, June-Aug until 19:00; Oct-March 10:00-17:00; last admission about 90 minutes before closing (though the Late Saver Ticket is sold one hour before closing for £9); audioguide-£3, but you get plenty of info without it; café/restaurant;

Modern Belfast

Titanic Trio

Most of us know the story of the *Titanic*, when the unthinkable happened to the unsinkable. Launched in Belfast in 1911, the *Titanic* was the largest and most celebrated luxury cruise liner of its time. Its sudden demise in 1912 is the most famous sea disaster of the modern era. Only 716 of the 2,260 aboard were rescued; 70 percent of the first-class passengers, with first dibs on the few lifeboats, survived.

While everyone has heard of the *Titanic*, few know that it was the middle sister of three unfortunate ships, each built in Belfast by the prestigious Harland and Wolff shipyards for the White Star Line.

In 1910, the *Olympic* was the first of the three similar vessels to be launched. It soon collided with the naval cruiser HMS *Hawke* and returned to Belfast to be repaired with parts taken from the still-under-construction *Titanic.* When World War I began, the *Olympic* served as a troop transport ship. During the war, it struck and sank a German submarine (the U-103). After the war, it returned to commercial service and later collided with the *Nantucket Lightship* (killing seven). The Olympic's last voyage was in 1935; it was demolished in 1937.

The last of the three to be built was the *Gigantic* in 1914. But after the *Titanic* sank, its name was changed (while still under construction) to *Britannic*...which was thought to be a luckier name. It was repainted white and converted to a hospital ship at the start of World War I. In 1915, it was serving in the Aegean Sea when it hit a mine—or was struck by a torpedo from a U-boat. Fortunately, it had more advanced safety features than its two older sisters—it had enough lifeboats for all onboard, and was designed to sink more slowly. Only 30 of the almost 1,100 crew and medical staff died. In 1976, French underwater explorer Jacques Cousteau found the wreck of the *Britannic* 400 feet down and brought up a few of its artifacts.

A single human thread ties all three ships together. A stewardess and nurse named Violet Jessop was aboard the *Olympic* when it collided with the HMS *Hawke*. She was also one of the lucky few to be rescued from the *Titanic*. And yes, she was again among those rescued from the sinking *Britannic*. Talk about a buoyant personality...

located on Queen's Island, tel. 028/9076-6399, www.titanicbelfast.com.

Rick's Tip: *Go early or late as big bus-tour or cruise-ship crowds can clog the* **Titanic Museum** *exhibits from 10:00 to 14:00.* **Book ahead online** *to get the entry time you want.*

Getting There: From Donegall Square, take bus #26 or #26B (both stop behind Belfast Metropolitan College, infrequent buses on Sun), or go by taxi (£6 ride). The Titanic Quarter train station is a 15-minute walk to the south of the Titanic Belfast.

Tours: The Discovery Tour explains the striking architecture of the Titanic Belfast building and the adjacent slipways where the ship was built (£8.50, 1 hour, call ahead for tour times).

Visiting the Sight: The spacey architecture of the Titanic Belfast building is a landmark on the city's skyline. Six stories tall, it's clad in more than 3,000 sun-reflecting aluminum panels. Its four corners represent the bows of the many ships (most of which didn't sink) that were built in these yards during the industrial Golden Age of Belfast.

The exhibit's nine galleries are numbered differently than the floors, but it doesn't matter as you'll be routed on a one-way path through six floors. If you have any questions, there are helpful "crew" everywhere you look.

The "shipyard ride" near the beginning is a fun (if cheesy) five-minute experience. Six people share a gondola as you glide through a series of vignettes that attempt to capture what it was like to be a worker building the ship.

Continuing on, you'll find a big window overlooking the actual construction site (which you'll visit after leaving the building). Next, you'll see exhibits on the construction, historic photographs, proud displays of the opulence on board, the disaster (with Morse code transmissions sent after the ship hit the iceberg) and, in the 200-seat Discovery Theatre, the seven-minute *Titanic Beneath* video, with eerie footage of the actual wreckage sprouting countless "rusticles" 12,000 feet down on the ocean floor. Don't miss the see-through floor panels at the foot of the movie screen where the wreck passes slowly under your feet.

The last escalator leaves you on the ground floor facing the back door of the center. Step outside. Just beyond the door, in the pavement, is a big, stylized map showing the route of the *Titanic*'s one and only voyage. The brown benches are long and short—set up in dots and dashes to represent the Morse code distress transmissions sent on that fateful day. Just beyond two dashes, a few steps to the left, find the symbolic steel tip of the ship in the pavement and stand there looking out. This was where the bow was; the lampposts (stretching 300 yards before you) mark the size of the ship built here. Fifty yards ahead is a memorial with the names of all who perished.

Sectarian Neighborhoods in West Belfast

It will be a happy day when the sectarian neighborhoods of Belfast have nothing to be sectarian about. For a look at three of the original home bases of the Troubles, explore the working-class neighborhoods of Catholic Falls Road and Protestant Shankill Road (west of the Westlink motorway), or Protestant Sandy Row (south of the Westlink motorway).

Murals (found in working-class, sectarian areas) are a memorable part of any visit to Belfast. But with more peaceful times, the character of these murals is slowly changing. The Re-Imaging Communities Program has spent £3 million in government money to replace aggressive murals with positive ones. Paramilitary themes are gradually being covered over with images of pride in each neighborhood's culture. The *Titanic* was built primarily by proud Protestant Ulster stock and is often seen in their neighborhood murals—reflecting their industrious work ethic. Over in the Catholic neighborhoods, you'll see more murals depicting mythological heroes

Titanic Belfast

from the days before the English came.

Hop-on, hop-off bus tours regularly drive these roads. But taxi tours of Falls Road or Shankill Road are more interactive (quiz the cabbie, who grew up here) and allow you to pull over to take photos.

▲▲FALLS ROAD (CATHOLIC)

At the intersection of Castle and King streets, you'll find the Castle Junction Car Park. On the ground floor of this nine-story parking garage, a passenger terminal (entrance on King Street) connects travelers with old black cabs—and the only Irish-language signs in downtown Belfast. These shared black cabs efficiently shuttle residents from outlying neighborhoods up and down Falls Road and to the city center. This service originated almost 50 years ago at the beginning of the Troubles, when locals would hijack city buses and use them as barricades in the street fighting. When bus service was discontinued, local sectarian groups established the shared taxi service. Although the buses are now running again, these cab rides are still a great value for their drivers' commentaries.

Any cab goes up Falls Road, past Sinn Fein headquarters and lots of murals, to the Milltown Cemetery (£6, sit in front and talk to the cabbie). Hop in and out. Easy-to-flag-down cabs run every minute or so in each direction on Falls Road. Or, take a one-hour tour from a trained black-taxi cabbie (see page 277).

Visiting Falls Road: The Sinn Fein office and bookstore are near the bottom of Falls

Falls Road

Road. The **bookstore** is worth a look. Page through books featuring color photos of the political murals that decorated these buildings. Money raised here supports the families of deceased IRA members.

A sad, corrugated structure called the **peace wall** runs a block or so north of Falls Road (along Cupar Way), separating the Catholics from the Protestants in the Shankill Road area. The first cement wall was 20 feet high—it was later extended another 10 feet by a solid metal addition, and then another 15 feet with a metal screen. Seemingly high enough now to deter a projectile being lobbed over, this is one of many such walls erected in Belfast during the Troubles. Meant to be temporary, these barriers stay up because of old fears among the communities on both sides. In 2013, the Northern Ireland Assembly announced its ambitious goal to remove all of these walls by 2023, but a lack of resources and weak community unity have resulted in little progress.

At the **Milltown Cemetery,** walk past all the Gaelic crosses down to the far right-hand corner (closest to the highway), where little green railings set

Shankill Road

apart the IRA Roll of Honor from the thousands of other graves. These martyrs are treated like fallen soldiers. Notice the memorial to Bobby Sands and nine other hunger strikers. They starved themselves to death in the nearby Maze Prison in 1981, protesting for political prisoner status as opposed to terrorist criminal treatment. Maze Prison closed in the fall of 2000.

SHANKILL ROAD AND SANDY ROW (PROTESTANT)

A shared black cab brings you though the Shankill Road area (see page 277), but an easier and cheaper way to get a dose of the Unionist side is to walk **Sandy Row.** From Hotel Europa, walk a block down Glengall Street, then turn left for a 10-minute walk along a working-class Protestant street. A stop in a Unionist memorabilia shop, a pub, or one of the many cheap eateries here may give you an opportunity to talk to a local. You'll see murals filled with Unionist symbolism. The mural of William of Orange's victory over the Catholic King James II (Battle of the Boyne, 1690) thrills Unionist hearts. You'll find it at the northern end of Sandy Row at the corner with Linfield Road.

Central Belfast

▲▲CITY HALL

This grand structure's 173-foot-tall copper dome dominates the town center. Built between 1898 and 1906, with its statue of Queen Victoria scowling down Belfast's main drag and the Neoclassical dome

looming behind her, the City Hall is a stirring sight. Take a close look at the Queen Victoria monument and how it celebrates the industrial might of Belfast: shipping, linen (the woman with the bobbin), and education (the student).

A worthwhile, 16-room exhibit on Belfast's history and culture fills the ground floor of City Hall. It covers the history of the city, culture, industry, the WWII bombings, and the Troubles.

Cost and Hours: Free, daily 8:30-17:00; handy Bobbin coffee shop on ground floor, tel. 028/9032-0202, www.belfastcity. gov.uk/cityhall.

Tours: Free 45-minute tours of City Hall run Mon-Fri at 10:00, 11:00, 14:00, 15:00, and 16:00; Sat-Sun at 12:00, 14:00, 15:00, and 16:00 (fewer off-season); call or check online to confirm schedule.

Visiting City Hall: If you can't manage a tour, at least step into the main lobby to admire the marble-swirl staircase and the view up into the dome. In 1912, at the center of the marble floor design beneath the dome, Sir Edward Carson signed the Ulster Covenant—to be followed by 470,000 other Unionists at dozens of desks surrounding City Hall that day. Some signed with their own blood. The Covenant stated Unionists would use "all means necessary" (including the might of the 100,000-strong UVF militia) to resist the Home Rule bill that had just passed in Parliament. The bill would have given the entire island of Ireland limited autonomy from Britain. These Protestant Unionists did not want this new level of political distance from Britain and feared that "Home Rule is Rome Rule." They would have become the minority in a more independent Catholic Ireland. World War I interrupted the implementation of Home Rule, and the partition of Ireland followed shortly after the war's end.

LINEN HALL LIBRARY

Across the street from City Hall, the 200-year-old Linen Hall Library welcomes guests (notice the red hand

City Hall

1916

This pivotal year means vastly different things to Northern Ireland's two communities. When you say "1776" to most Americans, it means revolution and independence from tyranny (unless, perhaps, you're a Native American). But when you say "1916" to someone in Northern Ireland, the response depends on who's talking.

To Nationalists (who are usually Catholic), "1916" brings to mind the Easter Rising—which took place in Dublin in April of that year and was the beginning of the end of 750 years of British rule for most of Ireland (see sidebar on page 60). Some Nationalist murals still use images of Dublin's rebel headquarters or martyred leaders like Patrick Pearse and James Connolly. To this community, 1916 emphasizes their proud Gaelic identity, their willingness to fight to preserve it, and their stubborn anti-British attitude.

To Unionists (who are usually Protestant), "1916" means the brutal WWI Battle of the Somme in France, which began that July. Although both Catholic and Protestant soldiers died in this long and bloody battle, the first wave of young men who went over the top were the sons of proud Ulster Unionists. The Unionists hoped this sacrifice would prove their loyalty to the Crown—and assurance that the British would never let them be gobbled up by an Irish Nationalist state (a possible scenario just before the Great War's outbreak). You'll see Tommies heroically climbing out of their trenches in some of Belfast's Unionist murals. For the Unionists, 1916 is synonymous with devout, almost righteously divine, Britishness.

---

above the front door facing Donegall Square North; for more on its meaning, see the sidebar on page 290). Described as "Ulster's attic," the library takes pride in being a neutral space where anyone trying to make sense of the sectarian conflict can view the Troubled Images, a historical collection of engrossing political posters. It has a fine hardbound ambience, a coffee shop ('nice light lunches'), and a royal newspaper reading room.

Cost and Hours: Free; Mon-Fri 9:30-17:30, Sat until 16:00, closed Sun; 45-minute tours for £5—daily at 11:30, 17 Donegall Square North, tel. 028/9032-1707, www.linenhall.com.

GOLDEN MILE

This is the overstated nickname of Belfast's liveliest dining and entertainment district, which stretches from the Opera House (Great Victoria Street) to the university (University Road).

The **Grand Opera House,** originally built in 1895, bombed and rebuilt in 1991, and bombed and rebuilt again in 1993, is extravagantly Victorian and *the* place to take in a concert, play, or opera (ticket office open Mon-Sat 10:00-17:30, closed Sun; ticket office to right of main front door on Great Victoria Street, tel. 028/9024-1919, www.goh.co.uk). The recommended Hotel Europa, next door, while considered to be the most-bombed hotel in the world (33 times during the Troubles), actually feels pretty casual (but is expensive).

Across the street is the museum-like **Crown Liquor Saloon.** Built in 1849, it's now a part of the National Trust. A wander through its mahogany, glass, and marble interior is a trip back into the days of Queen Victoria, although the privacy provided by the snugs—booths—allows for un-Victorian behavior (consider a lunch stop—see "Eating in Belfast," later). Upstairs, the

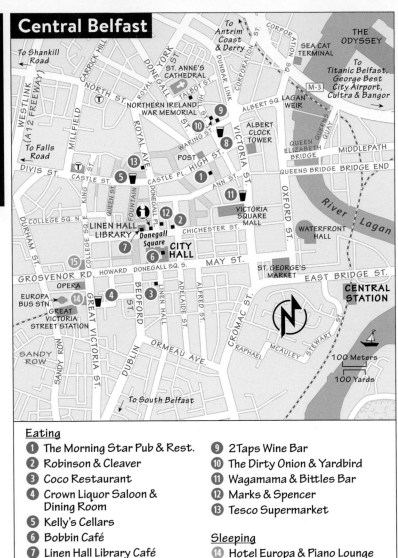

Central Belfast

Crown Dining Room serves pub grub and is decorated with historic photos.

Cathedral Quarter

This rejuvenating district is about a 15-minute walk north of City Hall, in the oldest part of the city. You'll find an unexpected cluster of culture that will make you rethink your preconceptions about Belfast. Besides being home to St. Anne's Cathedral, it's a memorable maze for a wander, where mind-bending murals put the "fun" in "funky" and show the artistic alternative to the sectarian murals found elsewhere. For the best scene, head for the intersection of Hill Street and Commercial Court and peek into nearby breezeways. It's also a good place for a lively dinner (see listings on page 291).

South Belfast
▲ULSTER MUSEUM
This is Belfast's most venerable museum. It offers an earnest and occasionally thought-provoking look at the region's history, with a cross-section of local artifacts.

Cost and Hours: £3 suggested donation; Tue-Sun 10:00-17:00, closed Mon; in Botanic Gardens on Stranmillis Road, south of downtown, tel. 028/9044-0000, www.nmni.com.

Visiting the Museum: The five-floor museum is pretty painless. Ride the elevator to the top floor and follow the spiraling exhibits downhill through various zones. The top two floors are dedicated to rotating art exhibits, the next floor down covers local nature, and the two below that focus on history. The ground floor covers the Troubles, and has a coffee shop and gift shop.

▲BOTANIC GARDENS
This is the backyard of Queen's University, and on a sunny day, you couldn't imagine a more relaxing park setting. On a cold day, step into the Tropical Ravine for a jungle of heat and humidity. Take a quick walk through the Palm House, reminiscent of the one in London's Kew Gardens,

but smaller. The Ulster Museum is on the garden's grounds.

Cost and Hours: Free, gardens open daily 8:00 until dusk; Palm House open daily 10:00-17:00, Oct-March until 16:00; tel. 028/9031-4762, www.belfastcity.gov.uk/parks.

LYRIC THEATRE
Located beside the River Lagan (near Queen's University), the Lyric Theatre is a Belfast institution. Rebuilt in 2011, it represents the cultural rejuvenation of the city—the building was partially funded by donations from actors such as Liam Neeson, Kenneth Branagh, and Meryl Streep. It's a good place to see quality local productions (tickets £15-25; box office open daily 10:00-17:00; 55 Ridgeway Street, tel. 028/9038-1081, www.lyrictheatre.co.uk).

Near Belfast
▲▲ULSTER FOLK PARK AND TRANSPORT MUSEUM
This sprawling 180-acre, two-museum complex straddles the road and rail line at Cultra, midway between Bangor and Belfast (8 miles east of town).

Cost and Hours: £9 for each museum, £11 combo-ticket for both, £29 for families; March-Sept Tue-Sun 10:00-17:00; Oct-Feb Tue-Fri 10:00-16:00, Sat-Sun 11:00-16:00; closed Mon year-round; check the schedule for the day's special events, tel. 028/9042-8428, www.nmni.com.

Palm House in Botanic Gardens

Ulster Museum

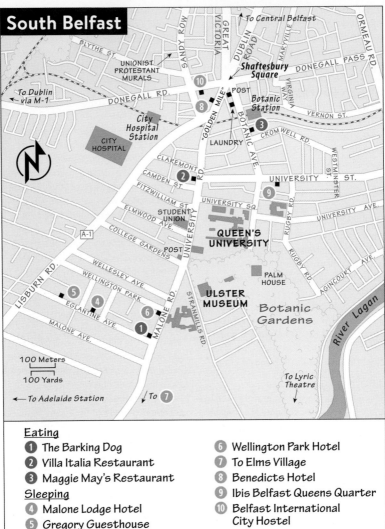

South Belfast

To Central Belfast

To Dublin
via M-1

Shaftesbury
Square

BLYTHE ST.

UNIONIST
PROTESTANT
MURALS

DONEGALL RD.

POST

Botanic
Station

City
Hospital
Station

CITY
HOSPITAL

LAUNDRY

CROMWELL RD.

CLAREMONT

CAMDEN ST.

FITZWILLIAM ST

ELMWOOD AVE.

STUDENT
UNION

COLLEGE GARDENS

POST

UNIVERSITY SQ.

QUEEN'S
UNIVERSITY

UNIVERSITY ST.

A-1

WELLESLEY AVE.

WELLINGTON PARK

EGLANTINE AVE.

MALONE AVE.

PALM
HOUSE

ULSTER
MUSEUM

Botanic
Gardens

River Lagan

SANDY ROW

GREAT VICTORIA

DUBLIN ROAD

MARYVILLE

DONEGALL PASS

ORMEAU RD.

VIRGINIA WAY

VERNON ST.

"GOLDEN MILE"

BOTANIC AVE.

WESTMINSTER ST.

RUGBY RD.

UNIVERSITY AVE.

RUGBY RD.

AGINCOURT AVE.

STRANMILLS RD.

MALONE RD.

UNIVERSITY RD.

LISBURN RD.

100 Meters

100 Yards

To Adelaide Station

To ⑦

To Lyric
Theatre

Eating
① The Barking Dog
② Villa Italia Restaurant
③ Maggie May's Restaurant

Sleeping
④ Malone Lodge Hotel
⑤ Gregory Guesthouse

⑥ Wellington Park Hotel
⑦ To Elms Village
⑧ Benedicts Hotel
⑨ Ibis Belfast Queens Quarter
⑩ Belfast International
City Hostel

Getting There: From Belfast, you can reach Cultra by taxi (£15), bus #502 (2/ hour, 30 minutes, from Laganside Bus Centre), or train (2/hour, 15 minutes, from any Belfast train station or from Bangor). Buses stop right in the park, but schedules are skimpy on Saturday and Sunday. Train service is more dependable (and more frequent on the weekend): Get off at the Cultra stop, which puts off between the

two parks, a bit closer to the Transport Museum than to the Folk Park.

Planning Your Time: Allow three hours for your visit, and expect lots of walking. Most people will spend an hour in the Transport Museum and a couple of hours at the Folk Park. You'll arrive (by rail or car) between the two museums a bit closer to the Transport Museum. From here, you have a choice of going downhill to the

Transport Museum or 200 panting yards uphill into the Folk Park. Assess your energy level and plan accordingly. Those with a car can drive between the museum and the folk park. Note that the Transport Museum is all indoors. The Folk Park involves more walking between buildings spread across the upper hillside.

Visiting the Museums: The **Transport Museum** consists of three buildings. Start at the bottom and trace the evolution of transportation from 7,500 years ago—when people first decided to load an ox—to the first vertical take-off jet. In 1909, the Belfast-based Shorts Aviation Company partnered with the Wright brothers to manufacture the first commercially available aircraft. The middle building holds an intriguing section on the sinking of the Belfast-made *Titanic*. The top building covers the history of bikes, cars, and trains. The car section rumbles from the first car in Ireland (an 1898 Benz), through the "Cortina Culture" of the 1960s, to the local adventures of controversial automobile designer John DeLorean and a 1981 model of his sleek sports car.

The **Folk Park,** an open-air collection of 34 reconstructed buildings from all over the nine counties of Ulster, showcases the region's traditional lifestyles. After wandering through the old-town site (church, print shop, schoolhouse, humble Belfast row house, silent movie theater, and so on), you'll head off into the country to nip into cottages, farmhouses, and mills. Some houses are warmed by a wonderful peat fire and a friendly attendant. Your visit can be dull or vibrant, depending upon whether attendants are available to chat. Drop a peat brick on the fire.

▲CARRICKFERGUS CASTLE

Built during the Norman invasion of the late 1100s, this historic castle stands sentry on the shore of Belfast Lough. William of Orange landed here in 1690, when he began his Irish campaign against deposed King James II. In 1778, the American privateer ship *Ranger* (the first ever to fly the Stars-and-Stripes), under the command of John Paul Jones, defeated the HMS *Drake* just up the coast. These days the castle feels a bit sanitized and geared for kids, but it's an easy excursion if you're seeking a castle experience near the city.

Cost and Hours: £5; daily 10:00-17:00, Oct-March until 16:00; tel. 028/9335-1273.

Getting There: It's a 20-minute train ride from Belfast (on the line to Larne). Turn left as you exit the train station and walk straight downhill for five minutes—all the way to the waterfront—passing under the arch of the old town wall en route. You'll find the castle on your right.

▲THE GOBBINS CLIFF PATH

Newly reopened in 2016, the Gobbins Cliff Path is an Edwardian adventure with

Ulster Folk Park and Transport Museum   *Carrickfergus Castle*

The Red Hand of Ulster

All over Belfast, you'll notice a curious symbol: a red hand facing you as if swearing a pledge or telling you to halt. You'll spot it, faded, above the Linen Hall Library door, in the wrought-iron fences of the Merchant Hotel, on old-fashioned clothes wringers (in the Ulster Folk Park and Transport Museum at Cultra), above the front door of a bank in Bangor, in the shape of a flowerbed at Mount Stewart House, in Loyalist paramilitary murals, on shield emblems in the gates of Republican memorials, and even on the flag of Northern Ireland (the white flag with the red cross of St. George). It's known as the Red Hand of Ulster—and it is one of the few emblems used by both communities in Northern Ireland.

Nationalists display a red-hand-on-a-yellow-shield as a symbol of the ancient province of Ulster. It was the official crest of the once-dominant O'Neill clan (who fought tooth and nail against English rule) and today signifies resistance to British rule in these communities.

But you'll more often see the red hand in Unionist areas. They see it as a potent symbol of the political entity of Northern Ireland. The Ulster Volunteer Force chose it for their symbol in 1913 and embedded it in the center of the Northern Irish flag upon partition of the island in 1921. You may see the red hand clenched as a fist in Loyalist murals. One Loyalist paramilitary group even named itself the Red Hand Commandos.

The origin of the red hand comes from a mythological tale of two rival clans that raced by boat to claim a far shore. The first clan leader to touch the shore would win it for his people. Everyone aboard both vessels strained mightily at their oars, near exhaustion as they approached the shore. Finally, in desperation, the chieftain leader of the slower boat whipped out his sword and lopped off his right hand...which he then flung onto the shore, thus winning the coveted land. Moral of the story? The fearless folk of Ulster will do *whatever it takes* to get the job done.

birds, beautiful scenery, and occasional rogue waves. Located 20 miles northeast of Belfast via Carrickfergus, this complex path—a mix of tunnel bridges, railings, and steps carved, hammered, or fastened to the cliff—was first opened in 1902, designed to boost tourism. Once popular, it fell into disrepair during World War II and was closed for decades. The newly reinforced path (which, to spoil all the turn-of-the-century fun, now requires helmets and guides) takes two to three hours to hike, and is awkward and steep in places, but not terribly strenuous. You'll spot puffins, cormorants, and kittiwakes in nesting areas along the way.

Cost and Hours: £10, visitor center open daily 9:30-17:30, required guided hikes generally hourly (weather permitting), book in advance as tours can fill up, tel. 028/9337-2318, 68 Middle Road, Islandmagee, www.thegobbinscliffpath.com.

Getting There: By car, take the A-2 from Belfast to Larne, turn right on B-90, and follow the signs to *Islandmagee* and *The Gobbins.* Without a car, take a train to Ballycarry (on the Larne line) and walk a mile to the center, or take a taxi (Ballycarry Cabs, tel. 028/9303-8131).

EATING

Downtown

The Morning Star is woody and elegant, with a **$$$ restaurant** upstairs (daily 12:00-22:00) and an **$ afternoon buffet** (Mon-Sat 12:00-16:00; down alley just off High Street at 17 Pottinger's Entry, alley entry is roughly opposite the post office, tel. 028/9023-5986).

$$ Robinson & Cleaver has a great central location, perfect for light lunches or tasty dinners. In good weather, their balcony has terrific views of City Hall (Mon-Sat 12:00-15:00, Wed-Sat also 17:00-21:30, closed Sun; Donegall Square North, a few doors east of the TI, tel. 028/9031-2666).

$$$ Coco Restaurant is a spacious, high-end place with a quirky sense of style serving reliably tasty modern Irish and Continental dishes. Their early-bird special makes it a budget find if you order before 19:00 (open nightly from 17:30, a couple of blocks behind City Hall at 7 Linen Hall Street, tel. 028/9031-1150).

$$ Crown Liquor Saloon, a recommended stop along the Golden Mile, is small and antique. Its mesmerizing mishmash of mosaics and shareable snugs (booths—best to reserve) is topped with a smoky tin ceiling (food served Sun-Thu 11:30-19:00, Fri-Sat until 17:00, 46 Great Victoria Street, across from Hotel Europa, tel. 028/9024-3187, www.nicholsonspubs.co.uk). The **$$$ Crown Dining Room** upstairs offers dependable meals

(daily 11:30-20:00, tel. 028/9024-3187, use entry on Amelia Street when the Crown Liquor Saloon is closed).

$$$ Europa Piano Lounge rests serenely above the lobby of the Europa Hotel, with refined service and possibly the best club sandwich in town. It's a great hideaway for quietly recharging your sightseeing batteries (daily 10:00-22:00, tel. 028/9027-1066).

$$ Kelly's Cellars, once a rebel hangout (see plaque above door), still has a very gritty Irish feel. It's 300 years old and hard to find, but worth it. The pub grub is basic, but the atmosphere is delicious (Mon-Sat 11:30-24:30, Sun 13:00-23:30; live traditional music Tue-Fri and Sun at 21:30, Sat at 16:30; 32 Bank Street, 100 yards behind Tesco supermarket, access via alley on left side when facing Tesco, tel. 028/9024-6058).

Lunch Spots: The **$ Bobbin Café** at City Hall is a good, cheap, and cheery little cafeteria serving soups, sandwiches, and hot dishes (open daily, same hours as City Hall). Across the street, the **$ Linen Hall Library Café** is more elegant (it's like eating with professors in a library) but with a more limited lunch menu (daily 9:30-16:00).

Supermarkets: Consider a picnic on the City Hall lawn with food from one of the following. **Marks & Spencer** has a coffee shop and a supermarket in its basement (daily until 18:00, WCs on second floor, Donegall Place, a block north of Donegall Square). **Tesco** is a block north of Marks & Spencer and two blocks north of Donegall Square (open slightly later than Marks & Spencer, Royal Avenue and Bank Street).

Cathedral Quarter

$$$$ Check out the lobby of **Merchant Hotel** (a grand former bank) for a glimpse of crushed-velvet Victorian splendor under an opulent dome, and consider indulging in Belfast's best afternoon tea splurge. Don't show up in shorts and sneakers (£25 for

Mon-Fri 12:00-16:30, £29.50 for Sat-Sun, reserve ahead for seating at 12:30 or 15:00, 35 Waring Street, tel. 028/9023-4888, www. themerchanthotel.com).

$$$ 2Taps Wine Bar is a whiff of Mediterranean warmth in this cold brick city. Try a cheerful tapas or paella meal washed down with sangria (Tue-Sun 12:00-21:00, closed Mon, 42 Waring Street, tel. 028/9031-1414).

$$ The Cloth Ear is a friendly, modern, often-crowded bar serving better-than-average pub grub from the kitchen of the posh Merchant Hotel next door (daily 12:00-20:30, 33 Waring Street, tel. 028/9026-2719).

$$ The Dirty Onion and **Yardbird** are a hip combo filling a dimly lit and woody warehouse with enthusiastic young-at-heart locals. The Yardbird (upstairs) serves the grub, specializing in rotisserie chicken that's "clucking good." The Dirty Onion (downstairs) is a popular pub that spills suds and live music into its packed outer courtyard on summer nights (daily 12:00-23:30, 3 Hill Street, tel. 028/9024-3712).

Victoria Square Area

Although Victoria Square is a big, modern mall, a couple of fun options are worth considering—one inside the mall (for food) and one next door (for drinks).

$$ Wagamama, part of a British chain, is a Japanese noodle bar located on the first floor of the mall. Hearty portions of chicken ramen, **yakisoba,** and cumin beef salad are menu highlights (Sun-Wed 12:00-21:00, Thu-Sat until 22:00, Victoria Square, tel. 028/9023-6098).

Bittles Bar is a good place to stop for a pint. It's a tiny, wedge-shaped throwback to Victorian days, hidden in the shadows on the east side of the mall next to the ornate, yellow Victorian fountain. The minuscule, terraced interior is decorated with caricatures of literary and political figures (daily generally 12:00 until late, no food, 70 Upper Church Lane just off Victoria Street, mobile 077-9396-2329).

Near Queen's University
$$$ The Barking Dog is closest to my cluster of accommodations south of the university. It's a trendy grill serving tasty burgers, duck, scallops, and other filling fare. If the weather's fine, the outdoor tree-shaded front tables are ideal for people-watching (Mon-Sat 12:00-15:00 & 17:00-22:00, Sun 12:00-21:00, near corner of Eglantine Avenue at 33 Malone Road, tel. 028/9066-1885).

$$$ Villa Italia packs in crowds hungry for linguini and *bistecca.* With its checkered tablecloths and a wood-beamed ceiling draped with grape leaves, it's a little bit of Italy in Belfast (Mon-Sat 17:00-23:00, Sun 12:30-21:30, 3 long blocks south of Shaftesbury Square, at intersection with University Street, 39 University Road, tel. 028/9032-8356).

$$ Maggie May's serves hearty, simple, affordable meals (Sun-Thu 8:00-22:00, Fri-Sat until 23:00, one block south of Botanic Station at 50 Botanic Avenue, tel. 028/9032-2662).

SLEEPING

Belfast is more of a business town than a tourist town, so business-class room rates are lower or soft on weekends. For cozy B&Bs, check out the Queen's University area or the nearby seaside town of Bangor.

In Central Belfast
$$$$ Hotel Europa is Belfast's landmark hotel—fancy, comfortable, and central—with four stars and lower weekend rates. Modern yet elegant, this place is the choice of visiting diplomats (breakfast extra, Great Victoria Street, tel. 028/9027-1066, www.hastingshotels.com, res@eur.hastingshotels.com).

$$$ Jurys Inn, an American-style hotel that rents 190 identical modern rooms, is perfectly located two blocks from City Hall (breakfast extra, Fisherwick Place, tel. 028/9053-3500, www.jurysinns.com, jurysinnbelfast@jurysinns.com).

South of Queen's University

$$$ **Malone Lodge Hotel,** by far the classiest listing in this neighborhood, provides slick, business-class comfort in 119 spacious rooms on a quiet street (elevator, restaurant, parking, 60 Eglantine Avenue, tel. 028/9038-8000, www.malonelodgehotel.com, info@malonelodgehotel.com).

$$ **Gregory Guesthouse,** with its stately red brick, ages gracefully behind a green lawn with 15 large, fresh rooms. It's a good value with subtle charm on a quiet street (family room, parking, 32 Eglantine Ave, tel. 028/9066-3454, www.thegregorybelfast.com, info@thegregorybelfast.com).

$$ **Wellington Park Hotel** is a dependable, if unimaginative, chain-style hotel with 75 rooms. It's predictable but in a good location (parking extra, 21 Malone Road, tel. 028/9038-1111, www.wellingtonparkhotel.com, info@wellingtonparkhotel.com).

$ **Elms Village,** a huge Queen's University dorm complex, rents 100 basic, institutional rooms (all singles) to travelers during summer break (July and Aug only, coin-op laundry, self-serve kitchen; reception building is 50 yards down entry street, marked Elms Village on low brick wall, 78 Malone Road; tel. 028/9097-4525, www.stayatqueens.com, accommodation@qub.ac.uk).

Between Queen's University and Shaftesbury Square

$$ **Benedicts Hotel** has 32 rooms in a good location at the northern fringe of the Queen's University district. Its popular bar is a maze of polished wood and can be loud on weekend nights (elevator, 7 Bradbury Place, tel. 028/9059-1999, www.benedictshotel.co.uk, info@benedictshotel.co.uk).

$$ **Ibis Belfast Queens Quarter,** part of a major European hotel chain, has 56 practical rooms in a convenient location. It's a great deal if you're not looking for cozy character (breakfast extra, elevator, a block north of Queen's University at 75 University Street, tel. 028/9033-3366, www.ibisbelfast.com, h7288-fo@accor.com).

¢ **Belfast International City Hostel,** big and creatively run, provides the best value among Belfast's hostels. It is located near Botanic Station, in the heart of the lively university district, and has 24-hour reception. Paul, the manager, is a veritable TI, with a passion for his work (private rooms available, 22 Donegall Road, tel. 028/9031-5435, www.hini.org.uk, info@hini.org.uk).

TRANSPORTATION

Getting Around Belfast

If you line up your sightseeing logically, you can do most of this flat town on foot. On wheels, you have several options. For most visitors, the Belfast Visitor Pass will save time and money. It combines iLink smartcards for local bus and train trips with sightseeing discounts (see "Sightseeing Pass," earlier).

By Train or Bus

Ask about **iLink smartcards,** which give individuals one day of unlimited train and bus travel. The Zone 1 card (£6.50) covers the city center, Cultra (Ulster Folk Park and Transport Museum), and George Best Belfast City Airport. The handy Zone 2 card (£11) includes Bangor and Carrickfergus Castle. The Zone 3 card (£14.50) is really only useful for reaching Belfast's distant international airport. Zone 4 (£17.50) gets you anywhere in Northern Ireland, including Portrush and Derry (£16.50 top-up for each additional day). Buy your iLink card at any train station in the city.

Pink-and-white city buses go from Donegall Square East to Malone Road and my recommended accommodations (any #8 bus, 3/hour, £2, all-day pass costs £4 Mon-Sat before 9:30—after 9:30 and on Sun it's £3.70). Sunday service is much less frequent.

For more information on iLink smart-cards, trains, and buses in Belfast, contact Translink (tel. 028/9066-6630, www.translink.co.uk).

By Taxi

Taxis are reasonable and a good option. For general transport, rather than the taxi tours described later, try **Valu Cabs** (tel. 028/9080-9080). Cabs charge a flat £3 rate for any ride (£3.40 from 22:00 to 6:00) and £2 per mile after that. If you're going up Falls Road, ride a shared cab (see page 277).

Arriving and Departing

For updated schedules and prices for both trains and buses in Northern Ireland, check with Translink (tel. 028/9066-6630, www.translink.co.uk). Consider a Belfast Visitor Pass (see page 276) if you're visiting just Belfast. Those going beyond Belfast can make use of the Zone 4 iLink smartcard, good for all-day train and bus use in Northern Ireland (see above). Service is less frequent on Sundays.

By Train

Arriving by train, you'll go directly to Belfast's Central Station (with an ATM in the lobby). From the station, a free Centrelink bus loops to Donegall Square, with stops near Shaftesbury Square (recommended hostel), the bus station (some recommended hotels), and the TI (free with any train or bus ticket, 4/hour, none on Sun; during morning rush hour, bus runs only between station and Donegall Square). Allow about £5 for a taxi from Central Station to Donegall Square, or £8 to my accommodation listings south of the university.

Slower trains arc through the city, stopping at several downtown stations, including Central Station, Great Victoria Station (most central, near Donegall Square and most hotels), and Botanic Station (close to the university, Botanic Gardens, and some recommended lodgings). It's easy and cheap to connect stations by train (£1.50).

From Belfast by Train to: Dublin (8/day, 2 hours), Derry (10/day, 2.5 hours), Portrush (15/day, 2 hours, transfer in Coleraine), Bangor (2/hour, 30 minutes).

By Bus

The Europa Bus Centre is behind Hotel Europa (Ulsterbus tel. 028/9033-7003 for destinations in Scotland and England).

From Belfast by Bus to: Portrush (12/day, 2 hours; scenic-coast route, 2.5 hours), **Derry** (hourly, 2 hours), **Dublin** (hourly, most via Dublin Airport, 3 hours), **Galway** (every 2 hours, 6 hours, change in Dublin), **Glasgow** (3/day, 6 hours), **Edinburgh** (3/day, 7 hours).

By Car

Driving in Belfast, although not as bad as in Dublin, is still a pain. Avoid it if possible. Street parking in the city center is geared for short stops (use pay-and-display machines, £0.30/15 minutes, one-hour maximum, Mon-Sat 8:00-18:00, free in evenings and on Sun).

By Plane

Belfast has two airports. **George Best Belfast City Airport** (airport code: BHD, tel. 028/9093-9093, www.belfastcityairport.com) is a five-minute taxi ride from town (near the docks) or a £2.50 ride on the Airport Express bus #600 (hourly from Europa Bus Centre). **Belfast International Airport** (airport code: BFS, tel. 028/9448-4848, www.belfastairport.com) is 18 miles west of town—a £7.50 ride on the Airport Express bus #300 (hourly from Europa Bus Centre).

NEAR BELFAST

BANGOR

To stay in a laid-back seaside home-town—with more comfort per pound—sleep 12 miles east of Belfast in Bangor (BANG-grr). It's a handy alternative for travelers who find Belfast booked up by occasional conventions and conferences. Formerly a Victorian resort and seaside escape from the big city nearby, Bangor now has a sleepy residential feeling.

Orientation

Arrival in Bangor: Catch the train to Bangor from either Belfast's Central or Great Victoria Street stations (2/hour, 30 minutes, go to the end of the line—don't get off at Bangor West).

Tourist Information: Bangor's TI is in a stone tower house (from 1637) on the harborfront (Mon-Fri 9:15-17:00, Sat from 10:00, Sun 13:00-17:00 except closed Sun Sept-April, 34 Quay Street, tel. 028/9127-0069, www.visitardsand northdown.com).

Helpful Hints: You'll find **Speedi-wash Launderette** at 96 Abbey Street, a couple of blocks south of the train station (Mon-Sat 9:00-18:00, closed Sun, tel. 028/9127-0074). **Kare Cabs** provides local taxi service (tel. 028/9145-6777 or 028/9181-8001).

Sights near Bangor

The eastern fringe of Northern Ireland is populated mostly by people who consider themselves true-blue British citizens with a history of loyalty to the Crown that goes back more than 400 years. Two sights within reach by car from Bangor highlight this area's firm roots in British culture: the Somme Heritage Centre and Mount Stewart House.

Getting There: Bus service from Bangor to these sights is patchy (bus #6; check schedule with Bangor TI). To rent a car for the day, try George Best Belfast City Airport, a 15-minute train trip from Bangor or a 10-minute ride from Belfast's Central Station.

▲MOUNT STEWART HOUSE

No manor house in Ireland better illuminates the affluent lifestyle of the Protestant ascendancy than this lush estate. After the defeat of James II (the last Catholic king of England) at the Battle of the Boyne in 1690, the Protestant monarchy was in control—and the privileged status of landowners of the same faith was assured. In the 1700s, Ireland's many Catholic rebellions seemed finally to be squashed, so Anglican landlords felt safe flaunting their wealth in manor houses surrounded by utterly perfect gardens. The Mount Stewart House in particular was designed to dazzle.

Cost and Hours: £9.50 for house and gardens; daily 10:00-16:30, closed Nov-Feb; 8 miles south of Bangor, just off A-20 beside Strangford Lough, tel. 028/4278-8387, www.nationaltrust.org.uk, enquiries@nationaltrust.org.uk.

Visiting the House: Hourly tours give you a glimpse of the cushy life led by the Marquess of Londonderry and his heirs over the past three centuries. The main entry hall is a stunner, with a black-and-white checkerboard tile floor, marble columns, classical statues, and pink walls supporting a balcony with a domed ceiling and a fine chandelier. In the dining room, you'll see the original seats occupied by the rears of European heads of state, brought back from the Congress of Vienna after Napoleon's 1815 defeat. A huge painting of Hambletonian, a prize-winning racehorse, hangs above the grand staircase, dwarfing a portrait of the Duke of Wellington in a hall nearby. The heroic duke (worried that his Irish birth would be

Gardens of Mount Stewart House

seen as lower class by British blue bloods) once quipped in Parliament, "Just because one is born in a stable does not make him a horse." Irish emancipator Daniel O'Connell retorted, "Yes, but it could make you an ass."

Afterward, wander the expansive manicured **gardens.** The fantasy life of parasol-toting, upper-crust Victorian society seems to ooze from every viewpoint. Fanciful sculptures of extinct dodo birds and monkeys holding vases on their heads set off predictably classic Italian and Spanish sections. An Irish harp has been trimmed out of a hedge a few feet from a flowerbed shaped like the Red Hand of Ulster. Swans glide serenely among the lily pads on a small lake.

SOMME HERITAGE CENTRE

World War I's trench warfare was a meat grinder. More British soldiers died in the last year of that war than in all of World War II. Northern Ireland's men were not spared—especially during the bloody Battle of the Somme in France, starting in July 1916 (see the "1916" sidebar on page 285). Among the Allied forces was the British Army's 36th Ulster Division, which drew heavily from this loyal heartland of North-

ern Ireland. The 36th Ulster Division suffered brutal losses at the Battle of the Somme—of the 760 men recruited from the Shankill Road area in Belfast, only 10 percent survived.

Exhibits portray the battle experience through a mix of military artifacts, photos, historical newsreels, and life-size figures posed in trench warfare re-creations. To access the majority of the exhibits, it's essential to take the one-hour guided tour (leaving hourly, on the hour). Visiting this place is a moving experience, but it can only hint at the horrific conditions endured by these soldiers.

Cost and Hours: £6.50; July-Aug Mon-Fri 10:00-16:00, Sat from 11:00, closed Fri Sept-June and Sun year-round; hourly tours, 3 miles south of Bangor just off A-21 at 233 Bangor Road, tel. 028/9182-3202, www.irishsoldier.org. A coffee shop is located at the center.

Eating and Sleeping

Be aware that most restaurants in town stop seating at about 20:30.

$$$ Bangla serves fine Indian cuisine with attentive service (open daily for lunch, Thu-Sun for dinner, 115 Main

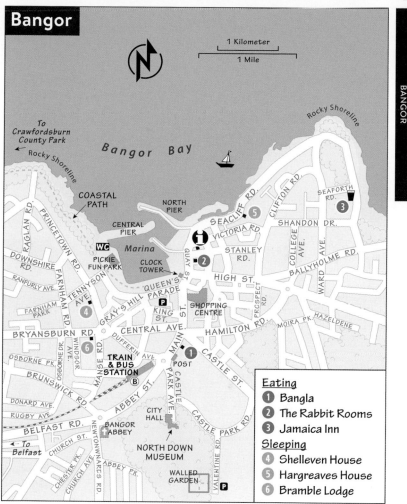

Bangor

1 Kilometer

1 Mile

To Crawfordsburn County Park
Rocky Shoreline

Rocky Shoreline

Bangor Bay

Rocky Shoreline

COASTAL PATH

NORTH PIER

CENTRAL PIER

SEACLIFF RD.

CLIFTON RD.

SEAFORTH RD.

WC Marina

PICKIE FUN PARK

CLOCK TOWER

QUAY ST.

VICTORIA RD.

SHANDON DR.

COLLEGE AVE.

RAGLAN RD.

PRINCETOWN RD.

DOWNSHIRE RD.

FARNHAM RD.

TENNYSON AVE.

GRAY'S HILL

QUEEN'S PARADE

STANLEY RD.

HIGH ST.

PROSPECT

BALLYHOLME RD.

WARD RD.

RANFURLY AVE.

FARNHAM PARK

KING ST.

SHOPPING CENTRE

HAMILTON RD.

MOIRA PK.

HAZELDENE

BRYANSBURN RD.

WINDSOR AVE.

CENTRAL AVE.

DUFFERIN AVE.

MAIN ST.

CASTLE ST.

OSBORNE PK.

BRUNSWICK RD.

MANSE RD.

TRAIN & BUS STATION

POST

PARK AVE.

CASTLE ST.

DONARD AVE.

RUGBY AVE.

BELFAST RD.

NEWTOWNARDS RD.

CITY HALL

CASTLE PARK RD.

To Belfast

CHURCH ST.

CHESTER PK.

CHURCH RD.

BANGOR ABBEY

ABBEY ST.

ABBEY PK.

NORTH DOWN MUSEUM

WALLED GARDEN

VALENTINE RD.

Eating
1. Bangla
2. The Rabbit Rooms
3. Jamaica Inn

Sleeping
4. Shelleven House
5. Hargreaves House
6. Bramble Lodge

Street). **$$ The Rabbit Rooms** serves hearty Irish food (daily, near the harbor at 33 Quay Street). The **$$ Jamaica Inn** offers pleasant pub grub and a breezy waterfront porch (188 Seacliff Road).

 $$$ Shelleven House is an old-fashioned, well-kept, stately place with 13 prim rooms (RS%, 61 Princetown Road, www. shellevenhouse.com). **$$ Hargreaves House,** a homey Victorian waterfront refuge with three cozy rooms, is Bangor's best value (RS%, 78 Seacliff Road, www. hargreaveshouse.com). **$$ Bramble Lodge** offers three inviting and spotless rooms (1 Bryansburn Road, tel. 028/9145-7924, jacquihanna_bramblelodge@ yahoo.co.uk).

Portrush
& the
Antrim Coast

The Antrim Coast is one of the most interesting and scenic coastlines in Ireland. Portrush, at the end of the train line, is an ideal base for exploring its highlights. Within a few miles of the train terminal, you can visit evocative castle ruins, tour the world's oldest whiskey distillery, catch a thrill on a bouncy rope bridge, and hike along the famous Giant's Causeway.

PORTRUSH & THE ANTRIM COAST IN 1 DAY

You need a full day to explore the Antrim Coast, so allow two nights in Portrush. In summer months, the long days this far north extend your sightseeing time (and most golf courses stay open until dusk).

Getting Around the Antrim Coast

By Car: A car is the best way to explore the charms of the Antrim Coast. Distances are short and parking is easy.

With a car, you can visit the Giant's Causeway, Old Bushmills Distillery, Carrick-a-Rede Rope Bridge, and Dunluce Castle in one busy day. Start with the Giant's Causeway, arriving by 9:00, when crowds are lightest; choose between a one-hour quickie visit or the scenic three-hour, five-mile "Clifftop Experience" guided hike (from Dunseverick Castle to the causeway).

Follow this with a tour of Old Bushmills Distillery (call ahead to reserve). For lunch, you can bring a picnic, or eat cheaply in either the visitors center at the causeway or the Old Bushmills hospitality room.

After lunch, drive to Carrick-a-Rede (about 20 minutes from the distillery). Note, though, that crossing the rope bridge requires timed-entry tickets, which can sell out in peak season (only available same-day and assigned starting at 9:30).

From here, hop in your car and double back west all the way to dramatically cliff-perched Dunluce Castle for a late-afternoon tour. The castle is only a five-minute drive from Portrush.

By Bus: In peak season, an all-day bus pass helps you get around the region economically. The **Causeway Rambler** links Portrush to Old Bushmills Distillery, the Giant's Causeway, and the Carrick-a-Rede Rope Bridge (stopping at the nearby town of Ballintoy). The bus journey from Portrush to Carrick-a-Rede takes 45 minutes (£6.50/day, runs roughly 10:00-18:00, hourly May-Sept, every two hours March-April, fewer off-season). Pick up a Rambler bus schedule at the TI, and buy the ticket from the driver (in Portrush, the Rambler stops at Dunluce Avenue, next to public WC, a 2-minute walk from TI; operated by Translink, tel. 028/9066-6630, www.translink.co.uk).

By Bus Tour: From Belfast, you can visit most Antrim Coast sights with a McComb's tour (see page 277). Those based in Derry can get to the Giant's Causeway and Carrick-a-Rede Rope Bridge with City Sightseeing (see page 315).

By Taxi: Groups (up to four) can reasonably visit most sights by taxi (except the more distant Carrick-a-

PORTRUSH & THE ANTRIM COAST AT A GLANCE

▲▲**Giant's Causeway** Otherworldly coastline of quirky geologic formations, breezy hikes, and mythological confrontations between Celtic giant rivals. **Hours:** Visitors center—daily 9:00-18:00, July-Aug until 19:00; causeway—always open for hiking. See page 307.

▲▲**Old Bushmills Distillery** The oldest whiskey distillery in the world (over 400 years old) where connoisseurs tour the production process and debate the merits of triple distilling. **Hours:** Opens Mon-Sat at 9:30, Sun at 12:00, last tour at 16:00; Nov-March opens Mon-Sat at 10:00, Sun at 12:00, last tour at 15:30--book ahead in summer. See page 310.

▲▲**Carrick-a-Rede Rope Bridge** Spectacular terminus of scenic coastal hike, drawing photographers, bird watchers, and thrill seekers. **Hours:** Daily 9:30-18:00, June-Aug until 19:00; Nov-Feb until 15:30. See page 311.

▲**Dunluce Castle** Historic and haunted Irish-Scottish hybrid fortification clinging to the peak of a sea stack while daring attack from any side. **Hours:** Daily 10:00-17:30, winter until 16:00. See page 312.

Portrush Victorian age working-class beach getaway and regional sightseeing base, complete with old-time arcade and world-famous Royal Portrush links golf course. See page 302.

Rede and Rathlin Island sailings from Ballycastle). Approximate one-way prices from Portrush: £6 (Dunluce Castle), £8 (Old Bushmills Distillery), £11 (Giant's Causeway). Try **Andy Brown's Taxi** (tel. 028/7082-2223), **Hugh's Taxi** (mobile 077-0298-6110), or **North West Taxi** (tel. 028/7082-4446).

PORTRUSH

Homey Portrush used to be known as "the Brighton of the North." It first became a resort in the late 1800s, as railroads expanded to offer the new middle class a weekend by the shore. Victorian society believed that swimming in salt water would cure many common ailments.

While it's seen its best days, Portrush retains the atmosphere and architecture of a genteel seaside resort. Its peninsula is filled with lowbrow, family-oriented amusements, fun eateries and B&Bs. Summertime fun seekers promenade along the tiny harbor and tumble down to the sandy beaches, which extend in sweeping white crescents on either side.

Students from nearby University of Ulster at Coleraine give the town a little more personality. Along with the usual arcade amusements, there are nightclubs, restaurants, summer theater productions, and convivial pubs that attract customers all the way from Belfast.

July and August are beach-resort boom time. June and September are laid-back and lazy. Families pack Portrush on Saturdays, and revelers from Belfast crowd its hotels on Saturday nights.

Orientation

Portrush's pleasant and easily walkable town center features sea views in every direction. On one side are the harbor and most of the restaurants, and on the other are Victorian townhouses and vast, salty vistas. The tip of the peninsula is filled with tennis courts, lawn-bowling greens, putting greens, and a park.

Tourist Information: The TI is located underneath the very central, red-brick Town Hall (July-Aug Mon-Sat 9:00-18:00, Sun from 11:00; shorter hours off-season and closed Oct-March; Kerr Street, tel. 028/7082-3333).

Laundry: Causeway Laundry offers full service (closed Sun, 68 Causeway Street, tel. 028/7082-2060).

Rick's Tip: Over a four-day weekend in mid-May, thousands of die-hard **motorcycle fans** *converge on Portrush to watch the* **Northwest 200 Race.** *Accommodations fill up a year ahead, and traffic is the pits (dates and details at www.northwest200.org).*

Sights
BARRY'S OLD TIME AMUSEMENT ARCADE

This fun arcade is bigger than it looks and offers a chance to see Northern Ireland at play. Older locals visit for the nostalgia, as many of the rides and amusements go back 50 years. Everything runs with tokens (£0.50 each, buy a pile from coin-op machines). Located just below the train station on the harbor, Barry's is filled with "candy floss" (cotton candy) and crazy "scoop treats" (July-Aug daily 12:30-22:00, weekends only Easter-May, closed Sept-Easter, www.barrysamusements.com).

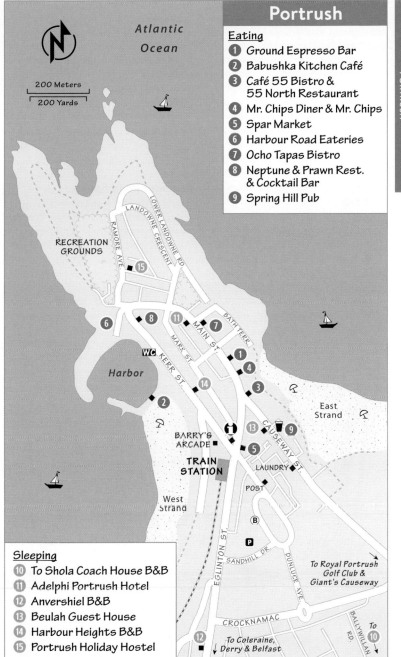

Portrush

Eating
1. Ground Espresso Bar
2. Babushka Kitchen Café
3. Café 55 Bistro & 55 North Restaurant
4. Mr. Chips Diner & Mr. Chips
5. Spar Market
6. Harbour Road Eateries
7. Ocho Tapas Bistro
8. Neptune & Prawn Rest. & Cocktail Bar
9. Spring Hill Pub

Sleeping
10. To Shola Coach House B&B
11. Adelphi Portrush Hotel
12. Anvershiel B&B
13. Beulah Guest House
14. Harbour Heights B&B
15. Portrush Holiday Hostel

ROYAL PORTRUSH GOLF CLUB
Irish courses, like those in Scotland, are highly sought after for their lush greens in glorious settings. Serious golfers can get a tee time at the Royal Portrush, which hosted the British Open in 1951 and is set to host it again in 2019 (green fees generally £190, less most days in off-season). Those on a budget can play the adjacent, slightly shorter Valley Course (green fees £25-£55, 10-minute walk from station, tel. 028/7082-2311, www.royalportrushgolf-club.com).

Eating
Lunch Spots
$ Ground Espresso Bar makes fresh sandwiches and *panini,* soup, and great coffee (daily July-Aug 9:00-22:00, Sept-June until 17:00, 52 Main Street, tel. 028/7082-5979).

$ Babushka Kitchen Café serves fresh sandwiches and creative desserts with an unbeatable view—actually out on the pier (daily 9:15-17:00, West Strand Promenade, tel. 077-8750-2012).

$$ Café 55 Bistro serves basic sandwiches with a great patio view (daily 9:00-

17:00, longer hours in summer, shorter hours off-season, 1 Causeway Street, beneath fancier 55 North restaurant, tel. 028/7082-2811).

$ Mr. Chips Diner and **Mr. Chips** are the local favorites for cheap, quality fish-and-chips (daily 12:00-22:00, 12 and 20 Main Street). Both are mostly takeout while the diner also has tables.

Groceries: For picnic ingredients, try **Spar Market** (daily, across from Barry's Arcade on Main Street).

Harbour Road Eateries
A lively quintet of restaurants clusters together overlooking the harbor. With the same owner, they all have a creative and fun energy, are often jammed with diners, and are basically open nightly from 17:00 to 22:00 (exceptions noted below).

$$ Ramore Wine Bar is a salty, modern place, with an inviting menu ranging from steaks to vegetarian food (also open for lunch, tel. 028/7082-4313). **$$ Coast Pizzeria** is a hit for its pizza, pasta, and burgers (tel. 028/7082-3311). **$$$ Harbour Bistro** is dark, noisy, and sprawling with a sloppy crowd enjoying chargrilled

Dining in Portrush

meat and fish (tel. 028/7082-2430). **$$
Mermaid Kitchen & Bar** is all about
fresh fish dishes with a Spanish twist and
great harbor views. (closed Mon-Tue, tel.
028/7082-6969).

$$$ Neptune & Prawn (just across the
inlet from the others) is the most yacht-
clubby of the bunch. Serving Asian and
other international food, with a fancy
presentation and many plates designed
to be shared, this place is noisy and high-
energy, with rock music playing (tel.
028/7082-2448).

Other Dining Options
off the Harbor

$$$ 55 North (named for the local lati-
tude) has the best sea views in town, with
windows on three sides. The filling pasta-
and-fish dishes, along with some Asian
plates, are a joy. Their lunch and early-bird
special (order by 18:45) is three courses at
the cost of the entrée (daily 12:30-14:00
& 17:00-21:00, 1 Causeway Street, tel.
028/7082-2811).

$$ Ocho Tapas Bistro brings sunny
Spanish cuisine to the chilly north,
featuring a great early-bird menu—
choose any three tapas from a varied list
(Tue-Fri 17:00-21:30, Sat-Sun 12:30-14:30
and 17:00-22:00, closed Mon, 92 Main
Street, tel. 028/7082-4110).

Pubs

Harbour Bar is an old-fashioned pub next
to the Harbour Bistro (see listing earlier).
Harbour Gin Bar (above Harbour Bar) is
romantic and classy—a rustic, spacious,
and inviting place with live acoustic folk
music from 20:30 (almost nightly) and a
fun selection of 45 gins.

Neptune & Prawn Cocktail Bar
(above the restaurant by the same name;
see listing earlier) has great views over the
harbor and is the most classy-yet-inviting
place in town for a drink.

Spring Hill Pub is also a good bet for its
friendly vibe and occasional live music (17
Causeway Street).

Sleeping

August and Saturday nights can be tight
(and loud) with young party groups.
Otherwise, rates vary with the view and
season—probe for softness. Most places
listed have lots of stairs. All but Shola
Coach House are perfectly central and
within a few minutes' walk of the train station. Parking is easy.

$$$ Shola Coach House is a memo-
rable treat that exceeds other B&B expe-
riences in Northern Ireland. About 1.5
miles south of town, it's easiest for drivers
(otherwise it's a 30-minute uphill walk
or £5 taxi ride). The secluded, 170-year-
old, renovated stone structure once
housed the coaches and horses for a local
landlord. The decor of the four rooms is
tasteful, the garden patio is delightful, and
Sharon and David Schindler keep it spot-
less (parking, no kids under 18, 2-night
minimum, 110A Gateside Road at top
of Ballywillan Road, tel. 028/7082-5925,
mobile 075-6542-7738, www.sholabandb.
com, sholabandb@gmail.com).

$$$ Adelphi Portrush is a breath of
fresh air, with 28 tastefully furnished mod-
ern rooms, an ideal location, friendly staff,
and a hearty bistro downstairs (family
rooms, 67 Main Street, tel. 028/7082-
5544, www.adelphiportrush.com, stay@
adelphiportrush.com).

$ Anvershiel B&B, with seven nicely
refurbished rooms, is a great value (RS%,
family rooms, parking, 10-minute walk
south of train station, 16 Coleraine Road,
tel. 028/7082-3861, www.anvershiel.com,
enquiries@anvershiel.com, Alan and Jan-
ice Thompson).

$ Beulah Guest House is a traditional,
old-fashioned place. It's centrally located
and run by cheerful Helen and Charlene
McLaughlin, with 11 prim rooms (parking
at rear, 16 Causeway Street, tel. 028/7082-
2413, www.beulahguesthouse.com, stay@
beulahguesthouse.com).

$ Harbour Heights B&B rents nine
retro-homey rooms, each named after a
different town in County Antrim. It has an

The Scottish Connection

The Romans called the Irish the "Scoti" (meaning pirates). When the Scoti crossed the narrow Irish Sea and invaded the land of the Picts 1,500 years ago, that region became known as Scoti-land. Ireland and Scotland were never conquered by the Romans, and they retained similar clannish Celtic traits. Both share the same Gaelic branch of the linguistic tree.

On clear summer days from Carrick-a-Rede, the island of Mull in Scotland—only 17 miles away—is visible. Much closer on the horizon is the boomerang-shaped Rathlin Island, part of Northern Ireland. Rathlin is where Scottish leader Robert the Bruce (a compatriot of William "Braveheart" Wallace) retreated in 1307 after defeat at the hands of the English. Legend has it that he hid in a cave on the island, where he observed a spider patiently rebuilding its web each time a breeze knocked it down. Inspired by the spider's perseverance, Robert gathered his Scottish forces once more and finally defeated the English at the decisive Battle of Bannockburn.

Flush with confidence from his victory, Robert the Bruce decided to open a second front against the English...in Ireland. In 1315, he sent his brother Edward over to enlist their Celtic Irish cousins in an effort to thwart the English. After securing Ireland, Edward hoped to move on and enlist the Welsh, thus cornering England with their pan-Celtic nation. But Edward's timing was bad—Ireland was in the midst of famine. His Scottish troops had to live off the land and began to take food and supplies from the starving Irish. He might also have been trying to destroy Ireland's crops to keep them from being used as a colonial "breadbasket" to feed English troops. The Scots quickly wore out their welcome, and Edward the Bruce was eventually killed in battle near Dundalk in 1318.

This was the first time in history that Ireland was used as a pawn by England's enemies. Spain and France saw Ireland as the English Achilles' heel, and both countries later attempted invasions of the island. The English Tudor and Stuart royalty countered these threats in the 16th and 17th centuries by starting the "plantation" of loyal subjects in Ireland. The only successful long-term settlement by the English was here in Northern Ireland, which remains part of the United Kingdom today.

It's interesting to imagine how things could have been different today if Ireland and Scotland had been permanently welded together as a nation 700 years ago. You'll notice the strong Scottish influence in this part of Ireland when you ask a local a question and he answers, "Aye, a wee bit." The Irish joke that the Scots are just Irish people who couldn't swim home.

inviting guest lounge, supervised by two tabby cats, overlooking the harbor. Friendly South African hosts Sam and Tim Swart—a photographer—manage the place with a light hand (family rooms, 17 Kerr Street, tel. 028/7082-2765, mobile 078-9586-6534, www.harbourheightsportrush.com, info@harbourheightsportrush.com).

¢ **Portrush Holiday Hostel** offers clean, well-organized, economical lodging for bottom-feeding vagabonds (private rooms available, tel. 028/7082-1288 or mobile 078-5037-7367, 24 Princess Street, www.portrushholidayhostel.com, info@portrushholidayhostel.com).

Transportation
Arriving and Departing

BY TRAIN OR BUS

The train tracks stop at the base of the tiny peninsula that Portrush fills (no baggage storage at station). The bus stop is two blocks from the train station.

Day Pass: Consider a £17.50 Zone 4 iLink smartcard, good for all-day Translink train and bus use in Northern Ireland (£16.50 top-up for each additional day; for more on iLink cards, see page 293). Translink's website has updated schedules and prices for both trains and buses in Northern Ireland (tel. 028/9066-6630,

From Portrush by Train to: Coleraine (hourly, 12 minutes), **Belfast** (15/day, 2 hours, transfer in Coleraine), **Dublin** (7/day, 5 hours, transfer in Coleraine or Belfast).

By Portrush by Bus to: Belfast (12/day, 2 hours; scenic coastal route, 2.5 hours), **Dublin** (4/day, 5.5 hours).

BY CAR

If driving on to Belfast from Portrush, consider the slower-but-scenic coastal route via the Glens of Antrim.

ANTRIM COAST

The craggy 20-mile stretch of the Antrim Coast extending eastward from Portrush to Ballycastle rates second only to the tip of the Dingle Peninsula as the prettiest chunk of coastal Ireland.

From your base in Portrush, you have a varied grab bag of sightseeing choices: Giant's Causeway, Old Bushmills Distillery, Dunluce Castle, Carrick-a-Rede Rope Bridge, and Rathlin Island.

It's easy to weave these sights together by car, but bus service is viable only in summer, and taxi fares are reasonable only for the sights closest to Portrush.

Sights
▲▲GIANT'S CAUSEWAY

This five-mile-long stretch of coastline is famous for its bizarre basalt columns. The shore is covered with largely hexagonal pillars that stick up at various heights. It's as if the earth were offering God a choice of 37,000 six-sided cigarettes.

Geologists claim the Giant's Causeway was formed by volcanic eruptions more than 60 million years ago. As the surface of the lava flow quickly cooled, it

Giant's Causeway, along the Antrim Coast

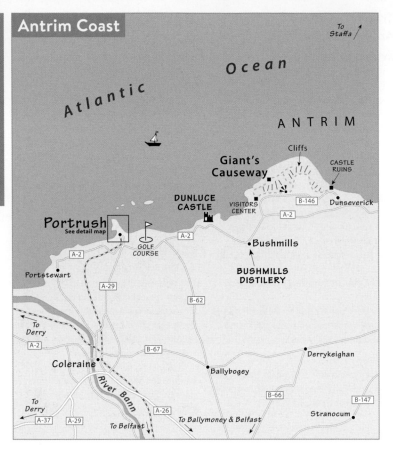

Antrim Coast

To Staffa

O c e a n

A t l a n t i c

A N T R I M

Cliffs

Giant's Causeway

CASTLE RUINS

DUNLUCE CASTLE

VISITORS CENTER

B-146

A-2

Dunseverick

Portrush
See detail map

GOLF COURSE

A-2

•Bushmills

A-2

Portstewart

A-29

BUSHMILLS DISTILERY

B-62

To Derry

A-2

B-67

Derrykeighan

Coleraine

Ballybogey

River Bann

To Derry

A-37   A-29

A-26

To Belfast

To Ballymoney & Belfast

B-66

B-147

Stranocum

contracted and crystallized into columns (resembling the caked mud at the bottom of a dried-up lakebed, but with far deeper cracks). As the rock later settled and eroded, the columns broke off into the many stair-like steps that now honeycomb the Antrim Coast.

Of course, in actuality, the Giant's Causeway was made by a giant Ulster warrior named Finn MacCool who knew of a rival giant living across the water in Scotland. Finn built a stone bridge over to Scotland to spy on his rival, and found out that the Scottish giant was much bigger. Finn retreated back to Ireland and had his wife dress him as a sleeping infant, just in time for the rival giant to come across the causeway to spy on Finn. The rival, shocked at the infant's size, fled back to Scotland in terror of whomever had sired this giant baby. Breathing a sigh of relief, Finn tore off the baby clothes and prudently knocked down the bridge. Today, proof of this encounter exists in the geologic formation that still extends undersea and surfaces in Scotland (at the island of Staffa).

Cost and Hours: The Giant's Causeway is free and open all the time. But in practice, anyone parking there needs to pay £10.50, which includes an audioguide (or guided walk) and entrance to the visitors center (daily 9:00-18:00, July-Aug until 19:00, Nov-April until 17:00, gift shop, café, tel. 028/2073-1855, www.nationaltrust.org.uk/giantscauseway).

Visiting the Causeway: For cute variations on the Finn story, as well as details on the ridiculous theories of modern geologists, start in the **Giant's Causeway Visitor Centre**. It's filled with kid-friendly interactive exhibits giving a worthwhile history of the Giant's Causeway, with a regional overview. On the far wall opposite the entrance, check out the interesting three-minute video showing the evolution of the causeway from molten lava to the geometric, geologic wonderland of today. The large 3-D model of the causeway offers a bird's-eye view of the region. There's also an exhibit about the history of tourism here from the 18th century.

The **causeway** itself is the highlight of the entire coast. The audioguide (included with the visitors center ticket)

highlights 15 stops along the causeway, each with a photo of the formation being described; all stops are shown on the map you'll receive with your ticket.

From the visitors center, you have several options for visiting the causeway:

Short and Easy: A **shuttle bus** (4/hour from 9:00, £1 each way) zips tired tourists a half-mile from the visitors center down a paved road to the causeway. This standard route (the blue dashed line on your map) offers the easiest access and follows the stops on your audioguide. Many choose to walk down and then take the shuttle back up.

Mid-Level Hike: For a longer hike and a more varied dose of causeway views, consider the cliff-top trail (red dashed line on your map). Take the easy-to-follow trail uphill from the visitors center 10 minutes to Weir's Snout, the great fence-protected precipice viewpoint. Then hike 15 minutes farther (level) to reach the Shepherd's Steps. Then grab the banister on the steep (and slippery-when-wet) stairs that zigzag down the switchbacks toward the water. At the T-junction, go 100 yards right, to the towering rock pipes of "the Organ." (You can detour another 500 yards east around the headland, but the trail dead-ends there.) Now retrace your steps west on the trail (don't go up the steps again), continuing down to the tidal zone, where the "Giant's Boot" (6-foot boulder, on the right) provides some photo fun. Another 100 yards farther is the dramatic point where the causeway meets the sea. Just beyond that, at the asphalt turnaround, is the shuttle bus stop.

Return to the visitor's center by hiking up the paved lane (listening to the audioguide at stops along the way). Or, from the turnaround, you can catch the shuttle bus back to the visitor's center (just line up and pay the driver).

Longer Hike: Hardy hikers and avid photographers can join the guided three-hour **Clifftop Experience** trek exploring the trail that runs along a five-mile section of the Causeway Coast, starting at the meager ruins of Dunseverick Castle (yellow dashed line on your map). Operated by the National Trust, the hike is led by a naturalist, who ventures beyond the usual big-bus tourist crowds to explore the rugged rim of this most-scenic section of the Antrim Coast. Expect undulating grass and gravel paths with no WCs and no shelter whatsoever from bad weather (£30, daily at 10:30, must prebook, no kids under 12, catch 5-minute ride on bus #402 from visitors center to Dunseverick trailhead, tel. 028/2073-3419, www.giants-causewaytickets.com, northcoastbookings@nationaltrust.org.uk).

This same hike could also be done on your own. Take the Causeway Rambler bus (see "Getting Around the Antrim Coast," earlier) or a taxi from Portrush to Dunseverick Castle (east of Giant's Causeway on B-146). Get off there and hike west, following the cliff-hugging contours of Benbane Head back to the visitors center. For more info on hiking the route without a naturalist, see www.visit-causewaycoastandglens.com and search for "North Antrim Cliff Path."

▲▲OLD BUSHMILLS DISTILLERY

Bushmills claims to be the world's oldest distillery. Although King James I (of Bible translation fame) only granted Bushmills its license to distill "Aqua Vitae" in 1608, whiskey has been made here since the 13th century. Distillery tours waft you through the process, making it clear that Irish whiskey is triple distilled—and therefore smoother than Scotch whisky (distilled merely twice and minus the "e").

Cost and Hours: £8 for 45-minute tour followed by a tasting; tours go on the half-hour Mon-Sat 9:30-16:00 (last tour), Sun from 12:00; Nov-March tours run Mon-Sat 10:00-15:30 (last tour), Sun from 12:00; tours are limited to 30 people and book up—reserve ahead in summer; tel. 028/2073-3218, www.bushmills.com.

Visiting the Distillery: Tours start with the mash pit, which is filled with a porridge that eventually becomes whiskey. (The leftovers of that porridge are fed to the county's particularly happy cows.) You'll see a huge room full of whiskey aging in oak casks—casks already used to

Old Bushmills Distillery

make bourbon, sherry, and port. Whiskey picks up its color and personality from this wood (which breathes and has an effective life of 30 years).

To see the distillery at its lively best, visit when the 100 workers are staffing the machinery—Monday morning through Friday noon. (The still is still on weekends and in July.) The finale, of course, is the opportunity for a sip in the 1608 Bar—the former malt barn. Visitors get a single glass of their choice. Teetotalers can just order tea.

▲▲CARRICK-A-REDE ROPE BRIDGE

For 200 years, fishermen hung a narrow, 90-foot-high bridge (planks strung between wires) across a 65-foot-wide chasm between the mainland and a tiny island. Today, the bridge (while not the original version) gives access to the sea stack where salmon nets were set (until 2002) during summer months to catch the fish turning and hugging the coast's corner. (The complicated system is described at the gateway.) A pleasant, 30-minute, one-mile walk from the parking lot takes you down to the rope bridge. Cross over to the island for fine views and great seabird-watching, especially during nesting season.

Cost and Hours: £7 trail and bridge fee; daily 9:30-18:00, July-Aug until 19:00, Nov-Feb until 15:30; last entry 45 minutes before closing, tel. 028/2076-9839, www.nationaltrust.org.uk. A coffee shop and WCs are near the parking lot.

Timed-Entry Tickets: Timed tickets are required to cross the bridge. Arrive as early as possible; they sell only 240 tickets (same-day only) for each hour-long entry window. Cruise groups and big buses arrive after 11:00. (If you're frustrated at the ticket booth, you're welcome to hike down to the bridge for free but won't be able to venture onto it.)

Nearby Viewpoint: If you have a car and a picnic lunch, don't miss the terrific coastal scenic rest area one mile steeply uphill and east of Carrick-a-Rede (on B-15 to Ballycastle). This grassy area offers one of the best picnic views in Northern Ireland (tables but no WCs). Feast on bird's-eye views of the rope bridge, nearby Rathlin Island, and the not-so-distant Island of Mull in Scotland.

Carrick-a-Rede Rope Bridge

Dunluce Castle

▲DUNLUCE CASTLE

These romantic ruins, perched dramatically on the edge of a rocky headland, are a testimony to this region's turbulent past. During the Middle Ages, the castle was a prized fortification. But on a stormy night in 1639, dinner was interrupted as half of the kitchen fell into the sea, taking the servants with it. That was the last straw for the lady of the castle. The countess of Antrim packed up and moved inland, and the castle "began its slow submission to the forces of nature."

Cost and Hours: £5, daily 10:00-17:00, winter until 16:00, tel. 028/2073-1938.

Visiting the Castle: While it's one of the largest castles in Northern Ireland and is beautifully situated, there's precious little left to see among Dunluce's broken walls.

Before entering, catch the eight-minute video about the history of the castle (across from the ticket desk). The ruins themselves are dotted with plaques that show interesting artists' renditions of how the place would have looked 400 years ago.

The 16th-century expansion of the castle was financed by treasure salvaged from a shipwreck. In 1588, the Spanish Armada's *Girona*—overloaded with sailors and the valuables of three abandoned sister ships—sank on her way home after the aborted mission against England. More than 1,300 drowned, and only five survivors washed ashore. The shipwreck was more fully excavated in 1967, and a bounty of golden odds and silver ends wound up in Belfast's Ulster Museum.

BEST OF THE REST

DERRY

No city in Ireland connects the kaleidoscope of historical dots more colorfully than Derry. From a leafy monastic hamlet to a Viking-pillaged port, from a cannonball-battered siege survivor to an Industrial Revolution sweatshop, from an essential WWII naval base to a wrenching flashpoint of sectarian Troubles...Derry has seen it all.

When Ireland was being divvied up, the River Foyle was the logical border between the North and the Republic. But, for sentimental and economic reasons, the North kept Derry, which is otherwise on the Republic's side of the river. Consequently, this predominantly Catholic-Nationalist city was much contested throughout the Troubles.

Even its name is disputed. While most of its population and its city council call it "Derry," some maps, road signs, and all UK train schedules use "Londonderry," the name on its 1662 royal charter and the one favored by Unionists.

The past 15 years have brought some refreshing changes. Most British troops finally departed in 2007, after 38 years in Northern Ireland. In 2011, a curvy pedestrian bridge across the River Foyle was completed. Locals dubbed it the Peace Bridge because it links the predominantly Protestant Waterside (east bank) with the predominantly Catholic Cityside (west bank). Today, you can feel comfortable wandering the streets and enjoying this "legend-Derry" city.

Orientation

The River Foyle flows north, slicing Derry into eastern and western chunks. The old town walls and almost all worthwhile sights are on the west side. (The tiny train station and Ebrington Square—at the end of the Peace Bridge—are the main reasons to spend time on the east side.) Waterloo Place and the adjacent Guildhall Square, just outside the north corner of the old city walls, are the pedestrian hubs.

Derry

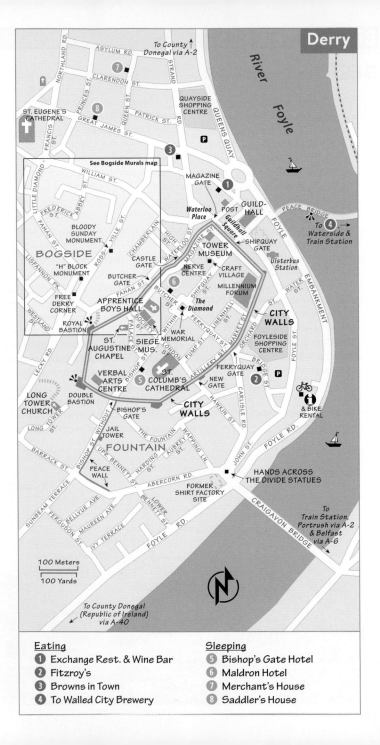

Derry

ASYLUM RD.
NORTHLAND RD.
CLARENDON ST.
PRINCES ST.
QUEEN ST.
STRAND RD.
River Foyle

ST. EUGENE'S CATHEDRAL
FRANCIS ST.
GREAT JAMES ST.
PATRICK ST.
QUAYSIDE SHOPPING CENTRE
QUEENS QUAY

LITTLE DIAMOND
See Bogside Murals map
WILLIAM ST.
ABBEY ST.
FREDERICK ST.
FAHAN ST.
ROSSVILLE ST.
BLOODY SUNDAY MONUMENT
BOGSIDE
"H" BLOCK MONUMENT
LISFANNON PK.
FREE DERRY CORNER
WESTLAND ST.
CHAMBERLAIN ST.
CASTLE GATE
BUTCHER GATE
FAHAN ST.
APPRENTICE BOYS HALL
SOCIETY ST.
ROYAL BASTION
LECKY RD.
ST. AUGUSTINE'S CHAPEL
PALACE ST.
SIEGE MUS.
BISHOP ST.
VERBAL ARTS CENTRE
DOUBLE BASTION
LONG TOWER CHURCH
LONG ST.
BISHOP'S GATE
JAIL TOWER
BARRACK ST.
BISHOP ST. WITHOUT
THE FOUNTAIN
FOUNTAIN
WAPPING LN.
UPR. BENNETT ST.
HARDING ST.
AUBREY ST.
ABERCORN RD.
PEACE WALL
FORMER SHIRT FACTORY SITE
SUNBEAM TERRACE
FERGUSON ST.
BELLVUE AVE.
MAUREEN AVE.
BENNETT ST.
LOWER BENNETT ST.
IVY TERRACE
FOYLE RD.

MAGAZINE GATE
Waterloo Place
POST
GUILD-HALL
Guildhall Square
MAGAZINE ST.
HIGH ST.
WATERLOO ST.
TOWER MUSEUM
NERVE CENTRE
SHIPQUAY GATE
SHIPQUAY ST.
CRAFT VILLAGE
MILLENNIUM FORUM
The Diamond
WITHIN
FERRYQUAY ST.
LINENHALL ST.
WAR MEMORIAL
PUMP ST.
LONDON ST.
ST. COLUMB'S CATHEDRAL
ARTILLERY ST.
NEW GATE
HAWKIN ST.
CITY WALLS
MARKET ST.
ORCHARD ST.
FERRYQUAY GATE
CARLISLE RD.
CITY WALLS

Peace Bridge
To Waterside & Train Station
Ulsterbus Station
WATER ST.
EMBANKMENT
FOYLE ST.
FOYLESIDE SHOPPING CENTRE
BRIDGE ST.
& BIKE RENTAL

HANDS ACROSS THE DIVIDE STATUES
JOHN ST.
FOYLE RD.
CRAIGAVON BRIDGE
To Train Station, Portrush via A-2 & Belfast via A-6

100 Meters
100 Yards

N

To County Donegal (Republic of Ireland) via A-40

Eating
1 Exchange Rest. & Wine Bar
2 Fitzroy's
3 Browns in Town
4 To Walled City Brewery

Sleeping
5 Bishop's Gate Hotel
6 Maldron Hotel
7 Merchant's House
8 Saddler's House

Day Plan: It takes a few hours to see the essential Derry sights: Visit the Tower Museum and catch some views from the town wall. With more time, spend a night in Derry, so you can see the powerful Bogside murals and take a walking tour around the town walls—you'll appreciate this underrated city.

Getting to Derry: Next to the river on the east side of town, Derry's little end-of-the-line **train** station has service to Portrush, Belfast, and Dublin. All **intercity buses** stop at the Ulsterbus Station, on Foyle Street close to Guildhall Square. **Drivers** stopping for a few hours can park at the Foyleside parking garage across from the TI.

Tourist Information: The TI sits on the riverfront and rents bikes, and can book bus and walking tours (Mon-Sat 9:00-18:00, Sun 10:00-17:00, closes earlier in off-season; 44 Foyle Street, tel. 028/7126-7284, www.visitderry.com).

Tours: For walking tours, consider **McCrossan's City Tours** (£4, tel. 028/7127-1996, mobile 077-1293-7997, www.derrycitytours.com, derrycitytours@aol.com) or **Bogside History Tours** (£6, mobile 077-3145-0088 or 078-0056-7165, www.bogside-history-tours.com). **City Sightseeing**'s double-decker buses are a good option for an overview of Derry (£12.50, tel. 028/7137-0067, www.city-sightseeingderry.com).

◑ Walk the Walls

• *This walk, lasting about an hour, starts on the old city walls and ends near St. Columb's Cathedral. It can be linked with the following Bogside Murals Walk.*

Squatting determinedly in the city center, the ▲▲ old city walls of Derry (built 1613-1618 and still intact) hold an almost mythic place in Irish history.

It was here in 1688 that a group of brave apprentice boys made their stand, slamming the city gates shut in the face of the approaching Catholic forces of deposed King James II. With this act,

the boys galvanized the city's indecisive Protestant defenders inside the walls. Months of negotiations and a grinding 105-day siege followed. The sacrifice and defiant survival of the city turned the tide in favor of newly crowned Protestant King William of Orange, who arrived in Ireland soon after and defeated James at the pivotal Battle of the Boyne.

Almost 20 feet high and at least as thick, the walls form a mile-long oval loop that you can cover in less than an hour. The most interesting section is the half-circuit facing the Bogside, starting at Magazine Gate (stairs face the Tower Museum Derry inside the walls) and finishing at Bishop's Gate.

• *Enter the walls at Magazine Gate and find the stairs opposite the Tower Museum. Once atop the walls, head left.*

Walk the wall as it heads uphill, snaking along the earth's contours. In the row of buildings on the left (just before crossing over Castle Gate), you'll see an arch entry into the **Craft Village,** an alley lined with a cluster of cute shops and cafés that showcase the economic rejuvenation of Derry (Mon-Sat 9:30-17:30, closed Sun).

• *After crossing over Butcher Gate, stop in front of the grand building with the four columns to view the...*

First Derry Presbyterian Church: This stately Neoclassical, red-sandstone church was finished in 1780. Over the next 200 years, time took its toll on the structure, which was eventually closed due to dry rot and Republican firebombings. But in 2011, the renovated church reopened to a chorus of cross-community approval (yet one more sign of the slow reconciliation taking place in Derry). The **Blue Coat School** exhibit behind the church highlights the important role of Presbyterians in local history (free but donation encouraged, closed Sat-Tue in summer and Oct-April).

• *Just up the block is the...*

Apprentice Boys Memorial Hall: Built in 1873, this houses the private lodge and meeting rooms of an all-male Protestant organization. The group is dedicated to the memory of the original 13 apprentice boys who saved the day during the 1688 siege. Each year, on the Saturday closest to the August 12 anniversary date, the modern-day Apprentice Boys Society celebrates the end of the siege with a controversial march atop the walls. The **Siege Museum** stands behind the hall, giving a narrow-focus Unionist view of the siege (£3, closed Sun, 18 Society Street).

Next, you'll pass a large, square pedestal on the right atop Royal Bastion. It once supported a column in honor of Governor George Walker, the commander of the defenders during the famous siege. In 1972, the IRA blew up the column, which had 105 steps to the top (one for each day of the siege).

• *Opposite the empty pedestal is the small Anglican...*

St. Augustine Chapel: Set in a pretty graveyard, this Anglican chapel is where some believe the original sixth-century monastery of St. Columba stood. The quaint grounds are open to visitors (closed Sun except for worship).

As you walk, you'll pass a long wall (on the left)—all that's left of a former **British Army base,** which stood here until 2006. Its dismantling—as well as the removal of most of the British Army from Northern Ireland—is another positive sign in cautiously optimistic Derry.

Stop at the **Double Bastion** fortified platform that occupies this corner of the city walls. The old cannon is nicknamed "Roaring Meg" for the fury of its firing during the siege.

From here, you can see across the Bogside to the not-so-far-away hills of County Donegal in the Republic.

Directly below and to the right are Free Derry Corner and Rossville Street, where the tragic events of Bloody Sunday took place in 1972 (see sidebar on page 319).

Down on the left is the 18th-century **Long Tower** Catholic church, named after the monk-built round tower that once stood in the area.

• *Head to the grand brick building behind you. This is the...*

Verbal Arts Centre: A former Presbyterian school, this center promotes the development of local literary arts in the form of poetry, drama, writing, and storytelling. You can drop in and see what performances might be on during your visit (closed Sun, www.verbalartscentre.co.uk).

• *Go left another 50 yards around the corner to reach...*

Bishop's Gate: From here, look up Bishop Street Within (inside the walls). This was the site of a British Army surveillance tower that overlooked the neighborhood until 2006. Now look in the other direction to see Bishop Street Without (outside the walls). You'll spot a modern wall topped by a high mesh fence, running along the left side of Bishop Street Without.

Siege-defending cannons atop walls

Bishop's Gate

This is a so-called **"peace wall,"** built to ensure the security of the Protestant enclave living behind it when the Troubles reignited almost 50 years ago. The stone tower halfway down the "peace wall" is all that remains of the old jail that briefly held rebels after a 1798 revolt against the British.

• *To do the Bogside Murals Walk from here, head through Butcher Gate and down the long flight of stairs (see next).*

❷ Bogside Murals Walk

The Catholic Bogside area was the tinderbox of the modern Troubles in Northern Ireland. Bloody Sunday, a terrible confrontation during a march that occurred nearly 50 years ago, sparked a sectarian inferno, and the ashes have not yet fully cooled. Today, the ▲▲ murals of the Bogside give visitors an accessible glimpse of this community's passionate perception of those events.

Getting There: The events are memorialized in 12 murals painted on the ends of residential flats along a 300-yard stretch of Rossville Street and Lecky Road, where the march took place. For the purposes of this walk, you can reach them from Waterloo Place via William Street. They are also accessible from the old city walls at Butcher Gate via the long set of stairs extending below Fahan Street on the grassy hillside.

The Artists: Two brothers, Tom and William Kelly, and their childhood friend Kevin Hasson are known as the Bogside Artists. For more about this unique trio, visit their website—www.bogsideartists.com.

The Murals: Start out at the corner of Rossville and William streets.

The Bogside murals face different directions (and some are partially hidden by buildings), so they're not all visible from a single viewpoint. Plan on walking three long blocks along Rossville Street (which becomes Lecky Road) to see them all.

From William Street, walk south along the right side of Rossville Street toward Free Derry Corner. The murals will all be on your right.

The first mural you'll walk past is the colorful ❶ *Peace,* showing the silhouette of a dove in flight (left side of mural) and an oak leaf (right side of mural), both created from a single ribbon.

❷ *The Hunger Strikers* features two Derry-born participants of the 1981 Maze Prison hunger strike, as well as their mothers, who sacrificed and supported them in their fatal decision (10 strikers died).

Smaller and easy to miss (above a ramp with banisters) is ❸ *John Hume.* It's actually a collection of four faces (clockwise from upper left): Nationalist leader John Hume, Martin Luther King Jr., Nelson Mandela, and Mother Teresa. The Brooklyn Bridge in the middle symbolizes the long-term bridges of understanding that the work of these four Nobel Peace Prize-winning activists created. Born in the Bogside, Hume still maintains a home here.

Now look for ❹ *The Saturday Matinee,* which depicts an outgunned but undaunted local youth behind a screen shield. He holds a stone, ready to throw, while a British armored vehicle approaches (echoing the famous Tiananmen Square photo of the lone Chinese man facing the tank). Why

Peace *mural in Bogside*

Bogside Murals Walk

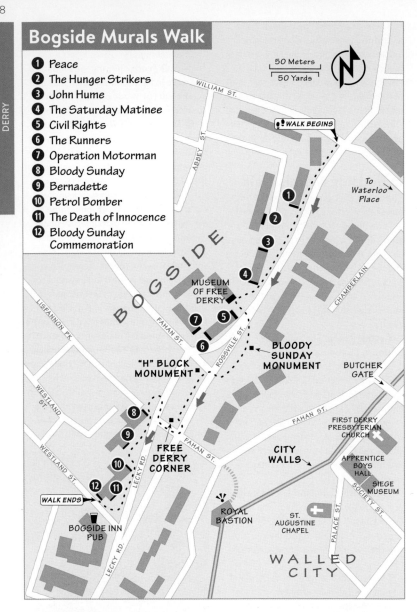

1. Peace
2. The Hunger Strikers
3. John Hume
4. The Saturday Matinee
5. Civil Rights
6. The Runners
7. Operation Motorman
8. Bloody Sunday
9. Bernadette
10. Petrol Bomber
11. The Death of Innocence
12. Bloody Sunday Commemoration

50 Meters
50 Yards

WILLIAM ST.

WALK BEGINS

To Waterloo Place

ABBEY ST.

B O G S I D E

CHAMBERLAIN

MUSEUM OF FREE DERRY

FAHAN ST.

ROSSVILLE ST.

BLOODY SUNDAY MONUMENT

LISFANNON PK.

BUTCHER GATE

"H" BLOCK MONUMENT

WESTLAND ST.

FAHAN ST.

FIRST DERRY PRESBYTERIAN CHURCH

FREE DERRY CORNER

CITY WALLS

APPRENTICE BOYS HALL

WESTLAND ST.

LECKY RD.

FAHAN ST.

SIEGE MUSEUM

SOCIETY ST.

WALK ENDS

BOGSIDE INN PUB

ROYAL BASTION

ST. AUGUSTINE CHAPEL

PALACE ST.

LECKY RD.

W A L L E D
C I T Y

Saturday Matinee? It's because the weekend was the best time for locals to engage in a little "recreational rioting" and "have a go at" the army; people were off work and youths were out of school.

Nearby is **5 Civil Rights,** showing a marching Derry crowd carrying an anti-sectarian banner. In the building behind this mural, you'll find the intense **Museum of Free Derry** (£6, open Mon-Fri 9:30-16:30 year-round, also open April-Sept Sat-Sun 13:00-16:00, 55 Glenfada Park, www.museumoffreederry.org).

Cross over to the other side of Rossville

Bloody Sunday

Inspired by civil rights marches in America in the mid-1960s, and the Prague Spring uprising and Paris student strikes of 1968, civil rights groups began to protest in Northern Ireland around this time. Initially, their goals were to gain better housing, secure fair voting rights, and end employment discrimination for Catholics in the North. Tensions mounted, and clashes with the predominantly Protestant Royal Ulster Constabulary police force became frequent. Eventually, the British Army was called in to keep the peace.

On January 30, 1972, about 10,000 people protesting internment without trial held an illegal march sponsored by the Northern Ireland Civil Rights Association. British Army barricades kept them from the center of Derry, so they marched through the Bogside neighborhood.

That afternoon, some youths rioted on the fringe of the march. An elite parachute regiment had orders to move in and make arrests in the Rossville Street area. Shooting broke out, and after 25 minutes, 13 marchers were dead and 13 were wounded (one of the wounded later died). The soldiers claimed they came under attack from gunfire and nail-bombs. The marchers said the army shot indiscriminately at unarmed civilians.

The clash, called "Bloody Sunday," uncorked pent-up frustration as moderate Nationalists morphed into staunch Republicans overnight and released a flood of fresh IRA volunteers. An investigation at the time exonerated the soldiers, but the relatives of the victims called it a whitewash and insisted on their innocence.

In 1998, then-British Prime Minister Tony Blair promised a new inquiry, which became the longest and most expensive in British legal history. In 2010, a 12-year investigation—the Saville Report—determined that the Bloody Sunday civil rights protesters were innocent and called the deaths of 14 protesters unjustified.

In a dramatic 2010 speech in the House of Commons, then-Prime Minister David Cameron apologized to the people of Derry. "What happened on Bloody Sunday was both unjustified and unjustifiable. It was wrong," he declared. Cheers rang out in Derry's Guildhall Square, where thousands had gathered to watch the speech on a video screen. After 38 years of struggle, Northern Ireland's bloodiest wound started healing.

Street to see the **Bloody Sunday Monument.** This small, fenced-off stone obelisk lists the names of those who died that day, most within 50 yards of this spot. Take a look at the map pedestal by the monument, which shows how a rubble barricade was erected to block the street.

Cross back again, this time over to the grassy median strip that runs down the middle of Rossville Street. At this end stands a granite letter **H** inscribed with the names of the 10 IRA hunger strikers who

died (and how many days they starved) in the H-block of Maze Prison in 1981.

From here, as you look across at the corner of Fahan Street, you get a good view of two murals. In ❻ *The Runners* (right), three rioting youths flee tear gas from canisters used by the British Army to disperse hostile crowds. Meanwhile, in ❼ *Operation Motorman* (left), a soldier wields a sledgehammer to break through a house door, depicting the massive push by the British Army to open up the Bogside's barricaded "no-go" areas that the IRA had controlled for three years (1969-1972).

Walk down to the other end of the median strip where the white wall of **Free Derry Corner** announces "You are now entering Free Derry." This was the gabled end of a string of houses that stood here more than 40 years ago. During the Troubles, it became a traditional meeting place for speakers to address crowds.

Cross back to the right side of the street (now Lecky Road) to see ❽ *Bloody Sunday,* in which a small group of men carry a body from that ill-fated march.

Near it is a mural called ❾ *Bernadette.* The woman with the megaphone is Bernadette Devlin McAliskey, an outspoken civil rights leader, who at age 21 became the youngest elected member of British Parliament. Behind her kneels a female supporter, banging a trash-can lid against the street in a traditional expression of protest in Nationalist neighborhoods.

❿ *Petrol Bomber,* showing a teen wearing an army-surplus gas mask, captures the Battle of the Bogside, when locals barricaded their community, effectively shutting out British rule.

Bernadette Devlin mural in Bogside

In ⓫ *The Death of Innocence,* a young girl stands in front of bomb wreckage. She is Annette McGavigan, a 14-year-old who was killed on this corner by crossfire in 1971. She was the 100th fatality of the Troubles, which eventually took more than 3,000 lives (and she was also a cousin of one of the artists). The broken gun beside her points to the ground, signifying that it's no longer being wielded. The large butterfly above her shoulder symbolizes the hope for peace. For years, the artists left the butterfly an empty silhouette until they felt confident that the peace process had succeeded. They finally filled in the butterfly with optimistic colors in the summer of 2006.

Finally, around the corner, you'll see a circle of male faces: ⓬ *Bloody Sunday Commemoration,* painted in 1997 to observe the 25th anniversary of the tragedy, shows the 14 victims.

Across the street, drop into the **Bogside Inn** for a beverage and check out the black-and-white photos of events in the area during the Troubles. This pub has been here through it all, and lives on to tell the tale.

While these murals preserve the struggles of the late 20th century, today sectarian violence has given way to negotiations. Former Nationalist leader John Hume once borrowed a quote from Gandhi to explain his nonviolent approach to the peace process: "An eye for an eye leaves everyone blind."

Sights

▲▲TOWER MUSEUM DERRY

Occupying a modern reconstruction of a fortified medieval tower house that belonged to the local O'Doherty clan, this well-organized museum provides an excellent introduction to the city. Combining modern audiovisual displays with historical artifacts, the exhibits tell the story of the city from a skillfully unbiased viewpoint, sorting out some of the tangled historical roots of Northern Ireland's Troubles. The museum is divided into two sections: the Story of Derry (on the ground floor) and the Spanish Armada (on the four floors of the tower).

Cost and Hours: £4, includes audioguide for Armada exhibits, daily 10:00-17:30, last entry one hour before closing, Union Hall Place, tel. 028/7137-2411, www.derrystrabane.com/towermuseum.

Eating and Sleeping

The trendy **$$$ Exchange Restaurant and Wine Bar** offers lunches and quality dinners in a central location near the river behind Waterloo Place (Queen's Quay). Busy **$$$ Fitzroy's,** tucked below Ferryquay Gate and stacked with locals, serves good lunches and dinners (2 Bridge Street). **$$ Browns in Town** is a casual, friendly lunch or dinner option (21 Strand Road). **$$ Walled City Brewery,** across the Peace Bridge, is a fun change of pace (closed Mon-Tue, 70 Ebrington Square).

$$$$ Bishop's Gate Hotel is Derry's top lodging option (fine bar, 24 Bishop Street, www.bishopsgatehotelderry.com). **$$ Maldron Hotel** features 93 modern

Operation Motorman *mural*

and large rooms (Butcher Street, www.maldronhotelderry.com). **$ Merchant's House** is a fine Georgian townhouse (16 Queen Street, www.thesaddlershouse.com); **$ Saddler's House** is a charming Victorian townhouse (36 Great James Street, www.thesaddlershouse.com).

Irish History and Culture

Ireland is rich with history, art, music, and language.

IRISH HISTORY

Prehistory

Ireland became an island when rising seas covered the last land bridge (7000 B.C.), a separation from Britain that the Irish would fight to maintain for the next 9,000 years. (Snakes were too slow to migrate before the seas cut Ireland off, despite later legends about St. Patrick banishing them.) By 6000 B.C., Stone Age hunter-fishers had settled on the east coast, followed by Neolithic farmers from the island of Britain. These early inhabitants left behind impressive but mysterious funeral mounds (passage graves) and large Stonehenge-type stone circles.

The Celts
(500 B.C.- A.D. 450)

More an invasion of ideas than of armies, the Celtic culture from Central Europe settled in Ireland, where it would dominate for a thousand years. There were more than 300 *tuatha* (kingdoms) in Ireland, each with its own *rí* (king), who would've happily chopped the legs off anyone who called him "petty." The island was nominally ruled by a single *Ard Rí* (high king) at the **Hill of Tara** (north of Dublin), though there was no centralized nation.

In 55 B.C., the Romans conquered the Celts in England, but they never invaded Ireland. Irish history forever skewed in a different direction—Gaelic, not Latin. The Romans called Ireland **Hibernia,** meaning Land of Winter; it was apparently too cold and bleak to merit an attempt at colonization.

The Age of Saints and Scholars
(A.D. 450-800)

When Ancient Rome fell and took the Continent—and many of the achievements of Roman culture—with it, Gaelic Ireland was unaffected. There was no Dark Age here, and the island was a beacon of culture for the rest of Europe.

Ireland (population c. 750,000) was still a land of many feuding kings, but the culture was stable.

Christianity and Latin culture arrived first as a trickle from trading contacts with Christian Gaul (France), then more emphatically in A.D. 432 with **St. Patrick,** who persuasively converted the sun- and nature-worshipping Celts. Legends say he drove Ireland's snakes (symbolic of pagan beliefs) into the sea and explained the Trinity with a shamrock—three leaves on one stem.

Later monks continued Christianizing the island. They flocked to scattered, isolated monasteries, living in stone igloo beehive huts, translating and illustrating manuscripts. Perhaps the greatest works of art from all of Dark Age Europe are these manuscripts, particularly the ninth-century Book of Kells (in Dublin).

By 800, **Charlemagne** was importing educated and literate Irish monks to help organize and run his Frankish kingdom. Meanwhile, Ireland remained a relatively cohesive society based on monastic settlements rather than cities. Impressive round towers from those settlements still dot the Irish landscape—silent reminders of this scholarly age.

Viking Invasion
(800-1100)

In 795, Viking pirates from Norway invaded, first testing isolated island monasteries, then boldly sailing up Irish rivers into the country's interior. The many raids wreaked havoc on the monasteries and continued to shake Irish civilization for two chaotic centuries. In 841, a conquering Viking band decided to winter in Ireland. The idea caught on as subsequent raiders eventually built the island's first permanent walled cities, Dublin and Waterford. The Viking raiders slowly evolved into Viking traders. They were the first to introduce urban life and commerce to Ireland.

Anglo-Norman Arrival
(1100-1500)

The Normans were Ireland's next aggressive guests. In 1169, a small army of well-armed soldiers of fortune invaded Ireland under the pretense of helping a deposed Irish king regain his lands. This was the spearhead of a century-long invasion by the so-called Anglo-Normans—the French-speaking rulers of England, descended from William the Conqueror and his troops.

By 1250, the Anglo-Normans occupied two-thirds of the island. But when the **Black Death** came in 1348, it spread rapidly and fatally in the tightly packed Norman settlements. The plague, along with Normans intermarrying with Gaels, eventually diluted Norman identity and shrank English control. But even as Anglo-Norman power eroded, the English kings considered Ireland theirs.

The End of Gaelic Rule
(1500s)

Martin Luther's **Reformation** split the Christian churches into Catholic and Protestant, making Catholic Ireland a hot potato for newly Protestant England to handle. In 1534, angered by **Henry VIII** and his break with Catholicism, the **earls of Kildare** (father, then son) led a rebellion. Henry crushed the revolt, executed the earls, and confiscated their land. Henry's daughter, **Elizabeth I,** gave the land to English Protestant colonists (called "planters"). The next four centuries would see a series of rebellions by Gaelic-speaking Irish-Catholic farmers fighting to free themselves from rule by English-speaking Protestant landowners.

Hugh O'Neill (1540-1616), a Gaelic chieftain angered by planters and English abuses, led a Gaelic revolt in 1595. At the Battle of Yellow Ford (1598), guerrilla tactics brought about an initial Irish victory. But after the disastrous **Battle of Kinsale** (1601), O'Neill ceded a half-million acres to England, signaling the end of Gaelic Irish rule.

English Colonization and Irish Rebellion
(1600s)

By 1641, 25,000 Protestant English and Scottish planters had settled into the confiscated land, making Ulster (in the northeast) the most English area of the island.

Then, **Oliver Cromwell**—who had pulled off a *coup d'état* in England—invaded and conquered Ireland (1649-1650) with a Puritanical, anti-Catholic zeal. Cromwell confiscated 11 more million acres of land from Catholic Irish landowners to give to English Protestants.

In 1688-1689, Irish rebels rallied around Catholic **King James II,** who had been deposed by the English Parliament. He wound up in Ireland, where he formed an army to retake the crown. The showdown came at the massive **Battle of the Boyne** (1690), north of Dublin. James and his 25,000 men were defeated by the troops of Protestant **King William III** of Orange. From this point on, the color orange became a symbol in Ireland for pro-English, pro-Protestant forces.

Protestant Rule
(1700s)

During the 18th century, urban Ireland thrived economically, and even culturally, under the English. Dublin in the 1700s (pop. 50,000) was Britain's second city, and one of Europe's wealthiest and most sophisticated.

But beyond Dublin, rebellion continued to brew. Irish nationalists were inspired by budding democratic revolutions in America (1776) and France (1789). Increasingly, the issue of Irish independence was less a religious question than a political one.

England tried to solve the Irish problem politically by forcing Ireland into a "Union" with England as part of a "United Kingdom" (**Act of Union,** 1801). The 500-year-old Irish Parliament was dissolved, with its members becoming part of England's Parliament in London. From then on, "Unionists" have been those who oppose Irish independence, wanting to preserve the country's union with England.

Votes, Violence, and the Famine
(1800s)

Irish politicians lobbied in the British Parliament for Catholic rights, reform of absentee-landlordism, and for **Home Rule.** But any hope of an Irish revival was soon snuffed out by the biggest catastrophe in Irish history: the **Great Potato Famine** (1845-1849). Legions of people (between 500,000 and 1.1 million) starved to death or died of related diseases. Another 1 to 2 million emigrated.

Ireland was ruined. Many of the best and brightest fled, and the island's economy—and spirit—took generations to recover. And culturally, old Gaelic, rural Ireland was being crushed under the Industrial Revolution and the political control wielded by Protestant England.

Easter Rising and War of Independence
(1900-1920)

As the century turned, Ireland prepared for the inevitable showdown with Britain. On Easter Monday, April 24, 1916, Irish nationalists marched on Dublin and proclaimed Ireland an independent republic. British troops struck back and in a week suppressed the insurrection. When the British government swiftly executed the ringleaders, Ireland resolved to win its independence at all costs.

In the 1918 elections, the separatist Sinn Fein party (meaning "Ourselves") won big, but these new members of Parliament refused to go to London. Instead, they formed their own independent Irish Parliament in Dublin. Then Irish rebels began ambushing policemen—seen as the eyes and ears of British control—sparking the **War of Independence** in 1919. The fledgling Irish Republican Army faced 40,000 British troops. A thousand people died in this multiyear guerrilla war of street fighting, sniper fire, jailhouse beatings, terrorist bombs, and reprisals.

Partition and Civil War
(1920-1950)

Finally, Britain agreed to Irish independence. But Ireland itself was a divided nation—the southern three-quarters of the island was mostly Catholic, Gaelic, rural, and for Home Rule; the northern quarter was Protestant, English, industrial, and Unionist. The solution? In 1921, the British Parliament partitioned the island into two independent, self-governing countries within the British Commonwealth: **Northern Ireland** and the **Irish Free State.**

Ireland's various political factions wrestled with this compromise solution, and the island plunged into a **Civil War** (1922-1923). The hard-line IRA opposed the partition. Dublin and the southeast were ravaged in a year of bitter fighting before the Irish Free State emerged victorious. The IRA went underground, moving its fight north and trying for the rest of the century to topple the government of Northern Ireland.

In 1949, the Irish Free State left the Commonwealth and officially became the **Republic of Ireland.**

Troubles in the North
(1950-2000)

The Republic moved toward prosperity in the second half of the century, but Northern Ireland—with a slight Protestant majority and a large, disaffected Catholic minority—was plagued by the **Troubles.** In 1967, organized marches and demonstrations demanded equal treatment for Catholics. Protestant **Unionist Orange-men** countered by marching through Catholic neighborhoods, provoking riots. In 1969, Britain sent troops to help Northern Ireland keep the peace.

From the 1970s to the 1990s, the North was a low-level battlefield, with the IRA using terrorist tactics to advance their political agenda. The Troubles, which claimed some 3,000 lives, continued with bombings, marches, hunger strikes, rock-throwing, and riots (notably Derry's **Bloody Sunday** in 1972).

Finally, after a string of failed peace agreements, came the watershed 1998 settlement known as the **Good Friday Accord** (to pro-Irish Nationalists) or the **Belfast Agreement** (to pro-British Unionists).

Global Nations
(2000 and Beyond)

After years of negotiation, in 2005 the IRA formally announced an end to its armed campaign, promising to pursue peaceful, democratic means. In 2007, London returned control of Northern Ireland to the popularly elected Northern Ireland Assembly. Perhaps most important, after almost 40 years, the British Army withdrew 90 percent of its forces from Northern Ireland that summer.

Now it's up to Northern Ireland to keep the peace. The 1998 peace accord gives Northern Ireland the freedom to leave the UK if ever the majority of the population approves a referendum to do so. At the same time, the Republic of Ireland withdrew its constitutional claim to the entire island of Ireland. Northern Ireland now has limited autonomy from London, with its own democratically elected, power-sharing government.

IRISH CULTURE

Irish Art

Megalithic tombs, ancient gold and metalwork, illuminated manuscripts, high crosses carved in stone, paintings of rural Ireland, and provocative political murals—Ireland comes with some fascinating art. Here are a few highlights.

Megalithic Period: During the Stone Age, 5,000 years ago, farmers living in the **Boyne Valley,** north of Dublin, built a "cemetery" of approximately 40 **burial mounds.** The most famous of these mound tombs is the passage tomb at Newgrange, part of Brú na Bóinne, which also features some of Europe's best examples of megalithic (big rock) art.

The Age of Saints and Scholars: Christianity grew in Ireland from St. Patrick's first efforts in the fifth century A.D. During this "Golden Age" of Irish civilization, monks, along with metalworkers and stonemasons, created imaginative designs and distinctive stylistic motifs for **manuscripts, metal objects,** and **crosses.**

Monks wrote out and richly decorated manuscripts of the Gospels. The most beautiful and imaginative of these illuminated manuscripts is the **Book of Kells** (C. A.D. 800). Crafted by Irish monks at a monastery on the Scottish island of Iona, the book was brought to Ireland for safe-keeping from rampaging Vikings. Many consider this book the finest piece of art from Europe's Dark Ages (now at Dublin's Trinity College Library).

The monks used Irish high crosses to celebrate the triumph of Christianity and to educate the illiterate masses through simple stone carvings of biblical themes. The **Cross of Murdock** (Muiredach's Cross, A.D. 923) is 18 feet tall, towering over the remains of the monastic settlement at Monasterboice. It is but one of many monumental crosses in Ireland.

Native Irish Art: The English suppressed Celtic Irish culture, replacing native styles with English traditions in architecture, painting, and literature. But in the late 19th century, revivals in Irish language, folklore, music, and art began to surface. **Jack B. Yeats** (1871-1957, brother of the poet W. B. Yeats), Belfast-born painter **Paul Henry** (1876-1958), and **Sean Keating** (1889-1977) were among the painters who looked to traditional Irish subjects for inspiration, focusing on Ireland's people, the country's rugged beauty, and its struggle for independence.

Trinity Library in Dublin

Stained-glass window, St. Mary Church, Cong

Traditional Irish Music

Traditional music is alive and popular in pubs throughout Ireland. "Sessions" (musical evenings) may be planned and advertised, or impromptu. Traditionally, musicians just congregate and play for the love of it. There will generally be a fiddle, a flute or tin whistle, a guitar, a *bodhrán* (goatskin drum), and maybe an accordion or mandolin.

The music often comes in sets of three songs. The wind and string instruments embellish melody lines with lots of tight ornamentation. Whoever happens to be leading determines the next song only as the current tune is about to be finished.

Percussion generally stays in the background. The *bodhrán* (BO-run) is played with a small, two-headed club. The performer's hand stretches the skin to change the tone and pitch. You'll sometimes be lucky enough to hear a set of bones crisply played. These are two cow ribs (boiled and dried) that are rattled in one hand like spoons or castanets.

Watch closely if a piper is playing. The Irish version of bagpipes, the *uilleann* (ILL-in) pipes are played by inflating the airbag with a bellows (under the elbow) rather than with a mouthpiece. The sound is more melodic, with a wider range than the Highland pipes. It takes amazing coordination to play this instrument well, and the sound can be haunting.

Occasionally, the fast-paced music will stop and one person will sing a lament. Called *sean nos* (Irish Gaelic for "old style"), this slightly nasal vocal style may be a remnant of the ancient tradition whose stories—often of love lost, emigration to a faraway land, or a heroic rebel death struggling against English rule—are always heartfelt.

Irish Literature

Since the Book of Kells, Ireland's greatest contributions to the world of art have been through words. After Christianity transformed Ireland into a refuge of literacy (while the rest of Europe crumbled into the Dark Ages), Charlemagne's imported Irish monks invented "minuscule," which became the basis of the lowercase letters we use in our alphabet today. The cultural importance placed on the word (spoken, and, for the past 1,500 years, written) is today reflected in the rich output of modern Irish writers.

William Butler Yeats' early poems and plays are filled with fairies and idyllic rural innocence, while his later poems reflect Ireland's painful transition to independence. Yeats' Nobel Prize for literature (1923) was eventually matched by three later, Nobel-winning Irish authors: **George Bernard Shaw** (1925), **Samuel Beckett** (1969), and **Seamus Heaney** (1995).

Dublin-born **Oscar Wilde** wowed London with his quick wit, outrageous clothes, and flamboyant personality. Wilde wrote the darkly fascinating *Picture of Dorian Gray* (1890) and skewered upper-class Victorian society in witty comedic plays such as *The Importance of Being Earnest* (1895). Meanwhile, **Bram Stoker** was conjuring up a Gothic thriller called *Dracula* (1897). Most inventive of all, perhaps, was **James Joyce,** who captured literary lightning in a bottle with his modern, stream-of-consciousness *Ulysses*, set on a single day in Dublin (June 16, 1904).

In recent decades, the bittersweet Irish literary parade has been inhabited by tragically volcanic characters like **Brendan Behan,** who exclaimed, "I'm a drinker with a writing problem." Bleak poverty experienced in childhood was the catalyst for **Frank McCourt**'s memorable *Angela's Ashes*. Among the most celebrated of today's Irish writers is **Roddy Doyle,** whose feel for working-class Dublin resonates in his novels of contemporary life (such as *The Commitments*).

Irish Language

The Irish have a rich oral tradition that goes back to their ancient fireside storytelling days. Part of the fun of traveling

Irish Words

Here are some Irish words you may encounter on your travels.

Irish	English
alt (ahlt)	cliff
an lár (ahn lar)	city center
ard (ard)	high, height, hillock
baile (BALL-yah)	town, town land
beag (beg)	little
bearna (bar-na)	gap
boireann (burr-en)	large rock, rocky area
bóthar (boh-er)	road
bun (bun)	end, bottom
caiseal (CASH-el)	circular stone fort
caisleán (cash-LAWN)	castle
cathair (CAHT-her)	circular stone fort, city
cill (kill)	church
cloch (clockh)	stone
doire (dih-ruh)	oak
droichead (DROCKH-ed)	bridge
drumlin (DRUM-lin)	small hill
dún (doon)	fort
fionn (fi-UN)	white, fair-haired person
gaeltacht (GAIL-takt)	Irish language district
gall (gaul)	foreigner
garda (gar-dah)	police officer
gort (gort)	field
inis (in-ish)	island
mileac (MIL-yach)	low marshy ground
mór (mor)	large
muc (muck)	pig
oifig an phoist (UFF-ig un fusht)	post office
poll (poll)	hole, cave
rath (rath)	ancient earthen fort
ros (ross)	wood or headland
sí (shee)	fairy mound, bewitching
slí (slee)	route, way
sliabh (sleeve)	mountain
sráid (shrayd)	street
teach (chockh)	house
trá (traw)	beach, strand

Gaeltacht Regions

AREAS SHOWN IN BLACK
ARE PART OF THE GAELTACHT

here is getting an ear for the way locals express themselves.

Irish Gaelic is one of four surviving Celtic languages, along with Scottish Gaelic, Welsh, and Breton. Some proud Irish choose to call their native tongue "Irish" instead of "Gaelic" to ensure that there is no confusion with the language spoken in parts of Scotland.

Only 165 years ago, the majority of the Irish population spoke Irish Gaelic. But most of the speakers were of the poor laborer class that either died or emigrated during the Famine. After the Famine, parents and teachers understood that their children would be better off speaking English if they emigrated to the US, Canada, Australia, or England. Children in schools wore a tally stick around their necks, and a notch was cut by teachers each time a child was caught speaking Irish. At the end of the day, the child received a whack for each notch in the stick. It wasn't until a resurgence of cultural pride in the late 19th century that an attempt was made to promote the language again.

These days, less than 5 percent of the Irish population is fluent in their native tongue. However, it's taken seriously enough that all national laws must first be written in Irish, then translated into English. Irish Gaelic can be heard most often in the western counties of Kerry, Galway, Mayo, and Donegal. You'll know you're entering an Irish Gaelic-speaking area when you see a sign saying Gaeltacht (GAIL-takt).

Irish Gaelic has no "th" sound—which you can hear today when an Irish person says something like "turdy-tree" (thirty-three). There are also no equivalents of the simple words "yes" and "no." Instead, answers are given in an affirmative or negative rephrasing of the question. For example, a question like "Did you mail the letter today?" would be answered with "I did (mail the letter)," rather than a simple "yes." Or "It's a nice day today, isn't it?" would be answered with "It is," or "'Tis."

Practicalities

TOURIST INFORMATION

Ireland's tourist offices—one for the Republic (www.discoverireland.ie) and one for Northern Ireland (www.discovernorthernireland.com)—offer a wealth of information. Before your trip, scan their websites.

In Ireland, a good first stop in every town is the tourist information office—abbreviated **TI** in this book. (The nationwide tourist-information number for travelers calling from within Ireland is 1-850-230-330.) Prepare a list of questions and a proposed plan to double-check. Pick up a city map, confirm opening hours of sights, and get information on public transit (including bus and train schedules), walking tours, special events, and nightlife.

TRAVEL TIPS

Time Zones: Ireland, which is one hour earlier than most of continental Europe, is five/eight hours ahead of the East/West coasts of the US. The exceptions are the beginning and end of Daylight Saving Time: Ireland and Europe "spring forward" the last Sunday in March (two weeks after most of North America) and "fall back" the last Sunday in October (one week before North America). For a handy online time converter, see www.timeanddate.com/worldclock.

Business Hours: In Ireland, most stores

Finding Your Irish Roots

Many come to the Emerald Isle to trace their Irish ancestry. But too few give it enough thought before they set foot on the old sod, and instead show up and start "asking around." While this approach may give you an opportunity to meet nice Irish people, preparation can save time and increase your chances of making a real connection to your Celtic roots.

Many think their Irish ancestors were from County Cork, because Cobh is listed as their emigration departure port. But Cobh was the primary departure port for the vast majority of Irish emigrants—regardless of where they had resided in Ireland. An even earlier wave of Irish emigrants (mostly Scots-Irish from Ulster) sailed from the port of Derry (the second busiest emigration port).

If you have an idea of what town your ancestors hailed from, go online and search for its location (www.google.com/maps is a good starting point). Correct spelling is essential: Ballyalloly is up north in County Down while Ballyally is down south in County Cork. There's a town named Kells in four different Irish counties.

Fáilte Ireland, the official government-sponsored Irish tourist board, is a safe bet for reputable genealogy sources (www.discoverireland.ie). Browse www.irishgenealogy.ie or www.ancestry.com. The recently enabled online access to both the 1901 and 1911 Irish censuses has been a boon (www.census.national archives.ie). However, it's not a perfect science: Many precious birth records (some dating back to the 1200s) went up in smoke when offices in the Four Courts building in Dublin burned in 1922 during the Irish Civil War.

Before you get to Ireland, contact the **Genealogy Advisory Service** at the **National Library** in Dublin (tel. 01/603-0213, www.nli.ie, genealogy@nli.ie) or the helpful genealogy search service in Cobh (tel. 021/481-3591, www.cobh heritage.com/genealogy, genealogy@cobhheritage.com). If you think your heritage might be Scots-Irish, check the **Discover Ulster-Scots Centre** in Belfast (tel. 028/9043-6710, http://discoverulsterscots.com, discoverulsterscots@gmail.com). Also consider the **Mellon Centre for Migration Studies,** near Omagh in Northern Ireland (tel. 028/8225-6315, www.qub.ac.uk/cms, mcms@librariesni.org.uk).

Another option is to hire a qualified expert for assistance; Fáilte Ireland may have a recommendation. If you're willing to invest in an experienced researcher, you may get better results. Consider Sean Quinn of **My Ireland Heritage,** who is based near Dublin in Trim, County Meath, but is able to work across Ireland (tel. 01/689-0213, www.myirelandheritage.com, sean@myirelandheritage.com). With a few emails, phone calls, and Internet searches, you may be rewarded with a pint shared with some Irish guy or gal who looks a lot like you.

---

are open Monday through Saturday from roughly 10:00 to 17:30, with a late night on Wednesday or Thursday (until 19:00 or 20:00). On Sundays, many shops are closed and public transportation options are fewer (for example, no bus service to or from smaller towns).

Watt's Up? Bring an adapter plug with three square prongs (sold at travel stores in the US) to plug into Europe's outlets. You won't need a converter, because newer electronics—such as tablets, laptops, and battery chargers—are dual voltage and convert automatically to Europe's 220-volt system. If your old hair dryer isn't dual voltage, buy a cheapie in Europe.

Discounts: Discounts (called "concessions" in Ireland) aren't listed in this book. However, many sights offer discounts for youths (up to age 18), students (with proper identification cards, www.isic.org), families, and seniors (loosely defined as retirees or those willing to call themselves a senior). Always ask. Some discounts are available only for citizens of the European Union (EU).

HELP!

Emergency and Medical Help

Dial 999 for police or a medical emergency. Or ask at your hotel for help—they'll know the nearest medical and emergency services. If you get a minor ailment, do as the locals do, and go to a pharmacist for advice.

Theft or Loss

To replace a passport, you'll need to go in person to an embassy or consulate office (listed below). If your credit and debit cards disappear, cancel and replace them. If your things are lost or stolen, file a police report, either on the spot or within a day or two; you'll need it to submit an insurance claim for rail passes or travel gear, and it can help with replacing your passport or credit and debit cards. For more information, see www.ricksteves.com/help.

Damage Control for Lost Cards

If you lose your credit or debit card, you can stop people from using your card by reporting the loss immediately to your card company. Call these 24-hour US numbers collect: Visa (tel. 303/967-1096), MasterCard (tel. 636/722-7111), and American Express (tel. 336/393-1111). In the Republic of Ireland, to make a collect call to the US, dial 1-800-550-000. In Northern Ireland, dial 0-800-89-0011.

Press zero or stay on the line for an operator. Visa's and MasterCard's websites list European toll-free numbers by country.

If you report your loss within two days, you typically won't be responsible for any unauthorized transactions on your account, although many banks charge a liability fee of $50. You can generally receive a temporary replacement card within two or three business days in Europe.

Embassies and Consulates

US Embassy in Dublin: Tel. 01/630-6200 (42 Elgin Road, http://dublin.usembassy.gov)

US Consulate in Belfast: Tel. 028/9038-6100, after-hours emergency mobile 012-5350-1106 (223 Stranmillis Road, http://belfast.usconsulate.gov)

MONEY

This section offers advice on how to pay for purchases on your trip (including getting cash from ATMs and paying with plastic), VAT (sales tax) refunds, and tipping.

What to Bring

Bring both a credit card and a debit card. You'll use the debit card at cash machines (ATMs) to withdraw local currency for most purchases, and the credit card to pay for larger items. Some travelers carry a third card, in case one gets demagnetized or eaten by a rogue machine.

What NOT to Bring: Resist the urge to buy **euros** before your trip or you'll pay the price in bad stateside exchange rates. Wait until you arrive to withdraw money. I've yet to see a European airport that didn't have plenty of ATMs.

Plastic versus Cash: Although credit cards are widely accepted in Europe, day-to-day spending is generally more cash-based than in the US. I find cash is the easiest—and sometimes only—way to pay for cheap food, bus fare, taxis, tips, and local guides. Some businesses

Exchange Rates

Check www.oanda.com for the latest exchange rates.

1 euro (€1) = about $1.20

1 British pound (£1) = about $1.30

The **Republic of Ireland** uses the euro. To convert prices in euros to dollars, add about 20 percent: €20 = about $24, €50 = about $60. Just like the dollar, one euro (€) is broken down into 100 cents. Coins range from €0.01 to €2, and bills from €5 to €500.

Northern Ireland uses the British pound sterling. To convert prices in pounds to dollars, add 30 percent: £20 = about $25, £50 = about $65. Coins range from 1 pence to £2, and bills from £5 to £50.

(especially smaller ones, such as B&Bs and mom-and-pop cafés and shops) may charge you extra for using a credit card—or might not accept credit cards at all.

I use my credit card to book hotel reservations, to buy advance tickets for events or sights, and to cover major expenses (such as car rentals or plane tickets). It can also be smart to use plastic near the end of your trip, to avoid another visit to the ATM.

Using Credit Cards: European cards use chip-and-PIN technology, while most cards issued in the US use a chip-and-signature system. Most European card readers can automatically generate a receipt for you to sign, just as you would at home. If a cashier is present, you should have no problems. Some card readers will instead prompt you to enter your PIN (so it's important to know the code for each of your cards).

At self-service payment machines (transit-ticket kiosks, parking, etc.), results are mixed, as US chip-and-signature cards aren't configured for unattended trans-

actions. If your card won't work, look for a cashier who can process your card manually—or pay in cash.

Using Cash Machines: European cash machines have English-language instructions and work just like they do at home—except they spit out local currency instead of dollars, calculated at the day's standard bank-to-bank rate. In most places, ATMs are easy to locate.

Avoid "independent" ATMs, such as Travelex, Euronet, Moneybox, Cardpoint, and Cashzone. These have high fees, can be less secure than a bank ATM, and may try to trick users with "dynamic currency conversion" (or DDC).

Dynamic Currency Conversion: Some European merchants and hoteliers cheerfully charge you for converting your purchase price into dollars. If it's offered, refuse this "service." You'll pay extra for the expensive convenience of seeing your charge in dollars.

Security Tips: Before inserting your card into an ATM, inspect the front. If anything looks crooked, loose, or damaged, it could be a sign of a card-skimming device. When entering your PIN, carefully block other people's view of the keypad.

ATMs are easy to find.

While traveling, be sure to use a secure connection if you need to access your accounts online (see page 346).

Pretrip Checklist

Report your travel dates. Let your bank know that you'll be using your debit and credit cards in Europe, and when and where you're headed.

Know your PIN. Make sure you know the numeric, four-digit PIN for all of your cards, both debit and credit. Request it if you don't have one and allow time to receive the information by mail.

Adjust your ATM withdrawal limit. Find out how much you can take out daily and ask for a higher daily withdrawal limit if you want to get more cash at once. Note that European ATMs will withdraw funds only from checking accounts; you're unlikely to have access to your savings account.

Ask about fees. For any purchase or withdrawal made with a card, you may be charged a currency conversion fee (1-3 percent), a Visa or MasterCard international transaction fee (1 percent), and—for debit cards—a $2-5 transaction fee each time you use a foreign ATM (some US banks partner with European banks, allowing you to use those ATMs with no fees).

Tipping

Tipping in Ireland isn't as automatic and generous as it is in the US. For special service, tips are appreciated, but not required. As in the US, the proper amount depends on your resources, tipping philosophy, and the circumstances, but some general guidelines apply.

Restaurants: At a pub or restaurant with waitstaff, check the menu or your bill to see if the service is included; if not, tip about 10 percent. At pubs where you order at the counter, there's no need to tip.

Taxis: For a typical ride, round up your fare a bit (for instance, if the fare is €9, give €10). If the cabbie hauls your bags

and zips you to the airport to help you catch your flight, you might want to toss in a little more. But if you feel like you're being driven in circles or otherwise ripped off, skip the tip.

Services: In general, if someone in the service industry does a super job for you, a small tip of a euro or two is appropriate...but not required. If you're not sure whether (or how much) to tip for a service, ask a local for advice.

Getting a VAT Refund

Wrapped into the purchase price of your Irish souvenirs is a Value-Added Tax (VAT); it's 23 percent in the Republic and 20 percent in Northern Ireland. You're entitled to get most of that tax back if you purchase your goods at a store that participates in the VAT-refund scheme. In Ireland, you do not have to meet a minimum purchase amount in order to qualify for a refund.

If the store ships the goods to your US home, VAT is not assessed on your purchase. Otherwise, you'll need to:

Get the paperwork. Have the merchant completely fill out the necessary refund document. You'll have to present your passport. Get the paperwork done before you leave the store to ensure you'll have everything you need (including your original sales receipt).

Get your stamp at the border or airport. Process your VAT document at your last stop in the European Union (the airport or border) with the customs agent who deals with VAT refunds. Arrive an additional hour early before you need to check in to allow time to find the customs office—and to stand in line. Some customs desks are positioned before airport security; confirm the location before going through security. It's best to keep your purchases in your carry-on. If they're too large or dangerous to carry on (such as knives), pack them in your checked bags and alert the check-in agent. You're not supposed to use your purchased goods before you leave. If you show up at customs wearing your new Irish sweater, officials might look the other way—or deny you a refund.

Collect your refund. Many merchants work with services, such as Global Blue or Premier Tax Free, that have offices at major airports, ports, or border crossings. These services, which extract a 4 percent fee, can refund your money immediately in cash or credit your card (within two billing cycles). If the retailer handles VAT refunds directly, it's up to you to contact the merchant for your refund. You can mail the documents from home, or more quickly, from your point of departure. You'll then have to wait—it can take months.

Customs for American Shoppers

You are allowed to take home $800 worth of items per person duty-free, once every 31 days. You can take home many processed and packaged foods: vacuum-packed cheeses, dried herbs, jams, baked goods, candy, chocolate, oil, vinegar, mustard, and honey. Fresh fruits and vegetables and most meats are not allowed, with exceptions for some canned items. As for alcohol, you can bring home one liter duty-free (it can be packed securely in your checked luggage, along with any other liquid-containing items). But if you want to pack the alcohol (or any liquid-packed food) in your carry-on bag for your flight home, buy it at a duty-free shop at the airport.

For details on allowable goods, customs rules, and duty rates, visit http://help.cbp.gov.

SIGHTSEEING

Sightseeing can be hard work. Use these tips to make your visits to Ireland's finest sights meaningful, fun, efficient, and painless.

Plan Ahead

Set up an itinerary that allows you to fit in all your must-see sights. For a one-stop look at opening hours, see the "At a Glance" sidebars for major destinations. Most sights keep stable hours, but you can easily confirm the latest by checking with the TI or visiting museum websites.

Many museums are closed or have reduced hours at least a few days a year, especially major holidays. In summer, some sights may stay open late. Off-season, many museums have shorter hours. Whenever you go, don't put off visiting a must-see sight—you never know if a place will close unexpectedly for a holiday, strike, or restoration.

Going at the right time helps avoid crowds. This book offers tips on the best times to see specific sights. Try visiting popular sights very early or very late. Evening visits are usually peaceful, with fewer crowds.

At Sights

Here's what you can typically expect:

Entering: Be warned that you may not be allowed to enter if you arrive 30 to 60 minutes before closing time. And guards start ushering people out well before the actual closing time, so don't save the best for last.

Some important sights have a security check, where you must open your bag or send it through a metal detector. Some sights require you to check daypacks and coats. (If you'd rather not check your daypack, try carrying it tucked under your arm like a purse as you enter.)

Photography: If the museum's photo policy isn't clearly posted, ask a guard. Generally, taking photos without a flash or tripod is allowed. Some sights ban photos altogether.

Expect Changes: Artwork can be on tour, on loan, out sick, or shifted at the whim of the curator. Pick up a floor plan as you enter, and ask museum staff if you can't find a particular item.

Audioguides and Apps: Many sights rent audioguides, which generally offer dry-but-useful recorded descriptions (sometimes included with admission). If you bring your own earbuds, you can enjoy better sound. Increasingly, sights offer apps—often free—that you can download to your mobile device (check their websites).

Before Leaving: At the gift shop, scan the postcard rack or thumb through a guidebook to be sure that you haven't overlooked something that you'd like to see.

Sightseeing Passes

Ireland offers two passes (each covering a different set of sights) that can save you money. The first is smart for anyone, and the second works best for two people traveling together. Twosomes who love to sightsee should get both passes.

Heritage Card: This pass gets you into 98 historical monuments, gardens, and parks maintained by the Office of Public Works in the Republic of Ireland. It will pay off if you visit eight or more included sights over the course of your trip (€40,

families—€90, student and senior discounts; comes with handy map and list of sights' hours and prices, purchase at first Heritage sight you visit, cash only, tel. 01/647-6592, www.heritageireland.ie, heritagecard@opw.ie). People traveling by car are most likely to get their money's worth out of the card.

Heritage Island Visitor Attractions Guide: Ambitious travelers covering more ground can grab this free map adorned with discount coupons (get it at any TI or participating site; skip the accompanying 56-page booklet sold online). The map doesn't overlap with the above Heritage Card sights and provides a variety of discounts (usually 2-for-1 entries, but occasionally 10-25 percent off) at 88 sights in both the Republic of Ireland and Northern Ireland. This is a great no-brainer addition, especially for two people traveling together (tel. 01/775-3870, www.heritageisland.com).

EATING

For years, Irish food was something you ate to survive rather than to savor. In this country, long considered the "land

The Good and Bad of Online Reviews

User-generated review sites and apps such as Yelp, Booking.com, and TripAdvisor can give you a consensus of opinions about everything from hotels and restaurants to sights and nightlife. If you scan reviews of a hotel and see several complaints about noise or a rotten location, it tells you something important that you'd never learn from the hotel's own website.

But as a guidebook writer, my sense is that there is a big difference between the uncurated information on a review site and a guidebook. A user-generated review is based on the experience of one person, who likely stayed at one hotel in a given city and ate at a few restaurants there (and who doesn't have much of a basis for comparison). A guidebook is the work of a trained researcher who, year after year, visits many alternatives to assess their relative value. I recently checked out some top-rated user-reviewed hotel and restaurant listings in various towns; when stacked up against their competitors, some were gems, while just as many were duds.

Both types of information have their place, and in many ways, they're complementary. If something is well-reviewed in a guidebook, and also gets good ratings on one of these sites, it's likely a winner.

local specialties wherever you happen to be eating.

When restaurant-hunting, choose a spot filled with locals, not tourists. Venturing even a block or two off the main drag leads to higher-quality food for less than half the price of the tourist-oriented places. Locals eat better at lower-rent locales.

At classier restaurants, look for "early-bird specials," which allow you to eat well and affordably, but early (about 17:30-19:00).

Tipping: At a sit-down place with table service, tip about 10 percent—unless the service charge is already listed on the bill. If you order at a counter, there's no need to tip.

Breakfast

The traditional breakfast, the "Irish Fry" (known in the North as the "Ulster Fry"), is a hearty way to start the day—with juice, tea or coffee, cereal, eggs, bacon, sausage, a grilled tomato, sautéed mushrooms, and optional black pudding (made with blood sausage). Toast is served with butter and marmalade. Home-baked Irish soda bread can be an ambrosial eye-opener for those of us raised on Wonder bread. This meal tides many travelers over until dinner. But there's nothing un-Irish about skipping the "fry"—few locals actually start their day with this heavy traditional breakfast. You can simply skip the heavier fare and enjoy the cereal, juice, toast, and tea (surprisingly, the Irish drink more tea per capita than the British).

Budget Eating

Picnicking saves time and money. Try boxes of orange juice (pure, by the liter), fresh bread (especially Irish soda bread), tasty Cashel blue cheese, meat, a tube of mustard, local-eatin' apples, bananas, small tomatoes, a small tub of yogurt (it's drinkable), rice crackers, trail mix or nuts, plain digestive biscuits (the chocolate-covered ones melt), and any local specialties. At open-air markets and supermarkets, you

of potatoes," the diet reflected the economic circumstances. But times have changed. You'll find modern-day Irish cuisine delicious and varied, and skillfully prepared with fresh, local ingredients. Irish beef, lamb, and dairy products are among the EU's best. And there are streams full of trout and salmon and a rich ocean of fish and shellfish right offshore. Try the

A new generation of Irish food

A hearty Irish dinner

can get produce in small quantities. Supermarkets often have good deli sections, packaged sandwiches, and sometimes salad bars. Hang on to the half-liter mineral-water bottles (sold everywhere for about €1.50); buy juice in cheap liter boxes, then drink some and store the extra in your water bottle. I often munch a relaxed "meal on wheels" in a car, train, or bus to save 30 precious minutes for sightseeing.

Pub Grub and Beer

If beer is not your cup of tea, don't wine about it. Pubs are a basic part of the Irish social scene, and whether you're a teetotaler or a beer-guzzler, they should be a part of your travel here. Whether in rural villages or busy Dublin, a pub (short for "public house") is an extended living room where, if you don't mind the stickiness, you can feel the pulse of Ireland.

I recommend certain pubs to eat in, and your B&B host is usually up-to-date on the best neighborhood pub grub. Ask for advice (but adjust for nepotism and cronyism, which run rampant).

Pubs are generally open daily from 11:00 to 23:30 and Sunday from noon to 22:30. Pubs that serve meals generally offer lunch from about 12:30 to 15:00, and dinner from 17:00 to 21:00. Outside of mealtimes, usually only snacks and simple sandwiches are available. And some pubs don't serve hot meals at all, and only have snacks.

Children can be served soft drinks and food in pubs (but may be seated in the restaurant section or a courtyard). You'll often see signs behind the bar asking that children vacate the premises by 20:00. You must be 18 to order a beer, and the Gardí (police) are cracking down hard on pubs that don't enforce this law.

Food: Pub grub gets better every year—it's Ireland's best eating value. But don't expect high cuisine; this is, after all, comfort food. For about $15-20, you'll get a basic hot lunch or dinner in friendly surroundings. Pubs that are attached to restaurants, advertise their food, are crowded with locals, and are more likely to have fresh food and a chef than sell lousy microwaved snacks.

Pub menus consist of a hearty assortment of traditional dishes, such as Irish stew (mutton with mashed potatoes, onions, carrots, and herbs), soups and chowders, coddle (bacon, pork sausages, potatoes, and onions stewed in layers), fish-and-chips, collar and cabbage (boiled bacon coated in bread crumbs and brown sugar, then baked and served with cabbage), boxty (potato pancake filled with fish, meat, or vegetables), and champ (potato mashed with milk and onions). Irish soda bread nicely rounds out a meal. In coastal areas, a lot of seafood is available, such as mackerel, mussels, and Atlantic salmon. There's seldom table service in Irish pubs. Order drinks and meals at the bar. Pay as you order, and only tip (by rounding up) if you like the service.

Drink: When you say "a beer, please" in an Irish pub, you'll get a pint of Guinness (the tall blonde in a black dress). If you want a small beer, ask for a glass, which is a half-pint. Never rush your bartender when he's pouring a Guinness. It's an almost-sacred two-step process that requires time for the beer to settle.

The Irish take great pride in their beer. At pubs, long hand pulls are used to draw the traditional, rich-flavored "real ales" up from the cellar. These are the connoisseur's favorites. Short hand pulls at the bar mean colder, fizzier, mass-produced, and less interesting keg beers. Stout is dark and more bitter, like Guinness. If you think you don't like Guinness, try it in Ireland. It doesn't travel well and is better in its homeland. Murphy's is a very good Guinness-like stout, but a bit smoother and milder. For a cold, refreshing, basic, American-style beer, ask for a lager, such as Harp. Ale drinkers swear by Smithwick's (I know I do). Caffrey's is a satisfying cross between stout and ale. Try the draft cider (sweet or dry)...carefully. The most common spirit is triple-distilled Irish whiskey.

You're a guest on your first night; after that, you're a regular. The relaxed, informal atmosphere feels like a refuge from daily cares. Women traveling alone need not worry—you'll become part of the pub family in no time.

Craic (pronounced "crack"), Irish for "fun" or "a good laugh," is the sport that accompanies drinking in a pub. People are there to talk. To encourage conversation, stand or sit at the bar, not at a table. It's a tradition to buy your table a round, and then for each person to reciprocate.

In 2004, the Irish government passed a law making all pubs in the Republic smoke-free.

SLEEPING

I favor hotels and restaurants that are handy to your sightseeing activities. Rather than list hotels scattered throughout a city, I choose hotels in my favorite neighborhoods.

Book your accommodations as soon as your itinerary is set, especially to stay at one of my top listings or if you'll be traveling during busy times (such as July and August in Dingle). See page 358 for a list of major holidays and festivals throughout Ireland; for tips on making reservations, see page 341.

The Republic of Ireland and Northern Ireland have banned smoking in the workplace (pubs, offices, taxicabs, etc.), but some hotels still have a floor or two of rooms where guests are allowed to smoke. If you don't want a room that a smoker might have occupied before you, let the hotelier know when you make your reservation. All my recommended B&Bs prohibit smoking. Even in places that allow smoking in the sleeping rooms, breakfast rooms are nearly always smoke-free.

Rates and Deals

I've described my recommended accommodations using a Sleep Code (see sidebar). The price ranges suggest an estimated cost for a one-night stay in a standard double room with a private toilet and shower in high season, include breakfast, and assume you're booking directly with the hotel (not through a booking site).

Once your dates are set, check the specific price for your preferred stay at several hotels. You can do this either by comparing prices online on the hotels' own websites, or by emailing several hotels directly and asking for their best rate. Even if you start your search on a booking site such as TripAdvisor or Booking.com, you'll usually find the best deal through a hotel's own website.

Types of Accommodations

Ireland has a rating system for hotels and B&Bs. These stars and shamrocks are supposed to imply quality, but I find that they mean only that the place sporting symbols is paying dues to the tourist board. These rating systems often have little to do with value.

Hotels

Many of my recommended hotels have three floors of rooms and steep stairs; expect good exercise. Older properties often do not have elevators. If stairs are an issue, ask about ground-floor rooms or choose a hotel with a lift (elevator).

In Your Room: An "en suite" room has a bathroom (toilet and shower/tub) attached to the room; a room with a "private bathroom" can mean that the bathroom is all yours, but it's across the hall. If you want your own bathroom inside the room, request "en suite."

Hotelier Help: Hoteliers can be a great help and source of advice. Most know

Friendly hotel staff

Sleep Code

Hotels are classified based on the average price of a standard double room with breakfast in high season.

$$$$	**Splurge:** Most rooms over €170/£140
$$$	**Expensive:** €130–170/£110-140
$$	**Moderate:** €90–130/£80-110
$	**Budget:** €50–90/£50-80
¢	**Backpacker:** Under €50/£50
RS%	**Rick Steves discount**

Unless otherwise noted, credit cards are accepted and free Wi-Fi is available. For the best deal, book directly with the hotel. Ask for a discount if paying cash; if the listing includes RS%, request a Rick Steves discount.

their city well, and can assist you with everything from public transit and airport connections to finding a good restaurant, the nearest launderette, or a Wi-Fi hotspot.

Hotel Hassles: Even at the best places, mechanical breakdowns occur: Air-conditioning malfunctions, sinks leak, hot water turns cold, and toilets gurgle and smell. Report your concerns clearly and calmly at the front desk. For more complicated problems, don't expect instant results.

To guard against theft in your room, keep valuables out of sight. Some rooms come with a safe, and other hotels have safes at the front desk. I've never bothered using one.

If you find that night noise is a problem (if, for instance, your room is over a nightclub), ask for a quieter room in the back or on an upper floor.

Checking Out: While it's customary to pay for your room upon departure, it

Making Hotel Reservations

Requesting a Reservation: For family-run hotels, it's generally cheaper to book your room direct via email or a phone call. For business-class hotels, or if you'd rather book online, reserve directly through the hotel's official website (not a booking agency's site). For complicated requests, send an email.

Here's what the hotelier wants to know:
- type(s) of rooms you need and size of your party
- number of nights you'll stay
- your arrival and departure dates, written European-style as day/month/year
- special requests (such as en suite bathroom vs. down the hall, cheapest room, twin beds vs. double bed, quiet room)
- applicable discounts (such as a Rick Steves reader discount, cash discount, or promotional rate)

Confirming a Reservation: Most places will request a credit-card number to hold your room. If you're using an online reservation form, look for the https or a lock icon at the top of your browser. If you book direct, you can email, call, or fax this information.

Canceling a Reservation: If you must cancel, it's courteous—and smart—to do so with as much notice as possible, especially for smaller family-run places (which describes many of the hotels I list). Cancellation policies can be strict; read the fine print or ask about these before you book. Many discount deals require prepayment, with no cancellation refunds.

Reconfirming a Reservation: Always call or email to reconfirm your room reservation a few days in advance. For B&Bs or very small hotels, I call again on my day of arrival to tell my host what time to expect me (especially important if arriving late—after 17:00).

Phoning: For tips on calling hotels overseas, see page 344.

can be a good idea to settle your bill the day before, when you're not in a hurry and while the manager's in. That way you'll have time to discuss and address any points of contention.

Big Modern Hotel Chains: Hotel chains—popular with budget tour groups—offer predictably comfortable, no-frills accommodations at reasonable prices. These hotels are popping up in big cities in Ireland. They can be located near the train station, in the city center, on major arterials, and outside the city center. What you lose in charm, you gain in savings.

Hotels usually have an attached restaurant, good security, an elevator, and a 24-hour staffed reception desk. Of course, they're as cozy as a Motel 6, but many travelers love them. The biggies are Jurys Inn (call their hotels directly or book online at www.jurysinns.com), Comfort/Quality Inns (Republic of Ireland tel. 1-800-500-600, Northern Ireland tel. 0800-444-444, US tel. 877-424-6423, www.choicehotels.com), and Travelodge (also has freeway locations for tired drivers, reservation center in Britain tel. 08700-850-950, www.travelodge.co.uk).

B&Bs

Compared to hotels, bed-and-breakfast places give you double the cultural intimacy for half the price. If you have a reasonable but limited budget, skip hotels and go the B&B way.

B&Bs range from large guesthouses with 10-15 rooms to small homes renting out a couple of spare bedrooms, but typically have six rooms or fewer. My top listings are run by people who enjoy welcoming the world to their breakfast table.

Many B&Bs take credit cards, but may add the card service fee to your bill (about 3 percent). If you do need to pay cash for your room, plan ahead to have enough on hand when you check out.

Some B&B owners are also pet owners. If you're allergic, ask about pets when you reserve.

Keep in mind that B&B owners are at the whim of their guests—if you're getting up early, so are they; and if you check in late, they'll wait up for you. It's polite to call ahead to confirm your reservation the day before and give them a rough estimate of your arrival time.

B&Bs serve a hearty "Irish fry" breakfast (for more about B&B breakfasts, see "Eating," earlier in this chapter). Because your B&B owner is also the cook, breakfast hours are usually abbreviated (typically about an hour, starting at about 8:00—make sure you know the exact time before you turn in for the night). It's an unwritten rule that guests shouldn't show up at the very end of the breakfast period and expect a full cooked breakfast. If you do arrive at the last minute (or if you need to leave before breakfast is served), most B&B hosts are happy to let you help yourself to cereal, fruit or juice, and coffee.

In the Room: Most B&Bs have a "tea service" in the room: an electric kettle, cups, tea bags, coffee packets, and a pack of biscuits.

Your bedroom probably won't include a phone, but nearly every B&B has free Wi-Fi (if they don't, I'll note it in the listing).

Electrical outlets sometimes have switches that turn the current on or off; if your electrical appliance isn't working, flip the switch at the outlet.

You'll likely encounter unusual bathroom fixtures. The "pump toilet" has a flushing handle that doesn't kick in unless you push it just right: too hard or too soft, and it won't go. (Be decisive but not ruthless.)

Most B&B baths have an instant water

Cozy B&B bedroom

heater. This looks like an electronic box under the showerhead with dials and buttons: One control adjusts the heat, while another turns the flow off and on (let the water run for a few seconds to moderate the temperature before you hop in). If the hot water doesn't work, you may need to flip a red switch (often located just outside the bathroom). If the shower looks mysterious, ask your B&B host for help... before you take your clothes off.

Americans often assume they'll get new towels each day. The Irish don't. Hang them up to dry and reuse.

Hostels

A hostel provides cheap beds where you sleep in a room with strangers for about €25-30 per night. Travelers of any age are welcome if they don't mind dorm-style accommodations and meeting other travelers. Most hostels offer kitchen facilities, guest computers, Wi-Fi, and a self-service laundry. Hostels almost always provide bedding, but the towel's up to you (though you can usually rent one for a small fee).

Independent hostels tend to be easygoing, colorful, and informal (no membership required; try www.hostels-ireland.com or www.hostelworld.com).

Official hostels are part of Hostelling International (HI) and share an online booking site (www.hihostels.com). HI hostels typically require that you be a member or pay extra per night.

Other Accommodation Options

Renting an apartment, house, or villa can be a fun and cost-effective way to go local. Websites such as Booking.com, Airbnb, VRBO, and FlipKey let you browse properties and correspond directly with European property owners or managers.

If you prefer to work from a curated list of accommodations, consider using a rental agency such as InterhomeUSA.com or RentaVilla.com.

STAYING CONNECTED

Staying connected in Europe gets easier and cheaper every year. The simplest solution is to bring your own device—mobile phone, tablet, or laptop—and use it just as you would at home (following the tips below, such as connecting to free Wi-Fi whenever possible). Another option is to buy a European SIM card for your mobile phone—either your US phone or one you buy in Europe. Or you can use European landlines and computers to connect. Each of these options is described below.

You'll find even more details about staying connected at www.ricksteves.com/phoning.

Using a Mobile Phone in Europe

Here are some budget tips and options.

Sign up for an international plan. Using your cellular network in Europe on a pay-as-you-go basis can add up. To stay connected at a lower cost, sign up for an international service plan through your carrier. Most providers offer a simple bundle that includes calling, messaging, and data. Your normal plan may already include international coverage (T-Mobile's does).

Before your trip, call your provider or check online to confirm that your phone will work in Europe, and research your provider's international rates. Activate the plan a day or two before you leave, then remember to cancel it when your trip's over.

Use free Wi-Fi whenever possible. Unless you have an unlimited-data plan, it's best to save most of your online tasks for Wi-Fi. You can access the Internet, send texts, and even make voice calls over Wi-Fi.

Most accommodations in Europe offer free Wi-Fi, but some—especially expensive hotels—charge a fee. Many cafés (including Starbucks and McDonald's)

How to Dial

International Calls

Whether phoning from a US landline or mobile phone, or from a number in another European country, here's how to make an international call. I've used recommended hotels in Dublin (tel. 01/679-6500) and in Belfast (tel. 028/9027-1066) as examples.

Initial Zero: Drop the initial zero from international phone numbers—except when calling Italy.

Mobile Tip: If using a mobile phone, the "+" sign can replace the international access code (for a "+" sign, press and hold "0").

US/Canada to Europe

Dial 011 (US/Canada international access code), country code (353 for the Republic of Ireland, 44 for Northern Ireland), and phone number.

▸ To call the Dublin hotel from home, dial 011-353-1-679-6500.
▸ To call the Belfast hotel, dial 011-44-28-9027-1066.

Country to Country Within Europe

Dial 00 (Europe international access code), country code, and phone number.

▸ To call the Dublin hotel, whether from Northern Ireland or elsewhere in Europe, dial 00-353-1-679-6500.
▸ To call the Belfast hotel from the Republic of Ireland or elsewhere in Europe, dial 00-44-28-9027-1066.

Europe to the US/Canada

Dial 00, country code (1 for US/Canada), and phone number.

▸ To call from Europe to my office in Edmonds, Washington, dial 00-1-425-771-8303.

Domestic Calls

To call within the Republic of Ireland or within Northern Ireland (from one Irish landline or mobile phone to another), simply dial the phone number, including the initial 0 if there is one.

▸ To call the Dublin hotel from Wexford, dial 01/679-6500.
▸ To call the Belfast hotel from Derry, dial 028/9027-1066.

More Dialing Tips

Republic of Ireland to Northern Ireland: To avoid international rates when calling from any Republic of Ireland phone number to a landline in Northern Ireland (prefix 028), you can dial 048, then the local number (skipping the access code, country code, and Northern Ireland's area code).

▸ To call the Belfast hotel from a Dublin landline, dial 048-9027-1066.

Dialing from Northern Ireland to Republic of Ireland
From a Northern Ireland phone number, dial 00-353, then the area code without its initial 0, and then the local number.
▶ To call the Dublin hotel from a Belfast number, dial 00-353-1-679-6500.

Irish Phone Numbers: Phone numbers in both the Republic and Northern Ireland can vary in length. I keep things simple by always dialing the full number (including the area code or prefix). Mobile phone numbers in the Republic start with 083, 085, 086, 087, and 089. Mobile phone numbers in Northern Ireland (and the rest of the UK) start with 07. Note that calls to a European mobile phone are more expensive than calls to a landline.

Toll and Toll-Free Calls: In the Republic, numbers starting with 1-800 are toll-free, but numbers starting with 15, 1850, or 0818 are toll numbers. In Northern Ireland, numbers starting with 080 are toll-free, but those beginning with 084, 087, or 03 are inexpensive toll numbers. Numbers beginning with 09 are pricey toll lines. International rates apply to US toll-free numbers dialed from Ireland—they're not free.

More Phoning Help: See www.howtocallabroad.com.

European Country Codes		Ireland & N. Ireland	353 / 44
Austria	43	Italy	39
Belgium	32	Latvia	371
Bosnia-Herzegovina	387	Montenegro	382
Croatia	385	Morocco	212
Czech Republic	420	Netherlands	31
Denmark	45	Norway	47
Estonia	372	Poland	48
Finland	358	Portugal	351
France	33	Russia	7
Germany	49	Slovakia	421
Gibraltar	350	Slovenia	386
Great Britain	44	Spain	34
Greece	30	Sweden	46
Hungary	36	Switzerland	41
Iceland	354	Turkey	90

have free hotspots for customers. You'll also often find Wi-Fi at TIs, city squares, major museums, public-transit hubs, airports, highway rest stops, and aboard trains and buses.

Minimize the use of your cellular network. Even with an international data plan, wait until you're on Wi-Fi to Skype, download apps, stream videos, or do other megabyte-greedy tasks. Using a navigation app such as Google Maps can take lots of data, so use this sparingly.

Limit automatic updates. By default, your device is constantly checking for a data connection and updating apps. It's smart to disable these so they'll only update when you're on Wi-Fi.

Use Wi-Fi calling and messaging apps. Skype, Viber, FaceTime, and Google+ Hangouts are great for making free or low-cost voice and video calls over Wi-Fi. With an app installed on your phone, tablet, or laptop, you can log on to a Wi-Fi network and contact friends or family members who use the same service. If you buy credit in advance, with some of these services you can call any mobile phone or landline worldwide for just pennies per minute. Many of these apps also allow you to send messages over Wi-Fi to any other person using that app.

Using a European SIM Card

With a European SIM card, you get a European mobile number and access to cheaper rates than you'll get through your US carrier. This option works well if you want to make a lot of voice calls or need faster connection speeds than your US carrier provides. Fit the SIM card into a cheap phone you buy in Europe in Europe (about $40 from phone shops anywhere), or swap out the SIM card in an "unlocked" US phone (check with your carrier about unlocking it).

SIM cards are sold at mobile-phone shops, department-store electronics counters, some newsstands, and vend-

Tips on Internet Security

Make sure that your device is running the latest versions of its operating system, security software, and apps. Next, ensure that your device and key programs (like email) are password- or passcode-protected. On the road, use only secure, password-protected Wi-Fi hotspots. Ask the hotel or café staff for the specific name of their Wi-Fi network, and make sure you log on to that exact one.

If you must access your financial info online, use a banking app rather than accessing your account via a browser. A cellular connection is more secure than Wi-Fi. Avoid logging onto personal finance sites on a public computer.

Never share your credit-card number (or any other sensitive information) online unless you know that the site is secure. A secure site displays a little padlock icon, and the URL begins with *https* (instead of the usual *http*).

ing machines. Costing about $5-10, they usually include prepaid calling/messaging credit, with no contract and no commitment. To get the best rates, buy a new SIM card whenever you arrive in a new country (although the EU caps the roaming fees that local providers can charge).

Public Phones and Computers

It's possible to travel in Europe without a mobile device. You can make calls from your hotel (or the increasingly rare public phone).

Most **hotels** charge a fee for placing calls—ask for rates before you dial. You can use a prepaid international phone card (available at newsstands, street kiosks, and train stations) to call out from your hotel. Some cards work in both the

Republic of Ireland and the UK—confirm before buying a card by checking for both an 1800 access number (used in the Republic of Ireland) and an 0800 access number (for the UK).

Public pay phones are hard to find in Northern Ireland, and they're expensive. You'll pay with a major credit card (minimum charge of £1.20) or coins (minimum fee of £0.60). Only unused coins will be returned, so put in biggies with caution.

Most hotels have **public computers** in their lobbies for guests to use; otherwise you may find them at Internet cafés and public libraries (ask your hotelier or the TI for the nearest location). On a European keyboard, use the "Alt Gr" key to the right of the space bar to insert the extra symbol that appears on some keys. If you can't locate a special character (such as @), simply copy it from a Web page and paste it into your email message.

Mail

You can mail one package per day to yourself worth up to $200 duty-free from Europe to the US (mark it "personal purchases"). If you're sending a gift to someone, mark it "unsolicited gift." For details, visit www.cbp.gov and search for "Know Before You Go."

The Irish postal service works fine, but for quick transatlantic delivery (in either direction), consider services such as DHL (www.dhl.com).

TRANSPORTATION

This section covers the basics on trains, buses, long-distance taxis, rental cars, and flights.

To see all of Ireland, especially the sights with far-flung rural charm, I prefer the freedom of a rental car. Connemara, the Ring of Kerry, the Antrim Coast, and the Boyne Valley are really only worth it if you have wheels.

The best overall source of schedules for public transportation in the Republic of Ireland as well as Northern Ireland—

including rail, cross-country and city buses, and Dublin's LUAS transit—is the Republic of Ireland's domestic website: www.discoverireland.ie (select "Getting Around" near the bottom of the page).

Taxis and Uber

Most Irish taxis are reliable and cheap. In many cities, couples can travel short distances by cab for little more than two bus or subway tickets. Taxis can be your best option for getting to the airport for an early morning flight or to connect two far-flung destinations. If you like ride-booking services like Uber, these apps usually work in Irish cities just like they do in the US: You request a car on your mobile device (connected to Wi-Fi or a data plan), and the fare is automatically charged to your credit card.

Trains

To research Irish rail connections online, you need to access two sites. For the Republic of Ireland, use www.irishrail.ie. For Northern Ireland, use www.translink.co.uk. For train schedules on the rest of the European continent, check www.bahn.com (Germany's excellent Europe-wide timetable).

It really pays to buy your train tickets online ahead of time. Advance-purchase discounts of up to 50 percent are not unheard of, but online fares fluctuate widely and unpredictably. Online and off, fares are often higher for peak travel on Fridays and Sundays. Be aware that very few Irish train stations have storage lockers.

Ireland Public Transportation

----- Rail
----- Bus (not all lines shown)
.... Boat

N

25 Kilometers

25 Miles

Dunfanaghy

Bunbeg

Burtonport

Letterkenny

Donegal

Enniskillen

Sligo

Belmullet

Ballina

Ballymote

Carrick-on-Shannon

Foxford

Boyle

Dromod

Castlebar

Westport

Knock

Strokestown

Claremorris

Roscommon

Longford

Letterfrack

Cong

Athlone

Clifden

Galway

Ballinasloe

Rossaveal

Athenry

REPUBLIC

Kilronan

OF

Aran Islands

Doolin

IRELAND

Cliffs of Moher

Atlantic
Ocean

Ennis

Nenagh

Killimer

Thurles

Shannon

Limerick

Tarbert

Limerick Junction

Cashel

Charleville

Tipperary

Cahir

Tralee

Clonmel

Dingle

Kerry

Farranfore

Mallow

Killarney

Midleton

Cahersiveen

Youghal

Kenmare

Blarney

Cork

Cobh

Waterville

Ringaskiddy

Ardgroom

Bantry

Kinsale

Skibbereen

To Roscoff &
Cherbourg,
France

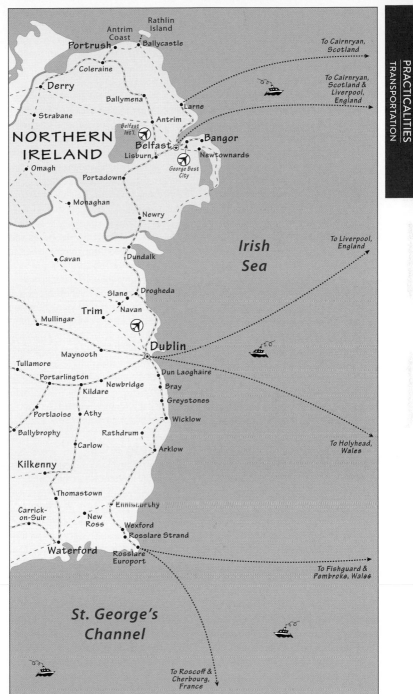

Rathlin
Island
Antrim
Coast
Portrush
Ballycastle
Coleraine
Derry
Ballymena
Larne
Strabane
Antrim
Belfast Int'l.
NORTHERN
Belfast
Bangor
IRELAND
Lisburn
Newtownards
Omagh
George Best
City
Portadown
Monaghan
Newry
Cavan
Dundalk
Slane
Drogheda
Trim
Navan
Mullingar
Dublin
Maynooth
Dun Laoghaire
Tullamore
Portarlington
Bray
Newbridge
Kildare
Greystones
Portlaoise
Athy
Wicklow
Ballybrophy
Rathdrum
Carlow
Arklow
Kilkenny
Thomastown
Enniscorthy
Carrick-
on-Suir
New
Ross
Wexford
Rosslare Strand
Waterford
Rosslare
Europort

To Cairnryan,
Scotland

To Cairnryan,
Scotland &
Liverpool,
England

*Irish
Sea*

To Liverpool,
England

To Holyhead,
Wales

To Fishguard &
Pembroke, Wales

*St. George's
Channel*

To Roscoff &
Cherbourg,
France

Rail Passes: For most travelers in Ireland, a rail pass is not very useful. Trains fan out from Dublin to major cities but neglect much of the countryside. But if a pass works for your itinerary, keep in mind that Eurail passes cover all trains in both the Republic and Northern Ireland, and give a 30 percent discount on standard foot-passenger fares for some international ferries. Irish Rail also offers a pass covering four consecutive days or five days of travel within a 15-day period in the Republic only (purchase at any major rail station in Ireland, http://www.irishrail.ie). For more detailed advice on train travel options in Ireland, visit www.ricksteves.com/rail.

Buses

If you opt for public transportation, you'll probably spend more time on Irish buses than Irish trains. But be aware: Public transportation (especially cross-country Irish buses) will likely put your travels into slow motion.

For example, driving across County Kerry from Kenmare to Dingle takes two hours. If you go by bus, the same trip takes almost four hours. The trip by bus usually requires two transfers, and the buses often take a rural milk-run route, making multiple stops along the way. Not every Irish coach trip will involve this kind of delay. But if you opt to go by coach, be realistic about your itinerary and study the schedules ahead of time. The Bus Éireann Expressway Bus Timetable comes in handy (free, available at some bus stations or online at www.buseireann.ie, bus info tel. 01/836-6111).

Buses are much cheaper than trains. Round-trip bus tickets usually cost less than two one-way fares. The Irish distinguish between "buses" (for in-city travel with lots of stops) and "coaches" (long-distance cross-country runs).

You may need to do some trips partly by train. For instance, if you're going from Dublin to Dingle without a car, you'll need to take a train to Tralee and catch a bus from there. Similarly, to go from Dublin to Kinsale without a car, take a train to Cork and then a bus; and from Dublin to Doolin, take a train to Galway or Ennis and then a bus.

If you're traveling up and down Ireland's west coast, buses are best (or a combination of buses and trains); relying on rail only here is too time-consuming. Note that some rural coach stops are by "request only." This means the coach will drive right on by unless you flag it down by extending your arm straight out, with your palm open.

Bus stations are normally at or near train stations. On some Irish buses, sports games are piped throughout the bus; have earplugs handy if you prefer a quieter ride.

Some companies offer **backpacker's bus circuits.** These hop-on, hop-off bus circuits take mostly youth hostelers around the country cheaply and easily, with the assumption that they'll be sleeping in hostels along the way. For example, Paddy Wagon offers three- to nine-day tours that can be combined into a longer tour covering Ireland (May-Oct, 5 Beresford Palace, Dublin, tel. 01/823-0822, www.paddywagontours.com).

Renting a Car

Travelers from North America are understandably hesitant when they consider driving in Ireland, where you must drive on the left side of the road. Irish government statistics say that 10 percent of all car accidents on Irish soil involve a foreign tourist. But careful drivers—with the patient support of an alert navigator—usually get the hang of it by the end of the first day.

Rental companies require you to be at least 21 years old and to have held your license for two years. Drivers under 25 may incur a young-driver surcharge. In the Republic of Ireland, you generally can't rent a car if you're 75 or older (unless you have a note from your doctor), and you'll usually pay extra if you're 70-74. Some companies in Northern Ireland won't rent to anyone over 69. (Note that you can't lease a car in Ireland.)

Research car rentals before you go. It's cheaper to arrange most car rentals from the US. Compare rates among several companies.

Most of the major US rental agencies (including Avis, Budget, Enterprise, Hertz, and Thrifty) have offices throughout Ireland. Also consider the two major Europe-based agencies, Europcar and Sixt. It can be cheaper to use a consolidator, such as Auto Europe/Kemwel (www.autoeurope.com) or Europe by Car (www.europebycar.com), which compares rates at several companies to get you the best deal—but because you're working with a middleman, it's especially important to ask in advance about add-on fees and restrictions.

Always read the fine print or inquire with the agent carefully for add-on charges—such as one-way drop-off fees, airport surcharges, or mandatory insurance policies—that aren't included in the "total price."

For the best deal, rent by the week with unlimited mileage. To save money on fuel, request a diesel car. In midsummer expect to pay at least $300 per week (more for an automatic), not including fuel and minimum insurance, for a basic compact-size car (like a Ford Focus 1.4-liter). With full insurance, the price of the same car increases by about $180 per week (even more for an automatic).

Almost all rentals are manual by default, so if you need an automatic, you must request one in advance. Be aware that cars with automatic transmission not only cost more to rent but also tend to be larger models, which aren't as maneuverable on narrow, winding roads. Weigh these considerations against the fact that in Ireland you'll be sitting on the right side of the car and shifting with your left hand... while driving on the left side of the road. The floor pedals are in the same locations

as in the US, and the gears are still found in the same basic "H" pattern as at home (i.e., first gear, second, etc.).

Picking Up Your Car: Big companies have offices in most cities, but small local rental companies can be cheaper. Some companies, such as Auto Europe (www.autoeurope.com) or Dan Dooley (www.dan-dooley.ie), will do longer-term rentals at a slight discount.

Compare pickup costs (downtown can be less expensive than the airport—but isn't recommended in congested urban Dublin), and explore drop-off options. Always check the hours of the location you choose: Many rental offices close from midday Saturday until Monday morning and, in smaller towns, at lunchtime.

When you pick up the rental car, check it thoroughly and make sure any damage is noted on your rental agreement. Find out how your car's lights, turn signals, wipers, radio, and fuel cap function, and know what kind of fuel the car takes (diesel vs. unleaded).

If your trip covers both Ireland and Great Britain (Scotland, England, and Wales), you're better off with two separate car rentals, rather than paying for your car to ride the ferry between the two islands. On an all-Ireland trip, you can drive your rental car from the Republic of Ireland into Northern Ireland, but be aware of drop-off charges (as much as $150-200) if you return it in the North. You'll pay a smaller drop-off charge (as much as $50-100) for picking up the car at one place and dropping it off at another within the same country (even picking up in downtown Dublin and dropping off at Dublin Airport). If you pick up the car in a smaller city, you'll more likely survive your first day on the Irish roads. If you drop the car off early or keep it longer, you'll be credited or charged at a fair, prorated price.

Car Insurance Options
When you rent a car, you're liable for a very high deductible, sometimes equal

Driving in Ireland

m = miles
h = hours
...... = ferry

Note: Your times may vary based on traffic, construction, and sheep on road.

to the entire value of the car. Limit your financial risk with one of these two options: Buy Collision Damage Waiver (CDW) coverage with a low or zero deductible from the car-rental company, or get coverage through your credit card (more complicated, and few credit cards now offer free coverage in Ireland).

Basic **CDW** includes a very high deductible (typically $1,000-1,500). Though each rental company has its own variation, basic **CDW** costs $10-30 a day (figure roughly 30 percent extra) and reduces your liability, but does not eliminate it. When you reserve or pick up the

car, you'll be offered the chance to "buy down" the basic deductible to zero (for an additional $10-30/day; this is sometimes called "super CDW" or "zero-deductible coverage").

If you opt for **credit-card coverage** (and your credit card is one of the few accepted for this type of coverage in Ireland), there's a catch. You'll technically have to decline all coverage offered by the car-rental company, which means they can place a hold on your card (which can be up to the full value of the car). In case of damage, it can be time-consuming to resolve the charges with your credit-card company. Before you decide on this option, quiz your credit-card company about how it works.

For more on car-rental insurance, see www.ricksteves.com/cdw.

Driving

Ireland's new motorways have vastly improved the cross-country driving experience and now link most major cities (Dublin, Belfast, Cork, Waterford, Limerick, and Galway). But the best intimate sites still require you to drive on narrow country lanes.

Note that your US credit and debit cards are unlikely to work at self-service gas pumps and automated parking garages, which use chip-and-PIN technology. Even a US card with a chip may not work, since most are chip-and-signature cards, but if you know your PIN, try it anyway. Luckily, the vast majority of Irish gas stations have a live attendant inside who can process your gas purchase (as long as it's not too late at night). The easiest solution is carrying sufficient cash.

An Irish Automobile Association membership comes with most rentals (www. aaireland.ie). Understand its towing and emergency road-service benefits.

Driving in Ireland is basically wonderful—once you remember to stay on the left and after you've mastered the roundabouts. Don't let a roundabout spook you. After all, you routinely merge into much faster traffic with cars slipping into your blind spot on American highways back home. The traffic in a roundabout has the right-of-way; entering traffic yields (look to your right as you merge). It helps to remember that the driver is always in the center of the road. And pay attention to the instructions painted on the pavement as you approach bigger roundabouts; they tell you which lane to be in for a destination well before you get to the actual roundabout.

Be warned: Every year I get a few emails from traveling readers advising me that, for them, driving in Ireland was a nerve-racking and regrettable mistake. If you want to get a little slack on the roads, try to time your car rental to begin on a Sunday morning when you can acclimate to driving on less congested roads at a mellower pace.

Road Rules: Don't drink and drive. The Gardí (police) set up random checkpoints. If you've had more than one pint, you're legally drunk in Ireland.

Be aware of typical European road rules; for example, many countries require headlights to be turned on at all times, and nearly all forbid talking on a mobile phone without a hands-free headset. In Ireland, you're not allowed to turn left on a red light unless a sign or signal specifically authorizes it, and on motorways it's illegal to pass drivers on the left. Seat belts are mandatory for all, and kids under 12 or under 1.5 meters tall (about 4 feet, 9 inches) must ride in a child-safety seat.

Ask your car-rental company about these rules, or check the US State Department website (www.travel.state.gov, search for your country in the "Learn about your destination" box, then click on

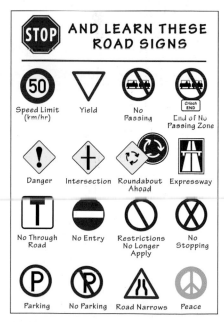

AND LEARN THESE ROAD SIGNS

Speed Limit (km/hr) · Yield · No Passing · End of No Passing Zone

Danger · Intersection · Roundabout Ahead · Expressway

No Through Road · No Entry · Restrictions No Longer Apply · No Stopping

Parking · No Parking · Road Narrows · Peace

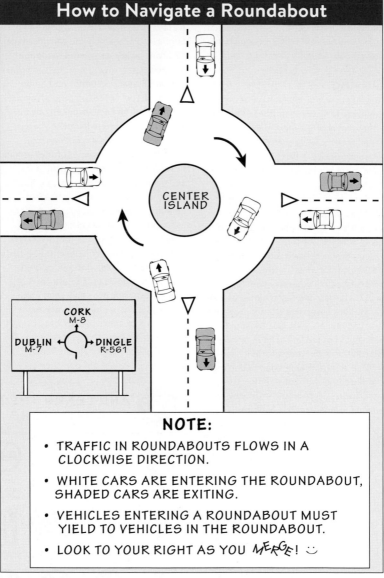

"Travel and Transportation").

Speed Limits: Speed limits are 50 kilometers per hour in towns, 80 kph on rural roads, 100 kph on national roads, and 120 kph on motorways. Note that road-surveillance cameras strictly enforce speed limits. Any driver (including foreigners renting cars) photographed speeding will get a nasty bill in the mail.

Navigation Maps and Apps: Plan to buy a good map. Ordnance Survey atlases are best (available in gas stations and bookstores).

The mapping app on your mobile

phone works fine for navigation in Europe, but for real-time turn-by-turn directions and traffic updates, you'll generally need Internet access. Helpful exceptions are Google Maps, Here WeGo, and Navmii, which provide turn-by-turn voice directions and recalibrate even when they're offline.

Download your map before you head out—it's smart to select a large region. Then turn off your cellular connection so you're not charged for data roaming. Call up the map, enter your destination, and you're on your way. View maps in standard view (not satellite view) to limit data demands.

Countryside Driving: When it comes to narrow rural roads, adjust your perceptions of personal space. It's not "my side of the road" or "your side of the road." It's just "the road"—and it's shared as a cooperative adventure. Buses always have the right of way on narrow rural roads, so you'll need to back up to give way.

Fuel: In Northern Ireland, unleaded costs about £1.20 per liter; in the Republic, unleaded is about €1.40 per liter. Diesel fuel pumps are black in Ireland.

Parking: One yellow line marked on the pavement means no parking Monday through Saturday during business hours. Double yellow lines mean no parking at any time. Broken yellow lines mean short stops are OK, but you should always look for explicit signs or ask a passerby.

Even in small towns, rather than fight it, I just pull into the most central parking lot I can find. As for street parking, signs along the street will state whether pay-and-display or parking disk laws are in effect for that area. The modern pay-and-display machines are solar-powered and placed regularly along the street (about six feet tall, look for blue circle with white letter *P*). I keep some extra coins in the console for these machines (no change given for large coins). The use of parking disks is less common these days, but if you need disks, they're sold at nearby shops. You buy one disk for each hour you want to stay. Scratch off the time you arrived on the disk and put it on your dashboard.

Flights

The best comparison search engine for both international and intra-European flights is Kayak.com. An alternative is Google Flights, which has an easy-to-use

Resources from Rick Steves

Begin Your Trip at www.RickSteves.com

My mobile-friendly **website** is *the* place to explore Europe. You'll find thousands of fun articles, videos, photos, and radio interviews; a wealth of money-saving tips for planning your dream trip; my travel talks and blog; and guidebook updates (www.ricksteves.com/update).

Our **Travel Forum** is an immense collection of message boards, where our travel-savvy community answers questions and shares personal travel experiences—and our well-traveled staff chimes in when they can help.

Our **online Travel Store** offers bags and accessories designed to help you travel smarter and lighter. These include my popular bags (which I live out of four months a year), money belts, totes, toiletries kits, adapters, guidebooks, planning maps, and more.

Choosing the right **rail pass** for your trip can drive you nutty. Our website will help you find the perfect fit for your itinerary and your budget: We offer easy, one-stop shopping for rail passes, seat reservations, and point-to-point tickets.

Guidebooks, Video, Audio Europe, and Tours

Books: *Rick Steves Best of Ireland* is just one of many books in my series on European travel, which includes country and city guidebooks, Snapshot guides (excerpted chapters from my country guides), Pocket Guides (full-color little books on big cities), and my budget-travel skills handbook, *Rick Steves Europe Through the Back Door.* A more complete list of my titles appears near the end of this book.

TV Shows: My public television series, *Rick Steves' Europe,* covers Europe from top to bottom with more than 100 half-hour episodes. To watch full episodes online for free, see www.ricksteves.com/tv. Or to raise your travel I.Q. with video versions of our popular classes (including my talks on travel skills, packing smart, most European countries, and European art), see www.ricksteves.com/travel-talks.

Audio: My weekly public radio show, *Travel with Rick Steves,* features interviews with travel experts from around the world. A complete archive is available at www.soundcloud.com/rick-steves, and much of this audio content is available for free, along with my audio tours of Europe's top sights, through my free **Rick Steves Audio Europe** app.

Small-Group Tours: Want to travel with greater efficiency and less stress? We offer tours with more than 40 itineraries reaching the best destinations in this book...and beyond. You'll find European adventures to fit every vacation length, and you'll enjoy great guides and a fun but small group of travel partners. For all the details, and to get our tour catalog, visit www.ricksteves.com or call us at 425/608-4217.

system to track prices. For inexpensive flights within Europe, try www.skyscanner.com.

Flying to Europe: Start looking for international flights four to six months before your trip, especially for peak-season travel. Off-season tickets can be purchased a month or so in advance. Depending on your itinerary, it can be efficient to fly into one city and out of another.

Flying Within Europe: If you're considering a train ride that's more than five hours long, a flight may save you both time and money. When comparing your options, factor in the time it takes to get to the airport and how early you'll need to arrive to check in.

These days you can fly within Europe on major airlines affordably for around $100 a flight. If you go instead with a budget airline such as Easyjet or Ryanair, be aware of the potential drawbacks and restrictions: nonrefundable and nonchangeable tickets, minimal or nonexistent customer service, pricey and time-consuming treks to secondary airports, and stingy baggage allowances with steep overage fees. If you've got lots of luggage, a cheap flight can quickly become a bad deal. To avoid unpleasant surprises, read the small print before you book.

Flying to the US: Because security is extra tight for flights to the US, be sure to give yourself plenty of time at the airport. It's also important to charge your electronic devices before you board because security checks may require you to turn them on (see www.tsa.gov for the latest rules).

HOLIDAYS AND FESTIVALS

This list includes selected festivals in major cities, plus national holidays (when banks and many sights close). Before planning a trip around a festival, verify its dates by checking the festival's website or TI sites (www.discoverireland.com).

Jan 1	New Year's Day
Late Jan	Temple Bar Trad, Dublin (Irish music and culture festival, http://templebartrad.com)
March 17	St. Patrick's Day (4-day festival in Dublin, www.stpatricksday.ie)
March or April	Easter weekend, including Easter Monday
Late March-early April	International Pan Celtic Festival, Carlow (www.panceltic.ie)
Early May	May Day; early May Bank Holiday (first Mon)
Late May	Spring Bank Holiday (last Mon)
Early June	June Holiday (first Mon)
Mid-June	Bloomsday, Dublin (James Joyce festival, www.jamesjoyce.ie)
Late June	Patrún Festival, Kilronan (*currach* boat races)
Late June	St. John's Eve Bonfire Night, Kilronan
July 12	Battle of the Boyne anniversary, Northern Ireland
Mid- to late July	Galway Arts Festival
Late July-early Aug	Galway Horse Races (www.galwayraces.com)
Early Aug	August Bank Holiday (first Mon)
Early Aug	Dingle Horse Races (www.dingleraces.ie)
Early-mid-Aug	Dingle Regatta (boat races)
Early-mid-Aug	Puck Fair, Killorglin, Kerry ("Ireland's Oldest Fair" and drink-fest, www.puckfair.ie)
Early-mid-Aug	Féile an Phobail, West Belfast (Irish cultural festival, www.feilebelfast.com)
Mid-Aug	Kenmare Fair (www.kenmare.com)
Late Aug	Late Summer Bank Holiday
Late Aug	Rose of Tralee International Festival (http://roseoftralee.ie)
Late Aug-early Sept	Blessing of the Boats, Dingle (maritime festival)
Mid-Sept	Galway Races (www.galwayraces.com)
Late Sept	Galway Oyster Festival (www.galwayoysterfest.com)
Late Oct	October Bank Holiday (last Mon)
Late Oct	Galway Races (www.galwayraces.com)
Dec 25	Christmas holiday
Dec 26	St. Stephen's Day; Boxing Day

CONVERSIONS AND CLIMATE

Numbers and Stumblers

- Europeans write a few of their numbers differently than we do. 1= 1, 4 = 4, 7 = 7.
- In Europe, dates appear as day/month/year. Christmas is always 25/12.
- Commas are decimal points and decimals are commas. A dollar and a half is $1,50, and one thousand is 1.000.
- When counting with fingers, start with your thumb. If you hold up your first finger to request one item, you'll probably get two.
- What Americans call the second floor of a building is the first floor in Europe.
- On escalators and moving sidewalks, Europeans keep the left "lane" open for passing. Keep to the right.

Clothing and Shoe Sizes

Shoppers can use these US-to-European comparisons as guidelines.

Women: For pants, dresses, and shoes, add 30 (US 10 = European 40). For blouses and sweaters, add 8 (US 32 = European 40).

Men: For shirts, multiply by 2 and add about 8 (US 15 = European 38). For jackets and suits, add 10. For shoes, add 32-34.

Children: Clothing is sized by height—in centimeters (2.5 inches = 1 cm), so a US size 8 roughly equates to 132-140. For shoes up to size 13, add 16-18, and for sizes 1 and up, add 30-32.

Metric Conversions

A **kilogram** equals 1,000 grams and about 2.2 pounds. One hundred **grams** (a common unit of sale at markets) is about a quarter-pound.

One **liter** is about a quart, or almost four to a gallon.

A **kilometer** is six-tenths of a mile. To convert kilometers to miles, cut the kilometers in half and add back 10 percent of the original (120 km: 60 + 12 = 72 miles). One **meter** is 39 inches.

Using the **Celsius** scale, 0°C equals 32°F. To roughly convert Celsius to Fahrenheit, double the number and add 30. For weather, 28°C is 82°F—perfect. For health, 37°C is just right. At a launderette, 30°C is cold, 40°C is warm (default setting), and 60°C is hot.

Ireland's Climate

First line, average daily high; second line, average daily low; third line, average days without rain. For worldwide weather statistics, check www.wunderground.com.

Dublin

J	F	M	A	M	J	J	A	S	O	N	D
46°	47°	51°	55°	60°	65°	67°	67°	63°	57°	51°	47°
34°	35°	37°	39°	43°	48°	52°	51°	48°	43°	39°	37°
18	18	21	19	21	19	18	19	18	20	18	17

Packing Checklist

Clothing

- ❑ 5 shirts: long- & short-sleeve
- ❑ 2 pairs pants or skirt
- ❑ 1 pair shorts or capris
- ❑ 5 pairs underwear & socks
- ❑ 1 pair walking shoes
- ❑ Sweater or fleece top
- ❑ Rainproof jacket with hood
- ❑ Tie or scarf
- ❑ Swimsuit
- ❑ Sleepwear

Money

- ❑ Debit card
- ❑ Credit card(s)
- ❑ Hard cash ($20 bills)
- ❑ Money belt or neck wallet

Documents & Travel Info

- ❑ Passport
- ❑ Airline reservations
- ❑ Rail pass/train reservations
- ❑ Car-rental voucher
- ❑ Driver's license
- ❑ Student ID, hostel card, etc.
- ❑ Photocopies of all the above
- ❑ Hotel confirmations
- ❑ Insurance details
- ❑ Guidebooks & maps
- ❑ Notepad & pen
- ❑ Journal

Toiletries Kit

- ❑ Toiletries
- ❑ Medicines & vitamins
- ❑ First-aid kit
- ❑ Glasses/contacts/sunglasses (with prescriptions)
- ❑ Earplugs
- ❑ Packet of tissues (for WC)

Miscellaneous

- ❑ Daypack
- ❑ Sealable plastic baggies
- ❑ Laundry soap
- ❑ Clothesline
- ❑ Sewing kit
- ❑ Travel alarm/watch

Electronics

- ❑ Smartphone or mobile phone
- ❑ Camera & related gear
- ❑ Tablet/ereader/media player
- ❑ Laptop & flash drive
- ❑ Earbuds or headphones
- ❑ Chargers
- ❑ Plug adapters

Optional Extras

- ❑ Flipflops or slippers
- ❑ Mini-umbrella or poncho
- ❑ Travel hairdryer
- ❑ Belt
- ❑ Hat (for sun or cold)
- ❑ Picnic supplies
- ❑ Water bottle
- ❑ Fold-up tote bag
- ❑ Small flashlight
- ❑ Small binoculars
- ❑ Small towel or washcloth
- ❑ Inflatable pillow
- ❑ Tiny lock
- ❑ Address list (to mail postcards)
- ❑ Postcards/photos from home
- ❑ Extra passport photos
- ❑ Good book

INDEX

MAP INDEX

Start your trip at

Our website enhances this book and turns

Explore Europe

At ricksteves.com you can browse through thousands of articles, videos, photos and radio interviews, plus find a wealth of money-saving travel tips for planning your dream trip. And with our mobile-friendly website, you can easily access all this great travel information anywhere you go.

TV Shows

Preview the places you'll visit by watching entire half-hour episodes of Rick Steves' Europe (choose from all 100 shows) on-demand, for free.

ricksteves.com

your travel dreams into affordable reality

Radio Interviews

Enjoy ready access to Rick's vast library of radio interviews covering travel tips and cultural insights that relate specifically to your Europe travel plans.

Travel Forums

Learn, ask, share! Our online community of savvy travelers is a great resource for first-time travelers to Europe, as well as seasoned pros. You'll find forums on each country, plus travel tips and restaurant/hotel reviews. You can even ask one of our well-traveled staff to chime in with an opinion.

Travel News

Subscribe to our free Travel News e-newsletter, and get monthly updates from Rick on what's happening in Europe.

Audio Europe™

Rick's Free Travel App

Get your FREE Rick Steves Audio Europe™ app to enjoy...

- Dozens of self-guided tours of Europe's top museums, sights and historic walks
- Hundreds of tracks filled with cultural insights and sightseeing tips from Rick's radio interviews
- All organized into handy geographic playlists
- For Apple and Android

With Rick whispering in your ear, Europe gets even better.

Find out more at ricksteves.com

Pack Light and Right

Gear up for your next adventure at ricksteves.com

Light Luggage

Pack light and right with Rick Steves' affordable, custom-designed rolling carry-on bags, backpacks, day packs and shoulder bags.

Accessories

From packing cubes to moneybelts and beyond, Rick has personally selected the travel goodies that will help your trip go smoother.

Rick Steves has

Experience maximum Europe

Save time and energy

This guidebook is your independent-travel toolkit. But for all it delivers, it's still up to you to devote the time and energy it takes to manage the preparation and logistics that are essential for a happy trip. If that's a hassle, there's a solution.

Rick Steves Tours

A Rick Steves tour takes you to Europe's most

great tours, too!

with minimum stress

interesting places with great guides and small groups of 28 or less. We follow Rick's favorite itineraries, ride in comfy buses, stay in family-run hotels, and bring you intimately close to the Europe you've traveled so far to see. Most importantly, we take away the logistical headaches so you can focus on the fun.

travelers—nearly half of them repeat customers—along with us on four dozen different itineraries, from Ireland to Italy to Athens.

Is a Rick Steves tour the right fit for your travel dreams? Find out at ricksteves.com, where you can also request Rick's latest tour catalog.

Europe is best experienced with happy travel partners. We hope you can join us.

Join the fun

This year we'll take thousands of free-spirited

See our itineraries at ricksteves.com

A Guide for Every Trip

BEST OF GUIDES

Full color easy-to-scan format, focusing on Europe's most popular destinations and sights.

Best of France
Best of Germany
Best of England
Best of Europe
Best of Ireland
Best of Italy
Best of Spain

COMPREHENSIVE GUIDES

City, country, and regional guides with detailed coverage for a multi-week trip exploring the most iconic sights and venturing off the beaten track.

Amsterdam & the Netherlands
Barcelona
Belgium: Bruges, Brussels, Antwerp & Ghent
Berlin
Budapest
Croatia & Slovenia
Eastern Europe
England
Florence & Tuscany
France
Germany
Great Britain
Greece: Athens & the Peloponnese
Iceland
Ireland
Istanbul
Italy
London
Paris
Portugal
Prague & the Czech Republic
Provence & the French Riviera
Rome
Scandinavia
Scotland
Spain
Switzerland
Venice
Vienna, Salzburg & Tirol

HE BEST OF ROME

he, Italy's capital, is studded with
an remnants and floodlit-fountain
res. From the Vatican to the Colos-
, with crazy traffic in between, Rome
derful, huge, and exhausting. The
ts, the heat, and the weighty history

of the Eternal City where Caesars walked
can make tourists wilt. Recharge by taking siestas, gelato breaks, and after-dark
walks, strolling from one atmospheric
square to another in the refreshing evening air.

d *Pantheon*—which
st dome until the
ly 2,000 years old
y over 1,500).

f Athens in the *Vat-
fies the humanistic
ce.

ladiators fought
nother, entertaining

Rome *ristoran*-

Rick Steves guidebooks are published by Avalon Travel,
an imprint of Perseus Books, a Hachette Book Group company.

POCKET GUIDES

Compact, full color city guides with the essentials for shorter trips.

Amsterdam	Munich & Salzburg
Athens	Paris
Barcelona	Prague
Florence	Rome
Italy's Cinque Terre	Venice
London	Vienna

SNAPSHOT GUIDES

Focused single-destination coverage.

Basque Country: Spain & France
Copenhagen & the Best of Denmark
Dublin
Dubrovnik
Edinburgh
Hill Towns of Central Italy
Krakow, Warsaw & Gdansk
Lisbon
Loire Valley
Madrid & Toledo
Milan & the Italian Lakes District
Naples & the Amalfi Coast
Northern Ireland
Normandy
Norway
Reykjavik
Sevilla, Granada & Southern Spain
St. Petersburg, Helsinki & Tallinn
Stockholm

Rick Steves books are available
from your favorite bookseller.
Many guides are available as ebooks.

CRUISE PORTS GUIDES

Reference for cruise ports of call.

Mediterranean Cruise Ports
Northern European Cruise Ports

Complete your library with...

TRAVEL SKILLS & CULTURE

Study up on travel skills before visiting "Europe through the back door" or gain insight on European history and culture.

Europe 101
European Christmas
European Easter
European Festivals
Europe Through the Back Door
Postcards from Europe
Travel as a Political Act

PHRASE BOOKS & DICTIONARIES

French
French, Italian & German
German
Italian
Portuguese
Spanish

PLANNING MAPS

Britain, Ireland & London
Europe
France & Paris
Germany, Austria & Switzerland
Ireland
Italy
Spain & Portugal

PHOTO CREDITS

Avalon Travel
Hachette Book Group
1700 Fourth Street
Berkeley, CA 94710

Printed in China
First printing May 2018
ISBN 978-1-63121-806-4
Second Edition

For the latest on Rick's talks, guidebooks, Europe tours, public radio show, free audio tours, and public television series, contact Rick Steves' Europe, 130 Fourth Avenue North, Edmonds, WA 98020, 425/771-8303, www.ricksteves.com, rick@ricksteves.com.

RICK STEVES' EUROPE
Special Publications Manager: Risa Laib
Managing Editor: Jennifer Madison Davis
Assistant Managing Editor: Cathy Lu
Project Editor: Suzanne Kotz
Editorial & Production Assistant: Jessica Shaw
Graphic Content Director: Sandra Hundacker
Maps & Graphics: David C. Hoerlein, Mary Rostad

AVALON TRAVEL
Editorial Director: Kevin McLain
Senior Editor and Series Manager: Madhu Prasher
Editor: Jamie Andrade
Associate Editor: Sierra Machado
Copy Editor: Kelly Lydick
Proofreader: Patrick Collins
Indexer: Stephen Callahan
Interior Design: McGuire Barber Design
Interior Layout: Tabitha Lahr
Cover Design: Kimberly Glyder Design
Maps & Graphics: Kat Bennett, Kathryn Osgood

Although the author and publisher have made every effort to provide accurate, up-to-date information, they accept no responsibility for loss, injury, mischievous leprechauns, or inconvenience sustained by any person using this book.

Let's Keep on Travelin'

Your trip doesn't need to end.

Follow Rick on social media!